A Garland Series

THE
RENAISSANCE
AND THE
GODS

A Comprehensive Collection of
Renaissance Mythographies, Iconol-
ogies, & Iconographies, with a
Selection of Works from
The Enlightenment

*Fifty-three Titles in Fifty-five Volumes Including
over 2,900 Illustrations, Edited with
Introductions by*
STEPHEN ORGEL
The Johns Hopkins University

THE GOLDEN BOOKE
OF THE
LEADEN GODS
London 1577

Stephen Batman

THE THIRD PART
OF. . .YVYCHURCH
London 1592

Abraham Fraunce

THE FOUNTAINE
OF
ANCIENT FICTION
London 1599

Richard Lynche

Garland Publishing, Inc., New York & London

1976

Library of Congress Cataloging in Publication Data

Batman, Stephan, d. 1584.
    The golden booke of the leaden gods.

    (The Renaissance and the gods ; 13)
    The third work, by V. Cartari, is a translation of
Le imagini de i dei gli antichi.
        1. Mythology, Classical. 2. Heresies and heretics.
I. Fraunce, Abraham, fl. 1582-1633. The third part of
the Countesse of Pembrokes Yuychurch. 1976. II. Car-
tari, Vincenzo, b. ca. 1500. Le imagini de i dei gli
antichi. English. 1976. III. Title. IV. Series.
BL720.B37   292'.1'3   75-27856
ISBN 0-8240-2062-6

Printed in the United States of America

Notes

Batman, *The Golden Book of the Leaden Gods.*
The first English iconography, written by an Anglican cleric and designed as a warning against paganism. Batman includes among his false gods a number of anabaptists and Roman Catholic theologians, though—as the book's title suggests—his attitude towards his classical material is exceedingly ambivalent. The book is largely based on Pictor's *Apotheoseos.* Our copy is from the Bodleian, shelfmark Douce BB.710.

Fraunce, *The Third Part of . . . Yvychurch.*
Most important of the English 16th-century mythographies, with moralizations based on Boccaccio, Comes, and Georgius Sabinus. We reproduce the British Museum copy, shelfmark 80.a.28.(2), and have replaced some badly-cropped pages with pages from the made-up copy in the Folger Library.

Lynche, *The Fountaine of Ancient Fiction.*
A truncated English version of Cartari. Our copy is from the Bodleian, shelfmark Douce L.191.

S. O.

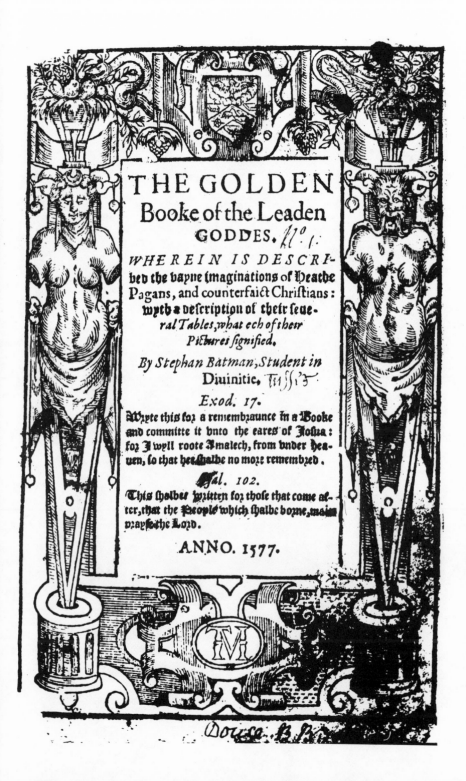

THE GOLDEN
Booke of the Leaden
GODDES.

WHEREIN IS DESCRI-
bed the vayne imaginations of Heathe
Pagans, and counterfaict Christians:
wyth a description of their seueral Tables, what ech of their
Pictures signified.

By Stephan Batman, Student in
Diuinitie.

Exod. 17.

Wryte this for a remembraunce in a Booke
and committe it vnto the eares of Iosua:
for I wyll roote Amalech, from vnder heauen, so that heeshalbe no more remembred.

Psal. 102.

This shalbee written for those that come after, that the People which shalbe borne, maie
prayse the Lord.

ANNO. 1577.

To the Right Honorable Lord

HENRY CARY, OF THE MOST NO-
ble order of the Garter Knight, Baron of Hunſdon,
Gouernour of the Queenes mateſties towne of Ber-
wycke, and Lorde Warden of the Eaſt Marches of Eng-
lande, agaynſte Scotlande, his ſinguler good
Lord and Mayſter: Stephan Batman wiſheth
the feruent zeale of Gods truth, & long continuaunce of proſperous health, vvith
encreaſe of much honour.

Allyng aduiſedly to
remembraunce(right Honorable)the worthy places of thoſe,
which by a ſpeciall prerogatiue,
and the prouident goodneſſe of
almighty God, are endued with
Magnanimity, and called to the hygheſt roomes of
Authority: I ſee and finde that by their wyſe and
prudent gouernmente, there is generallye cauſed a
publique peace both abroade, amonge ſtraungers,
and at home among our ſelues: and alſo I perceyue
and by experience do proue, that the bayte of their
cheereful countenaunce, allureth and winneth the
hartes of the Inferiours, to the imitation and admiration of like curteſie: And as anye occaſion is
offered, ſo do they teſtifye and geeue out (as tokens
of their good will & obedience)ſome yerely fruict,
more or leſſe, to confirme & (as it were) to ſeale
vp the vowed zeale of vnfeigned dutie, which they
faythfully, and hartely owe and beare vnto theire
Superiours. Such Nobleneſſe, Magnanimitie, Af-

fabilitie

fabilitie, & Curtesie, harbouringe wythin your L.
breast, hath also incited & emboldened me, now to
dedicate, and present, vnto your Honors view and
consideration, this smal Treatise of the putatiue &
imagined Gods of the Gentiles: a worke, as heretofore not gathered in oure vulgar tonge: So I trust
not so barrein of fruictfull documentes, but that it
maye seeeme both to sauour of no small paynes on
myne owne behalfe, and also to yelde out such other
instructions, as maye tende to sundrye Godlye pur-
poses, and to the betteringe of manye others.
VVherein we Christians, now lyuinge in the cleare
light of the Gospel, may euidently see, with what erroneous truperies, Antiquitie hath bene nozzeled:
in what foggy mystes, they haue long wandered: in
what filthye puddles they haue bene myered: vnder
what masking vysors of clouted religiös, they haue
bene bewytched: what traditions they haue of theyr
owne phantastical braynes to themselues forged: &
finallye into what Apostacye, Atheisme, Blasphemy,
Idolatrye, and Heresie, they haue plunged their
Soules, & affiaunced their beleeues. VVhose miserable captiuitie, so long and so manye yeres, vnder
the greuous yoake, and thraldome of oure deadlye
Enemie, and Capital foe Sathan, as wee are moste
pitifullye to bewayle: so are we most humblye, and
incessauntlye to prayse God for oure owne delyue-
raunce from the lyke slauerye, for the openinge of
our eyes and vnderstandings, & for the reuealing
of him selfe vnto vs, in his moste sacred and blessed
worde, the most perfect Touchstone, which vnfey-
                                               nedlye

nedly tryeth Truth and Simplicity, frō Falſhode &
Hypocriſie, Lighte from Darknes, Perfect honoure
from Superſtition, finally God and Godlines, from
the Deuil & Diuelishnes. Receyue therfore (right
Honorable Lorde) this poore pawne of my dutifull
hart, & vnder the Enſigne of your noble protectiō
shrowde it againſt the malicious Querkes of the
Sycophanticall Crewe, if any happen either to condemne my Enterpriſe, or impungue my honeſt meaning: which was, aud is, by shewing my ſelfe duti-
ful vnto you my Lord and Mayſter, to do good alſo
(as much as in me lyeth) vnto al others. Beſeching
Almighty God to continue and encreaſe his riche
bleſſinges vppon you, and after manye and flourishing daies here in this life ſpent, receyue you amōg
the trowpe of his holy and heauenly Inhabitaunts,
to reſt with him in his bleſſed Hierarchie for
euer. AMEN. At Newington the
8. of September. 1577.

Your Lordſhippes moſt humble
Seruaunt in the LORD,

Stephan Batman,
Miniſter.

To the wel diſpoſed Reader.

Ennes natures being as ſundꝛy and variable, as their Phiſnomies & faces bee diuers & diſagreable, ſmall maruayle is it, though, in iudgements and verdicts, they square frõ an vnity, and iump not together in one reaſonable accoꝛd of opiniõ.

Knowing therfoꝛe gentle reader, that there be as many Taſtes, as there be Mouthes: I loke not to be accompted ſo perfect a Cooke, as is able to ſeaſon foode and condimentes foꝛ euery palate & appetite: but referring the conſtruction of my goodwil, to the conſiderations of ſuch hũgry Stomakes, as cã and wil feede vpon and digeſt ſuch holeſome (thoughe homely) cheare, as is ſettte befoꝛe them: foꝛ the other coyer ſoꝛte, I pꝛofeſſe my ſelfe moꝛe redier to diſclayme acquaintaunce, then willing to ioine with thẽ in their ſo ſquemiſh affectiõs. A pꝛoofe of both theſe natured perſons, I am ſure in this boke to find: hoping as touching the cenſure, thereof, rather to fal into the hãdes of indifferente welwillers and by theym to be tryed, then, among thẽ which (lyke Aeſopes Dogge) lying in the Maunger wil neyther doe any thyng themſelues, noꝛ thynke wel of others, ꝑ ſweat foꝛ their cõmodyty. Which pooꝛe labour, if I perceiue to be wel accepted, I ſhalbe animated ſhoꝛtly to aduenture a further, paynfuller and greater Enterpꝛiſe.

Fare well.

Thomas Newtonus,
Cestreshyrius.

M E tibi, te(p mihi coniunxit amica voluntas,
Et firma à multo tempore amicitia.
Quam quoniã virtus, fuluo preciosior auro,
Mutuus ac fidè conciliauit amor,
Spero remansuram : quam me Iouis ira refringet,
Nec ferrum absumet, nec cariosa dies.
Cùmæ tuos limæ non dedignere labores
Submisisse meæ, verberibusæ meis,
Accipe, quæ nostræ iam sit sententia mentis,
Atæ infucati pectoris omen habe.
Crede mihi, tua cuncta placent, tua cuncta placebunt
Quæ dextræ scribis Palladis auspicijs.
Te morum candor, stylus, ingeniumæ venustat,
Te decorat Pithô, Suada, Minerua, Charis.
Te pudor ingenuus, te rara modestia adornat,
Te pietas, grauitas, te polit alma fides.
E rostris quoties verborum fulmina torques,
E grato toties manat ab ore lepos.
Curas, ne Stygius lupus insidietur ouili,
Romanusue pias rabula vexet oues.
Præstigias aperis, veterum et figmenta deorum,
Et pandis veræ relligionis iter .
Detegis horrendi fraudes Cacodæmonis atras,
Informas Iuuenes, erudis atæ rudes.
Ne dubites Batmanne igitur prodire in arenam,
Magna tibi accrescet gloria, magnus honos.
Iste tuus fœtus miro splendore superbit,
Multaæ in exiguo commoda fasce tenet.

Thomas Newton.

E. L. in the Authors
Commendation.

HE merites Fame (I say) that taketh payne,
Not for himselfe, but for his natiue Soyle:
Where one alone the profite shall not gayne,
But all may reape the sweete, of his sower toyle.
By all mens doome, that Man must needes haue prayse,
Who for behoofe of others, spendes his dayes.

Then since that all, by one, shall profite get,
Whats he disdaynes the trauayle of this wight?
Not one: vnlesse such Curres as stil do set
Themselues to byte at those, who bring to light
The slye deceiptes of their vngracious Crewe,
Who vertuous men to hurt do still pursue.

Braue golden workes m ay Jewels called bee,
That fine bene founde with shape of straunge deuise:
Such Jewels then, let not to viewe and see
No times then once, yea, more then twise or thryse :
For why? the rarenesse of this piece is such,
To view it stell, you cannot do too much.

For proofe, lo here that Jewell rare in sight,
This Booke beholde, that Leaden Gods contayne:
And how a Bat, like glittring Gold most bright,
Those glosinge Gods depaintes in colours playne :
That euery man, which doth his Booke beholde,
For guerdon will geeue it, the name of Golde.

Certes, such a worke in English neuer was
As this (though small) which doth vayne thinges bewraye
What then needes hee, that made the same once passe,
On Romish Curres, what they do barke or say :
No let them gnarle, and do the worst they can,
The Worke is good, the proofe shal prayse the Man.

FINIS.

THE

of the Leaden Gods.

IVPITER.

Vpiter was figured sytting *in Throne of Estate, with three eyes, and no Eares, al naked from the middle vpward, the rest couered: his Vysage resembling a womans countenaunce: in his right hand he held Lightening, and in the left, a Scepter. Standing or treading vpon Gyauntes: before him an Eagle, and a Page presentinge a cup of Golde. Ouer his head an Angel standing on a Globe holding a laurell Garland.*

Signification.

His sitting in Thzone, betokeneth his Kingdome to be durable, his thzee Eyes signifieth his meruelious Wysdome, by which hee ruleth Heauen, Sea, and Earth: his want of Eares declare him to be indifferent vnto all, not harkening moze to one, then to an other. The nakednesse of his vpper partes, and couerture of the nether, did purpozt him to be inuisible vnto mé, which dwel beelow, but visible to the heauenly myndes, wch are aboue. Hys womanly looke and full Bzeastes, intimate al thinges to be made & nourished by him. His Lightening in his right hand, dooth signifie his power, which lyke to Lightening peazceth thzough all: his Scepter betokeneth his pzouidence, by which, as by a Scepter hee disposeth wich hys

A cre-

The Golden Booke

creatures, as he thinketh best. His treading vpon Gi-
auntes doth declare him to be a punisher of the, which
are at defiaunce with him: by the Eagle is vnderstode
the Soule: for as the Eagle surmounteth all other
Birdes, and is swiftest, so much doth the minde sur-
passe the Bodye: by the Page, the simplicity therof:
intimating thereby, that if the Soule of Man, be free
from the querkes of dissembling phantasie, and as the
Eagle soareth aloft, so if the Soule of Man, shalbe occupied with heauenlye cogitations, that then shalbee
enioyed, the Cup of golde, whereby is signified the rewarde of Uertue, in the presence of Iupiter.

By the Angell is signified the swiftnesse of well doing. By the Globe vnder his feete, the small regarde
of worldlye Uanitie. By the Garlande, the endlesse
crowne of Immortalitie. The auncient Romans entituled him Optimus Maximus, because in very dede
it is better, and more acceptable, to profite many, the
to possesse great Wealth and reuenue.

IVNO.

I V N O was portraicted sitting vnder a Rayn-
bow, with a Crowne of white Lyllies on her head,
a Scepter in her right hand, and in her left hande
a payre of Sheares, on ech side a Peacocke: She had
for her footestoole a Lyon, her bodye couered ouer
with a fine Lawne.

Signification.

By Iuno is mente the Ayre, the Raynbowe betokeneth Rayne, whereof it is a token. Her Crowne of
Lyllies

Lyllies, signifieth the cause to bee in the Ayre, that ý Earth doth yelde foorth sweete Flowers: her Scep, ter is a representation of the power that is geeuen to the Ayre, aswel for preseruation, as encreasing of natural thinges. Her Sheares in her left hand sheweth Potencsse and Moystnesse of the Ayre, into which two qualitics it is sundered and parted. The two Peacockes are added, because theyr cry doth prognosticate chaunge of Weather. The Lyon is a figure of the Sunne, and the Lawne, of thynne Uapours: for the force and vertue of the Sunne is greatest, when hee entreth into Leo: hereby aduertising, that the heate of the Sunne draweth thyn vapors into the Ayre, where beeing congealed, by the extreeme colde of the middle Region, they are agayne by the scortchinge heate of the Sunne resolued into droppes.

The Poetes feigne this Iuno, to be sister and wyfe to Iupiter. I thinke because Iupiter beinge taken pro Aethere, and Iuno pro Aëre, they haue most semblable qualities and dispositions.

Iupiter and Iuno, are sayd to bee at variaunce, because Iupiter being hoat and drye, not hauing his heat repressed with moystnesse, all thinges are burned and parched: agayn, when Iunos moystnesse is not qualified with Iupiters heate, all thinges are drowned and ouerflowed: but when their qualities are with equal temperaunce combyned together, then the Earthe doth yelde her fruites with greate plentye and abundaunce.

APOLLO.

APOLLO was portraicted beardlesse, standing by a Bay tree, on whose toppe, stoode a Crowe.

The Golden Booke

Apollo treading on a Dragon hauing three heades. Vpon his head, a Crowne of burning Lampes, in his left hand an Harpe, and in his right hande, a Bowe. ~~Eivelohn 4 Aperta. cic. 41.7 i choint vst in Leurline~~

Signifycation.

BY Apollo is ment the Sunne, and being wythoute a Beard, Lustines of youth', which for the tyme is likened to the Sunne, whose beauty or pulchritude, is alwayes one: and standing by a Baye Tree, alwayes greene, Figureth the freshnesse of lustye Youthe: the Bay tree was first found, growinge on the Hyll Parnassus consecrated to Apollo, whose Uertue is not to be subiected neither to Beastes, nor Lightenings, as Authors haue reported. Tiberius, as often as it thundered, for his better preseruatiõ against the same, was crowned with the Baye, called among the Latines, Laurus. By the Crowne is signified Uigilancie to ouerlooke all things betime, as also the Crowe when hee is sicke, remouieth his disease by eating the leaues: Apollo hys treading vpõ the Dragon, betokneth the crooked course of the Sunne, into the twelue Signes of the Zodiake: the three heads of the Dragon, whereof the one is a Lyons, the other a Wolfes, the thirde the head of a Dogge, generally doth represent tyme: and particularlye, by the head of the Lyon, tyme present, the head of the Wolfe tyme paste, as it were so ouenlye snatched from vs: by the head of the Dogge is signified, tyme future or to come, because boped tyme flattreth ech estate accordyng to ech vocation, to gayn, or to reuenge: his burning Lampes in his crown resemble his diuers Beames, which geeue lighte to the

earth

earth: His Harpe in his left hand. betokneth the harmonie of ye celestial Spheres: & his Bow in his right hand, signifieth his wasting of some part of the Earth, by the Arrowe of extreeme and intemperate heate.

The Poets feygn, that Oenomaus, a king of Arcadia, counsayled by the Oracle, learned that he shoulde dye, when his daughter called Hyppodamia, shoulde take an Husbande (because of a Sonne which shoulde dispossesse him of his Kingdome) wherefore bee instituted and ordained a Game called the Running of the Chariotts, that who soeuer ouercame him by ouer swyftnesse, shoulde haue his Daughter, and whom he ouercame to be presentlye slayne. Hauing by his pollicy, subdued many, he hoped so to daunt ye courage of the rest, to be aduised of buyinge loue so deare, and thereby to stretch and lengthen his dayes to Nestors yeares: But Pelops far enamoured on Hyppodamia, by ye helpe of swyfte Coursers, ouerran Oenomaus Chariotts, and wan his Loue, or best beloued. Apollo for loue of his Uictorye gaue hym to his Mariage, his thre footed stoole, wrought out of fyne Gold, by Vulcan the Smyth: the Legs of the Stoole were Luste, Beautie, Strength. The Seate to sitte vppon, Ryches.

DIANA.

Diana was portraicted, standing in the middest of Satyres, Gods, and Nymphes of the Seas, Ryuers and Fountaynes, wyth three heades and two wynges, her bow was bent, and Quiuer by her side, she standing betweene a Panther, a Lyon, and a Shyppe.

Sygnifi.

The Golden Booke

Signification.

BY Diana is ment the Moone, her Garde of Satyres, Gods, and Nymphes, betoken all sortes of people vnder her Gouernment: and also her lighte euer Woods, Seas, & Fountaines : her iii. heades: the change of euery Moone into Calends, Nones, & Ides. Her winges betoken her swifte motion, because she finisheth her course twelue tymes in euery peare. Her bow & arrowes, represent the lpuelye effect & operatiō of her beames, aswel in quickning, as killing of moztal creatures. She hath a Pather on the one side, because the spots of that beast when it is yong, are bozned as the Moone in her first quarter, & in her rpper peares, her spots waxe round as the Moone in her ful: on the other side a Lyon which resembleth p Sunne, because the Moone hath no light of herselfe, but p which shee bozoweth of p Sunne. The Ship warneth Mariners in their courses to haue a special regard to the Mone, to the tydes and Floude guyded by her: who when the Seas in the night sparkle like Quickesiluer, it betokeneth tempeste to folow, geeuing Saylers warning to prepare foz Weather.

The Poetes faygue that Actæon, a man seekinge moze foz vaine pleasure and solitye, then Vertue, and of the progenie of Cadmus, after much wearynesse in folowing his houndes, sodainly espied Diana with her Dryades & Nymphes bathing, was foz his vnmanernerly biewing, trāsfozmed into an Hart, & so deuoured of his owne Dogs. Diana appellata est quod diem noctu efficiat, vel quasi Duana, quod duobus temporibus maxime cōpareat, die ac nocte.

Prudentius because he allowed the Goddesse Diana to be gouerner of both p Lightes, he being also a valiaunt

aunt & liberal Capitapne, esteeming Men before Money, and Valiauncie before Bryberye: and being fallen into great pouertie, not able to haue the funerall, of vayne brauerye, with more mourning Weedes, the mourning myndes, was neuerthelesse, by the earneste prayers of his Souldiers, by Titan and Cynthia caried into Cœlum Empyreum, for an immortall rewarde among the Gods for euer.

MERCVRIVS.

Mercurie was portraicted with winges at head and feete, wearing an Hat of white & blacke colloures: A Fawlchon by his side, in one hande a Scepter, & in the other a Pype, on the one side stode a Cocke and a Ramme, and close by his side a Fylcher or Cutpurse, and headlesse Argus.

Signification.

By Mercurie Marchauntes be ment. His wynges at head & feete betoken the expedition of Marchantes, which to gett worldly pelfe, post through all corners of the World: the whyte & blacke coloured Hat, signifieth their subtilty, which for greedines of gaine, spare not to face white for blacke, & blacke for white. By his Fawlchon is signified, goodes gotten by violence, when subtiltie cannot comprehend. His Mace is a token of peace, but the knot with two serpentes, clasping ech other aboute the sayde Scepter, doth intimate that no promise must be broken.

Hys

The Golden Booke

Hys Pppe refembleth Eloquence, which refrefheth the mynde, as Harmony ooth the eares.

The Cocke is fayoe to be the beft obferuer of tymes and feafons, warning Marchantes and trauelers, to fo2fake no oppo2tunity. The Ramme is a refemblauce of hys offyce, becaufe the Poets fayne Mercurie, to be Embaffaooure of the Goos: all are obeoient to hym, as the Flockes of fhepe, are to the Ramme: the figu-reo Cutpurfe, is a p2oofe that Mercurie was a thiefe: and Headleffe Argus, is a witneffe, that one Plague, bew2ayes a thoufand euilles. The Poets feigne that Argus the Sonne of Ariftor, had an hund2ed eyes, of al which, only two oio fleepe by courfe, fo that he was not to be take with al a fleepe: So fubtil was Argus, that what fraude foeuer was imagined, hee had poli-cie to defende it. Wherefo2e Iuno enuyinge Io (her b2other and hufband Iupiters Harlot) committed the keping of Io to Argus, fuppofing fo to be moft affured from euermo2e the hauing of Iupiters company. Iupi-ter to acquite Iunos p2actife, commaundeth Mercurye to take him to his Pppe, and with melodious foundes, b2ought Argus Eyes a fleepe: by which is fignified, what is hee that is fo circumfpect o2 aduifed, but that Flattrye o2 counterfeited perfwafion, at one time, o2 other may deceiue: which wo2ke being accomplifhed, hee ftryketh of Argus head, and fetteth Io, the tranf-fo2med Cow, at liberty. Iuno feeing this hap, in token of her good wyll, fets Argus eyes into the Peacockes tayle, fo2 a perpetual rememb2aunce of his trufty fer-uice.   A manifeft fhowe how vayne a thinge rewarde is, when it dyeth wyth the partie, from the pofteritie. As when Carnalia had flayne his freend Obliuios e-nempe, thereby receiuing his deathes wounde fo2 his laboure was rewarded with a Million of Gole: what

plea-

pleasure had bee thereof, beinge presented from the vse by death, and not geeuen to his familye.

MINERVA, OR

PALLAS.

PALLAS was portraicted all armed: her cou-
tenaunce menacing the beholder, hauing a Clo-
ke of three coulers, in her righte hande a Speare,
and on her lefte a Chriſtalline Target, emboſſed
with a Gorgons head. By her ſtoode a Greene Oliue
Tree, and a Dragon, with an Owle flyinge ouer
them.

Signification.

By Minerua is ſignified Wiſdome, ioyned to Force, to qualifie extremities. Pallas Armature doeth purpozte, that it concerneth a wyſe man to be fenced, alwell againſt frowarde affections, as the outward e-nemie: Her fierce Looke oz Countenaunce doth admo niſh vs, not to beholde ſinne, with gentill and amia-ble Countenaunce, but menacinge, and as it were with a Speare, to bydde and wage Battaple againſt it. Her Cloake of Whyte, Golden, & Purple, co-lours, ſetteth foozthe Wyſoome to the viewe of the eye. Foz the Whyte, betokeneth Simplicitie: the Golde, the glitteringe foze of Prudence, & the Pur-ple the pearcing brightneſſe of modeſt Gouernment.

The Golden Booke

By ý lõg speare is also signified, ý foresight of things to come. The Christalline Target, betokneth the warynesse of the wyse, in which as in a Glasse, he seeth to the bottome, the subtiltie of others : The Gorgons head warneth to vse Martiall Lawe, not in fostering, but in killing them at the first , whiche are knowen to be wylfull, and maupfest offendours . By the Oliue tree is signified peace, intimating that warre must neuer bee raysed , but when peace cannot otherwise bee mayntepned. The Dragon carieth a resemblaunce of prudence, for as hee, amonge all other Serpentes is most waking , so the Prudent is circumspect in al hys doinges.

The Owle representeth warynesse, because when all other sleepe, she waketh, and flying beholdeth that, which the common sort, neither do, nor can.

The Poetes faygne, Pallas to haue proceeded of Iupiters brayne, and neuer to haue had any mother , because the Athenians supposed the first sorts of men geuen to politike gouernmente , and wyse in foreseeinge Daungers to come, allowed the Lawes , and Statutes of Iupiter, calling them by the name of his daughter : the purpose of the Poete is, that for asmuch as Iuno, the wife of Iupiter was barren, for verye griefe shooke his head encountringe the wall, whence issued Pallas, & after gathering some courage to her self like Virago, steppeth foorth all armed, that which Lawe cannot wynne by lenitye: it must compel by force.

MARS.

MARS was portraicted al armed, his Chariot was drawen with two horses breathing Fyer.
                                        A wolfe

A VVolfe went befoore him with a Sheepe in hys mouth, and a Cocke following.

Signifycation.

Hys Chariot, Horſes, and Armour, betoken War, becauſe they be the chiefeſt furniture thereof. The names of the two Horſes are Feare, & Terrour, becauſe where Mars inuadeth, all thinges are lefte deſolate, & deſtroyed. The Wolfe with the Sheepe in his mouth repreſenteth Mars, whoſe Souldiers are as great raueners of other mens goodes, as the wolfe is of ſeely ſheepe. The Cocke followeth Mars, eyther becauſe he is a warlike Byrde, or ells that hee is meſſenger of the Sunnes approach, to the which Souldiers muſt haue a vigilant reſpect: vnleſſe they mynd to let paſſe, ſundrye and many good opportunities.

The Poetes faygne that Mars neuer had father, be cauſe he hated peace. Loquax requeſting of Mars the Countrye of the Pauperculans, hee aſked howe they ſhould then lyue, he ſayde by labour, then quoth Mars it is as fyt for thee, ſo to do, and get that thou haſt not, and they ſhall poſſeſſe that which they haue: hee not contented, by the determination of the Goddes, it was agreed, that hee ſhoulde not onely feede of the earthes encreaſe, but alſo that earth, ſhould ſo poſſeſſe him, as hee deſired: Loquax ſuppoſing the Pauperculans diſherited: hated the poſſeſſion, where hee beinge tyed lyke a Dog, was forced for hunger to eate the graſſe and in the ſame earth to be buryed, that hee ſo greedelye had coueted.

A good vvarning to beggers of ſtatutes penall: vvhere by the cómons are greatly impouerished, & their good kinges, neuer the better enriched,

B2 VE

The Golden Booke

VENVS.

*V E N V S was figured in a Garden of Flowers,
naked, with a Garlãd of Flowers and Roſes on
her head:her VV agon was drawen with two white
Swannes, and a payre of whyte Doues.*

Signification.

HEr Garland of Roſes doth ſignifie the ſuperfluity
which wantons require,and being naked, ẙ ſhame-
leſſe care of Virginitie : The Garden of Flowers,the
variable allurementes of amozous Louers, her Wagon betokeneth Pleaſure : the Swannes, ſtoutneſſe
of ſwift reuenge, and with as great myldeneſſe wyth-
out attempte, whoſe pzoperties bene diligentlp to defende theyz owne,and vſeth to ſinge befoze their death,
aduertiſing Louers to be conſtante: the Doues ſignifie mildeneſſe,chaſtitie,and continuaunce .

Tee Poetes faygne, of Paris, ſonne to Priamus, ẙ
Hecuba ,how ſhee dzeamed that ſhee bzought foozth a
Fpzebzande that ſet all Troie on fyer: Priamus mole-
ſted in mynde, commaunded that aſſone as the Boye
was bozne, to be ſlayn : but Hecuba being mooued tõ
a motherlye compaſſion, cauſed Paris to be nouriſhed
with a Sheepeard, who in continuaunce of tyme growinge to be a man: Iuno, Pallas,ẙ Venus, fel at contention foz a Golden Apple:on which this Poeſie was
wzytten: *Geeue it to whom thou lykeſt, if to*Iuno; *then
ſhalt thou bee Victorious, if to*Pallas,*then prudente and
wyſe to gouerne: If to*Venus,*then Knight ouer the fayreſt Lady in the worlde,in Luſt and Pleaſure.*

Paris

Paris beinge aſtonieð, to whom the Apple mought
beſt be geeuen, Iupiter eſpying his diſmay, willed him
to beſtow the Apple on whom he beſt lyked, who gaue
it to Venus.

So after ſweete Meate, came ſowꝛe Sauce, after
Laughinge Weepinge, to the vtter ruine of the Troians. Saplinge to Sparta bee eſpyed Menelaus
wyfe, whoſe Lecherous Luſt loſt himſelfe, his Parentage, and his countrye.

VVLCAN.

*VVLCAN was figured lympinge, wyth a blew
Hat on his head, a Hammer in his hand, prepared to the Forge lyke a Smyth.*

Signification.

BY Vulcan is ment Fier, & by his blew hat the ayꝛy
firmament, by his limping, the Renolucions of the
Heauens, which whē it deſcendeth to vs, looſeth much
of his foꝛmer ſtrength. By Vulcan is ſignifies laboꝛ,
by his hatte of blew, true dealing, by his Hammer, oꝛ
Sledge, the continuall toyle of Huſbandꝛye, aſwel by
the Plough in earing the tough earth: as by the Hammer in foꝛging of Mettall, whoſe foꝛce muſt bee pꝛepa
red aſwell to the mayntenaunce of the Pꝛince, as the
enriching of the ſubiect.

The Poetes faigne that Iupiter iarring with Iuno
his wyfe, fell from woꝛdes to blowes. Vulcan comming to the reſkue of Iuno, Iupiter waxed ſo angrye
that hee tooke Vulcan by the Legges, and flange him
into Lemnos, whom the Inhabitants receiued as ſent
from

The Golden Booke

from heauen and learned of him, to prepare Iron for necessary vses.

VESTA.

VESTA was figured like a Virgine, not suffering the holy Fyer to be extinguished.

Signification.

By VEsta (Vas) the vessel of Virginitie is signified: the Fyer resembleth the Sunne which maketh the Earth a mother of manye goodly Creatures.

In the Honour of Vesta, were ordayned sixe Uyrgins of her name, called *Vestales*, their office was to looke that the Fyer in the Temple neuer went out, so that, when so euer by their negligëce it was extinguished, they endured such punishment, as the hye Priest awarded: But if so it happened, that anye of theym, did suffer themselues to be spoyled of their Virginity, it was ordayned they shoulde bee burned quicke. So zealous were the Romans not onlye of the honour of their Goods, but also they helde Virginitie, for an exceeding Uertue. The Uirgins were chosen to serue this Goddesse betweene the sixte and tenth yeares of their age, from which tyme tyl after the expiration of 30. yeares, it was not permitted as lawfull to mary.

NEPTVNE.

NEPTVNE was portraicted in manlye forme naked, on the Sea horse most swyftlye floting

flotinge on the Seas, hauinge a forke on his shoul-
ders, the Tritones attending on hym.

Signification.

By Neptune is signified the swift passage of Ebbes
& Flouds, the Manlye forme purporteth the rage
of the bellowing Waues, and being naked the readi-
nesse of Shyppes to be smothe, and wel garnished, ells
is the swiftnesse stayde, when the outesioe is not free
from all annoyes: by the forcke is signified the furniture that good Shippes must haue, aswell in weapon
as tacklinge, thereby to preuente both Bellona, & Cyclops Seas, and Theeues. By the Tritones, skilfull
Maryners, Souldiers, and Munition.

The Poetes note that Neptune roade on an horse,
because when Athens was erected, Pallas & Neptune
were at stryfe aboute the naminge of the Cittie, after
many Wordes, the discorde was put to arbitremente
of the Gods: they awarded that which of theim coulde
finde out the moste profitablesse thinge for the life of
manne, he onlye shoulde haue the aucthoritye to name
the Cyttie. Neptune smote the ground w his Forke,
and foorthwith leapt out an Horse: But Pallas smy-
ting the Grounde with her Speare, sodeynlye sprong
foorth a Oliue treel, which the Goddes iudged to bee
more profitable to the vse of man. Pallas obteyninge
victorye called the Cittie Athens.

It was more by the fauour of the Gods, so to iudge
it, then it was to preferre the Oliue tree, before the
Horse.

An Epitheton.

Except by the Oliue tree is signified Uertue and by
the

The Golden Booke

by the horse type: Venusta Venus.

CERES.

CESES was figured havinge on her heade, a Crowne of wrythen Eares of Corne, in her right hande an handfull of Corne, and in the lefte the Herbe Poppye.

Signification.

CEres betokneth encrease of Grayne, becaufe fhe is called Dea Frugum, of the frugalitie which commeth of Earthe and Seede. The Crowne of Corne Eares betokeneth the encrease: þ Eares of Corne in her hand betokneth þ referued Seede, whereby doth follow the yeares encreafe.

By the Poppie is fignified the flouthfull or fleepye tyme to enfue, þ ech laborer may take heede to neglect no tyme: for as the Poppye is a caufer of fleepe: So Slouth is a vice that loofeth gaine. The Poppye alfo

called Papa-ver, with other weedes are fuffered to grow among the Corne, which muft be weeded foorth, for hyndring the Cornes encreafe.

The Poetes feigne that Saturne, Ceres father was a great deuourer of his Childgen: fo fayde by the Fygure Antithefis, for that the Earthe, as fhee yeldeth encreafe, doth receiue all into her agayne.

IANVS.

IANVS was portraicted double faced, & ftanding vpon twelue Alters, in his right hande hee helde

*helde a Keye with ξ & ε wroughte vppon it, in the
left hand a Barre, with this letter τ grauen on it.*

Signification.

His two Faces on both sides, aswell beehynde as
beefore, aduertiseth wiselye to consider thynges
aswell past, as to come, & standinge vpon Twelue Alters, admonisheth Princes, and Men of Honoure,
to bee constant in all theyre doynges, but moste especiall in Religion, as was I A N V S Kynge of
Italye : so named of Italus, from whom proceded
the name of the Countrye. The Keye in his ryghte
hande is a resemblaunce of policie, to open and bringe
to light, the treacherous deuises of diepe dissemblers.
The Letters ξ. and ε. sygnyfye 55. The letter τ. on
the barre three hundred, which Barre signified y Fortitude of a good prince in maynteyning Uertue & sup-
pressing vyce: By the number 355. the dayes of one
yeare, wherein no day ought to be ouerpassed, without
some exploite or good act.
The Romans in honour of Ianus, erected a beautifull
Temple, which in tyme of Warre stode wyde open, &
in tyme of peace it was alwayes shutte.

Ianus is supposed the firste beginner of letters and
skyll of the starres, taught the planting of the Uyne,
Deuided the twelue Monethes, and sundrye Domesticall skilles, for a common wealth, therefore double
faced, the Face of Gouernment, and the Face of Labour.

C SATVR-

The Golden Booke

SATVRNVS.

SATVRNE was portracted with a hoare head, but black bearded, & feeble footed. He held in his hand a Sythe of serpentine forme, leaninge on the sneathe or staffe. In his left hand hee helde an Infant, greedelye deuouringe it, his collour pale and wanne.

Signification.

SAturnus hoarynesse, betokeneth Winter: his black beard signifieth the Golden worlde, in which no mā was tormented with care: the earth yelding of it selfe sufficient, for euery mans contētation: his feeble feete resembled him to be the slowest of the seuen Planets, because he can finish his course in no lesse then thyrtie yeares, his pale and yealow collour, sheweth his cōplexion to be cold and dry: hys Sythe signifieth time, in the which, al thinges are mowen down, and wythered: hys greedy deuouring of the Childe, betokeneth the wastfull spending of thinges, before they come to growth whose mouthes be more plentye, then good condicions: deuouringe more at fewe Bankets, then their fathers got in fortie yeares.

GENIVS.

GENIVS was portraicted like a younge man hauing two VVinges, powring VVyne out of a
Bolle

Bolle , vpon an Alter.

Signification.

By Genius is fignified,the towardnes of quicke wittes,wherebyfundzye foztes of people are founde to exceede others : his Wings betoken the fwiftneffe of the mynde, as alfo the readyneffe,vpon whom he hath taken charge: he is fayed to bee the Sonne of the Immoztall God, becaufe hee is iopned to humaine foзme, called reafonable : His powzing wyne on an Alter,fignifieth the abundaunce of Ayzy moyfture,which doth foзce the barren earth,to yeld fooзth ech creature and fubftaunce.

Plutarch wzyteth that Iulius Cæfar had a mighty Genius alotted vnto him, by whofe helpe,he not onlie atchieued great Uictories in his lyfe, but was alfo reuenged en his murderers after his death: foз his Genius,fo purfued his confpiratours at the verye heeles, both by Sea,and Lande , that hee fuffered not one to remapne on lyue, which epther was a doer,oз a confpirour of the fact: fo likewife, after the fact of Robbers and wilful Murderers,in flyinge from place to place, they haue neuer beene at quiet, til death hath finifhed they deferued courfe.

PLVTO.

PLVTO was portraicted with a frowninge countenaunce,his feate was fiery: Cerberus was his footeftoole,in his right hand he helde a Scepter, & in his lefte , a Sowle : Proferpina with hellishe

C 2   *furies*

Furies, attendinge on hym.

Signification.

By Pluto is mente, the vnsaciable gotten ryches þ̃ faȝce possesseth , his Statelye countenaunce declareth , that woȝldlye Goodes make men pȝoude, arrogant, and ambicious : His fiery Seate, betokeneth the violence of the Ryche : His Scepter signifieth Welthye menns rule, ouer the Pooȝe. The Soule which he claspeth with his left hande, declareth, that vnsaciable desire oppȝesseth the pooȝe vnto Death , and by the Furies are mente, the cares which Ryches bȝynge with them. By Cerberus, the thȝee mischiefes whych do oppȝesse the simple, Flatterye, Hypocrisie and Oppȝession : fayȝe wooȝdes to allure , Hipocrisie to dissemble, Oppȝession to take bp vyolence, is signified.

The Poetes faygne Cerberus, to be Plutos Poȝter, of the Citty Dolor, who receiueth all those that Charon bȝingeth, hauing thȝee heades, the one of a Goate, the seconde of a Beare, the thirde of a Tyger, whereby is also signified, Lechery, Gourmandise, and Murder: dyuers haue framed diuers shapes, onely to paint foȝth the filthines of vice, the moȝe to terrify the folowinge Age. Fœlix quem faciunt aliena pericula cautum.

BACCHVS.

Bacchvs was portraicted with a graunde paunch, his Charyot was drawen with an Ownce and a Tygre, his head was horned, and crowned with an Iuye Garlande, in one hande a Bunche of Grapes, in the other a Cuppe, hauing to his Garde

an Ape loking in a glaſſe, a Hogge, a Lyon,
a VVolfe, and a Dolphyn.

Signification.

BAcchus Was the firſt that in Grece foud the manner of planting Uines, & the ſecret of preſſinge Wi-
nes, called Liber Pater, by an Adage, the father of Liberty. In vino veritas. When men bee dronken, they
diſcloſe all, as when the Wine is in, the witte is out:
al ſuperfluous banquetinges, and Riotous exceſſe are
called Conuiuia Bacchanalia, dronken feaſtes.

The Feaſtes of diuers ſpottes and colours, as is the
Dance, & Tigre, ſignifie the ſudry affectiōs of ð dronken, and the deſperate madnes that ſuche poſſeſſeth by
outragious deedes, in dronkēnes, his hornes portrait
the cuſtomes of the Auncients, whiche vſed hornes to
drinke in, in ſteade of Pottes, his ſtrayghte garlande
of Iuye reſembleth the kerchefes of ð dronkē, for they
were accuſtomed to bind their head the harder, therby
to ſtoppe the vapors from aſcending into their brayne.

The Ape, the Hogge, and the Lyon, the Woolſe, and
Dolphin, bewray the affections of the Dronken: for
ſome playe the Ape in imitating euery thyng. ſome the
Hog in returning to accuſtomed dronkennes, as filthy
affections: ſome the Lyon in executing of crueltp: ſome
the Wolſe in rauening and ſpoyling: ſome the Dolphin ouerwhelmed in Bacchus ſeas: the Ape looking
in a glaſſe, they vaine flatterp of deceiuable follp.

The Poets fayne that Semele, Bacchus mother, was
a woman very bewtiful, beloued of Iupiter. But Iealous Iuno impacient thereof, deuiſed with her ſelfe Semeles deſtruction, and taking to her the ſhape of Se-

C 3.   meles

The Golden Booke

meles Nurse, she telleth her $ it is greatly to be doubted whether hee who she toke for her Paramour & best beloued, wer Iupiter in dede or no: wherfore her aduise was that Semele shoulo desire of Iupiter, $ hee woulde company with her in suche & so great a maiestye, as hee was accustomed to vse with Iuno, called the Quene of Heauen. Shortly after, Iupiter resortinge to her, shee desired of him to graunte her one request, who promised by an oth that shee shoulde bee satisfied. Iupiters othe was by the Riuer Styx, Semele supposinge not to bee cyrcumuented by Iuno, and chargynge Iupiter with hys Othe to accompanye with her in all his Maiestye : but shee by reason that shee was Mortall, not able to sustayne his presence, died at the first sight thereof, and being younge with chylo at that instante through the clemecy of $ Gods, it was hatched, tyl it grew to a graunde paunch called Bacchus, wherby is also signified that corruption lyketh all thynges that are filthye.

BONA DEA.

BERECYNTHIA or *Bona Dea was por-trayted, sitting in her Chariot, on her head was a turretted, Crowne, her guard with drawn Swordes attending on her, her wagon was drawne by Lyons: but driuen by Cocks: she holding in her had a Key.*

Signification.

By Bona Dea, is ment the worlds lower part. Earth

and

and by the worlde all thinges earthy, ouer the which the Mone hath gouernment: by the Wagon, the swift course of all thinges issuing and growing forth of the same: her stately sitting betokeneth the firme ground wheron is builded Cityes and townes: by her Crown so signified: wearing on her heade, as on the vpper face of the Earthe all Edifices framed with mountaynes and vallels, as Castels & Fortes: her Guard with weapons drawen, betoken the spedy pace of workinge signes & seasons as wel in man as in beast, & al things crescet or growig, wherin is workig the spirit of life: by the weapons are signified the sodaynnes of deathe, warninge euery estate to take hede of time.

By the Liös the courage of souldiers to lose none opor tunitie. By the Cockes are ment the priestes of Berecynthia, Which must be vigilāt as ʒ. Cocks to admonish the people be time. By the Key, the openyng of ʒ secret and bidde natures of al things growing in, and vpon the earth: from whece ʒ Phisitiō learneth to heale the sicke, and the Chirurgiā to cure the wounded: as also the earth to be opened in the sommer, and shut in the winter, when she diminisheth of her increace, by the frosen and barren season.

The Poets faigne her to be the mother of the godds, because, the Earth is the mother of al creatures, into ʒ which they shal retourne againe.

HERCVLES.

HERCVLES was figured in a Lions skinne, and holding a Clubbe in his right hande.

Significvation.

HErcules apparayled in a Lions skinne, signyfyeth the

The Golden Booke

the valiant courage of a woozthy Captayne, also the
Prudencie wherewith his minde beinge furnished, he
subdued his outragious affections:the Club,signifieth
vnderstanding,thzoughe which the motions of wicked
affections are repzessed and vtterly vanquished.

Hercules was befoze the destruction of Troie, in the
third age of the wozld,gouerner among the Lybians,
& had victozye ouer many nations,and subdued diuers
Kingdomes,a Pzince of wozthye Fame, a mainteiner
of Uertue,and a punisher of Uice,such a one as hated
those y chose to steale by policye,rather then to win by
pzowesse.

The Poets sayne that the hill Atlas in Mauritania
was a hupge Giant which foz the height suppozted
the stars,& ouercome by Hercules, he wanne the countrye and people, also in the valey of the sayd mountain
was a pleasant plat,the Ladies wherof were thzee sisters Aegle, Erethusa,Hespertusa,commonly knowe
by these names of Hesperides,in this valley was the
sayned tree with golden Apples,kepte by a Dragon:
wherby is signifyed,the great riches that pzoceaded
of so fertill a soyle,& the couetus disozder of the inha-
bitantes,who by deuouring of others, consumed them
selues.

ÆSCVLAPIVS.

*ÆSCVLAPIVS was portraited crowned with
a Laurel, standing in a long gown,in one hãd
a box of oyntment, and in the other a staffe.*

Signification.

Æsculapius signifyeth Phisicias: his lawrel crown
the

the cure by many medicynes : his longe Gowne, ý mo-
desty that belonges to such skill. By the boxe of Oyntments, the readines of Salues foz bodely cure : foz in
Auncient times past, the Phisition, Chyzurgion, and
Apothecharie was the office of one man : and now foz
the most parte, ý Practice of thzee Theeues . Foz learninge, is Ignozaunce: Foz Cunning, Craft: Foz cure,
Spoyle: Foz Lyfe, Death. Such bee the fruictes, of
discepueable Practise : By the staffe, the stay of Age,
whereby is signified, ý Learninge, and Experience is
stayed by coūsayle, thozough the which cōmeth knowledge of thinges both Good and Euell.

The Poets fayne that Æsculapius was slaine of Iupiter, with Lightninge from Heauen, foz that by hys
Arte, he raysed Hyppolitus from Death to Life. Diana, seacretly louing Hyppolitus, desired Æsculapius
by his skill too reuiue him to hys fozmer Lyfe: Which
beinge donne, shee called him Virbius, as if shee should
haue sayd, bis vir, twice a man. Iupiter displeased foz
the Facte, deuided their loue, by Death: replying that
Phisike will not helpe where GOD is disposed to
plague.

FLORA.

FLora, was portraited with Flowers in her hand,
of Beanes and Pease, her Coat in as many colours
as the Raynebowe.

Signification.

FLora her coloured coate, signifieth the diuers hue ý
is geuē to Flowers; her Beanes & Pease declare a
custome

The Golden Booke

cuſtome of ꝑ Romayns, who eſteeme no moꝛe of Bau-
dery, then of Superſtition: Which to beare Ruſticall
Signes in hande, that Flora was Goddeſſe, as well
of Grayne, as Flowers: Yearely in Honour of ꝑ ſame,
they dyd Sparcle, Beanes and Peaſe, amonge the cõ-
mon People.

Thys Flora was a Famous Harlot, and exceading
Ryꝃe, Conſtitutinge at her Death, the People of
Rome to bee her Heyꝛe: Shee oꝛdayned foꝛ Euer, a
great Summe of Money, to be Imploied on Showes
and Playes. The oꝛdinaunce of a gentle Deuill, delu-
dinge many Fooles: of ſuch foꝛce is wycked Mãmon,
that hee can make an Harlot, counted foꝛ a Goddes.

Thus the Pope, and Poet, can make, both Harlot, &
Theefe, a Saynate.

ÆOLVS.

*Æolus was figured ſtandinge in the Mouth of
a Caue, in his hãd a Tortoyſe: Vnder his Feete
a payre of Bellowes.*

Signification.

BY Æolus, is ment the Winde: his ſtandinge in the
Mouth of a Caue, ſignifieth the Wind to be engendered, in holowe Vautes of the Earth: his ſhell Fiſhe
beinge a Toꝛtoyſe (whoſe Shel is not to bee perced)
betokeneth the foꝛce of Windes, farre to exceede the
foꝛce of Murall, oꝛ Metall: And as the ſofte Fiſhe, is
defended by the hard Shell from the violence of the
Winde, ſo all ſofte, and tender Seedes, are pꝛeſerued,
by cloſe

by close Earth. For that the harder thinges, the higher, and greatter, by the violence of the Winde, is oft ouerthrowen, Trees, Towers, & Hylles. His treading on the Bellowes, shewich ye force of engendered Windes, by thycke, Uapours, combininge the Windes into narowe roomes, as when the Apre is darkest then is it thickest, and the Windes greatest. Æolus rapgned in Æolia, an Ilande in Sicilia, ye sonne of Iupiter, whom Poettes fapne Kinge of Windes, becaufe he was ye first that gaue knowledge of weathers : he ruled the Iles, Lippara, Cræta, Strögyle, & Didyme, wherin were certaine fiery Hilles, like Etna, a man very amiable to his subiectes, and Debonaire to straügers : The Sauage People beinge taught by experieunce, of their Kinge Æolus, to marke the seasons, supposed him to bee the oꝛiginal of Weathers, & called him the God of Wind, and Tempest.

CVPID.

Cvpid was figured, vnder the Shape of a blynde Boye, hauinge VVinges at his Shoulders, and a Bowe in his hande, prest to Shoote.

Signification.

By Cupid, Loue is signified, and likened to a Childe, becaufe it is not able to resist Affection: also becaufe Loue maketh Oldemen, sometyme Foolishe as Boyes, in which foolishnes they become moꝛe Ignoꝛaüt, then Childꝛe, his Winges, betoken ye swiftnes of Loue, ye although the body be staied by foꝛce, yet is the Mind voyd of victoꝛy: By his Being blinde, ye fond affections of foolish Louers: foꝛ ye also loue is as fond in chosinge, as selfe will

vnaduifed.

The Golden Booke.

vnaduiſed in deliueringe: Yf it proceade of the man,
then is Beauty preferred before Honeſty: If of the
Woman, then vayne Brauery, before ciuell Modeſty.
For as a foule Whore, delighteth in a perſonable Mã,
ſo likewiſe a foule Knaue taketh pleaſure in a fayre
Whore. When the Dartes of ſuch Loue proceadeth,
it manifeſtly proueth, that Cupid of cupid is Blinde
in deede.

The Poets fayne that Cupids Bowe, ſignified, the
attemptes of Loue. And the Arrow, the force of Lo-
uinge: and the perringe to the Heart: the full conſent,
of the ſame. Alſo that Cupid was Venus ſonne, who
takinge vppon him the Shape of Iulus, ſo enflamed
the Heart of Dido with Æneas his Loue, that for
greiſe of Æneas Departure, ſhe ſlue her ſelfe.

VOLVPIA.

*Volupia was figured lyke an Empreſſe, but pale of
Countenaunce, treadinge Vertue vnder her
Feete.*

Signification.

By Volupia, Pleaſures bee ſignified: ſhee was figured lyke an Empreſſe: for that for ý moſt part, Men
in preferringe Pleaſures, ſubmit them ſelues, to their
delightes. Her pale Looke, ſignifieth, the feare that
Wantons lyue in, fearinge alwayes leaſt Fortune
ſhoulde turne her Wheele, and that Sorrowe ſhoulde
followe their delightes: as after ſweete Meate, ſowre
Sauce. Her tramplinge vppon Uertue declareth, that
they cannot be but deſpiſers of Uertue, which wil let
                                                    loſe

loſe the Raynes of their deſiers to fleſhly Appetite.

The Poetes fayne that Syrenes, the Daughters of Achelous, dwelled within a certayne Ilande betweene Italy, and Scicill, who with their ſwœtenes of Uoyce, allured ſuch as paſſed by: who no ſoner obtayned their cōpany, but were rewarded for their cōming tō preſēt death. Vlyſſes, occaſioned to paſſe by: τ to preuēt their Whoriſh illuſions, cauſed all his Saylers and Souldiers to ſtop their Eares, and him ſelfe to be bound to the Maſte of his Ship. By which Policy, bē eſcaped the perill. The Syrenes, for anger that they were preuented, flange themſelues headlonge into the Sea, whereby is deſcribed the property of Enuy, who wyll rather then bee banquiſhed from doinge of Miſcheiſe, further their pretence with their owne Death.

As ruſt conſumeth Iron, ſo doth VVrath, the Bones.

HARPOCRATES, AND ANGERONA.

HArpocrates, and Angerona, were figured in comely Apparell, holdinge their Fingers vppō theyr Mouth.

Signification.

They both reſemble Taciturnitie, and in beinge comely Apparelled ſign ſieth the graue modeſty of prudent Gouerners. By the holding of theire Forefingers on their Mouthes, ſheweth alſo the heedefulnes, that Men ought to haue, in ſpeakinge.

The

The Golden Booke.

The Poetes fayne that the Pyes Chatteringe bee-
tokeneth Ghestes: And Womens Bablinge, betokeneth folly: for sometimes both sortes, so trauayle wyth
a word, that they haffard both life & goods.

OSIRIS.

Osiris was figured with a Basket vpon his head,
in the which was a Serpent with three heades,
holdinge the Tayle in his Mouth.

Signification.

Osiris the God of ease or rest, figured slowe pacinge,
wyth a Basket on his heade: by his goinge is signified the carelesse dealinge of vnthrifty subiectes, & ser-
uauts, which are negligēt in þ Affayres of their Princes, & Maisters: By the Basket the bōdage of seruice
vnder the which, all are helde: By the Serpent with
thre heades, The first of a Lyon, þ second of a Dogge,
the thyrd of a Wolfe. The Serpent signifieth the prudence of Lawes, well to gouerne cōmon Wealthes:
The head of the Lion, the courage of þ kinge: the head
of the Dogge, the auctority of nobilitye, the watchful
barkinge of spirituality, to defende the oppressed from
enormities: the head of þ Wolfe signifieth oppressiō w
proceadeth from the Kinge, from nobility, from spirituality, from Officer in auctority: from the kinge whē
he graūteth ouer much liberty: frō the Nobility, whē
they regarde not magnanimity: frō spirituality, when
they defend not fidelity: from Officer in auctority, whē
by carelesse oppression, they cōsume pouerty. These .iij.

heades

heades iopned to on body, fignifieth, the mutuall ac-
cozd oz confanguinity in euills, which as the Serpent
dououringe herfelfe, by beginninge with her tayle, fo
are diuers Kindomes, by oppzeffinge comõ Wealthes,
made weake, and bzought to confufion. Ofyris, Raygn-
ned in Ægipt, whom, Typhon, his owne Bzother, to obtayne the kingdome, inuaded, & takinge Ofiris captiue,
murdzroufly cut him into. 25. peeces fendinge eache
peece to fundzy Confpiratours of his death, fuppofing
thereby to haue obtayned their greater fauours. But
Ifis, with the helpe of Oros her Sonne, reuenged her
Hufbandes death, by hanging Typhon on a Gallowes.
Foz fũdzy benefits that Ofiris had done to the Egyptians, they wozfhipped him as a God.

ISIS.

*ISis was proporcioned wyth a Cornet in one hand
and a Ship in the other.*

Signification.

ISis hath a Cozmet in one hand, becaufe her Pzeiftes
in their Sacrifices, did Honour her with the Melo-
dies of that inftrumẽt: the holding a Shipp in the other
hand, in honour of Ofiris, which foz her fake had paffed many and daungerous Seas. The Poetes fayne
that Iupiter companyinge with Io, otherwyfe called
Ifis, Iuno came vpon them, one fuch a fodayne, as foz
the hiedinge of the fact, he turned Ifis into a Cow, but
Iuno fufpectinge the matter, defired the Cow of Iupiter, and gaue her to Argus to be kept. But Mercury,
by the aduice of Iupiter, to fet Ifis at liberty, flue Argus.

gus. Iuno, for reuenge caused the ſtoute Fly, to ſtinge
and vexe Iſis, who beinge exceadingly tormented, fled
her ſelfe from place, to place, til at the laſt ſhe entered
Egipt, where being reſtored to her former Shape, ſhe
was Maried to Oſiris, and after her Death was made
a Goddeſſe.

PAN.

P *An was figured, with a longe Bearde and hornes*
on his head, his Feete were lyke vnto a Goat, hol-
dinge a Pype to his Mouth.

Signification.

By Pan, Shepheardes are ſignified and needeth no
explication, becauſe the whole deſcription, contay-
neth the Portrature of a Shephearde.

The Poettes fayne that Midas, a Rych Kynge of
Phrygia, obtayned of Bacchus, to haue any thing geué
him that hee woulde wiſhe. He therefore deſired that
what ſoeuer he touched, might bee turned into Gould.
Bacchus graunted the requeſt. Midas to try the truth,
touched not only Tymber, Stones, and Fruict, which
turned to Gold: But alſo his Meat, & Drinck: it repen-
ted him of his folly, & ſœinge himſelfe ſo ouermatched,
waxed penſiue, requiringe Bacchus to take frō him his
wiſh. Bacchus not hard to be intreated, cōmaunded Midas, to waſhe himſelfe in ẙ Riuer Pactolus, & he ſhould
be cured: he did ſo, and ẙ Riuer, ſithens hath had Golden Sandes. Afterward, when Phœbus, and Pan,
contended whether of theym two, ſhould be iudged
the

ỹ beſt muſician the hyl Tmolus being choſē foʒ iudge, gaue ſentence on Phœbus ſide: but Midas ſtanding by and not choſen foʒ a dayes man, very fooliſhly, pʒeferred Pan. Phœbus eſpying Midas to be a buſie body, foʒ his greate foliſhneſſe, gaue him a payʒe of Aſſes eares, but Midas ſo hydde theym, that none knew it but only his Barbour, and not mynvinge to conceale it. Neuertheleſſe not daring to repoʒt it, hee made a Uaulte, in the which he cryed, *Kyng* Midas *hath Eares lyke an Aſſe*, and after couerynge the ſame, with Earth in ſuch a Moyſte place where Reedes began to grow, oute of the whiche Caue, by ſhakinge too, and fro, hee ſounded fooʒth thoſe woʒdes, which the Barbour had infuſed.

CONCORDIA.

CONCORDIA *was figured lyke a comlye Matrone holdynge a Chayne, to the whyche were faſtned all kynd of Beaſtes by couples in theyr kynde ſittinge on Inſtrumentes: ſhe was alſo likened vnto the Storke.*

Signification.

COncorde ſignifieth all coequalities, aſwell of agreeinges in Beaſtes, Birdes, Serpentes, Woʒmes, Fiſhes, Fowles, as Man and Woman, kingdomes and Nacions: Being poʒtraicted lyke a comlye Matrone, ſhoweth thereby the modeſtye aſwell of the Mynde, as Apparel, to bee aduiſed in al thyngs, her Chayne alſo ſig.uifieth the foʒce of a Stable Mynde, in faſt lyncked experience: By the Beaſtes cöwpling

E　　　　　　　together

together, the accord that Nature yeldeth to her owne
kynde. By sitting on diuers Instrumentes, the sup-
pressing of vayne phantasie, not ouer much delighting
in naked comfort: for as euery Instrumēt (how braue
soeuer they be in show) be ingfolb discordāt in Note,
from the true concord in Musicke, is nothinge worth,
so Amities, Frendshippes, and Cordiall dealinges betweene man and man, being but to the vtter show, &
not from a faythfull harte, is then called Hypocrisie,
and breedeth dissention: For the Auncient Romaines
esteemed more a small Acte done in the furtheraunce
of the Common Wealth, then great showes of wordes called vayne Boastinge without Deedes.

In that Concord is fygured amonge the Pagans
in the shape of a Storke: it is to be shewed what her
properties are, which is, euery thirde yeare to caste
foorth of her Neast one of her Byrdes, from the house
or Tree, whereon shee buyldeth and breedeth, as a
recompence for her quiet sufferaunce: moreouer when
she is olde, she is fedde by her Younge with great di-
ligence.

The Kinges in tymes paste, carued in the toppe of
their Scepter, the similitude of a Storke, and in the
lower ende, the shape of the water Horse, signifyinge
thereby, to be mayntenours of peace, and bryvelers
of such, as shoulde vse vyolence to anye.

As the Storke is a deuourer of Serpentes, so
ought Kinges to bee destroyers of Theeues, Murderers and Robbers: and as shee is liberall in geeuing
her young, so ought Kinges and Princes, to rewarde
their Subiectes, not with the Goodes of others, but
with their own, and as the younge Storke doth feede
the olde, so ought the Subiectes beinge fedde by good
Lawes, rewarde their kinges with large Treasures:

for

foʒ where good Lawes are, there is none oppʒeſſion.

Sundʒie other haue figured Concorde in the foʒme of a Doue, oʒ Turtle, becauſe that ſhewing the Con-coʒde of faythfull Fidelitie, both kinge and Subiecte ought to hold the ſame trulye.

PROTEVS.

P*ROTEVS hath no ſhape or likeneſſe, becauſe the Poetes faygne that he was a God of the Sea, which could turne himſelfe into any ſhape, whether it were of flaminge Fyer, or of a Furious Lyon, a grunting Hogge, a running ſtreame, or any thinge ells, whatſoeuer him lyſted, which thinge Virgil ſignifieth in theeſe Verſes.*

Omnia transformat ſeſe in miracula rerum,
Ignemꝗ, horribilemꝗ feram, fluuiumꝗ liquentem:

*Hymſelfe he ſtraungely doth transforme
　into al ſhapes, and gleames:
Now lyke to Fyer, now like to Beaſt,
　now like to ſiluer ſtreames.*

Some thincke that by Proteus the dyuers affections, of manns mynde are ſignified: foʒ ſometwhyle wee take pleaſure, foʒ the chiefeſte felicitie, when in verye deede it is but a hoggiſh affection: otherwhyle Anger baleth vs, and maketh vs moʒe lyke Tygres, then men: ſomtimes Pʒyde aſſaulteth vs, and maketh vs moʒe hautie then Lyons: ſomtime ſwyniſh affecti-ons, and then we beecome moʒe Dʒonken then Hogs: as foʒ good cogitations, they haue ſmalle oʒ no dwel-linges in our harts, and that is ſignified by the water.

The Golden Booke

Wherfore, if wee wyll reape anye profite by Proteus that is, by these our dyuers affecticus, we must bzyole theym : For the Poetes faygne, that Proteus. neuer gaue foorth anye true Oracles, but when hee was forced oz constrayoed thereunto.

ASTRÆA.

SHee was portraicted in a Virgins Habyte with verye seuere countenaunce and comelye Gesture.

Signification.

By Astrxa is signified Iustice. She geeueth Iudges to vnderstand that they bee of Force against the wicked, but mercifull to the Penitente : as precise & vpright in Iustice, as otherwise graue and modeste in Apparell.

HARPYÆ.

HARPIAE were portraicted like Carmarãts in bodye, but strompetlyke faced, hauinge long and cruel tallantes,

Signification.

By the Harpyx shamelesse desperate iniuries are signified, which as vnder Feathers' are shadowed foz a season : By theyr whozishe Countenaunce, the canckered wzath of a malicious woman, as in Dalila, Mem.

Memphetica, Vasthi, Iuno, Semiramis, Cleopatra, &
Philamertia: by their longe and sharp tallentes, their
greedy despze, to gette in possession the goodes of o-
thers.

The poets fapgne, þ ther, are thzee sisters of them,
wherof the first is called Aello, which in our speche
signifieth a spoyler of men, by unsatiable whozecome.
The second is called Ocypite A spedy conueyer oz filcher, a hackney whoze, while she is in fact: she pyckes
the captiues purse.

The third called Celeno: which signifieth darke, be
cause the doinges of whozedome loue darknes & hate
the light.

PARCÆ

PARCAE wer thre sisters ef destinie, wheráf Clo
tho was figured holdinge the distaffe, Lachesis
drawing out the threed, and Atropos cutting
it of.

Signification.

The Poets fayne that these thze sisters betoken the
felicity and state of man, and the misery of man.

By the thzeedes, mans life is signifyed, foz warning
euerye estate to lyue well, so longe as Lachesis
dothe drawe the Threede, it geueth warnynge
that tyme be diligently spent, foz when Atropos commeth to cut the threed, thereby is signifyed the ende of
lyfe, thē is natures course ended: if þ thzeed be white,
it betokens felicity. If it be blacke, endless misery: þ
is, if the lyfe be virtuous, it obtayneth lyfe, if it bee
vitious, then foloweth death.

FRIAPVS

The Golden Booke

PRIAPVS.

A YOVNG man armed, hauing two winges, in his right hand, a veſſel: powringe forth water on a ſquare ſtone, on his left arme bearinge al ſortes of frutes, in his right hande a whippe of three cordes, haninge alſo a greene VVillow garland on his heade.

Signification.

THE poung man, betokeneth kyndled luſt, otherwyſe called the God of Lecherye: his two winges, ſwyftnes, to accompliſh carnal Venerie: the one wing is Flatterp, the other, is Force. The veſſel of water poured foorth on the ſtone, the multitude of wordes tending to no vertue: the ſquare ſtone, the ſtubburne and harde harted. By the holdinge of vaynzye fruites, the waſtful erpence that Leacherye vſeth by ryotous erceſſe.

By the whip, the ſharpe tople of beggerp, which followeth the haunters of ſuch art: By the three cordes hunger, ſickues & death. The Garlande of Willowe foreſhueth the ſharpe tyme of youthe, or ſtorpſhynge ſtrength.

The Poets faine Priapus to be the ſonne of Venus, which is Luſt following carnal deſpre. This Priapus was honowred for a god among the Gentiles, & prayed vnto by their women þ were barrayne, to the ende they might haue childzen.

GRATIAE

GRATIÆ

THE Three Graces were portraited naked with hand in hand, wherof two loked toward vs and the thyrd from vs.

Signification,

BY the three graces, thankfulnes, Bountefulnes and liberalitp is signifyed: fo2 in that one loketh frō vs, and two toward vs, we are let to weete, ý one benefyte, when it is bestowed wel, wil b2ing with him two home agayne .

They were po2trayted naked, becaufe benefytes muste not be coūterfaited, but done fo2 vertues fake. Theyr holding of one an other hand in hand, signifieth ý boūtie doth winne & couple mens hartes together. They also were portraited Lawghinge, becaufe the liberalitpe ý is commended, dothe p2ocede from a cherefull and wylling mynde.

The Poets fayne that the first fo2 her mery countinaūce, was called Aglaia ý fecond fo2 her fresh colour was called Thalia: And the thp2d fo2 her pleafantnes was called Euphrofine. Aglaia, signifyeth thankefulnes fo2 benefits receiued. Thalia, plenteoufnes by liberal reward, Euphrofine liberalitp whē nede is efpied.

Thefe p2efigure ý the benefits of ý mind, ought to bee no lesse liberal then ý p2oceding liberalitp, which p2oce deth frō fo2th of ý earth, & therfo2e called Gratiæ.

ORPHEVS

ORPHEVS was figured in a Philofophers wede, playing on a harpe with fundry fortes of beaftes and byrdes about him.

Significa-

The Golden Booke

Signification.

BY Orpheus is signifyed skil.ful musike, as wel by songe as instrument. By his Philosophers weede, the camly gesture that belongs to handling the instrument. By the harpe, the wyse sentences and sonets to the adorning of musike. By the beastes and byrdes, the delectable mindes of the simple unlearned.

The Poets faine that he was a peerelesse musition in so much, that at his playe, wild beasts would come aboute him, the byrdes stay their flightc, the waters, their flowinge, the trees bow down their toppes, and the mountaynes hoppe, whereby is sygnifyed the delightsome pleasures in al estates.

The Poets faygne that when his wyfe Euridice was dead, he went to Hell, to speake with her soule, where his swete musique so rauished the mayster Deupll, that hee consented to let Orpheus haue his wyfe, agayne, condicionallye þ shee should not loke backe til she were out of the infernal kingdome, which thing she not able to refrayne: he lost her agayne, Musique is delectable to the mynde, but carnally liked, is hurt to the soule.

PERSEVS.

PERSEVS had wyngs at his shoulders, a Falchion or Percian swoorde by his side, and flyinge Pegasus beatinge the grownd with his heeles.

Signifycation.

His winges betoken his shippes, by which he sayles
into

into Aſia:his ſwoꝛde ſygnyfieth his victoꝛye ouer Me-
duſa: his flyinge hoꝛſe, is a repꝛeſentation of Fame,
and ſpeedy purſuite after his enemies.

The Poets fayne Stheno, Euriale, and Meduſa, to
bee thꝛee ſiſters. euery hayꝛe on ech of their heades, to
to a Snake, and all ꝑ they looked vpon, they turned
into ſtones, by which ꝭ ſignified, their blaʒing Beau-
tyꝛ, to bee ſuch, and ſo greate, that they bereft oꝛ enamoured al that looked vpon them, ſo farre from wyt ⁊
vnderſtáding, by their alluring ſlights, ⁊ coũterfeyted
ſhewes, ꝑ therfoꝛe they were ſayde to bee tranſfoꝛmed
into ſtones, becauſe they ruled thẽ at their pleaſures.

The Poetes faygne Perſeus, to haue boꝛowed of
Mercurie, both Wynges, and Swoꝛd, and of Pallas a
Target, and ſo comminge ſodeulye, ſyndinge Meduſa
ſleeping bee cut of her heade, and ſhewed the ſame to
his enemies, at the ſighte whereof, they turned into
Stones.

The force of Forreyne helpe,
ech Countrye maketh ſtronger:
And force ſupplied when time doth laſt,
doth proſper it the longer.
The ſmyling ſhew, which treates a peace to be
Is treaſons fraude: let dayly prudence ſee.

FVRIÆ.

THe three Furies, Alecto, Tyſiphone, & Mæge-
ra, were portraicted with whyppes, in their handes: their hayres hyſſyng Serpentes, with haggiſh
F   lookes

The Golden Booke

lookes and gryeſlye countenaunces.

Signification.

By the Furies, the ſtynge of an euil conſcience is ſignified: their whippes betoken the Tormentes
which the wicked are forced to ſindure: theyr Serpen-
tyne hayres, doth intimate, that the Conſcience doeth
alwayes gnawe, and byte the harte of the vngodlye:
Their menacing looke and countenaunce, doth threa-
ten the grieſlye toyle in the ſecond Lyfe. Tullie in hys
Oration pro Roſcio, declareth after this ſorte.

Nolite putare, quemadmodum in fabulis ſæpenumero vi-
detis eos, qui aliquid impiè ſcelerateq, commiſerút, agita
ri et perterreritædis ardétibus: ſua quéq, fraus, ſuus terror
maxime vexat, ſuum quemq, ſcelus exagitat, amentiaq
afficit, ſua mala cogitationes conſcientiaq, animi terrent.
Hæ ſunt impijs aſſiduæ domeſticæq, furiæ, quæ dies nocteſq,
parentum pœnas à ſceleratiſſimus filijs repetunt.

In Engliſh thus.

Thinke not (as Poetes haue fayned) the wicked to
bee ſinged and ſcortched with Flaminge torches: it is
our owne guyle, that moſte doth beguyle vs, it is our
owne wickedneſſe, that doth moſt affright vs, it is our
own folly, that doth moſt caſt vs dovvne, and our own
thoughtes and wicked conſciences that doth tormente
vs. Theſe, theſe I ſaye are the continual boſome Furies, which day and night, cryeth for vengeaunce, and
puniſheth the ſinnes of lewd Parentes vppon theire
wicked chyldren.

The Poets fayne by theſe three Furies, the diuers
affectiõs of þ mind, which force mẽ into ſuryy, ſ diuers
miſchiefes: the firſt is Anger, þ ſecond couetouſneſſe,
the thirde Luſt, wherof Anger deſireth to bee reuenged: Couetouſneſſe to poſſeſſe great riches: and Luſte
                                                    to en

to enioy Fleſhlp pleaſures.

CASTOR &POLLVX.

THeſe were figured like two Lampes, or Creſſet lightes, one on the Toppe of a Maſte, the other on the Stemme or foreshippe.

Signification.

BY the light firſt appearing in þ Stemme or forſhip & aſcending vpwarde, the Marpners hope of good lucke,for wpnde and weather layre to enſue: But if ether lights beginne at the Topmaſte, Boweſprpte, or Foreſhip,and deſcend downward into the Sea, it is a token of vehement tempeſt to folow.

Caſtor is ſuppoſed to be that light which aſcendeth & burneth cleare & bright. Pollux that which deſcendeth,and is more dymme,& ſtyncking,lyke Sulphur.

The Poetes faigne,that Caſtor & Pollux were the two brethren of Helena, who for their vnſaciable lecherie,and hotte burning luſtes,were tranſfigured by Apollo into two lightes, cōmitted to the gouernment of Nocturna,to be diſperſed into euerp coaſt for a plague & reuenge of the Troians deſtruction. By the encreaſed lightes is ment the fierp luſtes: the clearneſſe, that which proceedeth of Youth,which for a tyme ſeemeth delectable , & ſoone is quenched. The dymme lighte of Pollux ſigniſieth Age, and the Luſte thereof,to be more filthy,and therfore continuallp baniſhed of the Vertuous.

THe Athenians had for their God a gay Image, with a goldē tōgue, by which was signified that

F 2   neyther *neither Apparel nor outwarde comlyneſſe was any thinge worth, not hauing a Golden toung, VVherby is ſignified Truth.* Veritas temporis filia.

SEinge that wee haue ſpoken of manye DemiGods and Goddeſſes, conſider wel, by the Fygure followinge, of the one eternall, moſt mighty, moſt true and euerlpuinge God, by whoſe diuine ſufferaunce, manye thinges hath paſſed, and the former Ages meruelouſlye darkened, by the onelye crafte, and ſlye practiſes of our mortall enemie Sathan, the onely author of al errour and diſcorde. This Fygure is ſet betweene the Heathens, Pagans, and falſe Chriſtians, the more to blemiſhe their fooliſhe Imaginacions, for as before is deſcribed the Gods of the Gentiles: ſo foloweth after the Gods of the Romiſh Churche, to the ende that euery true Chriſtian, may the better dyſcerne the light from Darkeneſſe, and Truth from Falſhood: and conferring the vayne imaginacions of tyme paſt, with the true Touchſtone in tyme preſent, ſhal eaſelye eſpie, the broade way to deſtruction, through the which too manye haue paſſed: and now fyndinge the narrow waye to ſaluation, may euermore be the redier to prepare them ſelues to the Hauen of Peace, which God in mercye graunt, for his onelye ſonne Ieſus Chriſte his ſake aſſiſting vs with his holy ſpyryte now & euer. Amen.

A Fygure on fyue Letters, of the Eternitie vnder which is comprehended the Hypocryſie of the Church, the loſing of Sathan, and the appearinge of the Goſpell.

C. is the capital letter of Chriſtus, two V.V. endwiſe ioyned maketh an X. which is in nūber 10, ſ figure of the Law, nature & grace ſo ioyned togethers, called

called the law of the tenne commaundementes ; which
being geuē after creatiō, called DIES, stanos in in .2.
place: the 3 letter I. which is in number one, repꝛesen-
ting the beginning, and ending applied to the 3 person
which is Homo, who being made in Dics, which woꝛd
carieth also his pꝛoper signification, as of 4 letters 4
Elementes, ⁊ then secōdly the woꝛd Homo of the same 4 letters, the 4 cōplexiōs ⁊ hauig life in it selfe foꝛ
a tyme by creation, generation, ⁊ pꝛocreatiō, is said to
be ꝑ, which Homo signifieth, which is mā: first Earth,
Water, Aire, Fyer: the Melācholy, sleumatike, sāgui-
ne ⁊ choler so cōpouded as a liuing creature exceding
all other. Fy the thyꝛd and last figure whiche is one, ⁊
the first from the beginning is made 3 by the same, as
by the figure moꝛe playnely appeareth vnder ꝑ which
is figured, Christus, Dies, Homo. cupplinge it selfe
into humanity: woꝛketh redēption through moꝛtifica-
tiō, ⁊ resurrectiō. The hebꝛew Schin W signifieth the
coniunctions of the diuine persons as the former in re-

dēptiō father, Son, ⁊ Holi ghost by C.X.L. These bewraye false religion, Apostacy ⁊ Hypocrisy by Chꝛyst
in tyme among men.
The

The Golden Booke

The letter C,one hundred: the letter X,tē,the letter
I, one:which make one Hundred and eleuen: ý two
letters V V,as thus X makes an X,which is tenne:
and one ten makes foure V,V,V,V,which is twētý:
in the whole thýztý. The letter X turned euery way,
makes four tennes,which is 40.in ý whole,70:to 70
ad,C,X I.tĕ in al maketh 181.The gather together ý
Hebrew nūber ⌣ which is.CCC.¢ ý chared ⫯lod
which makes 10.that is in all 491,ad to euerye letter
single in the square one thousande, to the number of
491, and you shall fynde ç 4 9 1. from the whyche
tyme depnge erpzzed,to the ende and seconde com-
mynge of CHRIST persecution is to bee loked
foz

Vnfold me this, and tel me playne:
  VVhether the Gospel shal remayne.
If thou say no,then hast thou lied,
  for truth it selfe the same hath tryed.
Sathan was bound a thousand yeres,
  His members are worse then himselfe.
Sathan dayely among men apperes ,
  Romes treasure is turned to pelfe.

Many nations and Citties had a wonderful great de
light in themselues,foz that they were cōsecrated vnto certayne Gods Athens was cōmended of Minerua,Delos the Ilād of Apollo ¢ Diana. Cicero against
Verres pzaysfeth al Sicilia, but especiallye ý mount Etna,foz that it was cōsecrated vnto Ceres, as thoughe
it were wholy nothyng els,but an house oz temple of
Ceres. How much moze honourable is it ,foz those
which be Chzistians in name,to be the same in deede,
the childzen of the one and the euerliuing GⅮⅮ,
                                                    whiche

ẘ is bleſſed foꝛ euer, aṁꝛ. Foꝛ amongꝭ the gentiles ſuch
regarde was had vnto vertue, that they dedicated to ꝑ
vertuous, ꝑ reward of three goddeſſrs.
The firſt Strenua whereby is mente Dexterity oꝛ valiant dealinge.
The ſeconde Agenoria, whiche ſignifyeth virilitye
oꝛ manhode tendynge to   Actiuitye and valiant-
nes.
The thyꝛd Stimula which ſignifyeth a ſpurre, the
agility ⁊ quicknes to vertuous exerciſes. Seing therfoꝛe that the Gentiles and heathniſh people in auncie-
ent times paſt, haue ſo pꝛeferred vertue, that not onely they haue executed their lawes by puniſhinge the
ungodlye: but alſo haue lefte in Tables, wꝛitten,
paynted and grauen, the ſubſtaunce of that which
they pꝛofeſſed foꝛ a perpetuall recoꝛde of theyꝛe liues
and conuerſations, howe much moꝛe oughte wee that
are Chriſtians eſteme of the moſt deuine tables geuē
by God to Moſes. wherein was dꝛawen by the finger
of the almighty, the happie gouernment of mannes
felicitye? Alſo what pictures canne moꝛe admo-
niſhethen the grauen, wꝛittē and pꝛynted charcctes
and bokes of gods eternal woꝛd and goſpel confirmed
by a gloꝛious victoꝛy, ouer a tiranous death, to beholde
one another it ſhal ſuffice whether the deedes frō the
mynde be aunſwerable to the Image of the bodye oꝛ
not: but being founde farre otherwyſe as euery man
and woman, nation ⁊ people, wil decke and make com-
ly the earthy body by waſhing, bathing ⁊ curious clo-
thing, cleſing ⁊ bꝛuſſhing ꝑ ſpots of dyrt ⁊ duſt, ſo is it
behoueful to euery chriſtian ſo to clenſe his mynd and
conſcience from euel thoughts and woꝛkes, as maye
pꝛepare the ſoule with adoꝛned vertues befoꝛe God ẘ
moꝛe Diligēce thē ꝑ garmēts befoꝛe woꝛldly graciual
Pꝛinces

princes the neglecting wherof, prouoked God almighty, first of all after mans pryde began to growe on the
earth, so for to reiect him from his fatherly compassion, that his holy spirite no soner being absent, Sathā
presently steps in, and so fillinge the mynde wyth vayn
cogitaticns, whch presently began inuocations to di-
uyls, honours to spirites, & worshipinge of creatures,
neuerthelesse in ỹ midest of the which sin, there amōg
some remayned the sparkes of treue seruice, by the
which although outwarde Idolatrous, yet inwarde
by lawes, & constitutions verteous this Straūge entermixed stratageme engēdred after a time Hypocrisie
which left at ỹ last ỹ act of doing Iustice, & by vsyng ỹ
bare shew, became Infideles: through the which Sa-
thans kingdome increased, & Gods people became few
Till by the comming of our Blessed Sauiour many
were restored agayne, as by the disputation betwene
Adrianus & Epictetus is somewhat to bee parcepued
and after the end thereof shall solowe the Goddes of
Supersticion.

☞ The Capital God in his right fashion.

Adrianus out of Vege-
tius de re militari.

WHAT matter is it, yf thou vnlose thy gyrdle
for vs, thou thy selfe shal not bee vnclothed,
regard that body by the which thou mayste
be taught.

Epictcus It is an Epystle.

A. VVhat is an Epistle?

E. A silent mesenger.

A. VVhat is a Picture?

E. A glosing treuth.

A. VVhy doste thou tearme it so?

E. Because wee see paputed Apples, flowers, lyuinge creatures, Golde, and Siluer, and they are not the very true, & selfe same thinges.

A. VVhat is Goulde?

E. The bond Slaue of Death.

A. what callest thou Siluer?

E. The place of Enuy.

A. what is Iron?

E. An Instrument for euery Arte.

A. VVhat is a Sworde?

E. The Ruler of Force, the stay of Tentes in Battaile.

A. VVhat is a Fensor?

E. A manquellour without offence.

A. VVho are those, that beinge in health, are sicke?

E. They that are busie in other Mens matters.

A. Hovve can a man laboure, and not be vveary?

E. By gayninge.

A. VVhat is Frendship?

E. A concorde, or agreeing.

A. VVhat is that which in length exceadeth al other thinges?

E. Hope.

A. VVhat is Hope?

E. A slumber to a Watchman: and a doubtful Chaunce to him that looketh for it.

A. what thinge is that which a man canot behold?

E. The Mynde of an other.

A. In what thinge doth a man offend?

E. In lust.

A. VVhat is lust?

E. A secret stearinge of the Body to Ill: A corruptible heate, the Originall to Leachery.

A. VVhat is Liberty?

E. Innocency.

G　　VVhat is

The Golden Booke

A. VVhat is cōmon aſwel to a King as to a wretch?

E. Byꝛth, and Death.

 A. VVhat is the beſt thinge, and worſt thinge?

E. A Wooꝛde.   (to an other ?

 A. VVhat is pleaſaunt to one, & diſpleaſaunt

E. Bondage againſt liberty: pꝛoſperity to the healthy: To a Kinge, no company: to a Begger, no Almes.

 A. VVhat is that which is euer?

E. Lyfe.

 A. VVhat is Lyfe?

E. The oꝛiginall of all beginninges.

 A. VVhich is the beſt Lyfe?

E. Felicity.

 A. VVhat is the moſt certayne thinge of all?

E. Death.

 A. VVhat is Death?

E. A perpetuall ſecurity.

 A. VVhat is the generall Death?

E. The ende of all thinges that euer were: a thinge to bée feared of none that lyueth well: the Enemy of lyfe: a God ouer liuinge Creatures: a feare of the Parētes: a pꝛaye to the Childꝛen: the cauſe of makinge Teſtamentes: a Speach after life is departed: the very laſt Mourninge: a foꝛgetfulnes, after a Remembꝛaunce: the light Toꝛch of the laſt Fyꝛe: a burden foꝛ a Graue: a title of a Toumbe, & Death is the ende of all euil.

 A. VVhy are the Dead crowned? (lyfe.

E. It is a Witnes ꝑ they haue paſt the bitter courſe of

 A. Why are the Thūbes of the dead boūd together?

E. Becauſe they may knowe themſelues to be equal after Death.

 A. VVhat is the fatall fier?

E. A contentinge of the Dettour: A paymēt of ꝑ debt.

 A. VVhat is a Trompet?

a miⱦture

E. The ſtirringe vp to battayle: the warninge to fight: a mixture of Swordes: a lametacion of dead Corſes.

A. VVhat is a Pooreman?

E. A deſert Well: whom al the Paſſengers behold and leaue it ſtill in his place.

A. VVhat is man?

E. A Man is like to a Hotehouſe : the firſt roome is warme, where the bodies are annoynted : ſo an Infant beinge borne, is firſt annoynted: the ſeconde for the bodyes to ſweat in, is Youth : ſo are the bodies ſubiect, & therefore equall to diſtemperatures.

A. VVhat is mans ſtrength?

E. Like a rotten Apple, eyther they fall downe when they are throughly ripe : Or if they falle before, they falle hardly.

A. VVhat is man in Age?

E. A Candle placed agaynſt the Winde : a Soiourner in Earth, the very Image of the Lawe: a Stable of miſery, a bond ſlaue to death: a delayer of life, with whom Fortune dalieth.

A. VVhat is a VVoman?   Litigious:

E. A neceſſary euil: for vnneceſſary cauſes: a touchſtone to ſhew y colour of Gold, & Siluer : a burdē to beare childrē of two ſortes: men & womē : Baſtards & Hermaphroditical childrē, hauing. 1. mother, & 2. fathers.

A. VVhat is a VVoman. Coniunctiue.

E. The piller of the houſe: the Ioy of the Huſband, the comforte to children, the Storehouſe of Generation, & the Augmentour of Poſterity.

A. VVhat is Fortune?

E. Shee is a noble Matrone y applieth herſelfe to her ſeruaūts: the next marke wout Iudgement: a chalice of outward egoods, to ſhineth on him, on whom it happeneth, and darknech him, from whom it flyeth.

The Golden Booke.

A. Howe many Fortunes bee there?

E. As many as fond heades hath inaentions: yet sayd to bee thꝛee: one blinde that applyeth herselfe where shee list: An other Mad, that taketh away agayne the Giftes by her geuen: The thirdis Deaffe, that neuer will harken to the Pꝛayers of the miserable.

A. VVhat are the Gods?

E. The very signes of our Eies, the powers of ý minD, if thou be afrayd of the, that is feare: If thou refraine of thine owne accoꝛd, that is Religion.

A. VVhat is Religion?

E. A Doctrine established in thy minde, vnto the which is geuen reuerence, either good, oꝛ bad.

A. VVhat is good?

E. That which was neuer Ill.

A. VVhat is Euill?

E. That which hateth good.

A. VVhat is the Sunne?

E. The light of the Woꝛlde, which geueth and taketh away the day, by the which we know the course of the howers.

A. VVhat is the Moone?

E. The Adder of the Day, the Eye of the Light, the Light of Darcknesse.

A. VVhat is Heauen?

E. A high, and mighty Roofe, a pured Ayꝛe.

A. VVhat are the starres?

E. The bestenies of Men, safe Hauens to ý Mariners.

A. VVhat is the Earth.

E. The Barne of Ceres. A mansion place foꝛ Lyfe.

A. VVhat is the Sea?

E. A way vncertayne.

A. VVhat is a Shippe?

E. A wandꝛinge house, a dwellinge place, where thou
lyst, the

lyſt, the power of Neptune, a table for the courſe of the yeare.

A. VVhat is a Mariner?

E. I louer of the Sea, a forſaker of the firme Lande, a Cōtemner of Lyfe, ꝣ Death, a Cliēt of the Waues.

A. VVhat is ſleepe?

E. The Image of Death.

A. VVhat is the Night?

E. A reſt for the Labourer, ꝣ a Gayne for the Robber.

A. VVhy was *Venus* paynted naked?

E. Becauſe loue is naked, ꝣ becauſe Venus doth leaue thoſe naked, whom naked thinges delight.

A. VVhy was *Venus* maried to *Vulcan?*

E. That declareth all loue to be ſtirred vp by Heate.

A. VVhy was *Venus* Squint Eyed?

E. Becauſe ſhe wanted good Conditions.

A. VVhat is Loue?

E. A vexation of an Idle Breaſt, in a Child it is ſhame, in a Virgin, a bluſhinge ſecret: In a Woman madneſ: In a Youngeman heate: In an Oldman a laughinge-ſtocke: in the mockinge of the Vice, a heinous crime.

A. VVhat is God?

E. He which ruleth all thinges.

A. VVhat is Sacrifice?

E. An Offeringe vp of Incence.

A. VVhat is without a Companion?

E. A Kingedome.

A. VVhat is a Kingdome?

E. A part of the Gods.

A. VVhat is a Kinge?

E. The head of the publique light.

A. VVhat is the Senate?

E. An Ornament of the Citty: The Brightnes of the Cittyzens.

VVhat is a

The Golden Booke.

A. VVhat is a Souldiour?

E. The Bulwarke of the Realme, the Defender of a Coũtry: a Honourable seruice, a Messenger of Might: In some Countries, a People naught set by.

A. VVhat is Rome?

E. The Fountayne of the Empyre: a mother of Motions: a Possessour of substaũce: a hostage for Romaines, a consecration of eternall peace.

A. VVhat is *Rome*, sithens it ruled by religion?

E. The Foũtayne of Ciuil dissentiõ, poured into sũdry Kingedomes: A Brothell house for Whores mayntenaunce: A Sãctuary for Murtherers, & Theeues: A Pardon for homicide, the Temple of Idolatry: A depriuation of Uertue: the execrable face of alł furies.

A. VVhat is Victory?

E. An Enemy to Warre: a Louer of peace.

A. VVhat is Peace?

E. A quiet liberty.

A. VVhat is the Courte Haule?

E. A place for Frablers.

A. VVhat are frendes?

E. Goulden Images.

A. VVhat is a friende?

E. He that healpeth in time of necessity.

A. VVhat are Flatterers?

E. They that catch men like Fishes.

A. VVhat is the best case?

E. He which doth good to most: and harme least?

STEPHANVS

THAT THE HOPE OF IMMOR-
tality, hath conuerted many from
Infidelity.

OUr almighty God hath made a plentifull worlde: But miserable fooles, maketh it to seeme scarce: when the hidden goods, bewrayeth the Gatherers. All thinges created in the Worlde, is fructfull.

Therefore,

Man being in the World, is fruitful.

VVherein?

Either in number of Uertues, through ẙ which bee shal lyue. Either in the number of Uices, by ẙ which he shal dye: and this is called Gayne.

A. VVhat doth a man gaine by getting the world?

E. The losse of his Soule.

A. VVhat is the losse of the Soule?

E. The excludinge from endlesse Ioye.

A. VVhat is Ioye?

E. The Iewell of health.

A. VVhat is health?

E. The perfection of peace.

A. VVhat is peace?

E. The whole rest of immortalitie.

A. VVhat is immortality?

E. The endlesse Ioye called felicity, which was from beyonde tyme, and euer shalbe.

A. By whom is mortality crowned?

E. By Immortality: who as cheife Creatour, chooseth whom hee wil and leaueth what he list.

A. VVhat is a Creator?

(shalbe.

E. The originall of all thinges, that euer were, is, or

A. VVhat is his name?

E. God almighty.

A. And why?

E. Because he is the same, frõ whõ, ẙ in whose power, are al thinges in subiection, Man, Beaste, Fysh, Foule, Serpent, Worme, Flyes, Heauen, and Earth, Hell, Sinne, the Deuill, and Deathe, who seeth all thinges before they were, what they are, and what they shaibet who also sayeth, seeke not out those thinges, which are aboue thy capacity, because they are not subiect to thée,

The Golden Booke

Stephanus Verses conclu-
dinge these questions.

The Tiger fierce, doth followe kinde,
The Doue by flyght, doth seeke her rest,
The blessed ones, doth shewe their mynde,
Although of euill bee possest.

The Haughty Rocke though fast hee stande,
Is subiect to the quakinge Earth.
The vile surmise of wicked Man,
Is forst by kinde to lose his Breath.
Striue not therefore agaynst the Streame,
The foode yealdes such as laboure gleane.

Uorax the capitall God
of Supersticion,

SO called of deuouringe, oppzessinge and consuming
by takinge with vpolence the Landes and Goods of
Kinges, and People, by persecutinge, foz the truthes
pzofession, by killinge to suppzesse, and darken the be-
rity, foz ý custome claymeth auctozity, after the which
followeth Superiozity, which beinge obtayned, conté-
neth Equality, and so remayneth as highest till the almighty frustrate such Arrogancye.

Frauncis.

ITem that he sitteth in the first degré, & chéefest place
in Heauen, & hath his Seate in the Highest Place.
That

that Fraunces is Chriftes Chauncellour, Treaſorer, his banner bearer, & counſapler, & that he beareth, the wounds ipke Chriſt: & where as Lucifer was ỹ high-eſt ſette in the heauen, being longe ſithens diſplaced, Fraunces hathe his roome, implping, ỹ there is foũd none like him, for hee, hathe obſerued the lawe of the higheſt.

Item that the doue ſeut from Noe out of the Arcke, ſigniſieth the order of the barefoote Friers: alſo that, in al things, Fraruncis was like the ſonne of God, whe-ther this be horrible blaſphemp, let al that be of God, Iudge.

Pope Gregorie the.9.made him a Sainct.

A Confirmation.

FRyer Loy ſaw Chriſt crucified goinge before, and Frauncis talkinge with hym, & that Frauncis tur-ned the Ryuer Tiber into Oyle, it map be thought he kplled a number of Fyſhe, but poyſoned mo Soules. an vncharitable miracle.

Of Frauncis Byrthe by Miſtris Picha his Mother I omitte, and infinite other Fables, becauſe he muſt geeue place to moe.

F. Gyles.

FRyer Gyles was rapt into Heauen.

Dunſtane.

SAynct Dunſtane, helde the Dyuell by the noſe with a payre of Tonges, by which is ſignified the ſtrẽgth of holy churche: in the which act, the Legende ſetteth
ħ   foorth

The Golden Booke

foozth this toy to small commendacions: as also in the Alcharō of the Barefoote Fryers.

Such a number of preposterous Godds are to bee found: so Saincted & made by the maylter Demon, ÿ to wzyte them al, woulde contayne an huge volume.

These haue I sette onlye to sharpen the myndes of wel disposed, the better to consider of the rest: & therfoze the moze earnestly pzay to God almightye, foz Iesus Chzistes sake, to keepe vs from such seruile bondage, as our fozefathers haue long continued in, & daylye imploye oure studies and wylles to his gloze, in which so doing, our assurance shalbe perpetual, which God in mercy graunt.

Item in the Reliques of Rome, the Pageaunte of Popes, the Fozest of Hystozies, the Secretes of Nature, and Anotomie of the Masse, are all readye touched the supersticious Gods and Sainctes of Romayne factions. I therefoze omitte the same, shewinge thee whyther to resozt, as also the pzincipal Authozs, from whence they were first had.

Legenda Sanctorum.   Brunellus.
Legenda aurea,   Mystery of Iniquitie.
Sermones discipuloū.
Catalogus glorię Mundi.
Vita Sancti Patricij.   Vita Christi.
The Flower of the Commaundementes.
Vitæ Patrum.
Methodi⁹ de Reuelationb⁹. with many others, wherby the tyme present maye beholde as in a Chzistall Glasse lyke true traueylinge Pilgrimes, aswell the freckles of counterfeit perswasions, as also the great spottes of cozrupt Religion, which being thus espyed, by the ayd of the thzee Gzaces, Fayth, Hope, & Charitie, we may attayne to the heauen of celestial perpetuitie.

A reca

A Recapitulation of the Sectari-
an Gods, by whose Heresies, much harme hath
growen, to Gods true Church.

WHen the Image of the beast, a formed shape had foūd,
Thē straightwais he became to geue the church a wound:
Which church new erected, by force was put downe
By PAPA the great God, which weares the triple crowne.

HIs heresye was and is of the Sacrament, that ꝑ
Sonne of God, boꝛne of the Uirgin Mary, was ⁊
is, in the Sacramentel of theyꝛe abbominable Alter,
Fleshe, Bloud, ⁊ Bones: also they hold, that it is law-
ful to haue Idols in Churches, to geeue reuerence to
Saynctes canonized: also they holde, ꝑ it is no sinne
to murder the pꝛofessours of Gods woꝛde and Uerity,
replying that there is none other Uerity, Doctrine, oꝛ
Chꝛistianitie, then what pꝛoceedeth out of theyꝛe Dia-
bolical Synagogue: neither any other religion to bee
holden foꝛ truthe, but that which pꝛoceedeth from Rome. The Popes Apparel domesticall, is a purple uel-
uet Cappe, edged with Armine, oꝛ other rych Furres,
hys vpper Garment, a Red oꝛ Purple cloake, euen tō
his elbowes, vnder ꝑ which is a blacke silke Uesture, ⁊
vnder the Uesture a whyte lynnen Garment, edged tō
Golde ⁊ hunge with pendentes oꝛ belles, his Pontificall adourninge is a tryple Crowne of great rychesse,
set with Stones of peerelesse value: his vpper Garment, is a Cope, moꝛe woꝛth then his Condicions: hee
is caried on the Backes of foure Deacons, after the
maner of carping Whytepot Queenes, in Westerne
Maygames.

              H2   Basilides

The Golden Booke
Baſilides.

BAſilides, the name of an Heretique, who affirmed that Chꝛiſt was not crucified, but Simon Cireneus, who, as ꝑ Euāgeliſtes wꝛpte, was cōſtrapned to beare the Croſſe, when our Sauiour wared fapnt, thꝛough effuſion of bloude by his ſcoꝛginge. He held that it was no offence to denpe Chꝛpſte in the tpme of perſecution: hee denied the laſte reſurrection: hee alſo affirmed, ꝑ Uirginitie was of no greater merite, then Marpage, but equall with it. Hee was aboute the peare of oure Loꝛde. 110.

Cataphriges.

Theſe Heretikes, tooke their name of one Montanᵘ of Phrigia, and Archheretique, who affirmed that the Holpe Ghoſte was geeuen to him, and not to the Apoſtles. They Baptized not in the name of the Trinitie: and bſed to Baptpʒe men after they were dead. They did alſo condemne the ſeconde Mariage. This Sect began in the peare. 170.

Apelles.

Thps fellowe began his Hereſie in Greece, hee denyed the knowinge of God, as that hee knewe not the God whom hee woꝛſhipped, and that Chꝛiſte was not berp God in deede, but a phantaſie appearing bnto men as a man, he was about the peare. 174.

Pharifees.

PHarifees were befoꝛe Chꝛiſt his cōming. 125. peres:
they

they tooke their names of Phares, seperating them as
a people moze woztby then other, taking vpon theym
Pharah oz Pharasch of expouding the law of Moses
and the Pzophets. They beleued that god alone was
onely the true god, and that Chzystes comming should
be pzofytable foz them, and yet when hee came, they
persecuted him: they were pzoud bosters of their deedes. There garmentes were large and wide, and on
the skyrtes of their gownes were bzoad gards, wheron were wzitten sundzy Charectes in the Hebzew, and
they named these, Philacteria.

Saduces.

These had theyz name of Zedec, whiche signifyeth
rightfulnes, and called themselues Zedechim, that is
iust & right. These spzang vp after the Pharesies: they
beleued that body & soule should both perish together,
and that neither the godly should receiue any reward,
foz his good wozkes, noz the wicked shoulde recepue
pain foz his euil dedes, otherwise the in this life. They
held that ther was neither hel noz Heaue, nether Angel noz spirite: and that it was in our owne powers, either to haue felicity oz misery. They were enemies a-
gainst the Pharises, and yet with the Pharases agre-
ing to persecute Chzist Iesus.

Essees

Were a kynd of sect, hating mariage, they came to
gether in great companies and held opinion that euil
soules were dispersed in the Ocean seas, there to bee
tozmented by the tempestes.

Cerdo

The Golden Booke

Cerdō.

An heretike of Cerdonia who affirmed that Chryſt was neuer borne of a woman, and that he had no fleſh, nor ſuffered any paſſiō, but that he feined to ſuffer: he denyed Godto be þ father of our lord Ieſus Chryſt, and þ God was knowē and Chriſt bnknowē: god was holy, Chriſt he ſaid to be bnholy: he denied the old Teſtamēt, ſaying that it was the worke of an other God, ꝯ not of the bniuerſall God: which other God was the beginning of the bniuerſal miſchiefe: he was after Chriſt our lorde 144 yeares.

Valentinianus.

This Heretyke held that Chriſte did paſſe throughe the Uirgin , as the Wynde paſſed throughē a Pype.

Martion.

This heretike was Diſciple to Cerdō, born in Cinope, a Citty of PONTVS who beinge at Epheſus in þ time of S. Iohn the Euangeliſte, fayned that there were 2. Gods: the one the maker of the lawe and worlde, the other to bee more mightye (the father of our lord Ieſu) He bilde that ſoules are ſaued, but the bodies riſe not agayne. He diſalowed of Wedlocke.

Sabellicus.

A Notable Heretike denyynge Ieſu Chriſt to bee any of the three perſons, and that he was not þ ſonne

sonne of God.

Manes.

AN Heretyke which affirmed himselfe to bee lyke chziſt, ſ ſomtime to be cōſozter that was pzomiſed to come.

Arrius

This mā was a Pzieſte in the church of Alexandria in ẏ pere of our Lozd. 320. his erroure was ẏ the Sonne was not equal tō the father in Deitie, noz of ẏ ſame ſubſtaunce: but that he was a very creature: hee infected a merueilous great nūber tō his Hereſy, foz ẏ which the great connſaile of Nice was boldē by ẏ Emperoure Conſtantinus Magnus: himſelf being pzeſent tō 318 Byſhopes. Afterward Arrius hozribly finiſhed his lyfe: foz by going to the ſtoole, his guttes went frō him, and ſo hee died.

Donatus.

This Heretike affirmed that any cōgregation with out him ẏ his Sectaries were not Chriſtiā ẏ that in the church were none eupll, but all good, and that they onely pertained to the Church: he was a Numidian bozne, aboute the pere of oure Lozde 353.

Macedonius.

BEing at Conſtātinople he mainteined the hereſie of Arrius.

Eunomi-

The Golden Booke
Eunomius.

An enuious heretike of Arrius sect, wherunto he added, that the sonne was in euery thing, vnlike vnto ye father: & that the holy Ghost had no medlig with the father nor the sonne: he affirmed that all which belue the
fayth ye he taught should be saued, yad, they committed
neuer so great sinne, & continued therin: he was about
the yere after Christe. 353.

Pelagius

Pelagius was an other Archeheretike his opinion
was, that manne is iustifyed by his own workes & not
by fayth in Christ. Thys Atheist was about the yere
of our L. 388.

Eutices

Was an Abbot of a Monastery in Constantinople
about the yere of our Lord 450. He affirmed ye Chryst
had but one only nature, that is to say diuine or of god,
like as he was one person.
This heresye was condemned in the Counsaile of
Ephesin, & Eutices sent into exile.

Iohn A leyd

This Rustical hedgegod was at Munster in VVest-
phalia by occupati on Tailour naming biselfe king of
new Ierusalem: a ringleader of ye Anabaptistes: he so
seduced

ſeduced the people, ẏ he brought them to vtter cõfuſiõ: he denied Baptiſme to Infants: hee had one Gnipperdolling to his Prophet, & Cretching to his cõpaignis, his end was to bee ſterued to death in an Iron cage. before this Heretique, was borne two Swordes: which betokened the Gouernment of two Kingdomes, Heauen, and Earth: A round Globe, with a Croſſe: and a Sworde thruſt through the Globe, ſignifyinge that he was Kinge ouer the whole Worlde.

Dauid George.

THis Blaſphemous fellowe, an other Heretike, naming himſelfe to be ẏ Meſſias, was borne at Delph in Holland: He ſaide that hee was Gods Nephew, and talked with wylde Beaſtes, and Byrdes in their Language, receyuinge his foode of theym. Hee ſayde that Heauen was empty, and that he was ſent to chooſe & apoinct the children of God with other vaine and abſurd tromperies. After chaunging his name to Ihon a Bruges, he came to Baſill in Swizerland, & there after. 12. yeares died: His Errowre was, that by hym came ſaluation: and after three yeares, after his burial he ſhould riſe agayne. Ere two yeares were finiſhed he was taken vp, and with his Coffyn, hanged on a Gallowes.

Henry N.

THis ſtrauagant Heretike, Henry Nicolas, otherwiſe called Harry Claſh a Fleming ſuppoſed, hath by the healpe of others, ſent forth, diuers blaſphemous

I   Bookes,

The Golden Booke

Bookes to the great hurt of many lightbrayne Chri-
ſtiãs. And by his diſciple one Chriſtopher Vitell, Iop-
ner, one altogether vnlearned, ſaainge that he is ſom-
what erroniouſly, Bewitched hath géeuen foorth certayne bookes here vndernamed: naminge themſelues,
& their Adherentes the Family of Loue. They fayne a
Gouernment of Immortality, to be by their deſkpinge
immortality: they côfeſſe thêſelues to be têpted: wherfore they appoynet, auricular confeſſion, (nothinge to
the forgeuenes of ſinnes): They ſinne til they come to
their perfection: then ſinneleſſe: and ſo able to bringe o-
ther to the ſame, beinge of their Family: They wyll
haue nothinge to be diſlyked, y is done by their Elder.

The ſayd. H. N. was firſt of Amſterdame and driuē
from thence, becauſe of his Errours, and went to Ro-
terdam, and from thence to Collen: From whence pro-
ceaded al theſe wicked Errours. The names of his cô-
uerted ones, be of. 3. degrees.
1. The côminalty of the holy ones,
2. The vpright vnderſtandinge ones,
3. The illuminate Elders.

The names of. H. N. his Bookes bearinge
the name, of the Family of Loue.

The cryinge Voyce.
The firſt Epiſtle and firſt exhortation.
A Dialogue betwene the Father & the Sonne.
The true and ſpirituall Tabernacle.
The publiſhed peace vpon Earth.
The Euangelium Regni.
The declaration of the Maſſe.
The newe Ieruſalem.
The prophecie of the ſpirit of loue.
The Glaſſe of righteouſneſſe.

Certayne p-

Certaine vpstart Anabap-
tisticall Errours,

That Christe tooke not flesh of the blessed Virgin
Mary.

That Infantes of the Faythfull ought not to be baptized.

That a Christian man, may not bee a Magistrate, or
beare the Sworde and office of auctority.

That it is not Lawfull for a Christian to take an oth.

THese hellish sortes of Errours are more preposterous & wicked, then y lawes or statutes of y Pagās, al
though in the respect of any cōmendatiō: bad is y best:
for as the diuel, aucthor of all mischiefe beganne to in-
fect the former Age with illusions, so now in these la-
terdayes he hath almost poysoned the remained seeds,
with al abhominations.

First in Delphos, then in Euboea, at Nasamone, and
among the Dodonean Okes, throughe whose hudge boughes, the whistlinge woos seemed to yeld forth y
Thondringe clamour of Deuplles: then began worshipping of formed shapes, as of Saturn in Italy, of Iupiter in Candie, of Iuno in Samos, of Bacch' in India,
and at Thebes, of Isis, & Osyris in AEgipt, of Vesta at
Troia, of Palas Tritonia amoug y Aphricās, of Mercury in Frāce, & Germany, of Minerua at Athens, of
Apollo at Delphos, at Chio, at Rhodes Patra, Troa-
da Thymbria, of Diana in Delos, & in Scythya, of Ve-
n' in Paphos Cyprus, Gnydos and Citheros, of Mars
in Thracia, of Priapus in Hellespētus, of Vulcane in

The Golden Booke

Lypara and Lemnos: Symon Magus at IERVSA-
LEM, MACHOMET in Mecha, PAPA
in ROME, who as the former Pagans set vp Images of theyr fathers to be honoured: so likewyse hath ye
pestilēt Church of Superstition mayntayned Idolls,
ye very ceremonies of the heathē pagans: stocks, stones,
gold, siluer, ꝝ other metal to be worshipped. This apish
religiō, neuerthelesse being espyed, is suffred ꝝ of some
laughed at, but not subuerted: so whilethe world bal-
teth betwene two opiniōs, suffring ye Mōster to rule as
him listeth, all are so stayned, some wt Idolatry, some
wt supersticiō, some with Schisme, Arrianisme, Apos-
tacie aud infidelity, ye frō King to Priest, ꝝ frō Priest
to People, ꝝ head is Hypocrisie. I do most earnestly be-
sech thee, deere bought Creature: better to consider
of God his Benefices, and holy religion, lest he make
thee partaker, with the greater people (at this-day) the
Armenians, Arabians, Persians, Syrians, Assyrians,
Medes, Ægyptians, Namidiās, Lybians, Moores, Bra-
silians, Tartarians, Scythians, Æthiopians, Faythlesse
Christians, Romaynes, ꝝ an Iufinite number of Kingdomes and people, which doe far surmount the armye
of true Christians, and so seclude thee from his fauour
and Kingedome, by harkeninge to fantasy ꝝ omitting
the verity. The only good God, and merciful father e-
uermore pardon our offences, and defend vs from this
yoke of counterfayted carnality, both now and euer.

Banaster.

This irreligious captife, belde an Oppinion, that no
man ought to feare God. ꝝc.

Euri

Eurynomus.

A Deuill, who as the Aunciont Greekes fuppofed, did eate and confume, the flefh of Dead men, leauinge the bones bare : Who n they paynted in a figure terrible, hauinge longe Teeth oz Tufkes, fyttinge in the Skin of a Vultur, of coloure betweene Blacke, & Yealow. A fit God foz fuch Companions.

SEra nimis Vita eft craftina, viue hodie.
To mozowes Lyfe is to late, lyue to day.

AS God is good, and beft of all,
   So man is ill, and fubiect thrall.
Ill by good, is made better,
   Then man to God muft bee detter.

Though all be many, and one be few,
   And fewfte make many returnde to one,
Then many men earthy what do they fhew,
   Sith all and euery ftandes not alone.

One is fayd fimple, where moe are in place,
   The moe thought the ftroger, each caufe to defed.
One God and one Kyng, yet ftil kepes the grace:
   Creation and kingdom bryngs al to an end.

The one fro beginning which al things haue made,
   VVil euery other fo gather to gether,
               That each

The Golden Booke.

That each thinge in his kynde clearely shall vade,
The worldes beautye beginneth to wither,

Then shall this summething a nothing make,
VVhen all shalbe vacant, as when he began,
Of nothinge, in no place, cannot lesse be.
VVhen that which was, is not, as soules shal thē see,

FINIS.

The names of the Authours, out of whom
this worke is gathered.

 Ndreas Theuet
Aristoteles.
Alex. Aphrod.
Aristophanes.
Apollodorus.
Apuleius.
Albertus Magnus.
A. Gellius.
Aratus.
Beatus Rhenan.
Cicero.
Catullus.
Cornelius Tacitus.
Cælius Rhod.
Censorinus.
Diodorus Siculus.
Erasmus Rot.
Eusebius.
Euclides.

Lactant. gram.
Lactant Firmian.
Lucianus.
Marcus Varro.
Martianus.
Manilius.
Martialis.
Macrobius.
Naso.
Orpheus.
Propertius.
Plinius.
Palephatus.
Pindarus.
Plato.
Plutarchus.
Phornutus.
Pontanus.
Prolemæus

Fulgens

VVith many others.

FINIS.

Imprinted at London in Fleete-
ſtreete, neare vnto Saynct Dunſtanes
Churche, by Thomas Marſhe.

ANNO DOMINI.
1577.

Cum Priuilegio Regiæ
Maieſtatis.

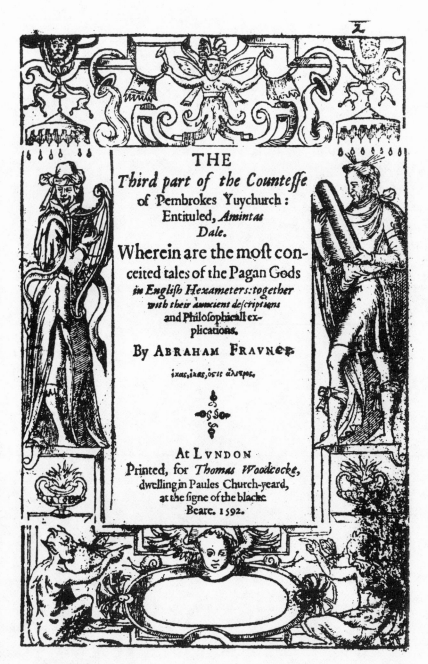

THE
Third part of the Countesse
of Pembrokes Yuychurch :
Entituled, *Amintas*
Dale.

Wherein are the most con-
ceited tales of the Pagan Gods
in English Hexameters: together
with their auncient descriptions
and Philosophicall ex-
plications.

By ABRAHAM FRAVNCE

ἵκας, ἵκας, ὅςις ἀλιτρος.

At LVNDON
Printed, for *Thomas Woodcocke*,
dwelling in Paules Church-yeard,
at the signe of the blacke
Beare. 1592.

Illuſtriſsimæ, atque ornatiſsimæ Heroinæ,
pia, formoſa, erudita : Domina Maria,
Comitiſſæ Pembrokienſi.

NYmpha Charis Chariton, morientis imago Philippi,
Accipe ſpirantem poſt funera rurſus Amintam:
Accipe nobilium dulciſsima dogmata vatum,
Delicias, Muſas, myſteria; denique, quicquid
Græcia docta dedit, vel regia Roma reliquit,
Quod fructum flori, quod miſcuit vtile dulci.

Deuotiſſ:

Ab. Fr.

¶ The Third part of the
Counteſſe of Pembrokes *Yuychurche.*
Entituled, Amintas Dale.

NOw that ſolempne feaſt of murdred *Amyntas* aproached:
And by the late edict by *Pembrokiana* pronounced,
Yuychurches nymphs and paſtors duely prepared
With fatall Garlands of newſound flowre *Amaranthus,*
Downe in *Amyntas* dale, on *Amyntas* day be aſembled.

Paſtymes ouerpaſt, and death's celebration ended,
Matchles Lady regent, for a further grace to *Amyntas*
Late tranſformd to a flowre; wills euery man to remember
Some one God transformd, or that transformed an other:
And enioynes each nymph to recount ſome tale of a Goddeſſe
That was changd herſelf, or wrought ſome change in an other:
And that as euery tale and hiſtory drew to an ending,
Soe ſage *Elpinus* with due attention harckning,
Shuld his mynd diſcloſe, and learned opinion vtter.

Thirſis turne was firſt: whoe after his humble obeiſſance
Made to the Lady regent, thus fram'de himſelf to be ſinging.

When noe fyre, noe ayre, noe earth, noe water apeared,
Confuſd fyre, rude ayre, vaſt earth, dull water abyded.
Water, th'earth and ayre and fyre extreamely defaced,
And fyre, th'earth and ayre and water ſowly deformed.
For where water or earth, where ayre or fyre was abyding,
Fyre, ayre, earth, water were alſo ioyntly remaynyng.
Fyre and ayre and earth with a ſhapeles water abounded,
And earth ayre and fyre, that ſhapeles water aforded,
Euery one was in all, and all was in euery one thing,

Euery

Soe each one made all, made this rude All, to be nothing,
Nothing els but a heape, but a masse, but a lump, but a cluster;
Cluster, lump, masse, heape, where seedes of things disagreeing
Fyre, ayre, earth, water lay all confusd in a corner.
Hoate things fled fro the colde, dry could not abide to be moystned,
Hard contemned soft, and light fro the heauy retyred.
Noe peace, noe concord, noe good conformable order,
Nought but warrs and iarrs, all strife, and all on an vproare.
Noe aire transparent, noe Sunne was cause of a daylight,
Noe nights-light *Phœbe* was a chearfull guide to the darcknes;
Earth was not yet firme, fire could not yeeld any sparkles,
Water would not flow: til sou'raigne God *Demogorgon*
Ends these broyles, brings peace, setts euery thing in an order.
Heau'n fro the earth he dyuides, and earth fro the water he parteth,
And pure Christall skye from grosse thick ayre he remoueth.

These things thus distinct, in seu'rall places he setleth,
Light fyre mounteth aloft, and lyfts it-self to the heauen,
Ayre next in lightnes, next him was placed in highnes,
Grosse earth drew downeward, and stayd herselfe by the centre,
Water cleaues to the earth, and there as a border abydeth.

Fyre, ayre, earth, water were euery howre in an vproare,
Whilst they lay on a heape, and all dwelt ioyntly togeather;
Fyre, ayre, earth, water were brought to a peacable order,
When they lodged apart, each one in seueral harbor.
Thus by a disioyning, Elements were mightily ioyned,
And by disunyting vnyted syrmely for euer.

Each part thus placed, round earth was cast in a compas
Lyke to a globe or a ball, that noe syde might be vnequall.
Then were swelling Seas powrd foorth in places apoynted
Here and there by the earth; whose braunches duly dyuyded
Kyngdomes from kyngdomes: then first came springs fro the mountayns,
Pooles were pitcht in moores, and lakes lay downe by the valleys,
Ryuers flowd by the fyelds with a thowsand slippery wyndings,
Some suckt vp by the earth, some ran to the sea with a restles
race, his shoare for a banck with billowes mightyly beating.
Then fyelds stretcht themselues, then meddowes gan to be flowring,
Greene leaues cou'red trees, and trees gaue shade to the forrests,
Mountayns mounted aloft, and dales drew speedyly downewarde.

Ouer sea and earth, the relenting ayre he reposed,
And there foggs and mystes and clustred clowds he apoynted.
Thence come thunder-clapps, thence lightnings, there be the blustring
Wyndes, whose roaring blasts would teare this world in a thousand

Peeces, might they rage at randon: but the prefixed
Coaftes are known, for thefe fowre brawling brethren apoynted.
Eurus flew to the Eaft, where *Memnons* mother arifeth,
Sweete *Zephyrus* to the Weaft, where Sunnes reuolution endeth,
Cold *Boreas* to the North, whence frofts are dayly proceeding,
Moyft *Aufter* to the South, where fhowres are euer abounding.

Next to the ayre, bright sky, as a royall throane he repofed,
And eache parte thereof with ftarrelight all to beefprinckled.
Thus was an ougly Chaos transformd at laft to a braue worlde,
Soe braue, that t'was a world foe woorthy a world to be feeing.
Euery quarter of it with fuch lyue things was adorned,
As were conuenyent and feemely for euery quarter.
Gods dwelt in bright skyes, and Chriftall-mantled *Olympus*,
Fowl es did fly by the ayre, and Fifhes fwam by the waters,
Mylde beaftes fed by the fyelds, and wylde beafts rangde by the Forrefts.

But man was wanting, who might be the abfolut owner,
And haue perfect rule and iurifdiction ouer
Mylde beafts and wylde beafts, and Foules and flippery fifhes.
At length Man was made of mould by the crafty *Prometheus*,
Crafty *Prometheus*, whoe by degrees contriued a picture,
And gaue life to the fame with fyre that he ftole fro the heauens.
And, where other beafts lay poaring downe to the grownd-wards,
Man with a greater ftate had a looke lyft vp to *Olympus*,
Whence his better part was then but lately deryued.
This was an age of gold, then was *Saturnus* an Emprour,
Sythe-bearing *Saturne* rul'de iuftly without any iudges,
Noe lawes, noe lawyers were then, yet noebody lawleffe,
Noe theeues and robbers were hangd, yet noebody robbed,
Noe bloody manqueller was kyld, yet noebody murdred.
Vndiffembled loue and playne fymplycyty ruled,
Vncorrupted fayth and pure fynceryty raigned.
Hart conceaud noe harme; tong, harts interpreter only,
Playnly without any glofe or diffimulation op'ned
Harts harmeles conceipts: hands, true and trufty to practyfe,
Did, what his hart contryu'd, or tong had truly delyu'red.

Pinetrees pitcht vpon hills, gaue wonted grace to the hill-topp,
Not with gaping gulfs of *Auernus* dayly bedafhed,
But with trickling fhowres of *Olympus* fweetly bedeawed.
Euery man kept home, and where he receau'd a beginning,
There did he make his graue, and drew his dayes to an ending.
Noebodie was foe mad by the ragged rocks to be ranging,
And with clowds, windes, feaes, nay heau'n and hell to be ftryuyng,

Onely

Only to spy and ly, and feede fooles eares with a wonder,
How fro *Geneua* to *Gaunt*, from *Gaunt* he repair'd to *Vienna*,
How fro the Turk to the Pope, fro the Pope to the Souldan of *Ægipt*,
And at laſt came back fro the newfound world as an old foole,
With fowre Dutch-french woords, with a ſtrange-cutt beard, or a Caſſock.
Noe townes were walled, noe walls were loftyly towred,
Noe towres were planted with diu'ls inuention ord'nance.
Euery buſh was a bowre, and euery ruſtical harbor
Was fort ſufficient, where noe force was to be feared.
Deaths-forerunner Drum did ſownd no dreadful Alarum;
Noe man-murdring man with a teare-fleſh pyke, or a pollax,
Or blood-ſucking ſweard was known by the name of a Sowldyer.
Peace made euery man ſecure, ſecuryty careles,
Careleſnes cauſd myrth, myrth neuer dreeds any danger.
Fruytefull ground vntorne, vntutcht, was free fro the plough ſnare,
And ſelf-ſufficient, of her owne ſelfe yeelded aboundance.
Noe new-found diſhes were ſought, noe coſtly deuiſes
Farr-fetcht and deare bought : men ſimple lyued a ſimple
Lyfe, vſd ſymple ſoode, ſloe, nutt, plum, ſtraubery, apple,
Ackorne falln fro the oake, and blackbery pluckt fro the bramble.
Tygers were then tame, ſharpe-tusked boare was obeiſſant,
Stoordy Lyons lowted, noe woolf was knowne to be mankinde,
Beares did bow at a beck, no ſerpent breathd any poyſon.
Spring was ſtill-ſpringing, whole yeare was wholly a ſpring-tyme,
Euer-ſhyning ſunne with clowds was neuer eclipſed,
Euer-flowring flowrs with froſts were neuer anoyed.
Lyfe-breathing *Zephyrus* with ſweete blaſt charyly foſtred
Euery fruite, which th'earth of her owne free bounty aforded.
Yea good-natur'd ground at laſt gaue plentiful harueſt,
Neuer ſowd, ſtill mowd, not tyld, yet ſyld with aboundance.
Then floods flow'de with mylke, each wel-ſpring then was a wyne-ſpring,
Euery greene-hewde tree bare ſweete and ſugered honny.
Happy the age, and happy the men, that lyu'd in a happy
Age : age all of gold, where noe bad thing was abyding,
All of gold indeede, where each good thing was abounding.
  But when good *Saturne* by force was dryu'n to *Auernus,*
And vſurping *Ioue* did rule and raigne in *Olympus*,
Golden dayes were gone, and ſiluer time was aproaching,
New Lords made new lawes : th'owld ſpring tyme *Iupiter* altred,
And chang'd it to a yeare, and new-made yeare he dyuyded
In fowre parts, each part with a ſeu'rall ſeaſon apoynted,
Warme Spring, hoate Sommer, cold wynter, changeable *Autumne*.

Then swelting doggstarre, then scalding breath of *Apollo*,
Then northern *Boreas* causd better bowres to be builded.
Then ground gan to rebell, from a mother changd to a stepdame,
Naught but thorns and weeds of her owne accord she aforded,
But by force constraind and by compulsion vrged:
Now plow's chaynd to the yoake, and yoake bound fast to the oxen,
Now are furrowes drawn, and seede cast into the furrowes.
Iupiter of purpose made fruitefull ground to be sruyteles,
And sowld nought for naught, and sweetenes mixt with a sowrenes,
Least that too much ease might make men stil to be careles,
Whereas want breedes care, and care coynes dayly deuises.

Next came brazen tyme, whose hoate and furius of-spring
With bould brazen face, was greedily geu'n to reuenging,
Yet not past all grace. Last age was named of Iron,
And her cursed brood in like sort framed of Iron,
Merciles, hard, vniust, vnkinde, vntractable, hatefull,
Ireful, of Iron ful, yea too ful of ire, ful of Iron,
Faith, and truth, and shame, for shame lay downe in a dungeon,
And in-came whooredome, pride, robbery, treacherie, treason.
Grownd with ditch and hedg was now exactly dyuyded,
Shippe with waues, and sayles with wyndes were all to be tossed,
Sea scowrd with rouers, land scowrged dayly by robbers,
Myne, not thyne, came in; Myne and thyne, quite was abandond.

Corne is now contemnd, and fruitefull tree's but a tryfle,
Their minde's all on mynes of brasse, lead, copper, or Iron,
Or gold, gold farre worse, then brasse, lead, copper, or Iron.
Earth's very bowells now are torne eu'n downe to *Auernus*,
All for gold, gold worse then a thousand feends of *Auernus*.
First, was an age of gold, then golden goodnes abounded,
Last, was an age for gold, for then gold only triumphed.
Weake are thrust to the wall, and strong men striue to be mighty,
Mighty men hope to be Kings, and Kings still looke to be emprours,
Might rule's right, lust law, rage reason, worlde's at a world's ende,
World runs all on wheeles: guest fear's to be robd as he sleepeth,
Hoast can skarce trust guest; wife longs for death of her husband,
Husband loath's his wife, and brethren skarcely be brethren.
Infamous stepdames keepe cups with poyson abounding
For theyr sons in law: and sons (ô viperus of-spring)
Dayly before theyre dayes wish fathers dayes to be ending,
All's turnd vpside downe. At last *Astraea* departed,
And from damnable earth, to the spotles skie she remoued.
Then came gryesly Gyants, and needes would clymbe to *Olympus*

With mounts on mountaines,till thundring *Ioue* in a fury
Brake their scorched bones, and bullwarkes all to be battred :
Whose congealed bloud transformd to a most bloody offspring
By th'earth theire mother that causd that desperat vproare,
Stil contemned Gods,and heauens dayly maligned.
Wherewith *Ioue* incenst,and moou'd of late,by *Lycaons*
Owtrage,ouer-whelmd whole earth with a mightyly flowing
All ouer-flowing water :soe that,not a man now,
But good *Deucalion* was lyuing, and not a woeman,
But good *Pyrrha* remaynd,which mankynde newly repayred,
And,by casting stones,brought foorth soe stoany an offspring.

THis*is hauing made an end of this tale to the content of the hearers generally;* Elpinus *began thus to worke vpon it. Poets and Painters(men say) may well goe together,sith pen and pencill be both alike free, and doo equally challeng the selfesame prerogatiue.* Cicero *reporteth, that* Fabius *a famous Romaine,thought it an especiall commendation, to be surnamed* Pictor. *And,* Antiquissimum è doctis fuit poetarum genus, *saith the same* Cicero. *When I talke of Painters, I meane not the ridiculous fraternitie of silly Wall-washers : neither doe I euer once thinke of our loftie rimers,when I make mention of Poets. Yet a wall may bee colored by an elegant Painter, but the conceite and elegancie is more then the colour : and poets (seeking as well to please,as to profit) haue well made choyce of verse, yet the making of a verse is no part of Poetrie: otherwise, the sweete and inimitable poeme of* Heliodorus *should be no Poeme,and euery vnreasonable rimer should weare a Lawrell garland. Both poetry, a speaking picture, and paynting, a dumbe poetry, were like in this,that the one and the other did vnder an amyable figure and delightsome veyle,as it were,couer the most sacred mysteries of ancient philosophie. Nay, Py:..agoras himselfe by his symbolicall kinde of teaching, as also* Plato *by his conceited parables and allegoricall discourses in his bookes called,* Phædrus, Timæus, *and* Symposium, *may make any man beleeue, that as the learned Indians,* Æthiopians, *and* Ægyptians *kept their doctrine religiously secret for feare of prophanation, so the Grecians by their example, haue wrapped vp in tales,such sweete inuentions, as of the learned vnfolder may well be deemed vonderfull,though to a vulgar conceit,they seeme but friuolus imaginations. Yea that song of the most wise* Salomon,*called for the excellencie thereof the song of songs, is altogether mysticall and allegoricall, least any man thinke my speech but a tale, in attributing so much to poeticall tales : which, mee thinkes,may well bee compared to sweete grapes couered with leaues and braches,or to the old* Sileni,*which being but ridiculous in shew, did yet inwardly conteine the sacred image of some God. He that cannot conceaue any sufficient cause which might induce antiquitie to deale thus warilie in matters of* *such importance, let him knowe, that* rerum 'ευαγία, *the picturing, fashioning, figuring, or, as it were, personall representing of things in verse after this manner, is most effectuall and auayleable, to moue mens mindes, to stirre vp delight, to confirme memorie, and to allure and entice our cogitations by such familiar and sensible discourses, to matters of more diuine and higher contemplation. Poeticall songs are Galeries set forth with varietie of pictures, to hold euery mans eyes, Gardens stored with flowers of sundry sauours, to delite euery mans sence, orchyards furnished with all kindes of fruite, to please euery mans mouth. He that is but of a meane conceit, hath a pleasant and plausible narration, concerning the famous exploites of renowmed* Heroes, *set forth in most sweete and delight some verse, to feede his rurall humor. They, whose capacitie is such, as that they can reach somewhat further then the external discourse and history, shall finde a morall sence included therein, extolling vertue, condemning vice, euery way profitable for the institution of a practicall and common wealth man. The rest, that are better borne and of a more noble spirit, shall meete with hidden mysteries of naturall, astrologicall, or diuine and metaphysicall philosophie, to entertaine their heauenly speculation. That this is true, let vs make triall, and first in* Saturnus *and* Chaos, *offered vnto vs by* Thirsis : *whereof, before we speake, it shall not be amisse to note this generally, for the better concealing of ensuing particularities.* Iupiter, Iuno, Neptune, Ceres, *with the rest, are therfore called Gods and goddesses, for that in the superior and fierie region of the ayre noted by* Iupiter, *in the inferior, represented by* Iuno, *in the bowells of the earth, figured by* Ceres, *in the deapth of the Seaes, shadowed by* Neptune, *and so in others, there is,* τὸ θειον, *a certaine celestiall and diuine power, so called by* Hippocrates, *and by the ancient Poets more particularly expressed by the sundry titles of seuerall Deities proportionable thereunto. And, if the copulation or coniunction of these deified elements obserue the natural order of generation, it is called of the Poets a mariage of such a god and goddesse: if it swarue and degenerate from the wonted course of nature, they tearme it adulterie and libidinous loue, & the parties, louers, not man and wife, as in the former kinde of copulation: so that, no mā hath cause to think it a ridiculous repugnancy & impossibilitie, whē as Poets in their songs make mention of the loue, mariage, procreation, affinity, offspring, pedegrees, and discents of their superior & inferior gods.*

    Now for the transformation of Thirsis *his* Chaos, *true it is, that* Ouid *much after this manner discourseth of the creation of the world, of the reducing of the confused* Chaos *into distinct formes, of* Prometheus *his framing of man of the very earth it selfe: which things, no doubt, as also the distinction of times into foure seuerall ages, of gold, siluer, brasse, and yron, were taken, (although in part mistaken) out of the sacred monuments of* Moyses. Leo Hebræus, *out of some anciēt Poet, whom he calleth* Pronapides, *reporteth another history of the same matter, albeit not after the same manner.* Demogorgon, *saith he, the great and terrible God of heauen and earth, accompanied only with* Æternitie & Chaos,

perceaued

perceaued on a time, an outragious vprore and tumult stirred vp in the bely and
bowels of the forenamed Chaos: therefore, to ease her, he stretched forth his
owne hand and opened her wombe, ꝛ hence presently came forth a filthie and deformed offspring, called Litigiū, Strife: which no sooner apeared, but immediatly
it bred brabbles, made a foule stirre, stird vp contentions, and stroue to mount
vp toward heauen, but that by Demogorgon he was ouerruled, and throwne
downe to the lower partes & elementall regions. Chaos as yet had not ended her
chile-bearing labor & trauaile, but was troubled with heauie burdens, fainty
sweats, languishing groanes,& fierie tormēting agonies; so that Demogorgon
could not for pitie withdraw his helping hand, till by his assistance, she had
brought forth Pan, with his three fatall sisters, and also Erebus, Æther, and
Dies. Pan found such fauour, that Demogorgon committed vnto him the
whole charge of his familie, commaunding his three sisters continually to waite
and attend vpon him, as his handmaydes: And thus was Chaos at last deliue-
ted, and eased of her childe-birth. By Demogorgon, or peraduenture, Demiur-
gon, is here vnderstood that one & only creator of al, to whom Æternitie is in-
separably conioyned, sith himselfe is, was, and will be eternall and euerlasting.
Chaos, in this eternall societie obteineth the third place, because she is that common, confused, and vndistinct matter, which the ancient Philosophers made Co-
eternall with the Creator: calling the one, the Father, the other the mother of al.
things formed; yet so, as they alwaies esteemed Demogorgon the chiefe and
efficient,& Chaos only the subsequent and secondary cause in this procreation.
The reason why they ioyned Chaos with the Creator as a companion from all e-
ternitie, was this: they thought it proceeded from him by a certaine eternall generation: so proceeding, as eternall, because alwaies proceeding; yet so eternall,
as proceeding, because not of her selfe proceeding, but from the procreator. And
as they made Chaos proceede from Demogorgon eternally without limitati-
on of time, so they affirmed, that he afterwards framed all things of this vn-
formed Chaos, not eternally, but in time. The tumult and vprore styrd vp in the
bowels of Chaos is her naturall inclination and desire of bringing forth things
variable and disagreeing. The hand of Demogorgon, which opened her bely, is
that celestiall power, reducing the vniuersall and confused possibilities of Chaos,
to distinct formes and actuall particularities, and giueth vs also to vnderstand,
that this first production of things, was not vsuall and accustomed (as naturall
generation is, which afterwards succeeded this supernaturall creation) but
strang and wonderful,& did therefore require the vse of Demogorgons hand,
that is, the most mighty and effectuall instrument of all others. Strife came
first forth: for from prima materia that first and generall matter of all that
was made, the diuision and distinction of things, which before were confused and
vndistinct, proceeded: & this diuision is called strife; sith it conuerseth among
foure striuing & contrary elemēts, the one alwaies maligning & repugning the
other. His face was ougly & deformed: for discord and diuision causeth defect,

want

want, & imperfection, as vnion & concord, are the authors of blessednes, beauty, and perfection. Strife striuing to get vp to heauen, was thrown down to the earth: for in the celestiall bodies there is noe discord, noe repugnancy, and therfore conseqently, noe destruction or mortalyty; effects thereof: but only in these earthly and inferior matters, contynually subiect to infynite decayes and dissolutions, caused by oppositions and contrarieties. The burdens, sweatings, groanings, and agonies of Chaos, are the euer-strugling and contending natures of the fowre elements, heauy earth, moyst water, breathing ayre, and consumyng fyre: for pacification whereof, Pan was borne, which in Greeke, signifieth, All: and betokeneth that generall and vniuersall power of nature, ruling and gouernyng whatsoeuer proceeded from Chaos; and quyeting those disagreeing qualities of the repugnant elements. Whereupon it is here sayd, that after Stryfe, came, Pan; syth after discord, comes concord, and succeedeth in place therof. Togeather with Pan, the three fatall Ladies of Desteny, Clotho, Lachesis, and Atropos were borne, attending on Pan, the God of vniuersall nature. κλωθώ, soe called of turnyng, noteth the continuall motion and reuolutiō of things present, and turneth and spinneth the present threede of lyfe. λάχεσις is the production and drawing foorth of that which is to come, preparing and keeping diligently the threede of lyfe which yet remaineth to be turned and spunne. ἄτροπος, as if a man would say, irremeable, irreuocable, and immutable, representeth what is past, which neuer returneth: and this last Lady hath dispatched, finished, and cut of the threede committed to her charge to be spunne. In Latine they are called Parcæ à parcēdo, of sparing, by the contrary, as some thinke, because they spare not, as lytle Iohn was called soe in iest, being a man of a wonderfull great stature. Scaliger lyketh not this cōceipt, sith they spare indeed rather the otherwise, one of thē only cutting of lyfe, whereas the other two maynteyn and preserue it. Varro thought they were in Latine called Parcæ à pariendo of bringing foorth, whereupon their particular names were framed accordingly, of the tymes of byrth, the one being of the auncient Romayns called Nona, the other Decima, of the nynth and tenth moneth, in the which vsually by course of nature the childe is borne: yet, because whosoeuer is borne, is borne to dye, the third was named Morta, of the Latyne Mors, which signifyeth Death, represented by the third fatall Lady. Claudian in his Poeme de raptu Proserpinæ, maketh them all attend on Pluto, soe doth Fulgentius, because their dominion is most ouer these terrestiall and inferior bodies, figured by Pluto and his infernall kingdome. Agayne, these Ladyes drawe foorth the threede of mans lyfe, and mans lyfe is long or short, according as the body is framed of a strong or weake matter, which earthly matter is subiect to Pluto. The first hath care of mans byrth, the second of his lyfe, the third of death. The first is yong, the second of myddle age, the third very owlde: the yong Lady holdeth the distaffe and draweth the flaxe, the myddle hath a spyndle and windeth vp the threede, the owld sister with her Sheares snappeth the threede in two.

two. Homer *in his hymne to* Mercury *maketh them winged, for tyme flyeth, and death draweth on. They are here sayd to be borne of* Chaos, *sith in that first distinction and separation of things out of that confused heape and* Masse, *euery particular matter had his peculier desteny allotted vnto it : others would haue them to be borne of* Erebus *(the most hidden and remote part of the earth) and of* Darcknes : *that, by the obscurity of the father and mother, wee may imagine how difficult, nay how impossible a thing it is, to search out the hidden causes of* Desteny. *There bee also some that make them the daughters of* Iupiter *and* Themis, *the rulers and directers of fatall iustice and vniuersall prouidence.*

Plato *in the tenth booke of his common wealth, maketh them the daughters of ineuitable* Necessity, *placing between their knees, the great Spindle of adimant, reaching from the arctike to the antarctike Pole : they sit on a throne, equally distant one from an other, couered with white roabes, crowned with diademes, singing proportionably to the heauens harmony, things that are past, present and to come : they all ioyntly togeather with their mother* Necessity, *turne this spindle,* Clotho *with the right hand,* Lachesis *with the left,* Atropos *with both, as appeareth there in* Plato *more plentifully, in imitation wherof, as should seeme,* Ouid *in the last book of his transformations, bringeth in* Iupiter *talking with* Venus *concerning the immutable decrees of these inexorable Ladies, written in Iron, brasse, and Adamant.*

> Talibus hanc genitor : sola insuperabile fatum
> Nata mouere paras? intres, licet, ipsa sororum
> Tecta trium : cernes illic molimine vasto,
> Ex aere, & solido rerum tabularia ferro :
> Quae neq; concussum caeli, neq; fulminis iram,
> Nec metuunt vllas tuta atq; aeterna ruinas.
> Inuenies illic incisa Adamante perenni
> Fata tui generis.

Hereupon doth Capella *call them* Ioues *scribes ; for that they register his decrees in these euerlasting tables.* Catullus *in his wedding song of* Peleus *and* Thetis *(which noteth the generation of things, for* ὕλος *is slyme, and* Thetis *water, whereof all things are made, yet by an efficient ; and therfore all the gods were at that wedding, except* Discord, *the only cause of dissolution) maketh their heads to be bound with a white fillet or lawne : some othersgiue thē garlands of* Daffadil.

The sixt childe that Chaos *brought foorth to* Demogorgon, *was named* Erebus , *a certaine naturall power incident to euery inferiour thing, and, as it were, cleauing and adherent thereunto : and this , in the terre-*
striall

ſeriall globe, is the very matter it ſelfe, wherof things are made, the only cauſa of gene ration, corruption & all other alterations in theſe inferior bodies: but in Man, the μικροκοσμος, or little world, it ſignifieth that naturall appetite, and continuall deſire, which man hath to obteyne new matters ; whereupon the Poets haue alſo fayned, that this Erebus had many children, as Labour, Enuy, Feare, Deceipt, Fraud, Obſtinacy, Pouerty, Myſery, Famyne, Lamentation, Sicknes, Death, and ſuch like, whoſe mother they made Darknes, or Night, who bare to Erebus her huſband this loathſome broode, according to thoſe verſes of Claudian *in his firſt inuectiue againſt* Ruſinus.

Glomerantur in vnum
Innumeræ peſtes : Erebo quaſcunq; , ſiniſtro
Nox genuit fœtu ; nutrix diſcordia belli,
Imperioſa fames, lætho vicina ſenectus,
Impatienſq; ſui morbus, liuorq; ſecundis
Anxius, & ſciſſo mœrens velamine luctus,
Et timor, et cæco præceps audacia vultu,
Et luxus populator opum, cui ſemper adhærens
Inſælix humili greſſu comitatur egeſtas,
Fædaq; auaritiæ complexæ pectora matris
Inſomnes longo veniunt examine cyræ.

The two laſt chilaren of Demogorgon, were Æther and Dies, the ſuperirior region of the ayre, and the brightnes of the day : who, of brother and ſiſter, became man and wife, and begat Cælius or Cælus, the heauen : which name was firſt attributed to Vranius, Father of Saturnus, king of Creete. This Vranius, for his excellency, was deemed rather cæleſtiall, (as his name importeth) then any earthly creature : repreſenting that æthereall purity by his diuine wiſedome, and the cæleſtiall light and brightnes, by his vertuous conuerſation: this is the hiſtoricall ſence : now for the Allegoricall conceipt, it is moſt manifeſt : for Cælus, the heauen, including and concluding euery thing, is therefore called the ſonne of Æther and Dies, for that his nature is æthereall by reaſon of his moſt ſubtile and ſpirituall perſpicuity ; and alſo bright and lightſome by the plentifull and abundant light of thoſe ſo many radiant ſtarres wherewith it is ſweetly garniſhed. And as Vranius himſelf for his vertue was called Cælus, heauen, ſoe Veſta his wife, becauſe ſhe was a fruitefull and happy mother, was called Terra, the Earth. Of theſe two, Saturnus was born, wholy addicted to huſbandry and tilling of the earth, and of nature ſlowe and heauy, like the earth. Allegorically thus ; Saturnus is Sonne to Cælus, becauſe he is the firſt Planete, and neareſt to the higheſt heauen. He is alſo ſonne to the earth, as in moſt of his naturall proprieties reſembling the earth. Firſt his color is pale and leaden, like the earth : Secondly, as the earth of all other Ele ments is moſt groſſe and heauy, ſoe Saturne among other Planets is moſt ſlowe in finiſhing his reuolution, as requiring full thirty yeares for the accompliſhing of the ſame; whereas Iupiter endeth his in twelue yeares, Mars in two, Sol, Venus, and Mercury in one, and Luna, the Moone, in one moneth only. Thirdly Saturne by his influence worketh ſuch a conſtitution and temperature in mens bodies, as is altogeather agreeable with the qualities of the earth, to wette, cold and dry, making them in whom he is predominant, ſad, melancholicall, graue, heauy, pale, giuen to huſbandry, building, and ſuch like exerciſes. Whereupon he is figured as an olde man, ſad, euil-fauoured, muſing, badly cloathed, with a ſithe in his hand, a ſit inſtrument for his earthly practiſe. He afordeth a reaching wit, profound cogitations, perfect knowledge, ſage and graue aduice, conſtancy of minde and perſeuerance: by reaſon that the earthly nature of his mother is qualified and tempered with that of his cæleſtiall Father. Laſtly, as of his Father he cauſeth perfection and excellency of minde, ſo by his mother he is the author of deformity and deſtruction of the body.

His wife was called Ops, his owne ſiſter, borne of the ſame Father and Mother. Allegorically, Opis ſignifieth help or aſſiſtance, noting the ayde and furtherance of the earth herſelf towards the tilling of ſyldes, building of howſes, and founding of Cities. Soe is ſhe worthily both ſiſter to Saturne, as borne of Cælus, whoſe influence is the beſt mainteyner both of huſbandry and earthly habitations: and alſo wife to Saturne, for that as he is the agent, ſoe herſelf is the patient in huſbandry and fortification. Saturne bereft his father Cælus of thoſe inſtruments which are fit for generation: Cronos, that is, Saturne, is time, time is the meaſurer of the worlds motion; therfore, as one world, ſoe one time, one Saturne; and Cælus can get no more like him, ſith all is now ſpent and conſumed vpon him. Saturne fearing the prediction of Oracles, that his owne ſonne ſhould expell him out of his kingdome, conſulting with his brother Titan, reſolued to deuoure all the ſonnes, that his wife Opis ſhould beare vnto him; and for that intent commaunded her to ſhew him euery childe immediatly after the birth thereof. She firſt brought foorth Iupiter and Iuno: Iuno being a girle, and therefore not to be deuoured, was preſented to her Father: but Iupiter was preſerued from his rage and fury by the noyſe of Cymballs & Taburs, which ſoe poſſeſſed Saturne his eares, that he heard not the yong infant Iupiter, cry. Saturne angrily and earneſtly demaunding where he was, his wife gaue him a Stone wrapped in a cloth, inſteede of the boy, which ſtone for haſte and rage, he ſwallowed, and afterwards vomited it vp againe, euen as he did all ſuch of his other ſonnes, whom he had deuoured. The like policy ſhe vſed in preſeruing of Neptune, making his father beleeue, that it was noe childe, but a yong colte, whereof ſhe was then deliuered, which Saturne thinking to be true, glutted the colt accordingly, Next to theſe were Pluto and his ſiſter Glauca borne: but Glauca being only ſhewed to Saturne, Pluto eſcaped aliue: all the reſt of his ſonnes he firſt deuoured, and preſently vomyted, as before is mencio-

ned. *Allegorically*, Titan, *the Sunne*, and Saturne, *Tyme*, *conspire together
and resolue, that all things in tyme borne, shall also dye in time.* For, *as the
deuouring continuance of outwearing time consumeth all things, so the life-giuing influence of the quickning sonne,is the chiefe cause of procreation: wherevpon it is vsually said,that* Sol & homo generant hominem, *The sunne and
man beget man. His daughters he deuoured not: for, time consumeth* indiui-
dua,*this thing,and that thing,but not the roote and ground of things, figured
by the femall sex.* Iuno *the ayre,with* Iupiter *the fire, and* Neptune *and* Pluto
*the water and earth,are not deuoured: for, the foure elements continue still:
but the rest are still subiect to continuall corruption: corruption I meane in
part,which is alwais a generation,of some other particularitie,not a totall or generall destruction: which is the cause,that time cannot digest and vtterly consume,but is enforced to vomite and restore euen those very bodies which hee
first deuoured, according to that ould ground which giueth vs to learne, that,
as nothing can be made of nothing,so nothing can be made to be nothing,*

Gigni
è nihilo nihil,in nihilum nil posse reuerti.

Homer *calleth* Iupiter αἰγίοχος, *for that he sucked Goates milke, the reason is
this, a Goate is euer climing and getting vpward, as* Iupiter *is,noting the fierie and highest part of the ayre.This ethereall and superior part of the ayre,was
thought of the Pythagoreans (by reason of the wonderfull celeritie and quick
dispatch of his motion and reuolution) to cause a most sweete and melodious
harmonie: whereupon* Iupiter *was reported to be preserued by the tinkeling
of Cymballs and sounding of taburs.*

Iupiter *is placed immediatly after* Saturne *in heauen, as* Iupiter *King of*
Creete,*succeeded his father* Saturne *in his kingdome. This Creetish King* Iupiter *for his bountifull and liberall nature was called by the name of that most
good and beneficiall planet* Iupiter; *euen as his father, for the causes rehearsed,was named* Saturnus. *Hee that hath in his natiuitie* Saturne *predominant ouer* Iupiter, *is like to bee endued with no excellent qualities, especially
those that vsually proceede from* Iupiters *influence,as* Iustice,liberalitie,mag-
nificence,pietie,fauour,beauty,riches,promotion,loue,and such like : all which
by the maligning nature of this damnifying planet* Saturne,*are altogether corrupted and depraued, as the* Creetish Iupiter *when he was but a tender infant,
was faine to be secretly conueyed away from his sterne and cruell father* Saturne, *who sought his destruction.* Saturne *being imprisoned and chayned by
the* Titanes, *was released by his dutifull and mercifull sonne* Iupiter,*who came
with a mightie army to the succor of his father. Allegorically,when the good
and beneficiall* Iupiter *in any mans natiuitie ouer-ruleth preiudiciall* Saturne,
*beholding the other planets with an amyable and fortunat aspect,which con-
foundeth the dead lookes and frowning face of* Saturne,*then is that man freed
from those* Saturnian *chaynes of calamitie and miserie, which otherwise he were*

subiect

subiect vnto. These Titanes *were the sonnes of heauen and earth, signifying the foure elements, which include in themselues a certaine terrene and earthly nature, and are therefore continually depressed and beaten downe by the power of the superior bodies : for, vapors by the heate of the sunne (the sunne is called* Titan *) are drawne vp, which when they approach neere the celestiall region, are repelled and driuen downe againe, or els resolued into pure and subtile ayre, and this mounting vp, and throwing downe is perpetuall.*

Iupiter, *when he had thus enlarged his father, vsurped his crowne and royall dignitie, bannishing* Saturne *into hell, or the infernall regions.* HISTORICALLY, Iupiter *hauing freed his father from thaldome, tooke vpon himselfe the dignitie and regiment of* Crete, *enforcing* Saturnus *to flie into* Italie ; *where he was honored liuing and dying as a God : for, such was the custome of that age, to attribute diuine honors and titles vnto them as Gods, of whom they receaued any goodnesse : as they did indeede of this* Saturnus, *who taught them how to till and manure the ground, to coyne money of mettale, which before was of leather, to leaue bushes and caues, and liue more ciuily and orderly, and to obserue certaine lawes and constitutions by him inuented, as appeareth by* Virgil. 8. Æneid. *who therefore calleth that time, the Golden age. Now in truth* Italy *was then far inferior to* Greece *in Wealth and Dignitie, and might therefore be called the infernall region, or base and lowe countrey in respect of* Saturns *florishing kingdome : as also, for that* Italie *is lower then* Greece, *as inclining more to the west ; and it is an vsuall thing, for men to call the East, the superior or higher region, and the West, the lower, downecast, and inferior ; or lastly, as* Varro *wil haue it,* qd latet Italia inter præcipitia Alpium & Apennini : *because* Italie *doth, as it were, lurke and lie hidden betweene the abrupt and high toppes of the* Alpes *& the Mountaine* Apenninus. *That this is true which I report, of his being in* Italie, *besides the testimonie of* Virgil *in the place aboue alleaged (where he saith that* Italie, *was named* Latium, à Latendo, *because* Saturne *did lurke and lie there, to hide himselfe from his sonne* Iupiter.) Ouid *also will beare me witnes, who in the first of his* Fasti , *concluding this matter, saith, that for an eternall memoriall of his arriuall and good institutions, the Italian posteritie in their money of mettale, figured the ship wherein he came vnto them.*

At bona posteritas puppim formauit in ære,
Hospitis aduentum testificata dei.

Allegorically , as before ; when in any mans action or natiuitie Iupiter *is predominant, then doth he controle* Saturne, *depriuing him of his power and dominion, and driuing him out as his inferior.* Sabinus *thinketh that* Saturne *was therefore saide to be driuen into the infernal dungeons, for that he is of all other Planets, the most remote and furthest from the earth, making that infinite and vnmeasurable height of Heauen, to be this* Tartarus, *this infernall or strange and far remoued region. But the most conceipted allegory for this*

pur-

purpoſe,is that folowing: for although that in Saturns *time and raigne, that is,by the influence and vertue of this Planet* Saturne, *the ſeede is preſerued in the bowels of the earth,and congealed or thickned in the bodies of ſenſible creatures at the firſt generation and conception;* yet when theſe things are brought forth and receaue increaſe and augmentation, then doth Iupiter ſhew himſelfe to be King, and dealeth all in all, driuing out olde Saturne into corners, and blinde and obſcure places,where the firſt ſeedes of things lie hidden, which only are ſubiect to Saturnus iuriſdiction.*

Time is ſwift and euerpaſſing without ſtay: which may bee the cauſe why Saturne *is changed to a ſwift courſer, when his wife tooke him dallying with* Philyra, *of whom he begat* Chiron *the Centaure as hereafter will appeare.*

Thus haue wee the good olde Saturne *in his ragges, with his foure children before him, his ... juming ſyth in his right hand,and a ſtone couered with cloth put to his mouth,with the left hand.*

Out of Euſebius, *he may be thus alſo figured: himſelfe couered with a long roabe: two eyes before,as many behinde: of which foure, two did euer watch, whileſt other two ſlept: foure wings were faſtned to his ſhoulders, two ſpread foorth,as though he were ready to flie,two pluckt in,as though he meant to ſtand ſtill: he had alſo two wings at his head. The foure eyes andwings note, that Time,though it ſeeme to ſleepe, yet alwaies watcheth and yet ſo watcheth,as it ſeemeth ſtill to ſleepe: and, as it ſtandeth, it flyeth away, andyet in flying, after a manner ſtandeth ſtill. The two wings at his head are ſaid to repreſent the intellectuall facultie and reaſonable power of mans minde, the old Philoſophers being of opinion,that the ſoule receaued from* Saturnes *ſpheare,the gift of reaſon and intelligence.*

Saturne *his wife had diuerſe names.* Rhea, ἀπὸ τῆ ῥεῖν *à fluendo: either becauſe euery thing floweth from the earth,as from a fountaine,or that the flowing raigne is made of vapors and exhalations from the earth.* Veſta *ſhe is alſo called,becauſe ſhe is* Veſtita, *that is, couered with corne and graſſe as with a veſture: or, quiâ vi ſtat, becauſe ſhe ſtandeth by her owne force,quaſi viſta,according to that of* Ouid *in his Faſti.*

Stat vi terra ſua,vi ſtando veſta vocatur,
    Cauſaq; par graij nominis eſſe poteſt. Vt ἰϛὰ ἀπὸ τῆ ἱϛαναι, *ducatur.*

The other Veſta, Cælius *his wife,differeth not much from this: but that ſhe ſeemeth to figure the very eſſence of the earth; and this, the fruitefull efficacy,operation,and aſſiſtance thereof,whereupon ſhe was called* Opis, *as I ſaide before, of helpe or aſſiſtance:* Cybele, *of a Phrigian Mountaine ſo called: or rather, as* Feſtus Pompeius *thinketh, ἀπὸ τῆ κίβε, ſignifying a Cube; ſith in olde time they did conſecrate a Cube vnto her: the reaſon was,for that a Cube which way ſo euer it be throwne,ſtadeth alwaies direct,repreſenting therfore, the not remoueable ſtability of the Earth.* Laſtly ſhe was called Magna mater, *the*

Satu
two
ture

great mother both of Gods and men, sith as well the Pagan Gods as men, being both mortall, must both acknowledge the earth their foundor and benefactor, whereof more in Taſſoes Meſſagiero. She is couered with a Diadem bearing diuers turrets; the circuit of her Crowne ſignifying the compas of the Earth, and her turrets, the ſtately buildings of the ſame, according to. that of Lucretius lib. 1.

    Muralique caput ſummum cinxére corona,
    Eximijs munita locis quòd ſuſtinet vrbes.

Her garment is all wrought with flowers and bordered with branches, noting, that all ſuch things proceede from the Earth. Her Chariot is drawne by Lions, on foure wheeles: the foure wheeles giue vs to vnderſtand, that although the Earth be immouable, yet all earthly things are in continuall motion and alteration, according to the foure ſeuerall conſtitutions and ſeaſons of the yeare. The Lyons note the mightie and Lyonlike operation of the celeſtiall bodies vpon the earth: or, that huſbandmens bodies muſt be ſtrong like Lions: or laſtly, that the ſtouteſt were tamed, and muſt liue and dye on and in the earth. Her ſcepter is a ſigne of earthly pompe and dignitie. Round about her be emptie and vacant ſeates; either, for that the earth hath alwaies places of habitation in ſtore for ſucceeding people; or, for that houſes, cities, and countries become many times deſolate by peſtilence, famine, ſword, fire, or otherwiſe; or, becauſe many regions were then thought to be vnhabitable. Iſidorus maketh her hold a key in one hand; for that the earth is, as it were, cloſed and ſhut vp in the winter, foſtring then and cheriſhing in her lap the ſeede, till ſpring time come, and then ſhe openeth her ſelfe : and therefore is April ſo called of Aperio, quaſi Aperilis, the open, or opening moneth, as Ouid doth expound it,

    Aprilem memorant ab aperto tempore dictum.

Coribātes her prieſts ſtand round about her, al in armour: & ſo ſhould euery mā, prieſt, ſwaine, or whatſoeuer, be ready with life and limme to defend his natiue ſoyle. The noyſe of Taburs had (as Ouid alſo teſtifieth) his beginning frō Iupiters birth, who, as I ſaid before, was by that meanes concealed frō his father Saturne: ſome referre the roundnes of the Taburs, to the roundnes of the earth, & others there be who think that the Taburs and Cymballs did note the windes, ſtormes, clouds, & thunders; al which come of the exhalatiōs of the earth, mounting vpwards. Pinus is ſacred vnto Cybele, for that Atis a ſweet young youth who ſhe loued, was by her transformed into the ſame for pitie, ſeeing the poore boy (being reiected of her for violating his vowed virginitie) plague his owne body, by cutting off thoſe partes wherewith he had offended. This Atis (ſaith Euſebius) repreſenteth flowers which are fayre in ſhew, but fade and fall away, before they bring forth any fruite, which is the cauſe, that he is ſaid to be depriued of his fructifying members, the tale is ſweetly told by Ouid in his bookes de Faſtis. Another Veſta they made to be Saturns daughter, ſignifying that vitall heate, which, diſperſed all ouer and through the bowells of the Earth, giueth life to *all earthly things, On her seruice attended the Vestall Virgins in* Rome, *so called of their Mistres* Vesta, *of whom also* Ouid *in the same booke hath learnedly discoursed; among other things, adding this,*

Nec tu aliud vestam, quàm viuam intellige flammam.

*

In Saturns *time, the harmeles simplicitie of his subiects gaue name to the golden age, as I said before; which by degrees declining to siluer, and brasse, in the end became all of yron.* Then did Astræa *leaue the polluted earth, and setled her selfe betweene the Starres called* Leo *and* Libra, *the* Lyon, *and the Balance, couering her face in the cloudes for griefe to behold such impietie. Allegorically,* Astræa, *of* Astrum, *a Starre, is celestiall and heauenly Iustice : a Iudge must be stout and of good courage, as a* Lyon, *least for feare of menaces he spare the due execution of iustice : yet he must also weigh each thing in an vpright ballance, that affection or corruption doe not peruert iudgement : Her face is couered with clouds : for, a Iudge must not behold the parties with affectionat and preiudicat eyes, seduced by wrath or drawne away by Partialitie.*

A Astræa *thus gone, the Giants began to rebell : a bloudie broode, borne of* Cœlus *his bloud, falling on the earth, when* Saturne *his sonne depriued him of his virility. Some other make them to be borne of* Neptune *and* Iphimedea: Neptunes *broode is furious and vnruly by reason of the superaboundant store of vnbridled humors : and* Ihimedea, *is nothing else but an obstinat and selfe-wild conceite and desire grounded in the minde, and not remoueable. These allegorically are seditious and rebellious subiects in a common wealth or schismaticall and hæreticall seducers in the Church.* Iupiter, *the King or supreame gouernour : the Giants, rebells or heretikes : the hills, their aspiring deseignes and accursed stratagems:* Ioues *lightning, the iust plague and confusion of such attempts : their serpentine feete signifie their pernicious and poysonable policies, and their monstrous and most degenerate deformitie in opposing themselues against the common wealth. The battaile was fought in* Phlægra *a sulphurus part of* Thessalia, *for* φλίγειν *is to burne. There is yet extant a fragment of* Claudian, *entituled,* Gigantomachia, *the bataile of the Giants, wherein many of their names are particularly set downe, the historicall truth is extant in* Theagenes *and* Eudoxus. *Of the Giants bloud came the bloud-thirsting* Lycaon; *in truth a tyran of* Arcadia, *who first did violate the lawes of truce and league by killing and sacrificing vnto* Iupiter, *a certaine hostage sent from the* Molossi : *whereon came the fable, that he set mans flesh before* Iupiter, *to trie, if he were a God or not. This* Lycaon *for his crueltie, is here transformed into a wolfe, which in* Greeke *is called* λύκος, *agreeable to his auncient name. That which foloweth of the generall deluge or inundation, is borrowed, by likelihood, out of* Moyses, *by adding thereunto the conceit of* Deucalions *and* Pyrrhaes *casting of stones behinde their backes for the renuing of our stony generation. For, both* Lucian *reporteth, that* Deucalion *entred an arke,* and beasts and fowles with him: and Plutarch, that he sent forth a Doue, which returning, brought a signe of the decreasing waters, all which agree with the historie of Noe. As for Deucalion he is said to haue raigned sometime in Thessalia, which being for the most part drowned by sodaine waters, himselfe and his wife Pyrrha assembled on Mount Parnassus all such as escaped: and by their wisdome (figured by the oracle from Themis) brought them to be sociable againe, and multiplie as they did in former times.

But all this while we forget the poore Prometheus, who yet lyeth groaning on the mountayne Caucasus, for stealing fyre from heauen to make his image lyue: and taketh it very vnkindely, that we haue, in this creation of the world, made noe mention of him, by whose bold enterprise, Man, the best part of the world, was both framed first, and quickned afterwards. Minerua, lyking Prometheus his woorke, bad him aske what he would that was in heauen, to furnish his begun woorkmanship: he aunswering, that, vnles he were there to see what was in heauen fit for his purpose, he could desire no certeyne thing, was brought vp thither by Minerua: where; seeing euery thing quickned with fire, he drewe secretly neere to the Chariot of the Sunne, and thence kindled a sticke, and with that fire gaue life to his image.

Historically, Prometheus is sayd to be the first who made any image of man, of clay, whence this poeticall imagination tooke his beginning, and by continuance of time grewe to this (by the accustomed policies of the olde deceauing serpent, who is euer ready to further Atheisme and Idolatry) that Prometheus was honoured as a God, and had Temples dedicated, and Altars erected for his seruice accordingly. As apeareth by Pausanias, who reporteth, that in the Academy of Athens, there was an altar consecrated vnto Prometheus, and that at certaine times apointed for that purpose, diuers men came thither, and there lighted a number of burning brands, running with them one after another all in a rowe to Athens, in such sort, that whosoeuer caryed his fire brand burning quite to the Citie, was reputed Victor: and if any mans brand were extinguished or put out by the way, he gaue place to his fellow folowing.

Allegorically, Prometheus is the fore-seeing and fore-knowing of thinges before they come to passe (for soe the very woord importeth.) as Epimetheus is the knowledge which we get by the end and euent of things already past & gone, whose daughter is Repentance. Prometheus was the sonne of Iapetus & Themis: Iapetus is nothing els (saith Proclus) but the most quick motion of heauen, ἀπὸ τοῦ ἰᾶσθαι καὶ πετέσθαι, of mouing and flying: An Eagle consumeth his hart, a wise mans minde is euer full of meditations: as much as by the day the Eagle deuoureth, somuch the night restoreth againe; soe, learned mens cogitations admit intermissions, but noe interruptions: he was bound to a piller, or columne; The minde is bound fast to the body, and there chained for a while: some make him bound to the Mountaine Caucasus, for that there he obserued the reuolution of the heauens: The yeelding and giuing place to the succeeding fea-

lowe or companion that runneth, meanes nothing els, but that the whole course of this present life, is full of woe and miserie, which when they are once ended, our race is ended also, and they that come after vs, take at our hands, as by tradition, the like fire brands of calamities, as we our selues sustained before. Remy Belleau *bringeth in* Prometheus *lamenting in his* Bergerie, *Thus,*

Noble race de dieux, semence Titannine,
Qui retires du ciel ta premiere origine,

And so foorth, as foloweth there in that his complaint: so passionate, as that I am sory not to repeat it, & yet so copious as that I haue no time to rehearse it: especially hauing spent somuch of the day about this outworn Chaos, *which, I hope, will therfore seeme pardonable, because the vnderstanding of all other poeticall tales and transformations by likelyhoode to be toulde, must needes receaue great light from that which hath beene spoken. Here good* Elpinus *paused awhile: and sith* Pan *had beene by him eftsoones mentioned in this his discourse, it was thought conuenient by the Lady Regent, that* Menalcas *his song should be spent on that subiect: who thus began accordingly.*

A Rcadian Syrinx was a Nymph most noble, amongst all
Naiades and Dryades, that, in olde times highly renowned
Arcadian fountaines and mountains euer aforded.
 Fleshly Satyrs, Fauni, Siluani dayly desired
Braue bony Syrinx loue, yet loueles braue bony Syrinx
Fleshly Satyrs, Fauni, Siluani dayly deceaued.
Syrinx tooke noe ioy in ioyes of Queene Cytherea,
But vowd life and loue, and hart and hand to Diana.
Lyke to Diana she lyu'd, for a virgins lyfe she professed,
Lyke to Diana she went, for in hunting roabes she delighted,
And with bow and shafts stil practysd lyke to Diana;
Onely the diffrence was, that, in-hunting-mighty Dianaes
Bow, was made of gowld, and Syrinx bow of a cornell:
Which noe great diffrence was not so greatly regarded,
But that Nymphs and Gods eu'n so were dayly deceaued,
And hunting Syrinx for mighty Diana reputed,
So nere by Syrinx was mighty Diana resembled.
 Pan, with a garland greene of Pinetree gayly bedecked
Saw this Nymph on a time come back from lofty Lycæus,
And his rurall loue in rurall sort he bewraied.
 Scarce had he sayd, Bony sweete: but away went braue bony Syrinx,
Went through hills and dales and woods: and lastly aryued,
Where gentle Ladon with mylde streames sweetely resounded,
Ladon stopt her course, Ladon too deepe for a damsell.
 Then, quod Syrinx, Help, deare sisters; let not a virgin,

Immaculate

Immaculate virgin by a rurall *Pan* be defyled.
Rather let *Syrinx* be a mourning read by the ryuer,
Soe that *Syrinx* may be a mayden reade by the ryuer.
By and by *Syrinx* was turnd to a reade by the ryuer:
By and by came *Pan*, and snatcht at a reade for a *Syrinx*,
And there sight and sobd, that he found but a reade for a *Syrinx*.
Whilst *Pan* sighs and sobds, new tender reades by the whistling
Wyndes, did shake and quake, and yeelded a heauy resounding,
Yeelded a dolefull note and murmur like to a playning.
Which *Pan* perceauing, and therewith greatly delighted,
Sayd, that he would thenceforth of those reades make him a *Syrinx*.
Then, when he had with wax, many reedes conioyned in order,
His breath gaue them life : and soe *Pan* framed a Pastors
Pipe, which of *Syrinx* is yet still called a *Syrinx*.

SHort & *sweet, quod* Elpinus; & *I meane not my self herein to be ouer-long.*
Pan *therfore is sayd to haue two horns on his forehead, reaching vp euen to
the heauens; a red & fiery face, a long beard hanging down on his brest, a staffe
and a Pipe compact of seauen reedes in his hande, a spotted and freckled skinne
on his body, crooked, rough, and deformed lymmes, and legges like a Goate.*
Cupid and Pan *contending for superiority,* Pan *had the woorst, and the worst
was this, that he extreamely loued* Syrinx, *who extreamely hated him. Besides
a certaine historicall discourse of an* Arcadian, *called* Siluanus, *who to ease his
Loue-fittes, was much addicted to Musike, and first (as is reported,) found out
the Pipe made of seauen reeds, there is in this tale a more philosophicall conceit.*
Pan *in Greeke, as I sayd, signifieth, All, and doth both by name & naturall lineaments betoken that vniuersall efficacy of nature, ruling and gouerning all. The
two horns on his forehead reaching vp to heauen, represente the* Arctike *and*
Antarctike *poles. His spotted skinne is the eight Spheare, distinguished with
those heauenly lights of innumerable starres. his fiery face, conteyning two
eares, two eyes, two nosethrills, and one mouth, proportionably shadow the fiery
and bright nature of the seauen Planets, His long bristled beard and bush, be
the beames of the Sunne, and other Planets and Starrs, whose influence is the
cause of earthly generations. His crooked, rough, and deformed lymmes, are
the foure Elements, and the bodies thereof made, which, compared with those
aboue, are altogeather rude and homely. His Goates feete & leggs note out the
crooked course of things terrestriall: for euen as Goats go neuer streight, nor continue any setled and direct course, but wander and skipp here and there; so, what
soeuer is vnder the Sphere of the Moone, obserueth no constant and immutable
proceeding, but confusedly changeth from this, to that, from that, to an other,
without any intermission. Pan was in loue with a spotles and pure virgin: vni-
versall nature affecteth and earnestly desireth a celestiall and perpetuall con-*

stancy in these inferior bodies. Syrinx *runs from* Pan *; soe doth immutable constancy forsake these inferior matters, which are dayly tossed to and fro, and continually subiect to tenthousand alterations.* Syrinx *in her maine flight is stopped and stayed by the Riuer* Ladon *: in like sort, the heauens and celestiall bodies (which by reason of their continuall motion are like to a Riuer) dooe stay and bridle that wandring and inconstant constancy of inferior bodies : and though the heauēs thēselues, by reason of their perpetuall motiō seeme somewhat varyable and inconstant, yet this their instability is indeed most stable, and motion immutable, noted by this spotles virgin transformed into reades, which being mqued and breathed vpon by the life-inspiring* Zephirus, *yeelde this sweete melody ; as those celestiall globes are said to doe, by the impulsion and direction of their intellectuall guydes and Spyrites. Hereupon is* Pans *pipe made of seauen reades, figuring that heauenly harmony of the seauen* Planets, *caused by their neuer-ending circumduction and reuolution.* Pan *lastly, besides his pipe, hath a staffe also,* Sith *by the stayed and setled motion of the seauen* Planets, *this vniuersall efficacie of nature ordereth the proceedings of these inferior bodies accordingly. The tale is told by* Ouid, *and* Achilles Statius.

*

Pans ture.

Mydas *the golden asse, and miserlike foole (who was faine to vnwish his wish of transforming euery thing into golde by his tutching thereof) preferred* Pans *rurall harmony before the heauenly skill of* Apollo, *and was therfore woorthily rewarded with asses eares for his labor : which deformyty, though for a time he concealed, by couering it with his purple bonnet, yet at last was discouered by his Barber, who neither daring to tell it any body, nor being able to keepe it secret, digged a pit in the ground, and therein whispered, That his master* Mydas *had asses eares : which pit being by him then filled vp with earth againe, brought forth a number of reedes, which blown by the winde, repeated the buried woords, vttered by the Barber, to weet, That King* Midas *had asses eares. A golden foole and a silken asse, may for the time be clad with purple, & delude the gazers on, but when the reades growe, that is, when after his death the learned begin to write, and lay him open to the world, then is his nakednes discouered.* Pan *commonly hath his garland of the leaues of a Pinetree : he was accompted the God of* Sheepe *and* Shepheards, *and kept in the woods. Such was* Siluanus, *who therfore had his name of* Silua, *signifying a wood.* Fauni *and* Satyri *may hether also be referred, whom* Iupiter *calleth rusticall and halfe-gods :* Ouid 1. Metamorphosean.

Sunt mihi semidei, sunt rustica numina Nymphæ,
Fauniq; , Satyriq; , et monticolæ Siluani,
Quos quoniam cæli nondum dignamur honore,
Quas dedimus certé terras habitare sinamus.

These Satyrs are sayd to be lytle Dandiprats, with two hornes, crooked noses, hayry and rough bodies, and goates feete. Plutarch writeth in Syllaes lyfe, that there was one of them caught not farre from Apollonia a city of Epirus, and brought to Sylla: which being by many interpreters demaunded who or what he was, vttred a kinde of voice, but such as no man vnderstood, it being a sound that resembled the neying of a horse togeather with the bleating of a Goate.

It is reported, that Antony the Eremite, saw and spake with such a Satyre in the Desert of Egipt: who confessed that himself and his fellowes were but mortall creatures, inhabiting the wilderness, although the Gentiles seduced and blinded did honor them as Gods, calling them Fauni and Satyri: adding farther, that he came as sent from his companions, desiring Antony to make intercession for them to his and their God, whom they did know and acknowledge, to haue come into the world to saue the world. Besides these rurall Gods, the auncient Poets perceauing that there was a life-giuing moysture and efficacie of humor, in trees, hilles, seas, flouds, lakes, wells, and such like, haue apoynted them their seuerall Nimphes and Deities, as Ladies of the same, hereof came these names, Dryades, Hamadryades, Ephidryades, Oreades, Napeæ, Naiades, Limniades, and such others. The Satyrs aboue spoken of, by reason of their wanton and lasciuious natire, are made companions of Bacchus; the drunken God: but sith by talking of Pan, I haue thoughs of them here, I meane to leaue both him and them to their forrests and rurall harbors.

Pan thus dispatcht, it was thought good; that Saturne his children should be remembred in order: and first, Iupiter, by Damætas, whose tale was much to this effect.

IOue, as he looked downe fro the skies, sawe beautiful Io,
Saw, and said, well mett, faire mayde, well woorthy the thundrer:
Toyle not thy sweete self, it's too hoate, come fro the scorching
Sunne, to the cooling shade: loe, here, and here is a harbor.
If thou darst not alone passe through these desolat harbors
Fo e feare of wilde beasts; let a God be thy guide by the forrest,
And noe trifling God, but a God that welds the triumphant
Mace, and hurls lightnings, and thunderbolts from Olympus.
Io fled for feare, for loue Ioue hastened after;
And for a quick dispatch, both lands and seas on a soddaine
Ouer-cast with a cloude, and soe caught beutiful Io.
In meane time Iuno Ioues wife lookes downe fro the heauens,
(Seeing lightsome skies at myd-day soe to be darkned,
Yet noe foggs or mystes from pooles or moores to be lysted)
Meruailes much, and asks, if her husband were in Olympus,
Who transformd some times to a Bull, some times to a golden
Showre, was woont each where such slippery prancks to be playing,

Ioue was not to be founde; why then,qd*Iuno*,without doubt
Fowly deceaued I am this day, or fowly abufed.
Down ftraight way fro the skies in a iealous fury,fne flingeth,
And thofe coofning clowdes,and darcknes roundly remoueth.
   Ioue forefawe this geare : and faire white bewtiful *Io*,
Straight with a tryce transformde to a fayre white bewtiful heyfar.
Iuno geu's good woords (although,God knows,with an ill will,)
And commends this Cow,and fais; o happy the Bullock
Whoe might once enioy this fayre white bewtiful Heyfar.
Then fhe begins to demaunde,who brought that Cow to the pafture,
Of what kynde fhee came,and what man might be the owner.
   Ioue,that he might fhyft off bufy *Iuno*,tow'ld her a lowde lye,
That nought els but th'earth brought forth that bewtiful Heyfar.
Iuno wel acquainted with her husbands wyly deuifes,
Askt this Cow for a guift : Then *Ioue* was brought to a mifchif:
What fhal he dooe?fhal he geue his louing *Io* to *Iuno*?
That were too too harde : fhal he not geue *Iuno* the Heyfar?
That would breede myftrufte : fhame fpurts on,Loue is a brydle:
And fhame-brydling loue,noe doubt, had laftiy preuayled,
But that,alas, if a wife,if a fyfter, a Lady,a *Iuno*,
Eu'n of a *Ioue*,of a Lorde, nay eu'n of a brother, a husband
Shuld be denyed a Cow,then might it feeme to be noe Cowe.
   Thus gate *Iuno* the Cowe : but yet fhee feared a Bull ftjl:
And,to be more fecure,fhe deliuered *Io* to *Argus*
For to be carefuly kept, whofe waking head had an hundred
Eyes; two flept by courfe, and but two only; the other
Stil kept watch and warde : Which way foeuer he looked,
Euer he lookt to the Cowe, *Argus* lookt euer on *Io*.
In day tyme fhee feedes,yet feedes ftil watched of *Argus*,
Feedes on boughes and graffe, (foode too too fowre for a fweete laffe)
Drincks of pitts and pooles,drinck noething fit for a damfell.
All night long fhee's tyde by the ouer-dutiful *Argus*,
And on bare could ground her tender fide fhe repofeth.
   When fhe begins her griefe,and woefull cafe to remember,
And would lyft vp her handes,to befeech vnmerciful *Argus*,
Noe hands are left her,to befeech vnmerciful *Argus*.
When fhe recounts her fmart,and meanes her woe to be vttring,
Io lowes as a Cow, infteede of an heauy bewayling,
Io the lowing Cow frights *Io* the laffe,by the lowing.
When to the fyluer ftreames of fathers brooke fhe repayreth,
Fathers fyluer ftreames fhewe daughters head to be horned,
Io the horned Cow,with her hornes feares *Io* the damfell.

Euery

Euery water-nymph ftil lookt and gazed on *Io*,
Neuer a water-nymph thought this fame Cow to be *Io*,
Inachus her father ftill lookt and gazed on *Io*,
Ioes owne father did neuer thinck her his *Io*:
And yet poore *Io* went euery day to the aged
Inachus: once himfelfe pluckt graffe, and gaue to the heyfar :
Io the guift for giuers fake, very kindly receaued,
And with ftrea ming teares her fathers hand fhe befprinckled,
Lykt and kiffed his hand : and would haue gladly reuealed
Her mifchaunce ; and this new transformation vttred,
But ftil, grones and lowes, infteede of woords, fhe deliu'red.
    At laft, two letters with her hoofe fhee prynts by the ryuer,
I, and, *O*, for a figne of late transfigured *Io*:
Inachus howld when he read this doleful letter of *Io*.
Inachus howld, and cride, and clipt disfigured *Io*,
Hangd on her horns and neck: and art thou *Io* my daughter?
Io my daughter, alas, ô moft vnfortunat *Io*.
Inachus euery where hath fought for beutiful *Io*,
And now findes her a Cow, infteede of a beutiful *Io*:
Io better loft then found : for I loft her a braue laffe,
But now haue found her, not a laffe, not a wench, not a woman,
Found her a Cow, dumbe Cow, whofe language is but a lowing :
Whereas I, fufpecting no fuch thing, fought for a husband
For my deare *Io*, and *Io* hoapte for a yong fon;
Io muft haue calues for fons, and bull for a husband:
    Inachus and *Io* thus leaning either on others
Neck, complaind and wept : then coms illuminat *Argus*,
And driues father away from daughters fight, to the fountains,
And driues daughter away from fathers fight, to the mountains.
    Iupiter impatient to behold difconfolat *Io*,
Commaunds *Mercurius*, to deceaue vntractable *Argus*:
Mercury putts on his hat, takes ftaffe and wings in a moment,
Flyes to the earth: where hat for a time, and wings he remoueth,
And th'inchaunted ftaffe, as a fheepehooke, only reteigneth,
And fo plods to the downe with an oaten pipe as a paftor,
And ftil playes, as he plods, which ftrange mirth greatly delighted
Cow-keeping *Argus* : who could not reft, til he called
Mercury vp to the mount. Now *Mercury* fits on a mountaine
Hard by *Argus* fide, and tells him there, of a purpofe,
This tale, and that tale : how worthily *Phœbus Apollo*
Plagued prowd *Niobe*, and *Pallas* fcorneful *Arachne*,
And each tale had a fong, and euery fong had a piping.

Argus

Argus twixt nodding and gaping laſtly demaunded
Who found out that pipe. Then *Mercury* gins to remember
Pan and *Syrinx* loue : but or halfe was brought to an ending,
Argus his hundred lights were all obſcur'd with a darcknes,
Al bade him good night. Here *Mercury* quickly repreſſed
Both his pipe and voyce, and ſlumbring *Argus* he bleſſed
With th'inchaunted ſtaffe, that much more ſoundly he ſleeped :
By and by, fro the neck, his nodding head he diuided,
And ſo by one clowd, one hundred ſtarrs he eclipſed.

Iuno was all in a chafe ; and *Argus* death ſhe bewayled,
And with ſelf-ſame eyes her Peacocks traine ſhe be-painted :
And made poore *Io*, poſſeſt with an helliſh *Erinnis*,
Run fro the eaſt to the weſt, and neuer finde any reſting :
Til by *Ioues* good meanes, fel *Iunoe's* fury relented,
Forgaue poore *Io*, and gaue her leaue to be lightned,
And, for a further bliſſe, to be call'd *Ægyptian Iſis.*

D Amætas *had now done: and* Elpinus *thus recontinued his intermitted labor.* Iupiter *in latine, is* quaſi Iuuans pater, *that is*, *a helping father. In greeke he is called* ζευ, ἀπὸ τὶ ζῶ, *à* viuendo *, of liuing, as being the autor and giuer of life. He reduced the old world from barbariſme to ciuilitie, he builded temples for the Gods, made lawes for men, and hauing ſubdued moſt part of the earth, diuided the ſame among his brethren and kinsfolke, reſeruing to himſelfe the mountaine* Olympus, *where he kept his court. Allegorically, theſe and the like be the effects and operations of this beneficiall planet* Iupiter. Olympus, *is of it ſelfe moſt high, paſſing the clowdes, the word is aſmuch to ſay in Greeke, as, all and wholly light and bright, and ſo taken for heauen.* Iupiter *is commonly pictured ſitting, ſith the eternall Monarch of heauen, and earth, is alwaies immutable, one, and the ſame, and neuer ſubiect to any alteration. His vpper parts are bare and naked, the lower, couered and concealed, ſignifying, that thoſe ſuperior and celeſtiall ſpirites conceaue the hidden myſteries of* Iupiter, *who will not diſcloſe himſelfe to mortall men, dwelling on earth ; and clogd with the heauie burden of a corruptible body. In his right hand he holdeth an all-ruling ſcepter, in his left, a ſin-correcting lightning and his* Ægle *ſtandeth by.*

*

Iupite
pictur

The ſcepter noteth a temperate rule and moderate gouernemont, correſpondent to the mylde nature of that mercifull planet : yet he wanteth not a lightning to plague the wicked, which is therefore aſcribed vnto him, ſith he is middle betweene Saturne *and* Mars, *whoſe contrary and repugnant qualities concurre both together in* Iupiter, *aſwell the extremity of colde from the circle of* Saturne, *as the furious heate from the ſpheere of* Mars *, whoſe conflict and*

D 3   *Bruslings*

strugling together causeth thunder and lightning. : whereof there bee three kindes. The first, bright and cleare, of a most wonderfull piercing and subtile nature, melting gold, siluer, and brasse in a purse, the purse neuer tutcht, destroying the childe in the mothers wombe, the mother no way hurt, killing and spoyling a man, his garments not somuch as schorched. The second is that which burneth, and is red: the third is somewhat moyst, and burneth not, but maketh black and blew: which was the cause that his lightning was called Trisulcum. The Ægle is his byrde, as being, by report, neuer tutcht with thunder, but looketh directly on the burning beames of the sunne, and is King of birds, as Iupiter is Monarch among the Gods. Among trees, the oake is sacred vnto him: because in olde time, the oake by her ackorns, is said to haue giuen life and foode, and Iupiter himselfe is the author of life. He maried his sister Iuno, so also called, à Iuuando, of helping. Allegorically, Iupiter noteth the celestiall and fierie region, Iuno the ayrie and inferior; and becaufe that celestiall is immediatly conioyned with this terrestriall, (and either of them is light and yeelding, leuis & mobilis) they are called brother and sister : and sith the celestiall by reason of his heate is the agent, and the inferior becaufe of her moysture the patient or recipient, they be therefore also Man and Wife, for without heate and moysture no procreation. But of Ioues mariage it were fitter time to speake, when Iuno his Wife comes in place. Now therefore to his Mynions and louetricks, which transformed him into sundry shapes of brute beasts: for this immoderate lust and wantounes, is not onely beastlike it selfe, but maketh them also beasts which giue themselues ouer thereunto.

For the matter remembred by Damætas, I haue heard, that the Phænicians did vsualy sayle to Argos in Greece ; and being there on a tims, when they had made shew of their marchandise, and diuers women of Argos (among which was also Io daughter to Inachus their King) came thither of purpose to buie ; the Phænicians tooke them away all to their ships, and brought them to Ægypt; where this Io was giuen in mariage to Osiris the Ægyptian King, surnamed Iupiter Ammon, as Diodorus Siculus maketh mention : and Io herselfe was afterwards among them honored for a goddesse, by the name of Isis. And becaufe the Ægyptians, in respect of husbandrie, did with diuine seruice and ceremonies honor a Cow, thereupon the fable tooke his ground, that Io being stolne by Iupiter, was transformed to a Cow. The impression of a Cowes hoofe, resembleth a greeke ω with an I in the middle : whereupon it is said, that Io with her foo e wrote her name on the banke of her fathers brooke. Natalis Comes maketh this ethicall moralization of it. The celestiall and heauenly power in Man, called reason or vnderstanding, figured by Mercurius, doth moderate, pacifie, and temper all those inordinate motions and affections proceeding from that other facultie of the minde, prouoking to wrath and anger. This cholerike and angry parte of mans minde as long as it resteth, may bee called Argus, sith ἄργος signifieth beauie, and

and slowe : but being once prouoked and incensed, it hath an hundred eyes looking to euery corner for reuenge, and cannot be quiet, till Mercury *dispatch him , that is , till Reason suppresse and keepe him vnder :* Pontanus *expoundeth it physically, making* Mercury *to be the sunne (by whose beames hee is euer lightned) the white Cowe the Earth ,* Argus *the Heauen , his eyes the Starres , which glister by night, but by the suns approach, are all dished and extinguished.*

Quin & Mercurium mutato nomine dicunt
Argum somnifero victum strauisse caduceo,
Insomnem, centumq; oculos, ac lumina centum
Pandentem, & niuex seruantem pascua vaccx.
Argus enim Cœlum est, vigilantia lumina flammx
Ætherix, & vario labentia sydera mundo.
Qux passim multa sublustris noctis in vmbra
Collucent, sed mox phœbo exoriente perempta
Torpent luce noua, & candenti lampade victa
Emoriuntur, & obscuro conduntur Olympo.

Iupiter *conueyed away* Europa, Agenors *daughter in a Ship called, The Bull, which was the cause why hee is saide to rauish her by transforming himselfe into a Bull. In that hee was turned to a golden showre to obtaine* Danae : *we see, that golde ouerruleth, and that, as* Cicero *somewhere saith,* Asellus auro onustus in castellum ascendere potest , *an asse loaden with golde will enter any strong holde. Or else* Danae *may represent mans soule, and* Iupiters *golden showre, the celestiall grace and influence deriued into our mindes from aboue.* Niobe , *for her excessiue pride and contempt of God , is worthily plagued, yea so extreamely plagued in those very thinges wherein she chiefely vaunted, that for very anguish of heart and vntolerable woe, shee is saide to bee turned to a dull and senceles marble stone. The like mischife befell* Arachne , *who being endued with excellent qualities, thought scorne of the goddesse which was her good Mistresse, and might haue beene her patronesse; and was therefore transformed to a spyder.*

Elpinus *hauing concluded this discourse, it was commaunded by the Lady regent, that because* Iuno *was by nature and mariage conioyned with* Iupiter, *they should also ioyntly be remembred, before any other of* Saturns *broode were medled withall.* Fuluia *therefore being apoynted for this narration, for that shee could not readily call to minde any memorable tale of* Iuno *herselfe, sang as foloweth of the Nymph* Eccho, *who was alwaies taken to be* Iunoes *daughter.*

Tiresias

Tiresias, *Iunoes* and *Ioues* iudge, blinde, yet a seer,
Foretolde *Narcissus* this destinie. *This pretie yong Boy*
Shalbe a man many yeares; if he neuer looke on his owne face.
This seemde strange for a while, but th'end proou'd all to be too true.
For, braue *Narcissus* (when he came at length to the sixteenth
Yeare of his age, and might seeme either a boy, or a batchler)
Had so louely a looke, soe sweete and cheareful a countnance,
That Nymphes and Ladies *Narcissus* dayly desired :
Yet soe loueles a looke, so prowd and scorneful a countnance,
That Nymphes and Ladies, *Narcissus* dayly refused.
Eccho once a day, the resounding *Eccho*, that aunswers
Euery question askt, and yet no question asketh,
Saw this gallant youth, as he hunted a deere by the forrest.
Eccho the tatling Nymph was a true bodie then, not an onely
Voyce, as now : although eu'n then that voyce was abridged
Like as now : and this was done by *Iuno* the Empresse,
Mother, as it was thought, to the prating Dandiprat *Eccho*.
For when *Ioue* with Nymphs himselfe did meane to recomfort
Here and there by the woods, and fetch his flings by the forrests,
Shee with a long discourse her mother *Iuno* deteigned,
Till Nymphs all were gone, aud *Ioues* deuotion ended.
    Iuno perceauing these tricks, cut short the deluding
Tong of pratling elf : yet pratling elf thus abridged
Of too much tatling and babling in the beginning,
Vseth her ould custome, by redoubling words in an ending.
Therefore when she see's *Narcissus* goe to the forrest,
Step for step thither by a secret path she repayreth,
Burning still for loue : and as she nearer aproacheth
Vnto the loued boy, soe she more mightily burneth.
How-many thousand times, poore soule, she desirde a desiring
And intreating speech to the wandring boy to be vttring?
But fatall nature would noe-way grant a beginning.
And yet, what nature permits, she greedily listneth
For some sound, which may make her to be quickly resounding.
    At last *Narcissus* from his hunting company straying
Wisht and sayd, O God, that I could see, some-body comming.
Eccho repeated agayne these last words, Some-bodie comming.
Some-bodie comming? Where? qd wandring hunter amased,
Come then apace : And, Come then apace, poore *Eccho* replied.
Narcissus wonders, lookes back, see's noe-body comming :
Why, qd he, callst-thou me, and yet stil runst fro my calling?
Cryest and fliest? And, Cryest and flyest? were dolefuly doobled.

Then

Then, qd *Narcissus*, let's meete, and both be together:
Eccho, these last words with most affection hearing,
Answered him fiue times, Let's meete, and both be together,
And soe runs to the boy, in a fond conceipt, fro the bushes,
Clips him fast by the neck, and offers friendly to kisse him.
But prowd boy, as prowd as fayre, disdainfuly frowning,
Flies from her embracements, and sayes, Let greedie deuouring
Boares and beares be my graue, if I euer yeeld to thy pleasure.
Eccho sayd nothing, but, I euer yeeld to thy pleasure.
And, for griefe and shame to be too too proudly repulsed,
Hides her-selfe in woods and caues, and dwels by the deserts,
And yet loues him still, still pines with vnhappily louing.
Careful loue, and sleeples cares brought *Eccho* to nothing,
Nothing but bare bones with an hollow heauie resounding.
For fiesh was cleane gone, and quite consum'd to a powder,
And life-giuing blood went all to an ayre from a vapor.
Yea, very bones at last, were made to be stones: the resounding
Voyce, and onely the voyce of forelorne *Eccho* remaineth:
Eccho remaineth a voyce, in deserts *Eccho* remaineth,
Eccho noe-where seene, heard euery where by the deserts.

   Iuno laught no lesse, then when shee saw in *Auernus*
Prowd *Ixions* wheele turne with reuolution endles.

   But th'ouer-weening princox, was iustly rewarded;
Who, for not louing others, soe loued his owne-self,
That selfe-will, selfe-loue, as he saw himselfe in a fountaine,
Made him loose himselfe, for a fading shade of his owne-self.

*THis tale being thus tolde by Fuluia, Elpinus tooke occasion thereby to dis-
   course of* Iuno *much after this manner.* Iuno, Ioues *wife and sister, as I
sayd before, is the Lady of mariage, and gouernesse of child-birth, called therefore* Lucina, à Luce, *sith she, as a cœlestiall midwife, helpeth to bring forward
the children* in lucem, *into light. These proprieties are assigned vnto her, for
that she resembleth the vertue and efficacy of the ayre, and al this inferior composition, as I haue already tolde.* Occanus *and* Thetis *brought her vp: the ayre
is made of water rarified and subtiled. She brought foorth* Vulcan *vnto* Iupiter: *the ayre incensed and made hoate, breedeth fire.* Homer *maketh* Iupiter *binde* Iuno *with a golden chayne, hanging two great masses of Iron at her
heeles, and that she thus tied, could be loosed by none, but by himself:* Iuno *is
the ayre; the two weights of Iron, be the earth and water, betweene which two
& the superior bodies she hangeth chayned: & this golden chayne is the cohœ-
rent concatenation and depending of things vnited so in order, as none but only
the almighty* Iupiter *can dissolue the same. The Peacock is* Iunoes *bird, and*

draweth her chariot: Iuno *is the goddesse of riches and honour, which are as glorious in shew, and as transitorie in truth, as the Peacoks spotted trayne, and make men as prowd and insolent, as a* Peacocke, *which in a vaunting and bragging conceipt, displayeth to the beholders, her feathers besprinckled with* Argus *his eyes. Her Nymphs and handmayds expresse the variable change & alteration of the ayre, portending either fayre or fowle weather, windes, stormes, rayne, hayle and such like: of whom* Virgil *maketh mention,* I. *Æneid. where* Inno *offreth* AEolus *the fayrest lasse of all her fourteene damsels.*

> Sunt mihi bis septem præstanti corpore Nymphæ;
> Quarum, quæ forma pulcherrima, *Deïopeiam,*
> Connubio iungam stabili, propriamq; dicabo,
> Omnes vt tecum meritis pro talibus annos
> Exigat, & pulchra faciat te prole parentem.

Iuno *might well command* AEolus, *the king of windes, sith winde is nothing els but the ayre stirred, or an exhalation blustring in the ayre: therefore in that place* Virgil *maketh him thus answere* Iuno.

> Tuus ô regina, quid optes,
> Explorare labor; mihi iussa capessere fas est.
> Tu mihi quodcunq; est regni, tu sceptra, Iouemq;
> Concilias, tu das epulis accumbere diuûm
> Nymborumq; facis tempestatumq; potentem.

Historically, AEolus *dwelling in a very hilly and windy countrie, perceaued and foretolde the mariners, by the flowing and reflowing of the seas, and such other Physical obseruations, what weather they should expect, noting and declaring vnto them before hand the sure and vnfallible tokens of the rising windes and tempests, whereupon he was called the king of windes, and his kingdome Æolia , of his name: where he with his regall mace in his hand, pinneth vp those blustring brethren in his dungeons, barred with huge hils and mountaynes, as there* Virgil *also beareth witnes.*

> Talia flammato secum dea corde volutans
> Nymborum in patriam, loca fœta furentibus austris,
> AEoliam venit: hic vasto rex *Æolus* antro
> Luctantes ventos tempestatesq; sonoras
> Imperio premit, ac vinclis & carcere frenat.
> Illi indignantes magno cum murmure, montis
> Circum claustra fremunt: celsa sedet *Æolus* arce,
> Sceptra tenens, mollitq; animos, ac temperat iras,

Ni faciat, maria ac terras cœlumq; profundum
Quippe ferant rapidi fecum verrantq; per auras.

The windes are painted winged, with swelling and puffing mouthes and cheekes, among the rest, Boreas hath this peculiar, that his feete be serpentine, according to his pinching and byting nature

The pi-
ctures c
the win

*

As Mercury *is* Iupiters *messenger, so is* Iris Iunoes. Iris *hath her name* ἀπὸ τῦ εἴρειν, *of speaking. for she speaketh and telleth when rayne is towards.* Iris *is the* Rayn-bow, *and* Iuno *is the ayre, wherein those raynie clowdes are clutte-red together.* Iris *is the daughter of* Thaumas *and* Electra: Thaumas *is the sonne of* Pontus, *the sea, or water: and* Electra *is the daughter of heauen, or the sunne.* Thaumas *signifieth wondring and admiration, of* θαυμάζειν, *and this bow, in truth, is euery way wonderful, by reason of those so many strange colours appearing therein.* Electra *is perspicuitie, or serenitie; of* ἤλιος, *the sunne, and* αἴθριος, *bright and serene: so this bow proceedeth from water and serenitie, to weete, from the reflexion of the sunnes beames, in a watery clowde.* Iuno *her selfe sitteth on a throne, with a scepter in her hand, a crowne on her head, and her* Peacocke *standing by her.*

Iunoes
picture.

*

Iupiter *iesting with* Iuno, *whether man or woman had more pleasure, the matter was referred to* Tiresias, *who had been both woman and man: but gi-uing sentence with* Iupiter, *was depriued of his sight by* Iuno. *It is not good therefore to iudge betweene our betters.* Tiresias *was a sage and contempla-tiue man: and such are commonly blinde to other matters, for that they scorne these inferior things, as hauing vowed their whole soules to more heauenly cogitations.* Eccho *is* Iunoes *daughter, for she is nothing els, but the reuerbe-ration and reduplication of the ayre.* Eccho *noteth bragging and vaunting, which being contemned and despised, turneth to a bare voyce, a winde, a blast, a thing of nothing.* Narcissus *is a louer of himselfe, and so it falleth out, that vaunting and bragging loues self-loue: He is turned to a flower, florishing to day, and fading to morrow, as such ouerweeners alwayes doe.*

Ixion *graced by* Ioue, *would needes dishonour* Iuno: Iupiter *framed a counterfait* Iuno, *in truth nought but a clowde: which* Ixion *vsing in stead of* Iuno, *begat the* Centaures. *This is a note of ambitious and aspiring loue,* And these Centaures *hereupon were called* Nubigenæ. *Historically they li-ued in high mountaines in* Thessalia, *which gaue occasion to this fiction. They were called halfe men, for that being practised in riding, they grew most ex-pert therein, sitting on horses continually, so that they seemed not men and hor-ses distinct, but a thing made of horse and man together. These rude fellowes enraged with wine and lust, set all on an vprore at* Pyrithous *his wedding.*

But

But to returne to Eccho, I remember an odde conceited dialogue betweene her & the affectionate louer, which as I heard it of late of a forren Pastor, so here for nouelties sake, I repeate it: that some of our company may another time either worke on the same ground, or lay himselfe a new foundation.

Valli, saffi, montagne, antri, herbe, & piaggie,
  Colli, selue, fontane, augelli, & fere,
  Satyri, Fauni, & voi ninfe leggiadre,
  Odite per pietà la pena mia.
Vdite come amor mi mena a morte
  Legato in duro e indiffolubil nodo? *odo.*
Voce odo; deh chi sei tu, che rispondi
  A l'amaro & dolente piànger miò? *Io.*
Ninfa sei forse? di, se ninfa sei
  Tu, che di questa voce formi il suono? *Sono.*
Ninfa sei dunq; ? deh dimmi anco il nome,
  Ch'io sappia chi si moue à pianger meco. *Echo.*
Hora poi ch'*Echo* sei, porgimi orecchio,
  Odimi, se l'udir non ti dispiace. *Piace.*
Tu vedi, com'io piango àmaramente,
  Deh mouati pietà del mio cordoglio? *Doglio.*
Se di me duolti, vuoi porger consiglio
  Al profondo pensier in cui m'inuoglio? *Voglio.*
Ma che premio fia'l tuo, se'l mio tormento
  In qualche parte almen per te si annulla? *Nulla.*
I'ti ringratio. Hor dunq; mi consiglia,
  Poiche piu altro premio non richiedi. *Chiedi.*
Tu vedi, Ninfa, com'amor mi strugge
  Ch'i'ò corro à morte, e à pena me n'aueggio? *Veggio.*
Che mi consigli? che faro perch'io
  Troui pietà là dou'amor mi chiama? *Ama.*
Vorrei saper che cosa è quest'amore,
  Questo, che tutto m'arde, e che m'infiamma. *Fiamma.*
Che fiamma è questa? come non finisce
  Di consumar, se mai non si rallenta? *Lenta.*
In che loco s'annida? oue soggiorna?
  Che parte è quella, ou'arde a mio dispetto? *Petto.*
Com'entra dimmi? oue troua la via,
  Perch'ella dentro al petto si trabocchi? *Occhi.*
Entra per gli occhi? parmi hauer inteso,
  Che molti per vdir s'namoraro. *Raro.*
Dimmi, che cibo è'l suo, doue si pasce,

Che par che di continuo ella m'acore? Core.
Se m'arde 'l cor! debbo durare ancora
   Al giogo, ou i'o mia libertà perdei? Dei.
Adunq; vuoi, ch'i'o stia nel mio pensiero
   Constante ancor, benche sia afflitto e stanco? Anco.
Tante lagrime spargo, e nulla gioua,
   Dimmi, sarebbe forse il pianto in vano? Vano.
Che farò dunq; acciò al mio casto ardire,
   Che m'arde, honestò premio si reserui? Serui.
Credi, che l'amor mio le serà grato,
   Et ch'ella fia del mio seruir contenta? Tenta.
Ogni via tentarò, se credi, ch'io
   Possa alcun premio riportarne poi. Poi.
Hor qual esser deuro, se pur talhora
   Il dolor mi sara tremante infermo? Fermo.
Ma che farò, s'egli cosi mi strugge,
   Ch'in pianto la mia vita si distempra? Tempra.
Com'io la temprerò, s'amor non cessa
   Di saettarmi da la terza Spera? Spera.
Dunq;, ninfa gentil, lo sperar, gioua,
   E la mortale passion raffrena? Frena.
Qual sia la vita mia, se senza speme
   Terrammi preso amor con man' accorta? Corta.
Se siano corti i giorni di mia vita,
   Non saran lieti almen, benc'hor m'attristi? Tristi.
Che spererò? mi lice sperar forse
   Che far mi debba vn giorno amor felice? Lice.
Vorrei saper chi mi darà speranza,
   Poich'a sperar la tua ragion m'inuita? Vita.
Vita haurà dunq;? haurò poi altro s'io
   Non mi las'io giamai mancar di Spene? Pene.
Pene? Sperando adonq; che mi gioua?
   Ma chi sia causa, che di pene i' tema? Tema.
Tema la causa fia? deh dimmi il vero,
   Dunq; tema potra farmi mendico? Dico.
Ahi lasso, ahi discortese, empio timore,
   Hor questo dunq; il mio piacer conturba? Turba.
Pommi far peggio? dimmi se puo peggio
   Seguir à queste membra afflitte e morte? Morte.
Morte? se dunq; il timor passa 'l segno,
   Talhor si more per souerchio amore? More.
Come lo scaccierò? l'alma si strugge,

      F

Che non lo vuole, piange, e si dispera. Spera.
    Tu pur dici ch'io spera, speme forse
Credi, che sola sia, ch'altri consola? Sola,
    Leuera tutto, o parte del tormento,
Lasso, che mi consuma, e'l cor mi parte? Parte.
    Adunq; la speranza per se sola
Beato non, potra far mi giamai? Mai.
    Ma oltre amore seruitute, e speme,
Che ci vuol? dimmi'l tutto a parte a parte. Arte.
    Chi mi dara quest' arte forsi, amore
Altri chi sia, se no' è amor istesso? Esso.
    Insegna dunq; amor, dunq; a gli amanti,
Amor del ver amor l'arte dimostra? Mostra.
    Dimmi di gratia, scopriro la fiamma,
ò mi consigli, ch'io non la discopri? Scopri.
    A cui debbo scoprirla? ad ogn'un forse?
ò bastera, che sol l'intenda alcuno? Vno.
    Vuoi che ad vn sol amico sia palese,
Celato à gli altri sia'l colpo mortale? Tale.
    Sapremo soli tre dunq; il mio ardore,
Se vuoi, che con vn solo mi consoli. Soli.
    Ma dimmi quale deue esser colui
à cui l'ardor secreto mio confido? Fido.
    Trouerans'in amor fedeli amici
C'habbin riguardo poi d'amico algrado? Rado.
    Come dunq; faro perche lo troui
Che sia fedel, si come si ricerca? Cerca.
    E s'io lo trouo, che potra giouarmi?
Forsi talhor la passion rileua? Leua.
    Hor questo che mi detti, dimmi'l modo
Vero d'amor, dimmi di gratia'l vero? Vero.
    Se questo è il vero modo, i' son felice,
Homai non temo, che'l dolor m'atterri. Erri.
    Perch' erro? forsi anchor altro ci vuole?
Perche senz'ale il mio pensier non vuole? Vole.
    Altro ci vuol ancor? non basta quello?
Deh dimmi'l ver, non mi lasciar incerto? Certo.
    Che ci vuol dunq; di per cortesia,
Perche di gioia sia l'alma conforte? Sorte.
    Sorte? hor altro ci vuol accioche in fine
Voglia, e speme in van nò starò in sorte? Sorte.
    In somma di, sopra tutto che gioua,
Perche no sia'l desir in darno, e sorte? Sorte.

Horresta in pace, ninfa, io ti ringratio,
Che co'l tuo ragionar par che nii auiui? Viui.

Philoueuia, being next by turne, was willed to remember what she could concerning the watery Nymphs & Ladies of the seas; that therby Elpinus might shew his conceipt touching Neptune, *the second heire of* Saturnus. *And this was her song.*

SCilla sate her down, then a mayd, now chang'd to a monster,
Sate her down on a banck with sea-borne Dame *Galathea,*
Down on a flowring banck, not far from sulphurus *Ætna.*
And there gan to recount ten thousand wilie deuises,
Wherewith poore young youths in scornful sort she deluded,
   Yea, but alas, sayd then, with a far-fet sigh *Galathea,*
They that seeke thy loue, yet suffer dayly repulses,
Beare mens face, mens heart, and so are safely repulsed.
But *Galathea* the wretch, (ó woful wretch *Galathea*)
Could not auoyd leawd lust and rage of lout *Polyphemus,*
Capten of *Ætna'es* feends, but alas, but alas with a danger,
Nay with a death, ô death: and there grief stopt *Galathea.*
   At length, inward woe with weeping somwhat abated,
Thus, for *Scillaes* sake her dearlings death she remembred.
   There was (woe worth was) was a fayre boy, beautiful *Acis,*
Acis, Faunus boy, and boy of louely *Simethis,*
Acis, Faunus ioy, and ioy of louely *Simethis,*
Best boy of *Faunus,* best boy of louely *Simethis,*
Most ioy of *Faunus,* most ioy of louely *Simethis:*
And yet better boy, and greater ioy by a thousand
Parts, to the blessed then, but now accurst *Galathea,*
Then to the syre *Faunus,* to the mother louely *Simethis.*
   As *Galathea* thus did loue her beautiful *Acis,*
So *Polyphemus* alas did loue his lasse *Galathea,*
And *Galathea* still did loath that lusk *Polyphemus.*
   O deare Lady *Venus,* what a souïraigne, mighty, triumphant,
And most imperious princesse art thou in *Olympus?*
This rude asse, brute beast, foule monster, sidebely *Cyclops,*
This *Polyphemus* loues: this grim *Polyphemus,* a mocker
Of both Gods and men: this blunt *Polyphemus,* a terror
Vnto the wildest beasts: this vast *Polyphemus,* a horror
Eu'n to the horrible hils and dens, where no man abideth,
This *Polyphemus* lou's, and doates, and wooes *Galathea*
Forgoes his dungeons, forsakes his vnhospital harbors,

Leaues his sheepe and Goates,& frames himselfto be finish,
Learns to be braue,forsooth;and seeks thereby to be pleasing,
Cuts his bristled beard with a syth,and combs with an Iron
Rake, his staring bush, and viewes himselfe in a fishpond; .
And there frameth a face, and there composeth a countnance,
Face for a diu'ls good grace,& countnance fit for a hell-hound.
His bloodthirsting rage, for a while is somwhat abated,
His brutish wildenes transformd to a contrary mildenes:
Strangers come and goe,sail-bearing Ships by the *Cyclops*
Passe and safely repasse, and neuer feare any danger;
This *Polyphemus* now, is changd from that *Polyphemus.*

   Telemus in meane time, as he sayld by Sicilian *Ætna,*
(Telemus in birds-flight had a passing singuler insight)
Came to the ougly Gyant,and said,that he should be depriued
Of that his one broad eie(which stood there filthily glooming
In middle forehead)by crafts-contriuer *Vlysses.*
Blinde foole,qd *Polypheme,*can a blinde man loose any eie-sight?
Poore *Polypheme* of his eye was by *Galathea* depriued
Long since,and cares not for crafts-contriuer *Vlysses.*

   Thus contemning that which after proued a true-tale,
Either in hellish caues his diu'lish carkas he rouzeth,
Or, by the shaking shore and sea-side lazily stalketh,
Or, very rockes themselues with a lubbers burden he crusheth.

   There was a hill, that stretcht with sharpned point to the sea-ward,
And had both his sides with *Neptune* dayly bedashed:
Hither he climes,and here his cart-load lims he reposeth,
Here his fellow Goates, and Rams, and Sheepe he beholdeth:
Then layes downe his staffe(his walking staffe was a Pine-tree,
One whole huge Pine-tree,that might wel serue for a main-mast
Vnto an *Armado)* and after, takes vp a iarring
Pipe(fit for piper *Polypheme,*fit lute for a lowby)
Compact of fiue-score and fifteene reedes, with a clumsie
Fist,and scrapes, and blowes, and makes so shameful an out-cry,
That both lands and seas did groane with a deadly resounding,
Hearing this fowle Swad such rustical harmony making;
For there vnder a rock, as I lay, and leaned in *Acis*
Lap,this song I did heare,and beare with a heauy remembrance.

   More white then Lillies, then *Primerose* flowre *Galathea,*
More fresh then greene grasse,more slyke & smooth thea cockle
Shell, thats washt and worne by the sea,more coy then a wanton
Kyd,more brigt then glasse, more ioy to the heart then a winters
Sunne,or sommers shade,more fayre and seemly to looke on

Then

Then ftraight vp-mounting plante-tree, more cleare then a Chriftall
Streame all froz'n, more woorth then a hoorde of melloed apples,
More fweete then ripe grapes, more foft then downe of a cignet,
And, (fo that thou couldft accept poore woorme *Polyphemus*)
More deare then Diamond to the louing woorme *Polyphemus.*

And yet more ftubborne then an vntam'de Ox, *Galathea,*
More light then floating billowes, more hard then an aged
Oake, more rude then a rock, more tough then twig of a Willow,
More violent then ftreame of a brooke, more fierce then a wilde-fire,
More fharpe and pricking then thorns, more prowd then a Peacock,
More fpiteful then a troaden fnake, more curft then a whelping
Beare, more deafe then feaes, and (which moft greeues *Polyphemus*)
More fwift-pac't then a Hart, then winged windes, *Galathea.*

O, but alas, run not, looke back, and know *Polyphemus,*
My bowre with maine rocks and mounts is mightily vawted,
That fcalding funbeames in fummer neuer aproach it,
And bluftring tempefts in winter neuer aroy it:
My trees bend with fruite, my vines are euer abounding
With grapes, fome like gold, fome others like to the purple:
And both golden grapes, and purpled grapes be referued
For my fweete purpled, my golden wench *Galathea.*
Thou with thine owne hands maift eafily pluck fro the bufhes
Blackbery, hipps, and hawes, and fuch fine knacks by the forreft,
Damfons, floes, and nutts : and if thou wilt be my wedded
Wife, each tree and twig, and bufh fhall bring thee a prefent,
Euery bufh, twig, tree, fhall ferue my wife *Galathea.*
All thefe fheepe be my owne, which quickly without any calling
Come and run to the pipe of their good Lord *Polyphemus :*
And many thoufands more, which either range by the mountains,
Or feede in valleys, or keepe their places apointed
And ftalls hard by my bowre : and if thou afke me the number
Of them, I know it not, for beggers vfe to be telling
How-many fheepe they keepe, my goodes, *Galathea,* be endles,
My fheepe nomberles : yet among thefe fo-many thoufand
Flocks of fheepe, not a fheepe did I euer prooue to be fruitles.
Thou thy-felf maift fee my goates and fheepe to be ftradling
With bagging vdders, thou maift fee how-many lambkins,
And yong kyds I doe keepe, kyds and lambs both of a yeaning,
Milke I doe neuer want, and part I referue to be drunken,
Part in curds and cheefe, with thrift I prepare to be eaten.

Neither fhall my loue *Galathea* be only prefented
With birds neafts, kyds, doues, and fuch like paltery ftale-ftuffe,

F   **And**

And common loue-toyes, which easily may be aforded
By each carters swaine : *Polyphemus* found on a mountaine
Two braue yong Beare-whelps, either so like to an other,
That who marks not well, will soone take one for an other :
These did I finde of late, and these doe I keepe for a token,
For to be playfellowes for my bonilasse *Galathea.*

O then scorne not me, scorne not my guiftes, *Galathea;*
This body shalbe thy spoyle, and this bloud shalbe thy bootie,
These sheepe shalbe thy goods, and these hills shalbe thy dowry.
Sweete pig, scorne not mee; for I know myselfe to be comely,
Often I looke in a lake, and set my selfe by a fishpond,
Making mine owne eyes of mine owne eyes the beholders,
And when I see my face, I delite my face to be seeing.
Looke how big I doe looke, how strong and stordily squared,
Mark how mighty I am : no thundring *Ioue* in *Olympus,*
(You fooles tell many tales of a thundring *Ioue* in *Olympus*)
No great thundring *Ioue* is greater then *Polyphemus.*
See what a swinging bush giues cou'ring vnto my countnance,
And, as a thickset groaue, makes dreadful shade to my shoulders.
My Flesh's hard indeede, all ouer-grown with a bristled
Hyde, and rugged skin; but that's but a signe of a mans hart,
And is no-more shame to the strong and stowt *Polyphemus,*
Then broade leaues to a tree, then faire long mane to a foming
Steede, then synnes to a fish, then feathers vnto a flying
Fowle, or woolle to a sheepe. One eye stands steedily pitched
In my front : but an eye, yet an eye as broade as a buckler.
And what, I pray you, hath this sunne any more but his one eye?
And yet he sees all things, and all things only with one eye.

Lastly, my syre *Neptune* with threeforckt mace, as a sou'raigne
Rul's in Sea's : and so shall sea-borne dame *Galathea*
By taking *Polypheme,* best ympe of Seaes, for a husband,
Haue also *Neptune,* chiefe Lord of Seaes, for a father,
Earth-shaking *Neptune,* that stroue with mighty *Minerua*
For the renowned *Athens* (as he often towld me his own-selfe)
And raisd vp *Troy* walls with threatning towres to the heauens:
With whose rage both Lands and seaes are fearefuly trembling,
At whose beck springs, wels, floods, brooks, pooles, lakes be obeying,
As soone as they heare his *Triton* mightily sounding:
Then, *Galathea* relent, and yeeld to thy owne *Polyphemus,*
Sith *Polyphemus* yeelds himselfe to his owne *Galathea,*
Sith *Polyphemus* yeelds: who cares not a rush for a thundring
Heu'n, and heauens King : thy frowning's worse then a thousand

Lightnings.

Lightnings and thunders. Yet I could forbeare thee the better,
If thou didst aswell scorne others, as *Polyphemus*,
But why should *Galathea* refuse well growne *Polyphemus*,
And yet like and loue and wooe, effœminat *Acis*?
Whome if I catch, Ile make him know, that great *Polyphemus*
Arm's as strong as great. Ile paunce that paltery princox,
Trayle his gutts by the fields, and teare his flesh in a thousand
Gobbets, yea ile powre his bloud, hart-bloud to the waters;
Eu'n thine owne waters, if I euer take *Galathea*
Dealing with that boy, dwarfe *Acis*, dandiprat *Acis*,
Elfe *Acis*: for I boyle with most outragius anger
And most raging loue: me thinkes whole sulphurus *Ætna*,
Ætna with all his flames in my brest makes his abiding,
And yet neither loue nor wrath can moue *Galathea*.

    Thus when he had this sweete loues lamentation ended,
Vp-gets th'one eyde feende, and rangeth abroade by the forrest,
Roaring out, as a bull, driu'n back with force from a heyfar:
And at length spies out vs two there downe in a valley,
Mee and *Acis* alas vnawares; and cries in a fury,
Endles griefe and shame confound forelorne *Polyphemus*,
If that I make not now your louetoyes all, to be ended.
This did he roare, but he roarde this with so hellish an outcry,
That mount *Ætna* with eccho resounds, and griesly *Typhoeus*
Groanes for feare, and breaths foorth flashing flames to the heauens,
Vulcan starts fro the forge, and *Brontes* runs fro the Anuile,
And swelting *Steropes*, with barlegd ougly *Pyracmon*
Leaue their Iron tooles: yea *Pluto* the prince of *Auernus*
Heard this yelling feende, and feared, least that his owne hound
Cerberus had broke loose with three-throate iawes to the heauens.

    Here I alas for feare, dopt vnderneath the reflowing
Waues, and poore *Acis* fled back, and cride, *Galathea*,
Helpe, *Galathea*, help; and let thy boy be receaued
In thy watery boures, *Polyphemus* murdereth *Acis*.

    Cyclops runs to a rock in a rage, and teares in a fury
One greate peece, as big as a mount, and hurl's it at *Acis*:
And but a litle peece thereof tutcht bewtiful *Acis*,
Yet that litle peece orewhelmd whole bewtiful *Acis*.

    Here I alas, poore wretch, wrought all that desteny suffred
For to be wrought, and caus'd his strength to be freshly renued,
His life eu'n by a death now more and more to be lengthned,
And his dearest name and fame to be dayly remembred,
And my selfe and him, by a heauy diuorce, to be ioyned.

E

His blood ſprang fro the lumpe ; his blood firſt cheerefuly purpled,
Then by degrees it changd, and rednes ſomewhat abated,
And lookt like to a poole troubled with raine from *Olympus*,
Afterwards,it clearde : then lumpe cloaue,and fro the cleauing,
Flowring reades ſprang forth,and bubling water abounded.
Beutiful *Acis* thus was then transformd to a horned
Brooke ; and yet this brooke tooke name of bewtiful *Acis*.
Acis a louing ſtreame,runs downe with a louely reſounding,
Downe to the great ſou'raigne of ſeaes with ſpeedy reflowing,
There,his yearely tribute to the three-forckt God to be paying,
And there,his *Galathea* for euermore to be meeting.

Here *Galathea* did ende : and coy dame *Scylla* departed :
Whom ſea-God *Glaucus* (new God,late made of a fiſher)
Lou'd,but vnhappily lou'd : and wept,when he ſaw her a monſter.

T*Hen, quoth* Elpinus , *Neptune was the ſecond of the three brethren and
ſons of* Saturne,*which had the whole frame of the world parted among them;*
Ioue *had the heauens,*Neptune *the ſeaes,all the reſt was* Plutoes. *Hiſtorical-
ly,as ſome thinke,* Ioue *had the Eaſt,* Pluto *the Weſt,* Neptune *the ſeacoſts:
howſoeuer,*Neptune *is ſoueraigne of the ſeas,who alſo many times ſhaketh with
his imperiall mace the very foundations of the earth,according to that of* Ouid,

> Ipſe tridente ſuo terram percuſſit,at illa
> Intremuit,motuq; vias patefecit aquarum.

*For, in coaſt adioyning to the ſea, earthquakes and inundations of waters are
moſt vſuall.* Homer *for this cauſe calleth* Neptune ινοσιγαιος, & ινοιχθων.Earth-
ſhaker. And as* Pallas *was preſident of Towres,and* Iuno *a gouerneſſe of Gates,
ſo* Neptune *had care of the groundworkes and foundations of buildings ; which
are neuer ſaid to be firme,vnles they be laide as deepe as the water. Therefore
as* Neptune *was hired by* Laomedon *to builde thoſe ſtately walls of* Troy, *ſo
in the ſubuerſion of the ſame,himſelf is as buſie afterwards,as apeareth by that
of* Virgil 2. *Æneid.*

> Neptunus muros,magnoq; emota tridente
> Fundamenta quatit,totamq; è ſedibus vrbem
> Eruit,&c.

For towres, Virgil 2. *Ægl.*

> Pallas quas condidit arces,
> Ipſa colat.

And 2. *Æneid.*

> Iam ſummas arces Tritonia,reſpice, Pallas
> Obſedit,nymbo effulgens,& gorgone ſæua.

For gates, Virgil 2. *Æneid.*

> hic Iuno Scæas ſæuiſſima portas.

Prima tenet, fociumq; furens à nauibus ignem
Ferro accincta, vocat.

Cymothoe, *is* Neptunes *feruant, fignifying the fwiftnes of the waues and billowes : for,* κυμα, *is a waue, and* θειν *is to run, as if a man would fay, a running waue.* Triton *is his trumpeter.* Plyny *reporteth that the* Vlyffiponenfes *fent ambaffadors to* Tiberius Cæfar, *giuing him to vnderftand, that in their countrey, there was one of thefe* Tritons *feene and heard finging : being a fea-monfter, refembling a man by his vpper partes, and a fifh by thofe belowe : his colour was like the fea-water; his skinne hard with fhels : and is called* Neptunes *trumpeter, to found the retreite, when his mafter would haue the fea to be calme; becaufe when he is heard thus finging, or feene apearing in the water, it is a figne of calme and fayre weather.* Neptunes *mace is alfo* Tridens; *three-forked, for that there is a triple and threefold vertue in waters, the firft in wells, which are fweete : the fecond in feaes, and they are falte: the third in lakes, being vnpleafant and vnfauory : or rather, becaufe euery one of the three brethren hath fomewhat to doe in euery part of the tripertite kingdome : which may alfo be a caufe why* Iupiters *lightning is alfo* Trifulcum, *and* Plutoes *Scepter* Tridens. *For albeit* Iupiter *is efpecially predominant in heauen,* Neptune *in the feaes, and* Pluto *in the lower regions, yet that almighty and all-ouerruling power is indifferently aparant in euery of thefe three kingdomes, and in heauen is called* Iupiter, *in feaes* Neptune, *below* Pluto, *whome therefore* Virgil *calleth* ftigium Iouem, *the ftigian* Iupiter.

Neptunes *wife, is* Amphitrite, *the water it felfe, gouerned by* Neptune, *noting the efficacie of nature ruling in feaes & deeps. She is called* Amphitrite *of compaffing, enuyroning, or turning about, as the fea embraceth and inclofeth the earth.* Neptune *had an infinite number of fons and daughters: moyfture is fit for generation; which was the caufe that* Thales *the* Philofopher *made water to be the ground and beginning of euery thing;* and Virgil *calleth the fea, the father of things,*

Oceanumque patrem rerum.

Oceanus *of* ωκυς, *fwift, for fo is the flowing of the fea. When* Neptune *was kept from* Saturnes *deuouring mouth, his mother fhewed a colt, infteede of him: and when* Pallas *and* Neptune *contended, who, as moft beneficiall, fhould giue name to* Athens, *he with his mace ftroke the earth, whence iffued a horfe: either for that a horfe is fwift, and the fea is violent ; or becaufe* Neptune *firft taught how to ride a horfe ; or by reafon that a horfe loueth plaines and large places, where free fcope is to run, as is the fea, for that caufe called,* æquor. *Therefore the* Romaine *fports called* Ludi circenfes, *wherein the race of horfes was vfual, were celebrated in honor of* Neptune ; *and* Horace *maketh* Vlyffes *his fonne fpeake thus to* Menelaus,

Non eft aptus equis Ithacæ locus, vt neque planis
Porrectus fpatijs, neque multæ prodigus herbæ,

F 3   Neptune

Neptune, *with his Queene* Amphitrite, *standeth in a great shell as in a chariot, drawne with two horses, whose hinder parts ende in fishes, a* Tridens *in his hand, a white and frothy crowne on his head; with hayre, beard, and roabe, of color like the sea-water.*

His Nymphs are called Nereides: *of which kinde,* Theodorus Gaza *saith, that himself sawe one cast on a shore: fashioned like a woman in her vpper parts, but ended like a fish.* Galathea *is so called of whitenes, and noteth the very froath of the Sea. Humor and moysture be the chiefe causes of augmentation;* Neptune *therefore, as hee hath many children, so hath hee some of them great and monstrous; among others,* Polyphemus: *who, though vast and rude, yet loued, (such is the force of loue) but loued like a lowte, such is the home-borne education of rurall clownes.* Polyphemus, *as the rest of that rout, was called* Cyclops, *of* κύκλος *and* ὂψ, *as hauing but one round eye in his forehead; in truth meaning a buckler, framed round like an eye, although* Seruius *doe otherwise expound it. Hee is reported to bee a bloudy and theeuish manqueller, robbing and spoyling all along the Sicilian shore: from whome* Vlisses *wiselie escaped, and was therefore said to haue bored out his great eye with a firebrand. This tyran* Polypheme *loued a noble Lady named* Galathea, *but could not obteine her: at last, vsing force for law, kept her violently: and perceauing that she affected one* Acis, *more then himselfe, murdered the youth* Acis, *and threw his bodie into a riuer, which thereof bare that name.* Allegorically, *as some will haue it,* Polyphemus *is a miserable and worldly keeper of sheepe and kine: he loueth* Galathea *the Lady of milke: and, knowing that moyst places be best for milke, cannot abide, that* Galathea *should come nere* Acis, *a riuer in* Sicilia, *whose naturall proprietie was saide to be such, as that it would drie vp and consume milke.*

Glaucus *loued* Scylla: *but being reiected of her, he intreated* Circe *to make her affectionate by charming.* Circe *at first sight falleth in loue with* Glaucus, *who in like sort refuseth her, whereupon she infecting the waters where* Scylla *vsually bathed herselfe, transformed her into a monster, which afterwardes became a rock. This* Glaucus, *perceauing the fish which he had caught, by tasting a certaine herbe, presently to leap againe into the water, himselfe, for triall, did pluck and eate, and by vertue thereof transformed, threw himselfe also into the sea: where he was deified. The tale is reported by* Ouid *in the end of the thirteenth and beginning of the fourteenth of his transformations, and expounded by* Tasso *in the second part of his dialogue, entituled* Gonzago, *ouero del piacer honesto: where, by the deified* Glaucus, *he vnderstandeth the intellectuall part and facultie of man: by the sea wherein he fisheth, the body and all bodily matters, being the matter subiect of naturall philosophie, and subiect to continuall alteration like the sea: by his fishing, the discoursing and sylogisticall reasoning of* Intellectus: *by his netts: the instruments of naturall*

Logick, by the fishe caught, those generall maximaes, and vniuersal grounds, and true conclusions and consequences: by the herbe which he did bite, the heauenly delite of contemplation, whereby he was made a God: by the casting of himselfe into the sea, his comming and descending from the quiet rest of contemplation, to the variable sea of action and operation figured also by the double shape and twoforked tayle of Glaucus *and the other sea-Gods. Thus doth* Tasso *transforme* Glaucus *to a God: and by a little turning of his exposition, he turneth him thus to a brute beast.* Glaucus, *by tasting the herbe, leapeth into the sea, together with his fishes: that is, by yeelding to the inchaunting force of pleasure, he so drowneth himselfe in the* Aphrodisian *sea of sensuality, that he becomes altogether beastlike.*

Historically, Scylla *and* Charibdis *were two rocks in the* Sicilian *sea.* Scylla *had that name* ἀπὸ τῦ σύλᾶι, *of spoyling; or* ἀπὸ τῦ σκύλλειν, *of vexing: or else* ἀπὸ τῶν σκυλάκων, *of whelps, or dogs, sith the beating of the waues vpon the rocke, made a noyse like the barking of curs.* Charibdis *was so called* ἀπὸ τῦ χάσκειν, *of gaping, and* ῥοιβδεῖν *to sup vp, or deuoure.*

By Typhoeus, Sabinus *vnderstandeth the burning and flaming exhalations, cause of that fire in* Ætna: *which clustred together, and wanting free passage, shake the earth,* τύφομαι, *is, to smoke. see* Virgil 3. Æneid. *and* Ouid. 5. Metam. *It seemeth, that the violent fury of the windes, is here also shadoed by* Typhoeus: *for his hands reach from East to West, and his head to heauen, agreeing with the nature of the seuerall windes blowing in euery coast of Heauen. His body is couered with feathers, noting the swiftnes of the windes: about his legs are crawling adders, so the windes are oftentimes pestilent and hurtfull, his eyes are red as fire, and he breathes flames out of his mouth; for, the windes are made of hoate and dry vapors.*

*

Acis *made a riuer, is said to be horned: Hornes are attributed vnto riuers, either because the crooked turnings and windings thereof resemble hornes, or for that the furious noyse of roaring and raging waters is like the belowing of a Bull, or lowing of an Oxe or Cowe. They are crowned with reades: reades grow plentifully in watery places, they are figured with long hayre and beard, like a man, alwaies lying, leaning on one elbow, or on some great vessell, whence water issueth aboundantly. I neede not make any explication hereof, all is so manifest.*

*

Among other sea-borne monsters the *Mermaides* must not be forgotten, *they had the face and proportion of women to the waste, & thence downewards, the resemblance of fishes: some others giue them wings, and scraping feete, like the feete of hens: they were three,* Parthenope, *that is,* Virgins face: Leucosia, *white and faire, and* Ligia, *which is, sounding. They were borne of* Achelous, *noting moysture, and the muse* Calliope, *that is, faire spoken: the one*

*fang, the other founded a trumpet, the third played on a lute, so sweetely, that
such as sayled, were enticed thereby to the dangerous rocks where they frequented.* Vlysses *being to passe that way, commaunded his companions to stop their
owne eares with wax, and then fasten him to the mast of the ship, least that inchaunting melodie might be their bane : which policie did so confound the Sirenes with shame and sorrow, that they thereupon threw themselues headlong
into the sea.* Ouid *maketh them* Proserpinaes *companions, who losing their
Lady and* Queene, *were thus made birds in part, and yet reteigned their former
face and beautie.* Suidas *saith, that in truth, they were certaine blinde and
dangerus rocks, which by the breaking and beating of the billowes, did make
such a sweetely resounding murmur, that it allured the passengers thither, to
their owne destruction. Whatsoeuer they were, Allegorically they signifie the
cosning tricks of counterfeit strumpets, the vndoubted shipwrack of all affectionat yonkers : and therefore is it said by* Virgil, *that the* Mermaydes *rocks are
all ouerspread with bones of dead men, whose destruction their deceaueable allurements had procured.* Xenophon *is of this minde, that the* Sirenes *did
learnedly and sweetely extoll the famous acts of renowned men: and that therefore* Homer *maketh them entertain* Vlysses *with their pleasing voyce, who indeede was for politick stratagems the chiefe ornament of* Greece *: and no
doubt, these sweete and glorious commendations of great mens exploites, are
the most effectuall charmes, to worke any impression in an heroicall minde, and
with this conceite of* Xenophon, Cicero *doth also agree. Besides these three
already named, some adde fiue others, that is,* Pisinoe *of τειθω, to perswade, and
νουs, the minde:* Aglaope *sweete of looke :* Thelxiope, *louely of looke; for θελγειν,
is to please and delite.* Thelxinoe, *delighting the minde: and* Aglaophone, *with
the pleasant voyce. They were tearmed* Sirenes, *of drawing, deteigning, and alluring men vnto them, as the* Greeke *word importeth.*

*

Of the marine monsters, Proteus *yet remayneth : who being* King *in* AE-
gypt, *did so wisely apply himselfe, and frame his wit to euery particuler accident, that he was said to turne and transforme himselfe to any kinde of shape.
Some referre this to the custome obserued of the* Ægyptian *kings, who neuer
came abroade, but hauing some one or other ensigne on their head, as a token of
their imperiall maiestie : and this they changed continually, sometimes vsing
the image of a* Lyon, *sometimes of a* Bull, *sometimes this, and sometimes that,
which variety gaue ground and occasion to this fable. It is reported, that hee
raigned in the Isle* Carpathus, *whereof, the* Carpathian *sea by* AEgypt, *had
his name : which because it had great store of sea-calues and other sea monsters,* Proteus *himselfe was called* Neptunes *heardsman, keeping his seaish
flocks.* Cornelius Gemma, *in his booke* de diuinis naturæ characterismis
allegorically expoundeth this tale out of the fourth of Virgils Georgicks, *making* Proteus, *a type of nature.* Plato *compareth him to the wrangling of brab-*

ling fophifters: and fome there be that hereby vnderftand, the truth of things
obfcured by fo many deceauable apparances: Laftly, there want not others,
which meane hereby the vnderftanding and intellectual parte of mans minde,
which vnles it ferioufly and attentiuely bend it felfe to the contemplation of
things, fhall neuer attaine to the truth, as Proteus would neuer reueale his
propheticall knowledge, but firft did turne and winde himfelfe euery way to efcape, vntil with bands he were enforced thereunto, as Homer (the firft author
of this inuention) in the fourth of his Odyffea difcourfeth at large.

Lady Proferpina, with her mother Ceres, fell to Amaryllis, who by talking
of them, difcourfed alfo of Pluto, and fo made an end of the three mightie Monarchs of the world.

PLuto the Duke of diu'ls, enrag'd with an hellish *Erynnis*,
  Gan to repyne and grudge, and moue a rebellius vprore,
For that he wanted a wife : and now eu'n all the detefted
Infernal rablement , and loathfome broode of *Auernus*
Cluftred on heapes and troupes and threatned wars to *Olympus*.
But *Lachefis*, fearing left laws layd down by the thundrer,
By the reuenging rout of feends might chance to be broken,
Fate-fpinning *Lachefis* cry'd out to the prince of *Auernus*.
  Sou'raigne Lord of damned Ghofts, and mightie Monarcha
Of *Stygian* darknes , which giu'ft each thing a beginning,
And by thy dreadful doome, doeft draw each thing to an ending,
Ruling life and death with iurifdiction endles;
O let thofe decrees and fatal lawes be obeyed,
Which wee three fifters for you three brethren apoynted :
Let that facred league and peace laft freely for euer;
Stay thefe more then ciuil warres, vnnatural vprores,
And inteftine broyls : aske *Ioue*, and ftay for an aunfwere,
Ioue fhall giue thee a wife. His rage was fomwhat abated,
Though not well calmed, yet he yeelds at laft to the fatall
Sifters intreating and teares ; although with an ill will
And a repyning heart, and *Mercury* fends to *Olympus*
With this round meffage : Tell *Ioue* that ftately triumpher,
Pluto cannot abide to be thus controll'd by a brother,
Imperius brother : who though that he maketh a rumbling
With fcar-crow thunders, and hurls his flames in a fury
On poore mortall men; yet he muft not think that *Auernus*
Vndaunted Capten, with buggs can fo be deluded.
Is't not enough that I liue in darkfome dens of *Auernus*,
Where fire, fmokes, & fogs, grief, plagues, & horror aboundeth,
Whil'ft vfurping *Ioue* keepes court in lightfom *Olympus*,

G   **But**

But that he muſt alſo forbid me the name of a husband,
And reſtraine thoſe ioyes which nature freely afordeth?
Seas-ſou'raigne *Nepiune* embraceth his *Amphitrite,*
And clowd-rolling *Ioue* enioyes *Saturnia Iuno,*
His wife and ſiſter, (for I let ſlip ſlipperie by-blowes)
But ſcorned *Pluto* muſt ſtil forſooth be a batchler,
Stil be a wiueles boy and childeles: But, by the dreadful
Streames of ſacred *Styx* I proteſt, if he yeeld not an anſwere
Vnto my full content, Ile looſe forth all the reuengful
Broode of damnable haggs and hel-hounds vp to the heauens:
Ile confound heau'n, hell, light, night, Ile caſt on a cluſter
Blisful *Olympus* bowres, with baleful dens of *Auernus.*

 Plutoes tale ſcarce tolde, light-footed *Mercury* mounting
Vp to the higheſt heau'ns, diſclos'd each word to the thundrer;
Who conſulting long, at laſt thus fully reſolued,
That *Stygian* brother, ſhould take *Proſerpina,* daughter
Vnto the Lady *Ceres,* pereles *Proſerpina:* matchles,
And yet fit for a match. Bloody *Mars,* and archer *Apollo*
Sought her a long while ſince; *Mars* big & fram'd for a buckler,
Phœbus fit for a bowe, *Mars* actiue, learned *Apollo:*
Mars offred *Rhodope, Phœbus* would giue her *Amyclas,*
And *Clarian* temples, and *Delos* fayre for a dowrie.
Lady *Ceres* caſt off bloody *Mars,* and archer *Apollo,*
Contemning *Rhodope,* deſpiſing proffred *Amyclas:*
And fearing violence and rape, commendeth her onely
Dearling and deare childe to the deareſt ſoyle of a thouſand
Louely *Cicil:* from whence with watery checkes ſhe returned
Vnto the towre-bearing *Cybele,* and lowd *Coribantes,*
On *Phrygian* mountains: Where ſhee no ſooner aryued,
But *Ioue,* ſpightful *Ioue* tooke opportunity offred,
And by the ſecret ſleights and wyles of falſe *Cytherœa,*
In mothers abſence her daughter alas he betrayed.

 Goe, qd he, my wanton, goe now whilſt mother is abſent,
Bring her daughter abroad to the flowring fields of a purpoſe;
Atropos hath decreed, that ſupreame Duke of *Auernus*
My brother *Pluto,* muſt haue *Proſerpina,* fatall
Orders muſt be obeyd : thy iuriſdiction hereby
Shalbe the more enlarg'd, and fame fly daily the further,
If very hell feele hell, taſte helliſh pangs of a Louer.

 Shee (for a word was enough) conueyd her away in a momēt,
And (for ſo *Ioue* would) *Pallas* with ſtately *Diana*
Ioynd as companions : all which three laſtly aryued

         There,

There, where Lady *Ceres* her daughters bowre had apoynted.
Wyly *Venus* drawes on simple *Proserpina* foorthwith,
Vnto the greene medows : herself went first as a leader,
Next came fayre *Phœbe*, and Ioue-borne *Pallas Athene*,
And shee between them both, who both thē rightly resembled,
Sweete yet sweetly seuere *Proserpina*: eu'n very *Phœbe*,
If that a bow were giu'n, if a target, *Pallas Athene*.
And sweete water-Nymphs by the careful mother apoynted,
Their mayden Princesse with a princelike company guarded:
Chiefly of all others, *Cyane* there made her aparance,
Whom for her excelling conceipt, and seemly behauiour,
Chiefely of all other well-Nymphs *Proserpina* loued.

There was a Christal brook by the fields, that ioyned on *Ætna*,
Called *Pergusa*, transparent down to the bottome;
Trembling leaues as a veyle, gaue cooling shade to the water,
Trembling leaues of trees, that crownd this lake as a garland;
Euery tree displayd his flowring boughs to the heauen,
Euery bow had a bird which therein made her abyding,
Euery bird on bow tooke ioy to be cherefuly chirping,
Euery chirp was a song, persuading all to be louing.
Fresh-colored medowes were ouer-spread with a mantle
Figured, and Diapred with such and so many thousand
Natures surpassing conceipts, that maruelus *Iris*
Was no maruel at al, and spotted traine, but a trifle,
Prowd-hart Peacocks spotted traine, compar'd to the matchles
Art, which nature shewd, in shewing so-many strange shewes.

Hither these Ladyes are come, and euery Lady
Plucketh at euery flowre; seeing each flowre to be more fayre,
More fresh, more radiant, more louely, then euery Lady.

In meane time *Pluto* wounded by wyly *Cupido*,
Intends his iourney to *Sicilia*; Griesly *Megæra*,
And fell *Alecto* his foaming steedes be preparing,
Steedes, that drank on *Lethes* Lake, and sed by the ioyles
Bancks of *Cocytus. Nycteus* and sulphurus *Æthon*
Swift, as a shaft; fierce *Orphnæus* with fearful *Alastor*,
Ioynd to the cole-black coach, drew neare to *Sicilian Ætna*;
And seeking passage, with strange and horrible earthquakes
Ouer-turnd whole townes, and turrets stately defaced.
Euery Nymph heard, felt, and fear'd this deadly resounding,
And dreadful quaking, but of all this deadly resounding
And dreadful quaking, not a nymph there knew the beginning,
Sauing onely *Venus*; whose heart with terror amazed,

Yet with ioy poſſeſt, was party to all the proceeding.

Duke of Ghoſts, miſſing of a way, through ſo-many by-waies,
And all impatient with loues rage, brake with his Iron
Mace, the rebelling rocks, and piearſt through th'earth to the heauens,
Heauens all diſmai'd to behold ſo helliſh an obiect.
Starres fled back for feare, *Orions* hart was apaled,
Charles-Wayne ran to the ſea, that he euermore had abhorred,
And by the yrkſome noyce, and neighing of the deteſted
And poyſned palfrayes of *Pluto*, laeſy *Bootes*
Tooke himſelfe to his heeles, and lingring wayne did abandon.
Baleful breath of night-borne courſers darkned *Olympus*
Chereful light, and loathed foame diſtild fro the bleeding
Bits, infected th'ayre: and th'earth all torne by the trampling,
Shakte and quakte for dread, and yeelded a heauy reſounding.

Ladies al ran away; *Proſerpina* laſtly remayned,
Whom *Stygian* coachman both ſought & caught in a moment.
Pluto droue on apace, *Proſerpina* woefuly wayling,
Cald and cryed, alas, to the Nymphs, to the maids, to the Ladies;
But Nymphs, Mayds, Ladies were all affrayd to be preſent,
And her mothers chance, ill chance, was then to be abſent.
Now *Stygian* raptor thoſe prayers lightly regarding
In reſpect of a pray and priſe ſo worthy the taking,
Chears and calls his dreadful ſteedes, and ſhaketh his out-worne
Bridle raynes, orecaſt with ruſt; and entreth *Auernus*,
All vnlike himſelfe, and much more milde then a *Pluto*.

Ghoſts and ſprytes came cluſtred on heaps, to behold the triumphant
Tartarean Capten, with ſoe great glorie returned:
Euery one was preſt, ſome bent their care to the courſers,   (bed.
Some to the coach, ſome ſtrawd ſweete flowr's, ſome lookt to the bride-
Elyſian Ladies with a ſpotles company wayted
On their new-come Queene, and carefuly ſought to recomfort
Thoſe her virgin feares and teares. Ghoſts wont to be ſilent,
Sang ſweete wedding ſongs, and euery nooke in *Auernus*
With banquets, meryments, and louelayes freely reſounded,
And whole hell for ioy was ſpeedily turnd to a heauen.
Æacus intermits his iudgements; ſtearne *Rhadamanthus*,
And auſtere *Minos* waxe milde : all plagues be remitted:
Tantalus eats and drinks ; Ixion's looſt from his endles
And ſtill-turning wheele, *Tityus* ſet free fro the *Ægle*,
Siſyphus extreame toyle by the rolling ſtone is omitted,
And *Danaus* daughters from running tubbes be releaſed.
Pale-ſac'te *Tiſiphone*, with ſnake-hayrd ougly Megæra,

And euer-grudging *Alecto*, fell to carousing,
And their burning brands embru'd with blood, did abandon.
Birds might easily passe by the poysned mouth of *Auernus*,
Men might safely beholde, and looke on stonie *Medusa*;
No consuming flames were breathd by fyrie *Chymera*.
Howling *Cocytus* with wine mirth-maker abounded,
Lamenting *Acheron* hart-chearing honny aforded,
And boyling *Phlegeton* with new milke chearefuly streamed:
Cerberus held his peace, *Lachesis* left off to be spinning,
And gray-beard feriman forebare his boate to be rowing,
All tooke all pleasure, and all for ioy of a wedding.

Lady *Ceres* all this meane time possest with a thousand
Careful mothers thoughts, thought euery houre to be twenty,
Till she returnd homeward: and home at last she returned,
At last, but too late, to her house, but not to her houshold:
Court was a wildernes, forelorne walkes, no-body walking,
Gates turnd vpside downe, hall desolat, euery corner,
Euery way left waste. But alas when lastly she entred
Persephone's chamber, seeing her curius hand-work,
And embroydred clothes, all ouer-growne by the copwebs,
But no *Persephone*; such inward anguish amased
Her distressed sprites, that neither a word fro the speechles
Mothers mouth could once come forth, nor a teare fro the sightles
Eyes; eyes, mouth, sence, soule, were nothing els but a horror:
Only she clipt, embrac't, and kist, and only reserued
Her sweete daughters work, poore soule, insteed of a daughter.

After long wandring, by chance shee found in a corner
Her deare daughters nurse, *Electra*, wofuly wayling,
With rent roabes, scratcht face, and beaten brest, for her only
Harts-ioy *Persephone*: whom shee as charily tendred,
As dearest mother could euer tender a dearest
Daughter: shee, when griefe and inward horror aforded
Time to reueale it selfe, this woful storie recounted
All at large: How *Persephone* was forc't to be walking
Greatly against her mind, and mothers wil, to the meddowes,
How foure black coursers conuey'd her away on a sudden,
No-body knew whither, nor what man might be the autors
How her companions were all gone: only the louing
And loued *Cyane*, for grief was lately resolued
Into a siluer streame; and all those sweetly resounding
Syrens, made to be birds in part, in part to be maydens,
And she alone was left, left all forelorne in a corner,

C

Mourning *Perfephone* and her fo heauy departure.

    Silly *Ceres* hearing thefe dead newes, all in a furie
Rayled on heau'n and earth, and ran to the fulphurus *Ætna*,
Lighted two Pine-trees, and day and night by the deferts,
Hils, dales, woods, waters, lands, feas, *Proferpina* fearched,
Searcht from th'Eaft to the Weaft: at laft, al weary with endles
Toyling and moyling, halfe dead for drink, fhe repayred
Vnto a poore thatcht coat, and knockt, and meekly defired,
That to a fchorched mouth fome water might be aforded.
Th'ould Beldam coat-wife brought forth a domefticalHotchpot,
Her chiefe food, both meat and drink, and gaue to the Goddes.
Faintly *Ceres* feeding by the coat, was fpy'd of a fawcie
Crackrope boy, who mockt, and cald her a greedy deuouring
Out-come witch in fcorne: Whereat this Lady agreeued,
And not forgetting *Latonaes* worthy reuengement
On Lician Lobcocks, (who fith they rudely denied
Water, were made frogs alwayes condemn'd to the water)
Threw in this boyes face all that was left of her Hotchpot.
Mocking gallowes thus by the Goddes ftrangely befprinckled,
Was transform'd to a S wyft; whofe back grew al to be fpeckled,
And his fpiteful breaft with wonted poyfon abounded.

    Through what lands and feas this Goddes wofuly wandred,
Twere too long to report : each part of th'earth fhe perufed,
Vainly perufed alas: and home at laft fhe returned
Back to *Sicil*; curfing, banning, and daylie reuiling
Euery foyle, but chiefly *Sicil*: Which now the detefted
More, then afore fhe defir'd: brake plowes, kild wearied oxen,
Blafted corne, bred weedes and tares, fent forth the deuouring
Foules, and too much drought, & too much raine from *Olympus*.
Fields for corne and graine of late fo greatly renowned,
Are to a barren wafte, and wilde heath fpeedily changed.

    Whilft childeles mother thus rageth, faire *Arethufa*
(Who by the fecret caues of th'earth from *Pifa* to *Ætna*
Fetcheth a reftles race) vp-lifted her head to the heauens,
And thefe firft tidings to the forelorne Lady reported,
How herfelfe of late taking her way by the fearfull,
Imperiured *Styx*, faw her loft childe in *Auernus*,
Somwhat fad, yet a Prince and fupreame Queene in *Auernus*;
Queene to the mighty Monarch & fou'raigne king of *Auernus*.

    Mournfull mother amas'd, for a while ftoode like to a fenceles
Stocke or ftone: at length, when fury remoued amafement,
Vp to the heau'ns fhe flies, & makes her moane to the thunder.

Lord and loue, qd fhee, vouchſafe at laſt to remember,
Take ſome care in time of poore *Proſerpina*, think her
If not mine, yet thine, and if thine, not to be ſtollen:
But let paſſe what's paſt, let rape and rage be remitted,
So that thy daughter from his helliſh dens be deliu'red.

T'were no diſparaging, qd *Ioue*, if prince of a mighty
Empire, *Ioues* brother might haue *Proſerpina*, ioyned
By both our conſents in wedlock : darkſom *Auernus*
Should haue no cauſe then to repine at lightſom *Olympus*.
Yet notwithſtanding, if thou ſtand fully reſolued,
And that my brother *Pluto* muſt needs be refuſed;
Then let *Perſephone* both mine and thine be reduced,
If ſhe be faſting yet : for ſo hath *Atropos* ordred,
And fatall orders are neuermore to be altred.

Mother was ful bent, to reduce her childe from *Auernus* :
Deſtinie did forbid : for that *Proſerpina* walking
In *Plutoes* Orchard, by chance (worſt chance of a thouſand)
Suckt ſeu'n Pomegranate kernels : and no-body knew it,
Sauing *Aſcalaphus*, who made it knowne to *Auernus*,
And ſtayd *Perſephone:* who then for a worthy requitall,
Foule-tungd *Aſcalaphus*, forthwith traſformd to a Scricheowle,
Foule and loathſome foule, whoſe neuer-luckily-ſounding
Voyce, brings baleful newes, and certaine ſignes of a vengeance.

Ioue tooke paines, made peace: firſt iuſtly the yeare he deuided,
Then, to the husband halfe, and halfe to the mother apointed,
and by theaſe good meanes cauſd euery part to be pleaſed.
Perſephone ſix moonths with her husband dwels in *Auernus*,
And ſix other months doth ſhew her ſelfe to *Olympus*.

Lady *Ceres* all griefe and all contention ended,
Sent forth *Triptolemus* with coach and corne to the people
Scattred in euery coaſt, whoſe foode was kernel of ackorne.
Triptolemus traueling through ſtrange lands, laſtly ariued
On *Scythian* borders : where *Lyncus*, falſly pretending
Life, intended death, and making ſhew of a friendly
Hoſt, his ſleeping gueſt vnawares had ſhamefuly murdred,
Had not Lady *Ceres*, his barbarus enuy preuenting,
Lyncus turnd to a *Lynx*, and his vayn-glory repreſſed,
Who of an others fact firſt autor would be reputed.

W*Ell, ſayd* Elpinus, *ſith* Amarillis *is ſafely returned from hell, I hope* Elpinus *may haue the like ſucceſſe: otherwiſe, ſo many fearefull monſters
and helliſh apparitions might well haue daunted a ſtouter heart then mine:*

Pluto

Pluto *then, you see, the third brother, rauished* Proſerpina: *the naturall efficacie and vertue of the earth (ſayth* Cicero, 2. de natura deorum*) draweth vnto it the rootes of corne, growing & increaſing in the bowels of the earth.* Ceres *her mother ſeeketh* Proſerpina, *and mourneth for her abſence: the corne purſueth and foloweth the ſeede : or, The earth ſeemeth to greeue, when the corne ſpringeth not vp in due time.* Proſerpina *was rauiſhed in* Cicil, *the deareſt ſoyle to* Ceres: *that was a moſt fruitful and fertile Iſland.* Arethuſa (*ſignifying the natural power and vertue of the ſeede and roote*) *is the firſt that tolde* Ceres *tydings of* Proſerpina : *In continuance and conueniencie of time, by that naturall efficacie and operation of the roote and ſeede , the grayne and corne it ſelfe appeareth & ſpringeth vp. Six moneths ſhe lies with her huſbād: al the winter time, whileſt the ſunne doth ſoiourne in the ſoutherne ſignes: ſix aboue with her mother, when the ſunne returneth to the northerne ſignes, bringing corne to ripenes and maturitie. She had this name* Proſerpina, *of the latine word,* Proſerpo, *which is to creepe forwards, becauſe the rootes creepe along in the body of the earth. She was gathering flowers when* Pluto *tooke her away, and kept her below; for then is that naturall vertue of the ſeede working, to produce afterwards the fruit and flowre accordingly.* Pluto *was accompted the Lord of riches aud treaſure :* Pluto *is the earth, whence al mettals are digged.* πλᾶτος *in* Greeke, *ſignifieth riches: and in latine they called him* Ditem, *to note,* Diuitias, *that is, Rich, alluding to riches. Some make him blinde , becauſe he dealeth partially in diſtributing riches , not according to deſert. And they giue him a key in his hand, ſith his helliſh gates are ſo ſurely locked , that the Ghoſtes once entring, can neuer poſſibly returne. He is called the God of Ghoſts, as ſome thinke, becauſe he firſt inſtituted the funerall obſequies and ſolemnities vſed at mens burials. He ſitteth as a prince on a throne, with a crowne on his head, a ſcepter in his hand, and* Cerberus, *his dogge, at his feete.* Cupreſſus *is ſacred vnto him, for it is vſed in funerals , and being once cutte, neuer buddeth or brancheth afterward.*

*

Proſerpina *being in hell, did eate : and, as ſome others report the tale, did eate poppie ſeedes; whoſe nature is to cauſe drowſines, ſleepe, ſtaying and reſting. So* Proſerpina *muſt ſtay below, till ſhe haue gotten roote and bee well and ſufficiently grounded. Her mother* Ceres *refuſed* Mars *and* Apollo : *for, wars, and ouer much heate of the ſunne, are both bad for corne and plenty.* Ceres, *by reporte, firſt found and taught the vſe of corne and grayne , and thereby brought men from that wilde and ſauage wandering in woods and eating of* Ackornes, *to a ciuil conuerſing, and more orderly dyet, and cauſed them to inhabite townes, to liue ſociably , to obſerue certain lawes and inſtitutions : and for theſe cauſes was her ſelf made a goddeſſe, figured like a matron, with a garland all of the eares of corne, hauing in one hand a little bundle of Poppie , as ſignes of fertilitie : and in the other hand a fire brand, wherewith ſhe ſought her*
daughter

*daughter. For in summer,when the beames of the sunne are hoate and burning,
the countreymen seeke and gather the corne, then full ripe and ready for the
sickle. Her chariot was drawne by two serpents or flying dragons : serpents are
so called à serpendo,of creeping and crawling in and out,as the rootes of corne
doe : or,for that the turning and winding bodies of dragons, resemble the crooked furrowes of the earth.* Ceres, *the earth,great by* Ioue, *the temperat heate
of the ayre,brought forth* Proserpina, *corne and graine : A sow was sacrificed
to* Ceres, *for she rooteth & spoyleth the corne: so was the goate to* Bacchus, *for
gnawing the vines: or, the sow is fruitefull, so is the earth; the sow euer wallo-
weth in the myre and earth,and* Ceres *herselfe noteth the earth.*

Besides Ceres,*there were other goddesses, that had care of the fruite of the
earth,as,* Pales,*that lookt to the Pastures, and was the Pastors goddes;* Pomona, *the Lady of Apples,hauing her name of the latine* Pomum,*which signifieth an apple.* Flora, *the goddes of flowres, and wife to* Zephyrus: Bona
dea, *the good goddes, (otherwise called* Fauna, à fauendo, *of cherishing and
fauouring) noting that quickning efficacy of the earth, which norisheth and fo-
streth the seede cast into the same.* Flora,*they say , in truth was a Romaine
strumpet,called* Laurentia; *who dying,left her wealth, which was excessiue, to
the people of* Rome,*who for her honor , made her a goddes of flowres, and called her* Flora , *of the word* Flos,*signifying,a flowre.*

Iupiter,*by report of* Plato,*perceauing that the auncient edict , commaunding euery man to be rewarded according to his desert , was not obserued, because men being aliue were iudged by liuing iudges : did enact,that none from
thenceforth should receaue triall,but after death: when all externall shewes of
birth,bewty,strength,riches,nobilitie and such like, were altogether remoued.
And that only his three sonnes,* Æacus,Minos, and Rhadamanthus (*whereof
the two last were borne in* Asia,*the first in* Europe) *should after their death,
repaire to a meadow,called The field of truth(where were two waies,the one leading to the* Elysian *fields, the other to the place of torment) and there sit in
iudgement of the spirites and ghosts of all, that had left their earthly mansion
and habitation.* Rhadamanthus *was apointed to giue sentence of such as came
from* Asia; Æacus *iudged those of* Europe : *and* Minos, *if any doubt or am-
biguitie arose,was the discusser and determiner thereof. This was* Ioues *decree,and thereupon,*Rhadamanthus *and* Æacus,*with their rods in their hands,
sit in iudgement,and* Minos *apart,with his golden scepter, seriously inquiring
into euery mans matter.* Historically, Minos and Rhadamanthus *were of*
Asia, AEacus *of* Europa, *all three iust and seuere; hereof came this tale. The
damned ghosts are committed to the* Furies *to be plagued in* Tartarus, *so called, because therein be many* τιεχμι. Auernus,*is the entrie to hell: historically,
it was a place,whence proceeded so noysome an exhalation , as that birds could
not flie ouer it,whereof it had that name in greeke,so saith* Virgil. 6. Æneid.

Ti
tu
C

Spelunca alta fuit, vastoq; immanis hiatu,
Scrupea, tuta lacu nigro, nemorumque tenebris:
Quam super, haud vllæ poterant impunè volantes
Tendere iter pennis, talis sese halitus atris
Faucibus effundens, supera ad connexa ferebat:
Vnde locum Graij dixérunt nomine Auernum.

Cerberus *is* Plutoes *dog, with three heades, watching that none goe out, but ready to let all in ; fawning on these, deuouring those, according to his name. For* κρεὸς ἐσς, *and, by a more easie contraction of the word,* κέρεϛς, *is a deuowrer of flesh, of* κρέας, *and* ἐδωρ: *wherefore some vnderstand by him, the all-deuowring earth, eating and consuming all earthly bodies. Others, by* Cerberus, *intend mans bodie, prest and appliable to all sensuall lust, but repugning and abhorring vertue and contemplation. His three heads be taken of some to represent those three necessarie euills, which withdraw men from contemplation, I meane, hunger, thirst, and sleepe: to all which, we must offer a morsell, as* Sybilla *taught* Æneas *in* Virgil, *we must yeeld, but not too much; so much only, as thereby nature may be susteined.* Natalis Comes *expoundeth it thus:* Cerberus *is* Couetousnes: *and a couetous man laughes when hee sees gold come in ; but it greeues his heart to lay out one penie. His three heads note the manifold guiles and deceites of couetous men,* Qui omnes pecuniæ vias norunt, *know all the waies in the world how to scrape coyne.* Cerberus *lyes in an hellish dungeon : a myser lurketh in corners, turning his rustie groates, without either profit to others, or pleasure to himselfe.* Hercules *drew him out of* Hell, *for, who can be a* Hercules, *and accomplish great matters, without money ? Or thus,* Hercules *bound and brought out* Cerberus, *that is to say, he bridled and kept vnder concupiscence, and therefore returned safe from* Hell : *but* Pyrithous *going thither of purpose to rauish* Plutoes Queene, *and so to satisfie sensualitie, was deuowred of* Cerberus : *or, lastly,* Hercules *is a learned and absolute* Thilosopher: *hee draweth the three-throated* Cerberus *out of* Hell, *by bringing to light the tripertite mysteries of Philosophie, naturall, morall, and dialecticall.* Cerberus, *for spite and rage, strugling with* Hercules, *did let his poysoned foame fall on the earth, whence proceeded the deadly* Aconitum, *for, what but rancor, can come frō a rancorous heart? Historically, as* Pausanias *reporteth, there was in a darke dungeō in* Tænarus, *leading to* Hell, *as the fame went, for the deepenes thereof, an hydeous and terrible serpent, which for his deadly poyson, and fearefull aspect , was called the Diuels dog, and was by* Hercules *drawne forth , and brought to* King Euristheus.

Acheron *had his name,* ἀπὸ τῦ ἀχ κρεῖ, *because there flowe the waues of miserie. This is the first riuer, that the* Ghosts (*hauing once tasted of* Lethe's *lake,) are to passe ouer : for, death aproaching, a certaine terror of conscience tormenteth*

tormenteth *vs, and this is* Acheron. *Styx, (as it were,* ϲϙϛϙϛ *odious and abhorred) is that hate and detestation, which euery man now dying, hath against such faults, as in his life time he committed. Styx ariseth out of* Acheron; *for, this detestation proceedeth from that griefe. Styx dooth nine times compas Hell: for, there is nothing but hatefull griefe, and wofull detestation.*

Iupiter *and the other Gods were woont to sweare by the riuer Styx; which was accounted the most religious oath; sith, as I saide, it noteth hate and detestation, a thing repugnant to the nature of the Gods. Some say, they vsed to sweare by water; because as water is the most ancient ground and beginning of things, so an oath should bee most strictly obserued and religiously honored, as a thing no lesse reuerenced, then water, the foundation of all : whatsoeuer was the cause, the matter is aparant by* Homer *and* Virgil *euery where, that they sweare by Styx, which therefore was called the imperiured riuer.* Ouid in Ibin.

Quique per infernas horrendo murmure valles
Imperiuratæ laberis amnis aquæ.

Achilles Statius lib. 8. *hath a discourse of a well called Styx, much like this.*

The Platonists *call the body a Hell; in respect of the minde, which being thither thrust downe, first, forgetteth all celestiall conceipts, drinketh of* Lethe, *and then passeth ouer* Acheron: *for, being bereaft of celestiall ornaments, it soroweth and greeueth, and therefore compast with Stygian waues, displeaseth itselfe, hateth and abhorreth his owne acts, howles, and makes pitifull lamentation; and that is* Cocytus, *of* κωκύω, *to howle and crie out, as* Plato *expoundeth it.*

Lethe *aboue mentioned, signifieth Obliuion; shee was sister to* Somnus, *sleepe: whereof there were two gates, the one of horne, the other of Iuorie: from that, came true dreames, false from this : for, as a candle inclosed in a lanterne made of horne, shineth and giueth light, because the matter is subtile and transparent, but contrarily in one of Iuory, because the matter is thick and condensate : so, if the bodie be temperate, the minde in dreames foreseeth the truth; but if it be troubled with surfeting, or otherwise, the dreames be false and confused.* Phlegeton *noteth the firie and fretting darts of griefe and vexation, and is also called* Pyriphlegeton, *of fire and burning.*

Charon *hath his name of ioy and gladnes : this gladnes carieth vs ouer* Acheron, *after wee haue lamented our owne faults.* Charon *is old; so graue and sage aduice is that, which worketh this repenting lamentation in vs.* Boccace, *by* Charon, *vnderstandeth time, and maketh him the sonne of Night and* Erebus. *The furies, so named of the latine worde* Furor, *noting*

madnes, be the *Ministers* of Pluto, *ready to execute his renenging wrath : the*
Athenians *called them*, σεμναὶ, *the seuere goddesses, the* Sicyonians *tearmed*
them, ἐυμενίδας, *milde and welwilling , by the contrary , meaning spitefull and*
cruell : or, simple milde, because Orestes *by* Mineruaes *aduice , pacified them*
at last, and was released of his rage and madnes. Their haire was all of crawling
snakes, their garment, a long black gowne , downe to the anckles , girt with a
snakie girdle, with serpents in the one hand, and a firebrand in the other, their
eyes, face, and teeth, portending malice and vengeance : they were three, Tisiphone, *of τίσις, reuenge, & φόνος, slaughter or murder* Megœra, *of μυγαίρειν, to en-*
uie: Alecto, *of ἀλήκτος, neuer ceasing, or neuer at rest. They are sometimes called*
Erynnæ, *of ἐρινύω, to be moued with great grudge and indignation : or, of this*
word, ἀεὶ, which signifieth cursing and banning, and ἀνύειν, which is, to heare,
for that they are euer ready to giue eare to such, as curse and call for vengeance:
or else, of ἔρα, that is, the earth, and ναίειν, to dwell, because they dwell in the dark-
some dens of the earth. Lactantius *compareth those three perturbations*
which tosse and turmoyle mens mindes, to weet, Wrath, Couetise, and Leachery,
to these three furies.

* * *

Much like in nature to these furies, were the Harpyes, *faced like Virgins,*
winged like birdes, with pale and hungry visages, and crooked scraping clawes,
deciphring flatterers, or rather, couetous and snatching worldlings. Harpyæ,
(*saith* Natalis Comes, *expounding it physically*) *haue this name of ἁρπάζω : no-*
ting the furious violence, and rage of the windes: the first was called Ocypete,
swiftly flying : the second, Aello, *that is, a storme or tempest: the third* Celæno,
the darkenes of the clowds driuen with windes. They were the daughters of
Thaumas *and* Electra, *by reason of the strange and wonderfull nature and*
might of the windes, which are eleuated and lifted vp by the beames of the
sunne from the purer & vpper-flowing water of the sea. Virgil *describeth them,*
3. æneid. as the most detestable monsters, that euer issued out of the Stygian
lak. Hither may be added those Haggs, *called* Lamiæ, *who with their sweete*
and maidenlike face, brest, and body, allure men vnto them, but with their ser-
pentine clawes destroy them afterwards.

* * *

Chimera's *vpper part was like a* Lyon, *the middle like a* Goate, *the lowest*
like a Serpent, *slaine by* Bellerophon. *Historically, it was a mountaine in Ly-*
cia, breathing out fire, whose top Lyons *did haunt, in the middle were pastures,*
where Goates *fed, and the foote was frequented by* Snakes *and* Serpents. Bellerophon *made it habitable, and was therefore saide to haue killed* Chimera.
Chimera, *the type of inordinate luste, κμι ἐρμος, first inuadeth men fiercely like*
a Lyon, *then wantonly and lasciniously like a* Goate, *afterwards brings poyso-*
ned sorrow and repentance, figured by snakes and serpents. Bellerophon *solli-*
cited to folly by Antia, *wife to* Prætus *King of the* Arigiui, *constantly refu-*

sed, whereupon she falsly accused him to her husband, of violence offered. Bellerophon by these meanes banished, passing through diuers dangers and perills, riding on the winged horse Pegasus, and bearing his terrible Gorgon, at last slew Chimera. He was called Bellerophon, either of one Bellerus, a Corinthian Prince, whom he vanquisht; or, of φόνος, and τὰ ζίσσας, for that hee rooted out euills and mischiefes: or else, you may so tearme him, as ἀναιρέτης, a wise and prudent counsailer, or ἀναιρεσιανδρος, as Homer speaketh. Palæphatus reporteth, that Pegasus was the ship that brought Bellerophon. Allegorically, by Pegasus borne of the blood of Medusa, we may vnderstand immortalitie and euerlasting fame. For, vertue ouer-comming all terrible things, figured by Gorgon, breedeth fame: and fame is eternised by the sounding voyce of Poets: which was the cause that the learned well, was said to be opened by the hoofe of Pegasus, striking the Parnassian mount. Medusaes hayre (either for that Neptune in Mineruaes temple vsed her irreligiously, as Ouid reporteth the tale 4. Metam. or, for that she gloried so much in her golden locks, as that she durst compare with goddesses) were turned into snakes, and the beholders thereof into stones. Medusa herselfe noteth lustfull beawty and voluptuousnes, turning men into stones; as making the greedy gazers thereon senceles and amased. None but Perseus, Ioues sonne, by Mineruaes help ouercame her: celestiall grace and wisdome are the onely meanes, to represse this inordinate affection. Some, by the three Gorgons, note the three faculties of the soule in man: Medusa, of the three sisters, was only mortall, figuring the sensible and liuing power, common to beasts, beheaded by Perseus, that is, kept vnder by the good Genius or celestial grace. The second was Stheno, the reasonable facultie of the soule, the third Euryale, the light infused and intellectuall part. They turne the beholders into stones; for we must kill Medusa, all perturbations, and be in that respect, as dead as stones, else wee cannot enioy this intellectuall light. The borowed and common eye, which all they vse by course, is this infused light, deriued from one of them vnto another. Perseus beareth Gorgon; hee maketh men wonder at his excellent prowesse: Historically, Athenæus reporteth, that in Lybia there was a kinde of beast like a calfe, killing with the very sight: one of them was brought dead to Marius, to Rome, his skinne being so diuersly colored, that none there, could gesse what beast it was, and that Perseus, by likelihood killed some of these, figured here by Medusa. Diodorus saith, that Gorgones were stout and warring women, the captaine whereof, Medusa, was slaine by Perseus. Others vnderstand the earth and earthly affections by Gorgon, dashed and daunted by Perseus borne of Ioue, that is assisted by his heauenly helpe and influence. But I see, that Chimera, hath brought me too farre out of my way: Ixion therefore (to come back where I was before) is, as I said already, plagued in hell, for his ambitious and aspyring arrogancie. The tale is notably well told by Remy Belleau, 2. iournée, de la bergerie, beginning thus.

Ie chante d'Ixion l'emprise audacieuse,
L'impudence, l'orgueil, & l'idole venteuse,
De la feinte Iunon, grosse de vent & d'aer,
Ouurage industrieux des mains de Iupiter &c.

Bartholomæus Annulus *in his* picta poesi, *hereby noteth a polluted conscience, which is euer his owne persecutor and tormentor, still flying, and yet still folowing himselfe, as Ixions wheele, that alwaies turns about, but neuer turns away.* Sisiphus, *being of Ioues counsaile, reuealed his secrets, and is therefore thus punished.* Lucretius *expoundeth it otherwise, of him that ambitiously gapeth after promotion, and is euer repulsed, toyling and moyling himselfe, with an endles rolling of a neuer-standing stone.*

> Sisiphus in vita quoque nobis ante oculos est,
> Qui petere à populo fasces, sæuasque secures
> Imbibit, & semper victus tristisque recedit.
> Nam, petere imperium, quod inane est, nec datur vnquam,
> Atque in eo semper durum sufferre laborem :
> Hoc est, aduerso nixantem trudere monte
> Saxum, quod tamen à summo iam vertice rursum
> Voluitur, & plani raptim petit æquora campi.

Others expound it so, as meaning by the stone, the studies and endeuours of mortall men : by the hill, the whole course of mans life : by the hill top, the ioy and tranquillitie of the minde : by Hell, the earth, and men on earth : by Sisiphus, *the soule and minde of man, which included in this prison of the body, striueth and contendeth by all meanes possible, to attaine to eternall rest, and perfect felicitie : which some repose in wealth, some in honor, some in pleasure : all which, hauing once gotten what they sought, begin againe as fast, to couet new matters, and neuer make an end of desiring : so that, he who first was wholly giuen to catch and snatch, being now growne to wealth, seeketh honor, and is as infinitely addicted to that vaine humor, as euer he was to the other miserable affection : this is the world,* omnium rerum est vicissitudo : *neither is it possible for any man (whilst he is a man) to enioy any setled felicitie in this life.*

Tityus *had his liuer, or, as some say, his heart, all day long deuoured by an* Ægle ; *or, as others report it, by a vultur : and, asmuch as was consumed in the day, somuch was restored in the night ; so that his torment was perpetuall. The liuer is the seate of lust and concupiscence, which in the night time suborneth vnchaste and wanton cogitations. Or physically thus,* Tityus *is the stalke or blade of corne, of* τῖτυς, *one letter being taken away : hee was borne of* Iupiter *and* Elara, *the daughter of* Orchomenus, *a riuer of Thessalia.*

falia. *This* Elara, *noteth the naturall humor and milke-white moiſture in the ſeede of corne: and without* Iupiter, *that is heate, and* Elara, *moyſture, the corne can neuer proſper.* Iupiter *therefore accompanying with* Elara, *when ſhe had conceaued, and was great, hid her in the ground, for feare of* Iuno: *ſhe in the ground was deliuered of* Tityus, *who being borne by his mothers death, was brought vp and nurſed of the earth . The ſence hereof is this, the ſeede is caſte into the ground, for feare of the iniury of the ayre, noted by* Iuno: *the mother dyeth, for the ſeede putrifieth :* Tityus *ſprings forth, being nurſed by the earth, and aſpyreth vp towards heauen, as though he were about to offer violence to* Latona, *and is therefore throwne downe and ſlaine by the darts of* Diana *and* Apollo : *that is to ſay, hee is ripened, and brought to maturity, by the heate of the ſunne, and moyſture of the moone, that at length hee may be cut downe by reapers. Vulturs conſume his liuer: for, the chaffe and huske is left to birds, as being not conuenient for bread to be made thereof. He is ſtretched forth in length, ſo as with his body he couereth nine acres of land : meaning that the corne thus ſowed and ſpringing vp, poſſeſſeth and ouerſpreadeth a great quantitie of grounde.*

Tantalus, *ſo named, as if a man would ſay,* ταλαντατω, *moſt vnfortunate and vnhappie, is the patterne of a miſerable and couetous wretch, who aſwell wanteth that which he hath, as that which he hath not : ſo* Horace *expoundeth it : But* Ouid *ſaith, he was thus tormented in Hell; to haue apples and waters alwaies before him, yet alwaies running from him, when he was about to reach them, becauſe of his blabbing tongue,*

> Quærit aquas in aquis, & poma fugacia captat
> Tantalus : hoc illi garrula lingua dedit.

Tantalus *was* Iupiters *ſon, a man fully inſtructed with naturall and celeſtiall Philoſophie, and is therefore ſaide to haue eaten with the* Gods, *and to haue feaſted and enterteigned them with a banquet ; ſith his whole delite was meditation and heauenly contemplation. In this banquet (to try whether the* Gods *knew all ſecrets) he killed and cut in peeces his ſonne* Pelops, *and ſet him before them among other diſhes:* Ceres *then preſent among the reſt, did taſte and eate the ſhowlder of* Pelops. *Philoſophers and learned men, whilſt they wholly addict themſelues to contemplation, neglecting their worldly and domeſticall affaires, looſe ſometimes their goods, ſometimes their children, or wife, or otherwiſe.* Ouid *telleth the tale in 6. Meta. adding further, that the* Gods *then pitying* Pelops, *vnited his torne members, and inſteede of the ſhoulder deuoured by* Ceres, *made one vp of Iuory, plaguing his father in Hell, for his offence: Some others make a ſtone hang ouer his head, ſtill like to fall and breake him to powder; to note out the continual labor and vexation of ſpirit, incident to euery man, that is ſeriouſly bent to earneſt meditation. He is ſaide* to haue imparted vnto men, Nectar and Ambrosia, the drinke and meate of the gods : because he did communicate among them, those hidden treasures of heauenly philosophie : for άμβεσπε is immortall, and Nectar hath in effect the same signification, noting, that the gods are immortall, and cannot dye, according to the verse,

Iupiter Ambrosia satur est,& nectare viuit.

Belides, or Danaides, were the fiftie daughters of Danaus; who killed their husbands all in one night, sauing only one; and are therefore enioyned to fill broken tubs with water still running out. Lucretius hereby vnderstandeth our vnthankfull mindes and vnsatiable desires, who still hauing, desire still to haue: so that nature powreth her infinite blessings into vs, as into broken vessels, which are euer empty and ready for more. It may signifie the whole estate of mans life, neuer setled, neuer satisfied, euer dooing and vndooing, and dooing almost all, to no purpose at al. It may also note the exchecquer or treasury of a prince, which like the sea, still receaueth, and is neuer full : or lastly, the nature of a blab, that is like a broken tub, plenus rimarum, full of sliftes, flowing out here and there, keeping nothing secret, that is imparted vnto him. With these and such like monsters, and monstrous torments, the poets haue furnished their hell. Virgil 6. aneid, setteth downe all most plentifully, placing at the very entrance and gate of hell, a rable of hellish haggs, as woe, reuenge, wrath, sicknes, old age, feare, famine, penurie, death, labor, sleepe, warre, discord, and such others. The torments aboue rehearsed, are apointed for the wicked and damned ghosts : the good and blessed spirits enioy euerlasting happines in the Elysian fields, a place seuered from the comfortles lodge of the damned.

The Sirenes (which I had almost forgotten) sought for, and folowed after Proserpina: strumpets and wanton huswiues folow riches & aboundance, figured by Proserpina, the Lady of fruite and corne, according to that olde saying, Sine Cerere & Baccho friget Venus.

The mocking boy made a Swift, Ascalaphus (borne of Orphne and Acheron) turnd to an Owle, the loutes of Lycia transformed to Frogs, and Lyncus, changed to a Lynx, are all tokens of iust plagues inflicted on such offendors.

Triptolemus, historically, in a ship bearing the name of the Dragon, brought store of corne to Athens, being in his time miserably plagued with famine.

These discourses thus ended, the Nymphs were suffered to rest for a time, and the Pastors enioyned freshly to pursue their interrupted narrations. Among whome Alphesibæus told this tale of his master Phœbus.

P Hœbus too too prowd for killing Pytho the serpent,
 Saw yong Lord of loue, with a bended bowe in Olympus:
And must boyes beare bowes, qd Apollo? must a Cupido
Leaue his mothers papps, and handle dangerus arrowes?

Leaue sharp tooles, poore child, and take vp a lamp or a firestick,
Kindle a foolish fire in a harebraine boy, or a frantick
Gyrle; or shoote at crowes, if boyes will needes be a shooting,
Such warlike weapons are far more meet for *Apollo*,
Who with a thousand shafts of late, confounded an ougly
Snake, whose poysned panch all ouerwhelmed a countrey.

Well, qd winged boy, content: let mighty *Apollo*
Shoote at snakes: and Lord of Loue at mighty *Apollo*:
And as much as a snake is lesse then mighty *Apollo*,
Soe much, Lord of Loue is more then mighty *Apollo*.

This sayd, yeelding ayre with fluttring wings he deuideth,
And *Parnassus* mount in a moment nymbly recou'reth:
There two feath'red shafts from painted quiuer he plucketh,
Of strong, yet diuers operation: one with a golden
Sharp head, breeding loue: and th'other fram'd with a leaden
Blunt head, feeding hate: Loue-breeder woundeth *Apollo*,
Hate-feeder *Daphne*: and eu'n as much as *Apollo*
Lou's *Daphne*, so much this *Daphne* hateth *Apollo*.
Daphne goes to the woods and vowes herself to *Diana*;
Phœbus growes starke wood, for loue and fancie to *Daphne*.

When that he looks on her haire, fayre haire and sweetly beseeming,
Though vndrest, vntrest, blowne here and there by the shoulders:
Then doth he think: ô if these loose, yet sweetly beseeming
Locks, were drest, and trest, and not left loose by the shoulders,
How-much more would they seeme fayre and sweetly beseeming?
When that he lookes on her eies, like sparkling stars in a frostie
Night: and lips, (yet lips to be kissed, not to be lookt on)
And armes all naked, fro the milk-white wrist to the elbow:
Then doth he think: If I ioy these outward partes to be viewing,
O, what a heau'n were it, those secret partes to be tutching?

O, what auailes it now, with scorneful words to be bragging,
And with winged boy, nay wicked boy, to be striuing?
O, what auails it now to be *Titan*, *Phœbus*, *Apollo*,
Bright, burning, radiant, with sight, light, beauty abounding?
Thou, whose beames did burne heu'n, earth, and watery Empire,
Art now scorcht, nay burnt, yea burnt to the bones with a wilde-fire:
Thou, who shouldst by right, be the due and daily beholder
Of both land and sea, doost now looke only on one thing,
Only vpon *Daphne*: fixing those eyes on a Virgin,
Which thou owst to the world: and getst vp rath in a morning,
For to behold her face: and goest downe late in an eu'ning,
Sory to leaue her sight: sometimes thy beames be eclipsed,

I

Thy

Thy face discolored, thy countnance chearful, apaled,
And makst mortal men with a soddayne terror amazed,
And all this for loue : for, loue makes strong to be weakned,
Loue all-seeing sunne, on a soddayne makes to be darkned :
    Simple *Daphne* feares, and flies, for feare, from *Apollo* :
Louer *Apollo* runs, and thus complains as he runneth.
O, stay deare *Daphne*, thy best friend hasteneth after,
Fly not away, sweet soule; for so sheep run fro the Woolu's-iawes,
Hart fro the greedy Lyons, and scaiful Doue fro the AEgle,
Euery one from a foe : but *Daphne* flies from a faithful
Friend, from a wounded soule, from a constant louer *Apollo*.
Looke to thy selfe, *Daphne*, take heede, for feare of a falling,
O, stay, haste makes waste, these thorns may chace to be pricking
Those thy tender legs, and all through fauk of *Apollo* :
O, these waies are rough, and ouer-growne with a thousand
Briers, if *Daphne* needs will goe, let her easily goe on,
Easily goe on afore, and Ile haste easily after.
And yet let *Daphne* not scorne to regard, to remember,
And mark wel, what he is, that beares such fancie to *Daphne*.
Noe brute mountaine bird, no swayne, no ristical Hoblob,
No threed-bare pastor, with an hyred flock by the forrest,
Prowd of a bawling curre, of a iarring pipe, or a sheep-hooke,
But burning *Tytan*, bright *Phœbus*, chearful *Apollo*.
Delos mine Honnor, my fame and glory denounceth,
And Clarian temples doe yeeld mee duetiful offrings.
Simple wench, God knowes, thou knowst not *Phœbus Apollo*,
And therfore thou runst as a simple wench, from *Apollo*,
Worlds sight, and worlds light, worlds comfort, *Phœbus Apollo*,
Soothsayer, singer, *Ioues* ofspring, *Phœbus Apollo*,
Yea, and most stedfast, most cunning archer, *Apollo*,
Had not that vile boy more stedfast hand then *Apollo*.
Healing hearbs, strange rootes, sweet balmes, odoriferus oyntments
Were found out, set forth, first taught by *Phœbus Apollo*,
And yet alas, not an hearb, not a roote, not a balme, not an oyntment
Is to be found that can cure cureles wound of *Apollo*.
    Phœbus spake; and more by *Phœbus* was to be spoken,
Daphne breakes his speech, and runs for life fro the speaker.
Sweet windes encountring *Daphne* (as loth to be leauing
So braue lasse, and glad such tender lims to be touching)
With milde blasts did blow her garments easily backward,
That bare skin, more white then snowe vntroadencapeared,
And wauing loose locks flew here and there by the shoulders.

Flight augments her forme, and bareſt parts be, the braueſt.
Flight augments his loue, and neareſt ioyes be the deareſt:
And as a nimble youth, as a youthful God, to the damſel
Strayght with might and mayne, and all inraged he flieth,
And leaues intreating and frames himſelf to a forcing.

Like as a light-foot hound, and trembling hare, in an open
Field, when as either runs, and either feares to be out-run,
Either runs for life, and either runs for a hares life,
Hare to prolong her life, and murdring hound to abridge it :
Hound thruſts forth his ſnowt, girds out, and greedily ſnatcheth:
Preſt to deuour poore hare; poore hare ſcarce fully reſolued
Whether ſhee's yet caught or not caught, ſhrinkes fro the murdrers
Teeth all on water : ſo *Daphne*, ſo was *Apollo*.
Feare driues on *Daphne*, and loue ſtil lifts vp *Apollo*:
Loue ſo lifts louer, that neare and nearer he vrgeth
Poore fainting *Daphne*, now hard at her heeles he aprocheth,
Eu'n ſo hard at her heeles, that *Daphnes* hayre by *Apollo*,
Daphnes ſcattered hayre was blow'n by the breath of *Apollo*.

Then weake and all ſpent, turning her face to the waters,
Pœnæus waters, there this laſt boone ſhe deſireth.
Father *Pœnæus*, lend helping hand to thy daughter,
If you brookes are Gods, and haue ſuch grace from *Olympus*,
Let this gaping earth conuey mee downe to *Auernus*,
Or, let this my face, too pleaſing face, be defaced,
Let this forme, which cauſd my former woe, be deformed,
And to an other ſhape by transformation altred.

Her words ſcarce vttred, lims al were ſtarck in a moment,
And her tender breaſt, all ouer-grow'n with a tender
Barck, and locks were leaues, & bare armes grew to be branches:
Swift foot was ſlow root, and crowne transformd to a tree-top;
In ſtead of *Daphne* by the riuer ſprang vp a Laurel,
Laurel freſh and fayre, as ſayre and freſh as a *Daphne*.

Phœbus comes ſweating and blowing vnto the new tree,
And, for his old loues ſake, beares endles loue to the new tree:
Yet, when he tutcht new tree, new tree was afrayd of a tutching;
Vnder a bark of a tree, *Daphne* was felt to be panting;
Yea, when he offred a kiſſe to the tree, in ſtead of a *Daphne*,
Tree bent back fro the kiſſe, and ſtarted aſide as a *Daphne*.

Well, qd he, though *Daphne* ſhall neuermore be *Apolloes*
Wife, yet *Daphnes* tree ſhall euermore be *Apolloes*
Tree, and deck both head, and hayre, and bow of *Apollo*.
Yea, thoſe noble Dukes, great Lords, and martial Emprors.

Daphnes

Daphnes Laurel leaues at feasts aud stately triumphings,
In signe of conquest, shall euermore be adorning :
And as *Apolloes* face is fresh and lyuely for euer,
So shall *Daphnes* leaues grow greene and louely for euer,
Thus did *Apollo* speak, and Laurell tree for a *Daphne*,
Bowes her top for a head, and condiscends to *Apollo*.

Daphne thus transformd : *Clymene* was lou'd of *Apollo*,
Lou'd, and bare him a son; *Phaeton*; too youthful a yonker,
Whose ouer-weening was his ouerthrow, by presuming
Rashly beyond his reach, his fathers coach to be guiding:
Like to the foolish boy, who mounting vp to *Olympus*,
Burnt his wings and wax, and soe fell downe to *Auernus*.

Y*Ou are a good scholler of the best master*, sayd Elpinus to Alphesibæus :
And your masters mother, as I haue heard say, was Thia, *that is, Diuine :
& his father*, Hyperion, *going ouer vs, or aboue vs, as the sunne doth. Some o-
thers make his mother to be* Euriphaessa, *late* Splendens, *glistering far and
neere : but the vsuall, and most receaued opinion is*, *that* Iupiter *begat both*
Sunne *and* Moone *of* Latona : *who being great, could finde no resting place, by
reason of* Iunoes *wrath: vntill at last she came to the wandring* Delos, *where
she was deliuered of them both. The reason alleadged by some, is this; after that
cōfused & vndistinct* Chaos *wherof al was made, called* Latona, λίθω, (*as* Plato
would haue it) à Latendo, *of lurking, and lying hid, and vnknowen: Light
(which chiefly proceeds from Sunne and Moone) was first framed by that all-
framing creator. They are sayd to be borne in* Delos (*an eminent and high
Island) because presently after the creation of light, things began to come to
light, to be seene, to be knowen, which first lay confused and not perceaued, in
the darkesome bottome of that all-including* Chaos. *Hereof came the name*
Delos, *of* δήλω, *to shew, or make playne and manyfest.*

Apollo *hath long yealow hayre : noting his rayes and beames, which heate
and hit, like dartes, a far off; and therefore is he called of* Homer ἰκόλος. *He is
young, fresh, and without any beard: for, his force neuer fadeth, and his heate
is always quickning. Therefore, the Tyran* Dionisius *did cut off* AEsculapius
*his golden beard, saying, It was no reason, that the sonne should haue such a
long beard, when as his father* Phœbus *had none at all. This perpetuall youth,
and neuer decaying nor declining validitie of* Phœbus *and other the Gods,
is figured by* Hebe : *signifieng the very flowre of youth, whom* Homer *for the
same cause maketh* Ioues *cup-bearer. This* Hebe *was* Iunoes *daughter : for,
of the temperature of the ayre proceede all heirbs and flowres:* Iupiter *is her
father : for, without the quickning heat of the ethereal region, no temperature
can be in the lower ayre : yet some there be that would haue her borne of* Iuno
without any father : Hebe *on a time, as she bare the cup to* Iupiter, *slipt, and in
falling,*

falling, discouered those secrets, which maydens are not willing to reueale; whereupon shoe was by Ioue depriued of her place, and Ganymedes *preferred thereunto. The sence whereof is this: when the flowers and leaues fall from trees, then doth the youth and honor of the hearbs and trees growe to decay; and* Ganymedes, *that is, winter, commeth in place.* Hebe, *they say, maried* Hercules; *the fame of valyant and heroical personages, is euer florishing.*

Others, by the rauishing of Ganymede *by Iupiter, vnderstand the lifting vp of mans minde from these earthly toyes, to heauenly conceipts: that* Ganymedes *may be deriued of* γάνυμαι, *to ioy and reioyce, and* μήδεα, *signifying aduice & counsaile, as though mans soule thus rauished by Ioue, might wel be sayd to enioy his heauenly comfort and counsaile,* γανύεαι μήδεα τῶ διι. Hebe *was framed like a sweet lasse: her roabes figured and flowred, & her head also adorned with a garland of sundry flowers. The* Corinthians *erected her a temple, in a certaine groue full of* Cipresse *trees: wherein such as escaped captinitie & thraldome, hanged vp their gyues and fetters in honor of* Hebe.

Hebes picture.

Phœbus *(so called, of the greeke words,* φῶς *and* ζωή, *light and life) is not onely young and fresh, but he is also the author of Physicke, the founder of musick, the gouernour of the Muses, and father of Oracles, all which excellencies proceede from the operation of the Sunne. His beames be pestiferous, if too hote, and therefore doth* Homer *make him plague the Grecian armie: but healthful, if moderate and temperate. Of this moderate heate of the Sunne, comes the temperature of the ayre: of a temperate ayre grow holesome hearbes and flowres, the simples and ingredients of euery physicall composition, and therefore* Phœbus *the author of physicke.*

Phlegias *is the heate of the Sunne; for,* φλέγειν, *is to burne: his daughter was* Coronis, *the ayre moderately moystned and heated,* ἀπὸ τῦ κεραννύαι: *of this* Coronis *and* Phœbus, Æsculapius, *the temperature of the ayre, is borne: whose daughters were two:* ὑγίεια, *soundnes of body or good health; and* Ίασω, *the efficacie of physicke in healing and curing mens bodies,* ἀπὸ τῦ ιασθαι, *which is, to cure. A* Esculapius *was slayne by angry* Ioues *thunder:* Phœbus *sory, and grieued for his sons death, slew in like sorte the* Cyclopes, *which made* Ioues *thunder: that is, the beames of the Sun, by degrees, doe consume that pestilent outrage of these contagious vapours and exhalations, causers of mortalitie. A* Esculapius, *being borne, was committed to* Chiron, *a most excellent Chirurgian, to be brought vp:* Chiron *was the sonne of* Saturne, *and the Nymph* Philyra: *for, knowledge and excellencie in physick, as in all other artes, is gotten by continuance of time and long experience: whereof* Saturne *representeth the one, and* Philyra *the other; so called of the greeke worde* φίλη, *a louer: and* ῥῖα *experience, as a louer of experience (the mother without doubt of Chirurgy) by taking away the first letter* π, *from πεῖρα, as if a man would say, φίλη, and, for the more easie and smoother pronunciation, φίλυρα. This* Chiron, is sayd to be halfe a man, and halfe a horse: sith surgery (and in olde times there was in effect no other part of Physick knowen but surgery) is auayleable aswell for horses and other beasts, as it is for man: and thus much to shew, that Phœbus is physicall. Now, he is also Musicall; and therefore Mercurie gaue him a Lute; whereon he playeth; alluding to the harmonie of the cœlestiall Globes, and the constancie and vniformitie, which the Sun obserueth most strictly in his course, as euer keeping the Eclipticall line: for which cause he is the master of the nine Muses, ruling the concent and melody of the nine Spheres. The Muses are the daughters of Ioue (for all goodnes comes of Ioue) and of Mnemosyne, Memory. Their nurse was Eupheme, Honor and Fame: for, Honos alit artes, honor and commendation is a spur to a student. They were nine, proportionably to the number of the Spheres, whose gouerning spirites the Platonists and Pythagoreans would haue them to be. Ουρανια, cœlestiall, was the first, referred to the immoueable Sphære, called ἀπλανης. Polymnia, to Saturne, a great singer, or singing much and of many matters. Cleio, to Mars, κλειος is glory and renowne. Melpomene, to the Sunne, singing, celebrating, extolling. Erato, to Venus, louing and amiable. Euterpe, to Mercurie, pleasant and delightsome. Thalia to the Moone, florishing. These be the eight Muses, as it were, the tunes of those eight Spheres, whereof is made the perfect concent and melodious harmonie, figured by the ninth, called Calliope, a sweete concent, the chiefe and guide of all the Muses, as Ouid witnesseth, 5. Metam:

> Dedimus summam certaminis vni,

meaning Calliope.   *and,*

> Finierat doctos e nobis maxima cantus:

to weete, Calliope.

They are called Musæ, of the verb μυω, which is, to teach and instruct a man in those things, that are sacred and holy, diuine and mysticall, whereof came the word mysterie. They are also called Camenæ, à canendo, of singing: and, Pierides, of the mount Pierius, where they were borne: They all, hand in hand, daunce in a round, and Phœbus in the middle: all liberall sciences are vnited and chayned together, the one depending on the other; noting that absolute ἐγκυκλοπαιδεια and coherent concatenation and continuation of all ingenuous erudition. Lastly, Phœbus is the father of Oracles and prophecies, the eye of the world, seeing and hearing all things first, as Homer was woont to say, and Ouid in imitation of Homer,

> Videt hic deus omnia primus.

Therefore Laurell is his tree, both for that it is always greene, and neuer toucht with lightning (noting that the fame of vertue and learning is euer flourishing, and neuer dyeth) as also hoate and odoriferous, and (as it is reported) causeth true dreames being applyed to a mans head and temples: and *being cast into the fire, portendeth good luck, if it make a great noyce, by crackling: bad, if either none, or but a little.* Coruus, *the Crowe is his bird: whose different chirps and prognostications of rayne, were obserued of sooth-fayers and diuiners, whose maister is* Apollo. Cicnus, *the Swan, is also his bird: the Swan is white and bright as the sunne;* a finger as Phœbus, *a fore-teller of his owne death, and so a diuiner as* Apollo. Cicnus *was king of* Liguria; *he loued Musick, and is therefore of Ouid turnd to a Swanne.* Laftly, *the cock is* Apolloes *bird, who dutifully faluteth him, and bids him good morrow euery morning. He is figured, a young fresh youth, hauing long hayre, no beard, a lute in the one hand, a bowe in the other, in a chariot drawen with foure coursers,* Pyroeis, Eous, AEthon, Phlegon, Ignitus, Matutinus, Ardens, Comburens, *being all Epithetes incident to the nature of the sunne: whose Pallace and Chariot are described by* Ouid : 2. Metam: *In Latine he is called* Sol, *quasi folus, alone and incomparable.*

*

Hercules *kild* Gerion, *and brought away his oxen: where, by* Hercules, *both* Pierius *and* Hesiodus *his interpreter, vnderstand the Sunne, sith he is the glorie and ornament of* Iuno, *that is, the ayre: for,* ἤρα, *is* Iuno, *and* κλεος, *is glory. And* Gerion, *they make to be winter, of γηρυω, which fig-nifieth to crye or roare, thereby noting the roaring and bluftring tempests of winter, which are calmed, and repressed by* Hercules, *that is to fay, by the heate of the Sunne. The Oxen be the crashes of thunder, whose feareful found resembleth the lowing of Oxen: and these thundrings are neuer lightly heard, but when* Hercules *hath flayne* Gerion; *when winter is ouerpast by the heate of the Sun.*

Apollo *being banished from heauen for killing the* Cyclopes, *fedde* Admetus *his Sheepe, Kine, and Oxen, by the riuer* Amphryfus. *Oxen fet foreward husbandry, and the vitall heate and influence of the Sunne, is the chiefe caufe of increafe: fo then,* Apollo *may well be called a paftor, becaufe, as* Pontanus *fayth, he feedeth and maintayneth all that liueth,*

Quòd pafcat quicquid fub cœli nafcitur oris.

The Affyrians *(by report of* Macrobius*) especially honoured one God aboue others, whom they named* Adad: *which fignifieth one: to whom they ioyned a Goddes, for a companion, called* Atargatis: *attributing all to these two: by whom they vnderstande the Sunne and the earth. The picture of* Adad *had his beames and rayes inclyning downewardes towarde* Atargatis, *shewing that the heauens worke on and in the earth, by influence from the sunne.* Atargatis *was fo framed, as that her beames afcended vp-wardes towardes* Adad: *notyng, that whatsoeuer the earth brought foorth, it came by operation of the cœleftiall vertue. Vnder* Atargatis *was a*

Lyon

Lyon, signifiyng, that she was the great mother of all things, Earth: who, as I shewed before when I spake of Cibele, *had her chariot drawen by Lyons.*

*

AEfculapius *was borne by the death of his mother, as* Ouid *telleth the tale in the second of his transformations: where, after th..: he had shewed, how* Apollo *in his furie flew* Coronis, *great with* AEfculapius *, hee addeth thus,*

23   Non tulit in cineres labi fua Phœbus eofdem
      Semina: fed natum flammis, vteroq; parentis
      Eripuit, geminiq; tulit Chironis in antrum. &c.

The vertue medicinable is hereby figured, drawen from the roots of hearbs, when the earth is pierced with the arrowes, that is, parched by the hoate beams of the Sunne. This is deliuered to Chiron, *the learned and experienced Phyfitian, who thereof frameth wonderfull compofitions.*

AEfculapius *is made fitting on a high feate, with a crowne of Laurell on his head, a long beard, a knotted ftaffe in his right hand (it is a difficult and hard matter to reftore decayed health) and a Snake in his left hand: a ferpent is quick of fight, and watchfull; fo muft a Phifitian be. A Snake may well bee taken for a figne of health; fith, as fhee by cafting her olde skinne, renueth her felfe, fo the fick and crafed body reftored to his former health, feemeth to be young agayne.*

*

The morning is the fore-runner to the funne, yet caufed of the funne. She is called the daughter of Thia *and* Hyperion, *fhe is ruddie like rofes, fhe hath yellow hayre, golden roabes, and fitteth on a golden throne.* Aurora *loued* Tithonus, Laomedons *fonne; becaufe he fett his wyfe from the* Eaft *; hee being extreamly olde, was turned to a Grafhopper: olde men neuer ceafe tatling and chirping. The diftinctions of times called howres,* Horæ, ἀπὸ τῦ ὡρῶω, *which fignifieth to keepe; doe guide, conferue and keepe in order all proceedings whatfoeuer, and are the daughters of* Ioue *and* Themis, *to weete,* Eunomie, Dice, Eirene: *for, no way better fhall a man perceaue the good or bad dealing of men, and the merciful or reuenging power of the Gods, then by the change of times & howrs: therefore they keepe heauen gates, and attend on the Sun, caufing fayre or fowle weather, when they luft, for the profite or plague of mortall men.*

*

Now to Alphefibœus *his tale.* Phœbus *kild* Pytho: *the heat of the Sun confumed thofe peftilent vapors left after the deluge, caufing putrefaction, fignified by this word,* πυθοι, *whereupon fome think, he was called* Apollo, *of the verbe* ἀπολλύωμι, *to kill.* Pontanus,

24   Tum tellus grauis imbre & adhuc ftagnantibus vndis
      Humide, anhela, vagos tollebat ad æthera tortus,
      Inuoluens cælum nube, & caligine opaca:

Hinc

Hinc ille immanis Python,&c.

This made Phœbus *vaunt : yet was he daunted by* Cupid, *and forced af-
fectionately to loue* Daphne, *daughter to the riuer* Penæus: *whereby is vnderstood, that naturall and radicall humor of the earth, proceeding from the waters and riuers, that moysten her and make her fruitefull. The sunne coue-
teth this moysture, sends downe his attractiue beames to draw it vp, resolues it
into vapors, and makes it fit for himselfe. On the other side, this moysture flu-
eth and withdraweth herselfe from the heate of the sunne, as from her deadly
foe. Againe, the violent and piercing beames of the sunne, compell this moysture to forsake the vppermost and superficiall parts of the earth, retyring backward into the deepest and remotest parts thereof. Which, being thither come,
and yet euen thither and there, persecuted by the scalding and searching rayes
of* Phœbus, *is at last, by the meanes of the celestiall powers, and help of the watery floods and riuers, defended from the violence of* Apollo, *and conuerted into fruitefull trees and plants.* Daphne *is transformed into a laurell tree, rather then any other, for that, by reason of her excellencie, continuance florishing
greenenesse, odoriferous sent, and naturall heate, shee aboue all other doth shew
her constitution to be tempered with due and proportionable commixtion of
terrene moysture and celestiall heate.* Daphne *is* Penæus *his daughter: for,
by the bankes and meddowes adioyning thereunto, an infinite number of lawrell trees were growing.* Apollo *garnished his Lute and Quiuer with Laurell leaues : so should only famous poets, worthy of Apollos Lute : and renowmed conquerors, figured by his Quiuer, be crowned with Laurel, in token of their
neuer-dying glory. Laurell is long kept ; so is the fame of learned and valiant
men : Laurell is alwaies greene: so is their praise eternall and euer-flori-
shing: Laurell is hoate and odoriferous: so dooth the heauenly-inspired spirit
of poets, and all-contemning courage of Heroicall mindes, breath foorth
the sweete sauour of vertues excellency: Lastly, Laurell is neuer tutcht with
lightning, and their names are neuer defaced by Obliuion.*

The other tale of youthfull Phaeton, *and his father* Phœbus, *may first
giue vs warning, neither to wish vnaduisedly, nor sodainely to yeeld to rash
demaunds : nor vnconsiderately to performe a promise foolishly made.* Phaeton, Semele, Theseus, *and others, by their owne wishes procured their owne
confusion.* Phaeton *was the sonne of* Phœbus *and* Clymene: *to weet the heat
and inflammation proceeding from the sunne. For* φαίθω, *is, to burne : and,* Clymene, *is the water,* ἀπὸ τε κλύειν, *to ouerflowe : and when these ouerflowing vapors eleuated by the sunne, are once inflamed, then doth this outragious heate
breake out.* Phaeton *fell downe into the riuer* Eridanus, *after extraordinary drought, folow commonly, inundations of waters.*

Phaeton *is beaten downe with thunder : for, these vapors raised vp by
the sunne, and by the enuironing coldnes of the middle region of the ayre,
thrust into a narrow straite ; by strugling for passage, cause thunder and lightning.*

ning, til the outrage of that heate bee so consumed. Phaetons *sisters,* Phaetusa *and* Lampetie *(noting heate and brightnes) did so sorowfully lament their brothers death, that, for pity, they were turned into poplar trees: that is, of this humor, and exceeding heate of the sunne, many kindes of trees and plants doe plentifully proceede.* Lucian *expoundeth it historically thus:* Phaeton *began seriously to obserue the course and reuolution of the sunne, but, preuented by death, could not finish his attempted enterprise. The ethicall moralization, (which* Ouid *himselfe tutcheth in his bookes* de Tristibus*) may be this:* Phaeton, *a youth, and therefore vnable to gouerne, will needes be a magistrate: but alas, it is too great a burden for his weake shoulders.*

> Magna petis, Phaeton, & quæ non viribus istis
> Munera conueniunt, nec tam iuuenilibus annis.

The gouernement and administration of a common wealth or kingdome, is a heauenly charge.

> Sors tua mortalis: non est mortale quod optas.

It is also as heauy as heauenly. The beginning and climing vp, is hard and difficult: the top thereof subiect to a thousand perills and dangers, which make euen the most experienced, much to feare: and the discent or comming downe is headlong.

> Ardua prima via est, & quà vix manè recentes
> Enituntur equi: medio est altissima cælo;
> Vnde mare & terras ipsi mihi sæpe videre
> Sit timor, & pauida trepidet formidine pectus.
> Vltima prona via est, & eget moderamine certo.

Besides this, in a common wealth, there be Bulls, Centaurs, Lyons, Scorpions, and such like; that is, sauage and rude people, vngentle, cruel, crafty, and ennious; to whose open violence and secreate supplanting the gouerner is euer subiect.

> Forsitan & lucos illic vrbesque deorum
> Concipias animo, delubraque ditia donis
> Esse: per insidias iter est, formasque ferarum.
> Vtque viam teneas, nulloque errore traharis,
> Per tamen aduersi gradiêris cornua tauri,
> Hæmoniosque arcus, violentique ora Leonis

Sæuaque

Sæuaque circuitu curuantem brachia longo
Scorpion, atq; aliter curuantem brachia cancrum.

Againe, the rude rablement of the vulgar sort, will hardly be maiStred, or brought to any conformitie.

Nec tibi quadrupedes animosos ignibus illis
Quos in pectore habent, quos ore & naribus efflant,
In promptu regere eSt : vix me patiuntur, vbi acres
Incaluére animi, ceruixque repugnat habenis.

TheSe and Such other imminent miSchiefes laid open by Apollo, *he falleth at laSt to intreating and perSwaSions, and fearefull cares of a louing father.*

Pignora certa petis : do pignora certa timendo,
Et patrio pater eSSe metu probor, aSpice vultus.
Ecce meos : vtinamque oculos in pectora poSSes
InSerere, & patrias intus deprendere curas.

But ambition can heare no reaSon, and Phaeton *will needs Sit in his fathers chariot.*

dictis tamen ille repugnat,
PropoSitumque petit, flagratque cupidine currus.

This chariot is the glorious type of earthly honor and dignitie: the axell tree all of golde, golden buck, golden Sollies of the wheeles, and Siluer Spokes: the collars, traces, and hownces glyStred with ChrySolites, *and other pretious Stones, which rauiSh the minde of the yonker* Phaeton.

Aureus axis erat, temo aureus, aurea Summæ
Curuatura rotæ, radiorum argenteus ordo:
Per iuga ChrySolithi, poStæq; ex ordine gemmæ
Clara repercuSSo reddebant lumina Phœbo.
And againe,
Dumque ea magnanimus Phaeton miratur, & optat. &c.

Phœbus *his horSes note the vulgar people, as I Said before, altogether fierce and outragious : the bridles are the Stay of gouernement.* Phaeton *thus being obStinate, & reSolued to be a ruler, is now inStructed how to rule. Spare the whip, reine them hard.*

Parce puer Stimulis, & fortius vtere loris.

The whip noteth a rigorous and tyrannicall kinde of commaunding and ouerruling: the reines, a moderate and temperate kinde of discipline. Mount not too high: fall not too lowe, keepe betweene both.

Altius egreſſus, cæleſtia tecta cremabis,
Inferius terras, medio tutiſſimus ibis.

Theſe præcepts ended, the yong headed officer, by the fauour and countenance of great men, is ſet aloft in his brauery.

Occupat ille leuem iuuenili corpore currum,
Statque ſuper, manibuſque datas contingere habenas
Gaudet, &c.

But when any tumult or ſedition is ſtirred vp among the people, then is he nobody, and eſteemed of nobody.

Sed leue pondus erat, nec quod cognoſcere poſſent
Solis equi, ſolitaque iugum grauitate carebat.
Vtque labant curuæ iuſto ſine pondere naues,
Perque mare inſtabiles nimia leuitate feruntur,
Sic onere inſueto vacuos dat in aere ſaltus,
Succutiturque altè, ſimiliſque eſt currus inani.

This happeneth to al ſuch magiſtrats as will not rule according to Apolloes rule. The ſunne indeede hath a contrarie motion to that of the heauen: but he trauerſeth the heauen gently, not croſſeth it ouerthwartly: and ſo muſt a ruler ouerrule the ſtubburne vulgar. Phaeton, poore youth, when all is on fire, all on an vproare, is at his wits end.

Tum verò Phaeton cunctis è partibus orbem
Aſpicit accenſum; nec tantos ſuſtinet æſtus.

Then Iupiter, at the pitifull complaint of the earth, that is, the commonwealth, coms to helpe.

Intonat, & dextra libratum fulmen ab aure
Mittit in aurigam. &c.

Where foloweth the miſerable end of theſe luſty commaunders, brought to vtter confuſion.

Illic fræna iacent, illic temone reuulsus
Axis &c.

When all is come to al, Phaetons *ambitious conceit, gaines naught but this, to comfort his destruction, that when by his aspiring, he hath procured his owne ouerthrow, men may say after his death, This felow caried a braue minde, and shott at mighty matters.*

Hic situs est Phaeton, currus auriga paterni,
Quem si non tenuit, magnis tamen excidit ausis.

The like folly and fall was that of Icarus, *who soared so high with his waxed wings, that he gaue name to the* Icarian *sea, wherein he was drowned.* Ouid 8. *Metam. sweetely telleth this tale, and in* 3. de tristibus, *as sweetely doth expound it.*

Sith Mercury *and* Apollo *were reconciled and made good friends, it was apointed, that* Damon *should ioyne* Mercury *to his companion* Phœbus : *who did it briefly, thus.*

L Ouely *Coronis* kild by the balefull darts of a louer,
   And tale-telling Crowe made black, for a worthy requital:
Yong *Æsculapius,* by repenting hands of *Apollo*
Cut fro the mothers wombe, was carefuly sent to the schoolehouse
Of Centaure *Chiron* to be taught : who made him a cunning
Surgeon; so cunning, that he dead men strangly reuiued.
Whereat *Ioue* incenst, with thunder fram'de by the *Cyclops,*
Stroake him dead himselfe, who cured somany deaths-wounds.
   Titan, sad to behold his son so spitefuly murdred,
On slaughtred *Cyclops,* his slaughter kindely reuenged.
Thundring *Ioue* much wroth, that such as fram'de him a thunder,
Sould suffer violence, and not from death be protected,
Expelled *Phœbus,* for a certaine time, from *Olympus.*
   Phœbus in exile now, contents himselfe with a pastors
Poore estate, and feedes *Admetus* flock, by the riuer
Amphrisus : so sweete and so secure is a pastors
Harmeles life : life next to the matchles life in *Olympus.*
   Once in an eu'ning-tide, whilst *Phœbus* lay in a valley,
And with rurall pipe bestowd himself on a loues-lay,
His sheepe (sheepe indeede, that leant no eare to a loues-lay)
Through *Pylian* pastures chaunst heere and there to be straying.
   Mercury, Ioues prety Page, fine-filcher *Mercury,* saw them,

K 2   Caught

Caught and brought them away, and kept them close in a thicket.
Phœbus knew nothing; for no-bodie saw, but an ould churle,
One ould canckred churle, which there kept *Mares* by the mountains,
Called bald *Battus:* whome *Mercury* friendly saluted,
Tooke him apart by the hand, and best perswasion vsed,
Gaue him a lambe for a bribe, and prayd him so to be silent.
Feare not, alas, faire sir, qd *Battus:* it is but a trifle,
Tis but a trick of youth, some stragling sheepe to be taking:
Kings may spare, and lend to the poore : And this very senceles
Stone (and points to a stone) of this fact shalbe reporter
As soone, as *Battus: Ioues Nuntio* gladly retired,
Yet, for a further proofe, both face and fashion altred,
And, as a countrey clowne, to a countrey lowt he returned.

Gaffer, I misse viue score vatt wedders : zawst any vilching
Harlot, roague this way of late ? canst tell any tydings?
Ichill geue the an eawe, with a vayre vatt lamb for a guerdon.
Battus perceauing his former bribe to be doobled,
Turnd his tale with a trice, and theast to the theefe he reuealed.
Vnder yonsame hill they were, yeare while, by the thicket,
And 'cham zure th'are there. Iste true, qd *Mercury* smiling,
Ist tr'ue, thou false knaue, and wilt thou needes be betraying
Mee to myself? and then false *Battus* turnd to a Tutch stone,
Tutch stone, yet true stone ; which each thing truely bewraieth,
And no-man thenceforth for no bribe falsely betrayeth.

At last, all brabling and altercation ended,
Mercury and *Phœbus* made friends, gaue one to another
Mutual embracements, and tokens : Pastor *Apollo*
Gaue his charmed staffe to the *Nuntio Mercury:* and the
Nuntio Mercury gaue his Lute to the Pastor *Apollo.*
Thus they parted friends : to the flock went Pastor *Apollo*;
Mercury sored aloft, til he seas'd on bewtiful *Herse,*
Sister of *Aglauros* possest with damnable enuie
And cursed Couetise, and worthily turnde to a black-stone,
Black-stone, signe of a minde all black and fowly defiled.

Not long after this, *Phœbus* with *Mercury*; ioyned
In faire-prowd *Chione : Chione* bare either a dearling :
Mercury, Autolicus did father, *Apollo, Philammon*;
Th'one well knowne for a theefe, and th'other fit for a fiddle;
But faire-prowde *Chione* was kild at last by *Diana.*

ELpinus *glad of so short a discourse, made as short worke in explication
of the same,* Mercury *was* Ioues *messenger indeede, yet not vsed onely by*
Ioue

Ioue, *but sometimes by other Gods also. His feete were winged, his hat win-ged,his face beardles,his body bare,but that he had a cloake cast ouer his shoul-ders,he held in his hand,a staffe called* Caduceus, *which* Phœbus *gaue him in exchange for his Lute: the serpents,winding it about, are a signe of concord; and the rod it selfe was borne of those who intreated of peace, called thereof* Caduceatores.*His winged hat and feete.shew, that speech and words (whereof* Mercury *is the best deliuerer)once being vttred,fly without returne,according to that of* Horace,

           Nescit vox missa reuerti.

    And else where,

      Et semel emissum volat irreuocabile verbum.

And Homer *calleth words,* ἔπεα πτερόεντα, *winged words.*

                                *
                                        Mer
     Mercury,*according to his diuers aspects,worketh diuers influences in mens* pictu
minds:if he be predominant, he afordeth eloquence,elegancy, learning,and espe-cially mathematicall knowledge. If he looke on Ioue *luckily, he giueth skill in* Philosophical *&* Theological *speculations : if on* Mars *happily,he maketh good* Physitians,*if vnhappily, he maketh thē either bad Physitians,or starke theeues : whēce came the fable,that* Mercury *begate on* Chione *a notable theefe, called* Autolicus, *as musical* Phœbus *by the same mother had fidling* Philammon. Mercury *therefore is a plaine turnecoate.good with good,bad with bad. Such as be Mercuriall, are commonly not very rich : yet they finde out now and then conceits and deuises to drawe money out of the chests of princes & mighty men; sith their crafty and cunning master* Mercury, *hath made them fit for the ma-naging of princes affaires. And this was the meaning of the tale,that maketh* Mercury *steale* Apolloes *cattell : for,* Apollo *noteth Kings & potentates,' and his flocks,are their wealth and riches, and the Mercuriall is the filcher. If,by chance, his Legierdumaine be perceaued,he can so finely smooth vp al by facilitie of discourse, that he neuer is vtterly disgraced by the mighty men. This their friendship and exchange noteth that incomparable vnion of* Iouial *intelligence with Mercuriall eloquence,the only flower of Kings courts,and felicity of com-mon wealths. The periured* Battus *is as worthyly plagued for his double tongue, as the blabbing clawback,and Brewbate* Crow,*for his long tongue.* Coronis *kild by* Apollo,*noteth the withered hearbs, by the withdrawing of the moysture to the rootes; whereof already in* Apollo. *Only this we may remember,that* Phœ-bus *killing* Coronis,*is a type of wrathfull iealosie,cause of present repentance. This tale (as also that of* Herse *&* Aglauros)*is in the second of* Ouids *trans-formations : and the other of* Chione,*(signifying,that pride will haue a fall)in the eleuenth.*

     Mercuries *reconciliation with* Phœbus *being thus briefely expoun-ded, it was thought good time, to talke of* Mars, *who, (as seemed by the late discourse) is also diuersly affected by or to the same* Mercurie. Condon *therefore , whose courage was most martiall , being hereunto apoynted, and remembring no famous transformation by him effected , did what hee could, and sang thus of* Mars, *and his Mistres* Venus.

WHil'ſt lymping *Vulcan* did lay on loade on his anuile,
 With ſweating Steropes, and fram'de *Gradiuus* a breaſt-peece:
Gradiuus tooke paines; and ſweete *Cytherea* belabr'ing,
With like endeauour made horned *Vulcan* a head-peece.

 Phœbus ſaw them firſt (*Phœbus* ſee's euery thing firſt)
Saw, and gree'ud very much, ſo ſhameful a ſight. to be ſeeing,
Ran to the forge ſtraightway, and there told al to the blackſmith,
Iunoes fayreſac't childe, *Cytherea'es* bewtiful husband.

 Mulciber aſtonied, ſtood ſtarck horne-dead for a long while:
Downe falls hart, downe falleth his head, downe falleth his hammer,
And no life, no ſoule, in ſenceles carkas apeareth.

 At laſt, fine ſmall nettes, and chaynes of wire he deuiſed,
So ſmall and ſo fine, that ſight muſt needes be deceaued;
Much more fine and ſmall, then fineſt threed of a copweb:
And ſo craſtily ſram'd, and with ſuch myſterie forged,
That, with a pluck they claſpt, with a tutch they ſpeedily cloaſed,
And held each thing faſt, and each thing greedily graſped.

 Theſe with ſleight and art on adultrous couch he repoſeth;
And, in a ſecreate place expects polluted adultreſſe,
And hoate raging *Mars:* who there lay louely together,
Either on others breaſt, and either in armes of another.

 When ſweete tickling ioyes of tutching came to the higheſt
Poynt, when two were one, when moyſture fully reſolued
Sought for a freer ſcope, when pleaſure cam to a fulnes,
When their dazeling eyes were ouer-caſt with a ſweete cloude,
And their fainting ſoules, in a ſleep, in a ſwowne, in a loue-trance:
Then was *Mars* faſt tide, faſt tide was dame *Cytherea*,
Then was *Mars* cooled, cooled was dame *Cytherea*.
Mars the adulter lay entangled with *Cytherea*,
And *Cytherea* lay entangled with the adulter:
Vulcans wires hold faſt, they lye vnſeemely together,
Either on others breaſt, and either in armes of another.

 Mulciber in meane time cauſd chamber dore to be open,
And calld Gods, to behold ſo ſtrange and louely a wonder:
Some laught, ſome ſmiled, ſome wiſhed ſo to be ſhamed,
No-body but *Neptune* could poſſibly pacifie *Vulcan*.

 Lady *Venus* let looſe, was ſpitefuly wroth with *Apollo*,
And his broode with luſt and rage ſhee dayly bewitched :

Sometime

Sometimes *Leucothoe* with an endles loue he defireth,
And fometimes *Clytie*, and fometimes louely *Coronis.*
Euery day new loue,new luft,new flames be prepared
By *Cytheraaes* meanes,for this tale-teller *Apollo.*

POore Vulcan, qd Elpinus,*was ouermatcht;and did therefore well to returne
to his forge,and not fight with* Mars, *the God of fighting.* Ioue,*they fay,
had* Minerua *without a mother,and therefore* Iuno *would needs haue* Mars
without a father. Mars *is that hote and furious difpofition , fit for wars. Hee
was borne in* Thrace, *a warlike and bloody countrey : his nurfe was called,*
Thero,*fignifyng fiercenes and cruelty : he is figured grim,fierce , and fterne,
all armed : his chariot is drawen by two horfes, which* Homer *calleth,Ter-
ror and Feare: his companions be,Feare,Fury, and Violence,and Fame,with
a trompet,goeth before,all eyed,winged,and clad with a thinne and fine roabe:
fhee is learnedly fet forth by* Virgil, 4. *Aneid: and fweetely by* Ouid, 12.
Metam.

Bellona,*fo called of* Bellum,*which is War,was a goddes,that entermedled
whith Martiall affayres alfo. She is paynted like a furious woman, with a
whippe in the one hand, and a firebrand in the other.*

Victoria, *Victorie; was paynted with a fweet Virgins face, winged, flying,
hauing a branch of Palme in the one hand , and of Laurel in the other; both
fignes of Victorie.*

Now to the fable of Mars & Venus. Venus,*that is to fay,Wanto:nes,ioyned
with* Mars, *which noteth hoate and furious rage,giuing themfelues ouer to ex-
ceffiue and inordinate pleafure; are by* Phœbus, *figuring the light of reafon,
accufed to* Vulcan, *who reprefenteth naturall heate; which is weakned by this
inordinate luft.* Vulcan, *by Phœbus his counfaile, linketh them together to
their fhame : for,when naturallheate is quailed, then the rage of luft is abated,
yrkefome repentance and languifhing debilitie enfuing thereupon.* Vulcan
*fheweth them both to be mockt of the Gods : the naturall heate complayneth,as
it were,and fheweth to all the other faculties (called Gods by reafon of their
heauenly frame and function) his decay and impotencie: whence foloweth of
neceffitie the impayring of all the other faculties: efpecially he calleth foorth*
Neptune, Mercurie, *and* Apollo;*fith* Neptune *by reafon of moyfture,noteth
the nourifhing power deriued from the Lyuer:* Mercurie, *the fenfible part proceeding from the brayne: and* Apollo *the vital and quickning vertue comming from the heart ; which three are extreamly preiudiced by immoderate
luft. No man could pacifie* Vulcan, *fauing only* Neptune : *nothing can
reftore the decay of nature, but fupply of moyfture and nourifhment.* Venus

Mars I
picture

Bellon
picture

The pi
of Victi

incensed,persecutes with deadly hate, the whole family of Phœbus, *for this discouery: for lust is a continuall aduersary to reason,euer maligning and opposing it selfe against all her proceedings: the tale is briefly tolde by* Ouid: 4. Metam: and more largely by* Homer, 8. Odyss: and otherwise expounded by Plutarch, in his discourse of* Homer. Ouid *in the fourth of his transformations largely discourseth, how* Leucothoe *was turnd to a sprig of franckencense, and* Clytic *to an hearb called* Heliotropium : *that noting the sweet and odoriferous influence of the Sun,this expressing the nature and name of that hearb, euer turning towards the Sun.*

The Nymphs were all this while behinde hand in their songes: therfore the pastors were now suffred to pawse for a season: Pallas,Diana, *and* Venus,*being referred to* Licoris, Arcsia, *and* Cassiopæa. Licoris *the mery lasse , sayd as followeth.*

WHen the rebelling broode of th'earth layd siege to the heauens,
   And *Ioue* all in vaine had wasted his ord'nary thunder,
Fire-forging *Vulcan* contriu'd new darts of a wondrous
Mixture,more violent then *Ioues* first ord'nary thunder.

When Gods thus victors were all secure in *Olympus,*
And new-found lightning had plagu'd the rebellius ofspring:
Ioue bade fire-cunning black smith, for a friendly requitall,
Aske and haue, what he would,and most sincerely protested
By *Stygian* waters, that nothing should be denied.

Ould limping Dottrel would needs ask Lady *Minerua,*
Of peace and of wars chiefe guide and Lady, *Minerua,*
Ioues ioy, borne of *Ioue,Ioue* only without any *Iuno.*

Well, qd *Ioue,*then speak and speede : if Lady *Minerua*
Yeeld her selfe to a smith, let a smith take Lady *Minerua.*

Vulcan limps on apace,prowd of so louely a Lady
And pearelesse Paragon: When he came at last to the Pallace,
And there found *Pallas,*th'ould buzzard gan to be bussing
Th'inuiolate Virgin : th'oulde sumbler gan to be fingring
Th'immaculate mayden : who by and by with a stately
Frowne,and austere looke, his rashnes boldly rebuked.
Black smith intreateth, prowd *Pallas* stoutly denieth,
Gray-beard contendeth,but manly *Minerua* repelleth.

   At last,with striuing and strugling stifly, the sharp-set
Ould fornicator was now so throughly resolued,
Fully resolued now, and now so fowly resolued,
That the resolued blood contending long for a passage,
Powr'd it self at length on th'earth,in steed of a *Pallas.*

Vulcan somewhat coolde, and seeing stately *Minerua*
Obstinat and peeuish, conuey'd himself to his hammers.

But

But the resolued blood which *Pallas* prowdly refufed,
Was fuckt vp by the earth ftraight way, and gladly receaued;
Wherof *Erichthonius* was borne, faire boy to the middle,
But fowle fnake downward. Which monfter, Lady *Minerua*
Gaue to the three fifters to be kept, inclofd in a casket,
With ftrayte commaundment, that none looke into the casket,
None peepe in to the childe, or fee fo fearful a monfter.
Pandrofos and *Herfe* kept tutch with Lady *Minerua*,
Curius *Aglauros* would fee what might be the matter,
And cheft vnclofed, difclofed a boy, with a ferpent.

There was a chatting Chough, which fpying down from an elmetree,
Saw all their dealings, and fhewd all vnto *Minerua*:
Who in ftead of thanks, this brew-bate crow did abandon,
And tooke *Nyctimene* transformd to an Owle, for her handmayd.
Thenceforth euery Chough, for a mock, was called a Iack-dawe;
And each prating Iack, beares yet this name of a Iack-dawe.

PAllas, qd Elpinus, *was* Ioues *daughter, borne of his head, without any mother: for, fapience and cœleftial wifdome is the gift of* Iupiter: *& her feate
is in the head: and women, though they haue many times too much witte, yet
haue they commonly as little wifedome. She was borne armed: wifdome is neuer weaponles; or, wifdome is the finew of warre.* Vulcan, *with an axe of A-
damant, did cut* Iupiters *head, whence* Pallas *proceeded, a pure and fpotles
Virgin. A Virgin; for, wantonnes and wifedome can neuer agree: Pure and
fpotles; for, that fuperior parte of the ayre, reprefented by* Iupiters *head, is
pure and incorruptible.* Mercurie *and* Minerua *were figured both together in
Vniuerfities; he noting eloquence, fhe fapience: that without this, is commonly
hurtfull, this without that, is feldome auayleable, both together are moft excellent. This was called* ἑρμαθήνη, *of* ἑρμῆς, Mercurie, *and* ἀθήνη, Minerua. *She had a
manly countenance and fierce: and glittering and flaming eyes. Her Helmet
was of gold: wifdome fhineth and is a gloriue protection. Her head is therwith
couered: wife men conceale their deuifes and cogitations; which was the caufe
alfo, why commonly there was on her helmet, the image of a* Sphinx, *betoken-
ing filence and fecrecie, hauing the head, face, and breaft of a mayden, the
wings of a bird, and the reft of the body like a Lyon: propounding obfcure rid-
dles, and deuouring thofe that could not vnfold them. Her fpeare is long: Valor and wifedome are mighty, and reach far. Her Shield is of Criftall: wifdome is bright and cleare. In her breaft-plate was* Gorgons *head: wifdome is
wonderfull to the wife, and maketh fooles amazed. The picture of* Pallas, *called* Palladium, *came downe from heauen into* Troy; *and, till it was gone,* Troy
*could not be taken: wifdome is cœleftiall, and the onely fafegarde of Cities, and
common wealths.*

I. 2   Pallas

Pallas *was so called because shee slew* Pallas *a Gyant: or, of shaking her speare,* ἀπὸ τοῦ πάλλειν τὸ δόρυ. Minerua, à memoria, *of memory, the treasury of wisdome : or,* à minuendo, *of diminishing: for, strength is diminished and weakned by earnest and continuall meditations: or,* à minando, *of menacing: for she is warlike as well as wise, and of* Bellum, *Warre, called also* Bellona: *though some distinguish them, making* Pallas *to note policie in wars; and* Bellona, *blood, slaughter, murder, and destruction.* Pallas *bare away the name of the city of* Athens, *by bringing foorth the* Olyue, *noting fertilitie, more beneficiall to Cities, then* Neptunes *horse, fit for warres: or, because students spend much oyle in their* Lamps, *as* Demosthenes *did, who was reported in al his life time not to haue consumed so much wine, as oyle: or, for that she first inuented the vse of oyle.*

*

ture
is
er.

Minerua *was also the Goddes of spinning, weauing, and curious working of cloath: and therefore was she figured sometimes with a distaffe in her hand. She reiected the Crow for his tatling: blabs be no companions for wise men, who vse to think before they speak, and yet not vtter all they think. In his place, she admitted the Owle, who seeth in darknes, and is solitary and silent: all which properties are agreeable to the conditions of a Philosopher & wise man.* Athens *was her chiefe delight:* Athens *was the most famous and learned Vniuersitie in all* Greece; *and she is the Lady of learning.*

*

ture
rua
li-

Now for the explication of this wooing of Minerua, Vulcan *must first be described: for, as by* Minerua, *the learned and witty contriuing of any worke is intended; so* Vulcan, *that is fire, is the instrument to effect these inuentions: and, because all thinges cannot be effectually wrought, which are cunningly deuised, therefore wooing* Vulcan *can neuer get* Mineruaes *good will. His hatte was of a skiecolor, bright and cleare, for, so is that cœlestiall fire of it selfe, but his feete are lame, and so is our earthly fire, impure, and not able to ascend vpwards directly, but shaketh and limpeth, this way, and that way, by reason of the terrene corruption: Or, if you take* Vulcan *for the naturall heate of mans body, then he may be therefore sayd to be lame, because this vitall heate doth increase, decrease, and alter, according to the difference of mens ages, and diuersity of the constitutions and complections of their bodies, and is neuer one and the same, or long like it self.* Iupiter *offended, to see this fowle babe* Vulcan *take his mothers part, threw him out of heauen: and he falling in the Isle* Lemnos, *brake his legge.*

Historically, he raigned in Ægypt, *was a stout warrior, halted by a wound receaued in battaile, & first found out the way to make armor of Iron; which gaue cause to these poeticall conceipts, calling him the black smith, forger of armor for all the Gods.* Vulcan *was maryed to* Venus: *for, without naturall heate, no procreation.* Vulcan *strugleth with* Minerua, *but to no purpose; for, of that æthereall fire, and subtile part of the skie, figured by* Minerua, *nothing is produced: But* Vulcan, *that is, the grosse and more earthly heate, powring himselfe on the earth, is the author of diuers and sundry procreations, noted by the diuers shape of* Ericthonius, *signifiyng strife, and the earth.* Ericthonius, *to couer his serpentine feete, inuented chariots to ride in. Historically, lame he was, and first author of chariots, by* Virgils *reporte: 3.* Georgic:

> Primus Ericthonius currus, & quatuor ausus
> Iungere equos, rapidifq; rotis insistere victor.

Vulcan *was also called* Mulciber, quasi Mulcifer, quià mulcet ferrum : *because the fire doth mollifie the hardnes of Iron, and maketh it malleable. He is paynted with a hat, as I sayd before, lame, black, swartie, filthy, for all the world like a smith at his forge.*

Next to Licoris *folowed* Aresia, *with a more pitifull-song, and fitter for her seuere and maydenlike disposition, wholly vowed to* Diana, *of whome she sang:*

L Ong, and far wandring *Cadmus* by the help of an earthborne
  Serpents broode, and good aduise of Lady *Minerua,*
Founded *Thebes* at last : but alas, no sooner he founded
Thebes, but vnhappy nephew, made grandsire *Cadmus* vnhappy.
Luckles, vnhappy nephew *Acteon,* ioyed in hunting,
Ouermuch hunting, til his own hounds hunted his own-self.
And yet no mischiefe did he work, but suffred a mischaunce,
No fault, but Fortune, causd his poore head to be horned.
  Acteon on a time from his house vntimely departed,
And to the green wood went with his hounds and huntf-men about him.
Morning all was spent, and *Phœbus* loftily mounted
Iust twixt East and Weast, drew euery shade to be shortest.
  Mates, sayd *Acteon,* it's now ful time to be resting;
Wee haue had good sport : now burning *Phœbus* on each side
Scalds vs, take vp toyles, and cease any more to be toyling;
Next day, eu'n by the break of day, wee'le back to the forrest.
  Acteons counsel was lik'te, his company rested,
Tooke vp tooles and toyles, and ceas't for a while to be toyling.
  There was a Dale, with Pine and Cypresse daintily shaded,
Called *Gargaphia,* sacred to the Lady *Diana.*
In whose furthest end was a playne and natural harbor,
And yet so pleasant, so sweet, so chearful a harbor,
That no arte could stayne this playne and natural harbor:

T

Harbor vauted aboue with bending bowes of a thousand
Tall trees: walled about with stones wrought only by nature,
And (which gaue most grace, and was to be chiefly regarded)
Watred sweetly within, with a bubling spring that abounded
with cleare cristal streames: whose brim was cherefuly mantled
With grasse, hearbs, and flowers: And here was lately ariued
Sou'raigne Lady regent of forrests, mighty *Diana*,
And her mayden troupes; with purpose there to be bathing
Their vnspotted limmes, all weake and weary with hunting.
And no sooner was that Virgin Lady ariued,
But quiuer, sharp dartes, and vnbent bow she deliu'red
Vnto her hand-mayd squire, who them with duety receaued.
Some pluck off buskins, some tuckt-vp roabes be remouing:
Nyphe brings water: *Crocale* stands still by *Diana*,
Fine-fingred *Crocale*, her loose hayre daintily tressing.
    But whilst Lady regent with a naked company guarded,
Washt her self in spring, and no-mans company feared,
In comes *Acteon*, from sleeping company seu'red,
In comes *Acteon*, by chance, to the company naked.
    Naked Nymphs seeing, that a man saw them to be naked,
Smote their naked breasts, and made so woful an out-cry,
That woods, wells, and caues in like sorte yeelded an out-cry:
And with naked breasts gaue cour'ing vnto the naked
Goddes their mistres, ioynd all in a round, in a compas.
But their matchles Queene, and Sou'raigne Lady *Diana*
Was too talle to be hid by that same company naked,
Ouer-lookt them quite, and so was seene to be naked:
And like scarlet clowdes, where *Tytans* beams be reflected,
Was their Mistres face, when she was seene to be naked:
Red for shame, and redfor griefe : for shame to be naked,
And for griefe much more, for griefe to be taken vnarmed.
Yet, thogh weaponles, she raught both hands to the wel-spring:
And *Acteons* face with water deadly besprinkling;
Now, sayd shee, go tel, that thou sawst Lady *Diana*
Naked, spare not a whit. This short narration ended,
Poore *Acteons* head with an ould Harts hornes she adorned,
Made eares sharp, nose flat, neck long, made armes to be spindle
Shancks, and fingers feet, and couered al with a specled
Hyde : and least any part of a Hart should seeme to be wanting,
Fearful thoughts, and fleeting legges are giu'n to the hartles
New hart *Acteon*, who feares, and flies by the forrest,
And, as he flies, wonders, that he flies so fast by the forrest.

But when he came to a brook,& saw his head to be horned,
And mouth enlarged, poore Hart,with terror amased
Whould haue cryed,Alas: but,alas,poore soule he deliu'red
Not so much as, Alas: sighs and brayes onely remayned
For to bewray his griefe,and teares powr'd foorth with abundance,
Trickling down his cheeks, not his own cheeks now,but a Harts cheeks.

Ofth'ould *Acteon,* th'ould minde now onely remayneth;
And this same ould minde is tost and turnd with a thousand
Conceits,cares,and feares. For, what shal he doe? shal he go home
Vnto the King and Queene,or wander alone by the desert?
Shame driu's *Acteon* fro the one;and feare fro the other:
Shame, on a King and Queene with a horned face,to be staring,
Feare,for a man forelorne by the desert stil to be wandring.

As thus he stood doubting, his dogs espied his horned
Head,light *Lælaps* first, with nimble-footed *Aello*
Called alowd to the rest; and then whole kennel aproached:
Nebrophonos, Dorceus, Harpya, Lycisca, Melampus,
Pamphagus, Agriodos, Pterelas, Hylæus, Hylactor:
These and as many more,through thick and thinne, by the wayles
Wayes, by the rocks and clyffes,by the hedge and ditch, by the desert
Run for a pray, and poore *Acteon* runs from his owne houndes,
And is chac'te himself, who was so lately a chacer,
Hunted of hounds himself, who that same day was a hunter:
Acteon makes sporte and play with his houndes in a morning,
And that selfsame day is a pray to his hounds by the eu'ning.
Oftentimes did he strayne himself, and sought to be speaking
Vnto his houndes,O leaue,leaue your vnnatural outrage,
Let your master alone : But no words could be aforded:
And the redoubled crie in mean time rang by the forrest.

Greedy *Melanchætes* did pinch him first by the haunches,
Next came *Theridamas : Oresitrophos* hangd by the shoulder.
These last,though latest, by crossing ouer a hill top,
Gayne-coapte *Acteon,* and held him fast,til his other
Hounds came trolling in: Who all so greedily fastned
On poore *Acteon,* that he scarce had so many morsels,
So many seu'ral bits, for so many houndes to be biting.
Acteon stil pluckt, stil powr'd foorth playnts to the forrest,
Groaned at euery gripe, and brayed at euery biting,
Groand as a man,brayd out as a Hart, and playnd as a Hart-man:
And on bended knees, with dolefull lookes he beholdes his
Hounds, and would, if he could, intreate and humbly beseech them.
But mery hunts-men cheare their houndes,and neuer imagin.

This

This to be *Acteon*: but looke each way by the forrest
For their *Acteon*; and hallow al by the forrest
For their *Acteon*,(*Acteon* shaked his horned
Head,when he heard his name) and al complaine,for his abfence
From fo goodly a fight,from fo vnlookt for a paftime;
Where poore *Acteon*,God knowes,did wifh to be abfent,
But was forced,alas,to be too vnluckily prefent,
And faw more then he fought,& felt much more thē he lookt for.
Curfed curres, Hell-hounds, their guts too greedily glutting,
Their Lord *Acteon*, inftead of a ftagge, be deuouring.
  So nothing but death, yea death by fo many deaths-wounds
Pleafd the reuenging minde of too too ftately *Diana*,
Yet not fo auftere , yet not fo ftately *Diana*,
But that her owld Mynion with a looke more louely regarding,
Beautiful *Endymion* fhe could finde time to be kiffing.

A Refia *had no fooner ended ; but* Elpinus,*feeing the day well fpent,began as* foloweth,*without expectation of any further commaund.* Diana *was fifter to* Phœbus, *and daughter to* Latona,*as I fayd before; Lady of hunting, regent of woods.* Diana *is fo called, as if a man would fay* Deuiana, *a ftragler or wanderer: for,the Moone ftrayeth from the Ecliticall line,as huntf-men wander in woods and forrefts,or els fhe may be called* Diana,*quià diem præcedit , becaufe fhe is, as it were, a fore-runner to the day. She is alfo called* Luna, *à luce, of her light:figured with a fweet and amiable looke, and maydenlike face, her garments tuckt vp, her quiuer on her back,a fire brand in her hand: noting either the pinching torments of child-birth, whereof fhe alfo (by reafon of her moyfture) is a Goddes, or the light which fhee afordeth for direction of men in the night feafon,whereof fhe is the gouerneffe. Her chariot is drawen by white* Harts; Harts *be fwift, and the* Moone *doth fooneft difpatch her reuolution. She is fifter to* Phœbus, *and therefore called* Phœbe,*for, fhe boroweth light from him; and they two equally deuide the time betweene them, hee ruling the day fhe the night. Her garment is changeable: the* Moone *hath diuers* φασις, *and apparitions. Her daughter was* Herfe,*that is* Deaw,*whom fhe conceaued of* Iupiter. *Her fhaftes note her influence.*

  She *is alfo called* Hecate. ιϰατον *fignifieth an hundred: which fimple & determinate number, is put for an infinite or great number : meaning,that the* Moone *hath many and infinite operations in and ouer thefe inferior bodies.She had three faces,called for that,* Triuia,Triformis,*and* Tergemina. *For,in heauen fhe is called* Luna, *in the woods* Diana,*vnder the earth* Hecate,*or* Proferpina. *That of thefe three faces,which was on the right fide , was the face and head of a horfe, figuring the fwiftnes of the* Moone *in ending her reuolution.*

The left was of a dogge, noting that when she hideth her self from vs she is then
Proserpina *with her hellish hounde : the middle was of a boare, signifying her*
iurisdiction in fields and forrests. When the Gods fled into Ægypt, *for feare of*
Typhoeus, *and euery one transformed himselfe to some vncoth shape,* Luna
turned herselfe into a cat; who seeth in the night, aswell as in the day : and
her sight doth increase: and decrease, accordingly and proportionably to the
Moone.

It is historically reported, that Cadmus *vanquishing one* Draco, *King of*
Beotia, *established himselfe in his throne : and that afterwards, being beset*
with the friends of the dead King, who all combined themselues together to re-
uenge his death, he politikely, with seditious rumors, set them together by the
eares among themselues, and so distracting and seuering their forces, easilie
ouercame them: and this he did, by the aduise of Pallas *: it being a part of wis-*
dome, by these meanes to weaken the aduersaries power, which otherwise vnited
would be more strong.   Others, by the dragons teeth sowed by Cadmus *in* Beotia, *vnderstand letters, which he first brought out of* Ægypt *into* Greece *:*
and, by the seditious and murdering brethren, they meane the men learned and
lettred the one still confuting and oppugning the other. Nazianzenus *hereby*
noteth them that abruptly climbe vp to honor and dignitie, from base and lowe
degree, without either vertue or erudition.

Actæon *fed and maintained a number of idle and vnthankefull persons, no-*
ted by his doggs. Others expounde it thus : we ought not to be ouer curious and
inquisitiue in spying and prying into those matters, which be aboue our reache,
least we be rewarded as Actæon *was.* Ouid. 2. de tristib.

Inscius Actæon vidit sine veste dianam:
Præda fuit canibus non minus ille suis.
Scilicet in superis, etiam fortuna luenda est,
Nec veniam læso numine casus habet.

Or lastly, thus, a wiseman ought to refraine his eyes, from beholding sensible
and corporall bewty, figured by Diana *: least, as* Actæon *was deuoured of his*
owne doggs, so he be distracted and torne in peeces with his owne affections, and
perturbations.   The names of his hounds are all set from the naturall quali-
ties and proprieties of doggs : Lælaps, Aello, Nebrophonos, Dorceus, Harpya, Lycisca, Melampus, Pamphagus, Agriodos, Ptcrelas, Hylæus, Hylactor, Melanchætes, Theridamas, Oresitrophos *: signifying, Swift, Tempest,*
Killbuck, Spy, Snatch, Woolfe, Blackefoote, Eateal, Sauage, Lightfoote, Wood-
man, Ringwood, Black, Kildeare, Hillebread.

Endymion *watching in the night, to obserue the course of the Moone in the*
Hill Latmos, *was said to be kissed of the Moone. Which may also be the cause*

why they of Theſſalia *were ſaide to force the* Moone *downe from Heauen,
with their charmes and incantations , for that they were very curious in
noting her nature and reuolution.* Endymion, *by ſome others,is a figure of
the ſoule of man, kiſſed of* Diana *in the hill, that is , raniſhed by celeſtiall
contemplation.*

Pan *enticed the Moone into the woods,by giuing her a faire fleece of white
wooll : that is to ſay , nature doth induce and perſwade the ſoule , by the gift
of ſenſible bewty, to come downe into this world of generation, and propagation
ſignified by the wood;* Virgil *hath ſome ſuch thing.* 3. *Georgecon.*

Munere ſic niueo lanæ (ſi credere dignum eſt)
Pan deus Arcadiæ captam,te,Luna,fefellit,
In nemora alta vocans;nec tu aſpernata vocantem.

Faire Venus *was now left for faire* Caſſiopæa : *who thus diſcouered the
loue betweene her and* Adonis.

Myrrha,the fathers hoore,and brothers mother,a myrrhor
Of moſt monſtrus luſt,was late transformd to a Myrrh-tree :
O how could ſweete Myrrh come from ſo ſinful a *Myrrha?*
Myrrha made Myrrh-tree,brought forth inceſtuus offſpring,
And yet moſt delicate,moſt ſweete,moſt bewtiful offſpring,
Dame *Natur's* dearling,heu'ns ioy,worlds woonder, *Adonis.*
Either take wings,bowe,and ſhafts from louely *Cupido,*
Or giue bowe and ſhafts,and wings to the loued *Adonis;*
And let louely *Cupid* ſtand hard by loued *Adonis*
Either on others ſide, and aske, who liſt,the beholders,
Which is louely *Cupid,* which is this loued *Adonis;*
Euery man will ſwere,that both àre louely *Cupidoes,*
Both are Lords of loue, and neither loued *Adonis,*
So like euery way were loue and loued *Adonis.*
Yea ſuch grace,ſuch face,ſuch eyes had loued *Adonis,*
That very *Enuies* eyes muſt needes praiſe loued *Adonis.*
Lord,how ſwift is time,and ſlideth away on a ſudden
Vnperceaud,vnſpide? That wretched,lewdly begotten,
Siſters,grandſires ſon,cloſd yeſterday in a Myrrhe-tree,
Borne but yeſterday,is now ſo louely an infant,
Sweete childe,tall ſpringall,braue youth; that Queene *Cytheræa*
Loues natures dearling,heu'ns ioy,worlds woonder *Adonis.*
Lord of loue,by a chaunce,as he playd with Queene *Aphrodite*
His louing mother,did raſe her breaſt with an arrowe.
Hence,qd Lady *Venus,* with this ſame paltery arrowe;

And putts back her son:but that same paltery arrow
Gaue her a deeper wound indeede,then first she beleeued.

Now *Cytherean* bowres and towres *Cytheræa* renounceth,
Fishy *Cnidos*,with watry *Paphos Cytheræa* refuseth,
Yea leaues heau'n it selfe for loue , for loue of *Adonis*.
Now she delites to be gay,and frames her lookes to be louely,
Trims and tricks her selfe,and all for loue of *Adonis*.
Sometimes downe by a well with *Adonis* sweetly she sitteth,
And on *Adonis* face in well-spring louely she looketh,
And then *Adonis* lipps with her owne lipps kindely she kisseth,
Rolling tongue,moyst mouth with her owne mouth all to be sucking,
Mouth and tong and lipps,with *Ioues* drinck *Nectar* abounding.

Sometimes, louely records for *Adonis* sake,she reciteth;
How *Leander* dyde, as he swamme to the bewtiful *Hero*,
How great *Alcides* was brought from a club to a distaffe,
How *Medea* the witch causd golden fleece to be conquerd,
What lost *Euridice*; who first came safely to *Circe*.

Sometimes vnto the shade of a braunched beech she repaireth,
Where sweete bubling brooke with streames of siluer aboundeth,
And faire-feathred birde on tree-top cherefuly chirpeth;
There her voyce,which makes eu'n *Ioue* himselfe to be ioying,
Vnto the waters fall,and birds chirpe ioyfuly tuning.

Sometimes vnto the woods,and pleasant parks she resorteth,
With tuckt-vp garments,and Quiuer,like to *Diana*,
And there harmeles game pursu's with loued *Adonis*,
Trembling hare,swift hart,and Roebuck loftyly horned:
As for Beares,and Woolu's,and such wilde beasts, she detested,
Lest any harme might chaunce,by the chace thereof,to *Adonis*.

Whilst that Lady *Venus* did thus conuerse with *Adonis*,
Making more account of a heauens-ioy,then a heauen,
Ioue sent forth summons through purple-veiled *Olympus*,
Forth-with commaunding all Gods and euery goddes,
There at a stately triumph,on a certeine time to be present.
Then was Lady *Venus* compelld to returne to *Olympus*
Greatly against her minde,and leaue her loued *Adonis*:
And yet afore she returnd,shee turnd herselfe to *Adonis*,
And thus tooke her leaue,last leaue of loued *Adonis*.

Sweete boy,sith that I must of force now goe to *Olympus*,
(Neuer afore did I so vnwilling goe to *Olympus*)
Make much of thyself, and ile make haste from *Olympus*.
Sweete boy,looke to thyself,goe not too oft to the forrest,
Where sharpe-tusked boares,and rau'nous woolus be resorting,

And

And ſtrong ſtoordy Lyons are each where fearefuly roaring.
Parks and launds are walkes more meete for yonker *Adonis*,
Harts and Hyndes are game more fit for gentle *Adonis*:
Tis no wit, ſweete boy, with a greater foe to be ſtriuing,
Tis no wit, to be ſtout with ſtrong, to be haughty with hardy :
Forbeare for my ſake, for my feare learne to be fearefull,
Meddle not with beaſts, whoſe euery limme is a weapon,
Euery ſtroake is death : leaſt too ſtowtharted *Adonis*
Buy his praiſe too deare : thy face, yeares, bewty, behauiour
Which poſſeſſe my ſoule, wil neuer moue the deuouring
Woolues, and briſtled ſwine, wil neuer finde any fauour
In blood-thirſting eyes of a rugged bare, or a raging
Ougly Lyon, moſt ougly Lyon ; whoſe merciles oſſpring
Chiefly of all other wilde beaſts *Cytberæa* deteſteth.
Then ſhe begins to recount, how fayre and ſwift *Atalanta*
Chaunſt at length in race to be ouercome, by the golden
Apples, which herſelfe of her owne grace, gaue to the thanckles
Hippomenes, whoſe loue was therefore turnd to a lewd luſt,
So lewd ; that *Cybeles* temple was ſowly defiled,
And themſelues to Lyons, for a iuſt plague, ſpeedily changed,
Drawing her chariot, whoſe church they lately prophaned.
     Then, qd ſhee, fly theſe ; and not theſe only, but all thoſe
Beaſts, that will not fly. Such counſel gaue ſhe *Adonis*,
But no ſuch counſel would ſerue too youthful *Adonis*.
For, no ſooner was ſweete ſea-borne Nymph *Aphrodite*
Conueyd in chariot by ſiluer ſwans to *Olympus*,
But to the wilde wood went too wilde and wilful *Adonis* :
Where, when his hounds on a time, by chaunce, had rowzed a wilde-boare,
Himſelfe ſets on firſt, and boare in a brauery woundeth.
Boare enrag'de, runs forth, with foaming tusk, to *Adonis*,
And teares thoſe very parts, thoſe tendreſt parts of *Adonis*,
Which were ſtil moſt deare to *Adonis* deare *Aphrodite*,
Teares, and wounds, and kills *Aphrodites* loued *Adonis*.
     And now, eu'n iuſt now, when wilde Boare murdred *Adonis*,
Ioues great gueſts were gone, and all ſolemnities ended,
And ſweete louely *Venus* from *Olympus* newly departed;
Thinking euery howre to be two, and two to be twenty,
Til ſhe beheld her boy : but alas too ſoone, ſhe beheld him :
Downe fro the skies ſhe beheld her long-lookt loued *Adonis*
Diſmembred, wounded, with his owne blood all to beſprinckled.
     Then to the dolefull dale, where murdred *Adonis* abideth,
Her milke-white courſers, with might and maine ſhe directeth,

Leaps downe, rents her roabes, and poore breast all to bebeateth,
Teares hayre, scratcheth face, and deathswound deadly bewaileth.

Hellish Fates, qd shee, though world be depriu'd of *Adonis*
Corps, and loued lymmes, by you ; yet world, to the worlds end,
In despite of you, shall yearely remember *Adonis*,
Yearely remember mee, by remembring yearely *Adonis*.
Yea, this purpled blood wil I speedily turne to a purple
Flowre ; which shalbe a grace to the ground insteede of *Adonis*.
If that *Apollo* could transforme his boy *Hyacinthus*
Into a flowre for a fame, to the mourning flowre *Hyacinthus*,
Which stil beares, ay, ay, in leaues, in signe of a wailing :
If that *Apollo* could his dolefull boy *Cyparissus*
Turne to a dolefull tree, to the ioyles deadly *Cupressus*,
Shall not Lady *Venus* doe the like for loued *Adonis?*

Then with life-giuing *Nectar*, sweete blood she besprinkleth,
And the besprinkled blood, with a round top swells, as a buble :
Purpled round by degrees, is speedily changd to a purpled
Flowre, that beares faire leaues, and fraile leaues ; euery winde-puffe
Blowes them away. So good things goe, so dyed *Adonis :*
Flowre fades, eye dazeleth, face wrinkleth, bewty decayeth.

CAssiopæa, *said* Elpinus, *hath so passionately discoursed of* Venus *and* Adonis, *that I feare me, vnder these names, she mourneth her owne loue, and
vttreth her owne affection. Howsoeuer it be ;* Saturnus, *that is,* Tyme, *with his
sithe, as I said elsewhere, cut off his fathers manlike parts : of which, cast into
the sea,* Venus *was borne. So* Saturne *destroyeth,* Venus *bringeth foorth ;
and both are necessary for the continuall propagation of these inferior bodies,
sith the corruption of one, is the generation of another.* Venus *is faire, bewty
enticeth to lust. She is naked, loue cannot be concealed. She is borne of the sea,
louers are inconstant, like the troubled waues of the sea : Hereof was shee also
called* Aphrodite, *of the froath of the sea, being like to* Sperma. *Shee is called*
Venus, *qd* ad omnia veniat, *or else,* à venustate : *Swans and Doues drawe
her chariot ;* Doues *are wanton, and* Swans *are white and musicall, both being
meanes to procure loue and lust.* Myrrha *is sacred vnto her, so is the rose also :
that, because it is thought to cause loue ; this, because it is fayre and fraile,
pleasant and pricking, hauing a thorne aswell as a flowre, as loue hath. In* Saxo-
ny, *she was figured naked, in a chariot drawne with two* Swannes *and two
doues, her head bound with myrtle leaues, a burning starre on her breast, a
globe representing the earth, in her right hand, and three golden apples in her
left : Behinde her were the three* graces, *back to back, hand in hand, and apples
in their hand.*

The

The firſt picture of Venus.

Now, for Venus *her loue to* Adonis, *and lamentation for his death : by* Adonis, *is meant the ſunne, by* Venus, *the vpper hemiſphere of the earth (as by* Proſerpina *the lower) by the boare, winter : by the death of* Adonis, *the abſence of the ſunne for the ſixe wintrie monetbs; all which time, the earth lamenteth :* Adonis *is wounded in thoſe parts, which are the inſtruments of propagation : for, in winter the ſon ſeemeth impotent, and the earth barren : neither that being able to get, nor this to beare either fruite or flowres : and therefore* Venus *ſits, lamentably hanging downe her head, leaning on her left hand, her garments all ouer her face.*

*

Pontanus *expreſſeth it thus,*

> Terra etenim ſolem queritur deſerta cadentem,
> Inuidit quem triſtis hyems, cui ſæuior apri
> Horret cana gelu facies, cui plurimus imber
> Crine madet, geminos & cùm malè contudit armos.
> Ac veluti virgo abſenti cum ſola marito
> Suſpirat ſterilem lecto traducere vitam,
> Illius expectans amplexus anxia charos:
> Cum grauidos aperitq; ſinus, & terra relaxat
> Spiramenta, nouas veniat quà ſuccùs in herbas,
> Diglomeratq; niues, & grandine verberat auras.
> Nam cùm ſol rebus præſit pater ipſe creandis,
> Vt ſeſe ad manes brumæ ſub frigore transfert,
> Tum tellus vidua ſulcos oblimat in alno,
> Et tandem complexa ſinum lætatur Adonim.

Adonis *was turnd to a fading flowre; bewty decayeth, and luſt leaueth the luſtfull, if they leaue not it.* Equicola, *expoundeth it thus :* Adonis *was borne of* Myrrha; Myrrhe *prouoketh luſt :* Adonis *was kilde by a boare, that is, he was ſpent and weakened by old age :* Venus *lamenteth, luſt decayeth.*

The companions of Venus *were the three Graces; virgins, free, mery, amiable, all ioyning together. So good turns muſt bee willingly aforded without grudging. Some make* Mercury *their leader, becauſe good turns ill beſtowed, he bad turns;* benefacta malè collocata malefacta arbitror, *therefore wiſdome and diſcretion. figured by* Mercury, *is here requiſite. The firſt of them is* Euphroſyne, *of* εὐφροσύνη, *to make mery, to cheare and comfort : the ſecond* Aglaia *of* ἀγλαΐα, *to bewtifie. The third* Pithus, *of* πειθώ, *to perſwade; or,* Thalia, *floriſhing, as others name her. Some make them winged, becauſe a good turne is litle worth, vnles it come quickly.*

Gratia

Gratia,quæ tarda eſt,ingrata eſt gratia : namque
Cùm properat fieri gratia,grata magis.

*Two of them looke towards vs,and one fromwards vs : we muſt yeeld double
thanks,and double requitall for good turnes. They be in greeke called* χαεɪηϛ,
ὑπι τὶ χαεɛ̑η, *of mirth and ioy.* Natalis Comes *referreth it to the tilling and
fertiltie of the earth.*

*

*The one hath in her hand a roſe,the ſecond a Dye,the third,a braunch of mir-
tle. The roſe noteth ioy : the Dye is a token,that they ought to come in courſe.
The myrtle,that they ſhould neuer be forgotten,but alwaies floriſh and continue
freſh and greene.*

Before wee leaue Venus, *wee muſt remember her ſonne* Cupido, *who, (to
omit the philoſophicall diſcourſes of the* Platoniſts *concerning diuers loues)
was pictured,a boy ; louers are childiſh : blinde ; they ſee no reaſon : naked ;
they cannot conceale their paſſions : winged ; loue ſoone flieth into our eyes
and ſoules,and louers are light,as feathers. His bowe and arrowes note, that
he hitteth a farre off:his burning lampe,the quickning light,and yet conſuming
heate of loue,* Dulcis amaror amor.

Venus *hauing brought forth* Cupid, *and ſeeing that he did not thriue, and
growe ; was told by* Themis, *that if* Eros *had* Anteros, *if* Cupid *had another
Cupid for his brother,who might contend in loue with him, he would doe well.*
Venus *hereupon,brought forth* Anteros, *and preſently* Eros *reuiued , loue was
luſty : and,as the one increaſed or decreaſed,ſo did the other,neuer deliting, but
either in others loue and liking.* Eros *was figured with a branche of palme in
his hand :* Anteros *contended to wreſt it from him,but could not. Hee that
will be loued,muſt loue :* vt amèris,amabilis eſto. *We muſt contend to ouercome and get the palme and victory,by louing more,then we be loued,ſo ſhall we
ſtill be loued more,* Fomes amoris amor.

*

Many yong wags wayte on great Cupido : *they are borne of Nymphs ;
yong , naked , and haue curled hayre , and changeable colored winges :
ſometimes with a lampe or a bowe , ſometimes without either bowe or
Lampe.*

Moſchus *in his wandring and fugitiue* Cupid, *maketh him not blinde, but
hauing bright and cleare eyes.* Taſſo *hath the like in Italian, to that of* Moſchus *in greeke.*

*The particuler hiſtories briefely tutcht in this tale, as by the way, may as
briefely be thus expounded.* Leander *and* Heroes *loue is in euery mans mouth :
the light of the lanterne or lampe extinct (that is , naturall heate fayling)*

luſt decayeth, and Leander toſſed with the cold ſtorme of old age, is at laſt drowned. Ouid *in his epiſtles paſſionately ſetteth it downe, and* Boſcan *hath made a
whole volume of it in ſpaniſh, entituled* Hiſtoria de Leandro y Hero, *beginning
thus,*

> Canta con voz ſuaue y doloroſa,
> O muſa, los amores laſtimeros,
> Que en ſuaue dolor fueron criados.
> Canta tambien la triſte mar in medio,
> Y à Seſto de vna parte, y d'otra Abido, &c.

Hercules *was alſo called* Alcides, *of* ἀλϰη *force and might: he was the ſun of*
Iupiter *and* Alcmena: μηνος *is ſtrength and prowes. So then,* Hercules *is the type
of a valiant, conſtant, and reſolute* Heros, *borne of* Iupiter, *that is, endued with
all heauenly qualities effected by* Ioues *influence, and ſo borne, as to purchaſe
himſelfe eternall fame and glorious renowne through the world by his admirable aduentures: which for that they were attempted and atcheeued by the mali-
tious inſtigation and prouocation of* Iuno; *himſelfe was thereof in Greeke named accordingly : for,* ἡρα *is* Iuno; *and* ϰλεος *glory, or renowne, as I haue already
mentioned : others had rather deriue the name,* ἀπὸ τῆς ἀρετῆς *which noteth vertue
& valor. In his infancie he ſtrangled two ſnakes; the meaning is, that he began
euen then to repreſſe wantonnes. Afterwards hee ſlew a* Lyon; *noting wrath,
pride, and crueltie; & ouercame* Hydra, *the almoſt inuincible, & ſtill breeding
beaſt,* Enuy. Hydra *lurked in moores & fennes;* Enuy *creepeth on the ground, in
baſe and abiect breſts.* Troy *could not be taken without his arrowes: his arrowes
are a figure of heroicall fortitude. He wreſtled with* Antæus, *who euer throwne
downe to the earth, receaued new ſtrength from the earth, till at laſt, hee lifted
him vp, and ſtrangled him in the ayre : ſo the ſpirit ſtill ſtriueth with the body,
but neuer can ouercome it, till he lift it vp ſo high from the ground, that with his
feete, to weete his affections, he receaue no new aſſiſtance from his mother the
earth.* Diomedes, *who fed his mares with mans fleſh, was by* Hercules *enforced to feede them with his owne body. By* Diomedes *mares, ſome vnderſtand
his whooriſh daughters, who robbed and conſumed all that came vnto them. He
killed the mighty* Hart, *he freed mens hearts from feare. He was euer couered
with the* Lyons *ſpoyle : a valiant man vſeth open and* Lionlike *prowesse, and
not treacherous and* foxelike *wiles. He brake one of the hornes of the huge riuer*
Achelous: *he reduced one part of the ſaide riuer into his woonted courſe, which
was the cauſe of great fertilitie to all the countrey : and therefore it is ſaide,
that the horne was dekt with flowres, and called* Cornucopiæ, *the Horne of a-
boundance. He fetcht away the golden apples of the* Heſperides, *kept by the
watching Dragon:* Heſperides, *the daughters of* Heſperus, *are the ſtarres:
their garden is in the weaſt, wherein grow golden apples : for ſuch is the nature
of the ſtarres, to gliſter like gold, and ſeeme round in ſhew like apples. They grow*

in the weast, because the stars neuer appeare, but when the sunne setteth, and that is in the weast: for, all the day long they are obscured, by the surpassing light of the sunne. The neuer-sleeping Dragon, that watcheth these apples & keepeth the garden, is the cyrcle, called Signifer. Hercules *brought these into* Grece, *that is, he brought* Astrologie *into his countrey. So was he, for the same cause, fayned to beare the heauens on his shoulders, whilst* Atlas *rested himself: because he learned* Astrologie *of* Atlas: *who is therefore sayd to holde vp the heauens, because he continually obserued the motions of the heauens, and was thereof called* Atlas, *of* α, *which here is a note of augmentation, and* τλᾶμι, *to beare and sustaine. The* Pleïades *and* Hyades *be called his daughters, because he first noted their course, and obserued their operation.* Ouid *in the fourth of his transformations maketh this* Atlas *to be a king of* Mauritania, *turned to a mountaine of his owne name, when* Perseus *had shewed him* Gorgons *head, for denying him entertainment. In trueth,* Atlas *is a most huge and high hill in* Mauritania, *so threatning the heauens, that it gaue beginning to this fiction. Sometimes* Hercules *is paynted olde and balde, with his club, bow, and shafts, & smal chaynes or wyres drawen from his toung, to othermens eares: signifiyng, that his sweete toung wrought more, then his strong body: and that the aged eloquence is most piercing and aualeable, as* Homer *maketh manifest vnder the person of olde* Duke Nestor. *

The | of He Galli

Thus did Hercules *his searching and heroicall heart leaue nothing vnattempted: but by his reaching capacitie, and inquisitiue speculation, pierced through heauen and hel: yet alas he that ouercame all, was at last ouercome himselfe: He that maistred men, was whipped by a woman, and enforced by her to spinne and handle a distaffe in stead of an Iron clubbe: so doth wantonnes effeminate the most warlike hearts, and so much harder it is, to resist pleasure, then not to be ouercome by payne. At length hauing passed through so many perils, and being infected with a shirt sent him from* Deïanira, *and polluted with the venymous blood of the* Centaure Nessus, *he burnt himselfe on the mount* Oeta: *that is to say, his terrestriall body being purged and purified, himselfe was afterwards deified and crowned with immortality.*

Medea *signifieth counsayle and aduice; the daughter of* Æeta, *and* Idya: *for* εἰδῄα, *is knowledge or vnderstanding, and knowledge is the mother of counsayle.* Medea *therefore (that is, such as are wise and aduised) leaueth her father, & teareth in peeces her brother and children: to weete, all such affections as might be a let vnto her, and flyeth away with* Iason, *the phisitian and curer of her infirmities,* ἀπὸ τῦ ἰᾶσαι, *to heale or cure. But when* Iason *giues himselfe ouer to filthines, then doth* Medea, *good counsel, flie away in her chariot drawne with winged Dragons, noting wisdome and policie.* Iason *was many wayes endangered, before he could atchieue the golden fleece: there is no man that can attayne to any excellency, without extraordinarie labour. The golden fleece noteth either great riches and treasure, or fame and immortality.*

Euridice, *the wife of* Orpheus, *figureth* Appetitum, *the coueting and desiring faculty in man. The serpent byting her heele, is affection & concupisence: for, veynes come from the heeles to those parts which are the instruments of lust. Therefore when* Thetis *washt her sonne* Achilles *in the Stygian waters, he was inuiolate and vnwoundable in euery part of his body, sauing only his heele, by the which she held him when she washed him, and in the same heele was hee wounded by* Paris *in the temple of* Apollo, *when he came to mary* Polixena, *that is to say, affection and lust to* Polixena *drew on his confusion.   In imitation whereof, the good* Thomalin *in the new Shepheards Kalender, singeth thus of the winged boy.*

        Therewith afrayd I ran away:
        But he that earst seem'd but to play,
            a shaft in earnest snatched:
        And hit me running in the heele;
        For then, I litle smart did feele,
            but soone the sore increased:
        And now itranckleth more and more,
        And inwardly it festreth sore,
            ne wot I how to ceafe it.

Orpheus *the husband of* Euridice, *an eloquent and wise man, so wrought the rude people, that he made them sociable and conformable: when he obteined the bringing backe of his wife from Hell, he was inioyned not once to looke back towards her: A wise man ought not to be withdrawen from his contemplation, by any passion or affection whatsoeuer.*

    Circe *may be either physically or ethically expounded: physically thus, She was called* Circe, à miscendo, *of mingling and tempring : for in the generation of bodies, these foure elements, as we call them, must needs bee tempered: which commixtion and composition is done by the influence and operation of the Sunne: and therefore* Circe *was borne of the Sunne and* Perseis, *the daughter of* Occanus. Perseis *or* Perse *is the humor and moysture of the Ocean, supplying the place of the matter or the woman, as the sunne is the efficient or the man.* Circe *had foure maydens, the foure elements: they gathered hearbs and flowres for her witcherie; these elements are autors of all motions and alterations.* Circe *her selfe is immortall; the generation of things is perpetuall. She transformed men into diuers shapes: for, as I sayd before, the corruption of one is the generation of another, not the same, but altred and transformed. She dwelt in the Isle* Æa, *so called of the groaning and wayling of mortall bodies, which by reason of the decay and dissolution of this bodylie composition, are subiect to diseases and griefes: for, ae, ae, ai, ai, signisieth,*

nisieth,

wisieth, alas, alas. She could not transforme Vlysses: the soule cannot be destroyed, though his companions, noting the elements coherent to the body, were changed. Shee wrought many wonders by inchaunting, she darkned the Moone, stayed the waters, dryed the fountaynes, burnt grasse and hearbes, and so foorth; vnorderly mixtion or composition, with abundance of vapours lifted vp, darken the moone, and worke twenty such like inconueniences. Ethically thus, lust is caused of heate and moysture, the Sunne, and Perseis: If she ouer rule vs, she transformeth vs into the shapes of seuerall beasts, according to the sundry beastly pleasures wherein we delight: vnles some heauenly helpe be aforded vs, as was to Vlysses. so Homer fayneth some of Vlysses companions to be deuoured by Polypheme the Cyclops, some by the Lestrigones, and some swallowed vp of Scylla, and such as were not dismayed with perils and daungers, did yet yeeld and giue ouer themselues to pleasure and sensualitie, whereof diuers became effeminate with the delicacie of the wanton Phæaces: and others in the region of the Lothophagi, by tasting forren fruit, did forget their own coutrey. The third sort, that resisted both pleasure & paine, was ouercome with couetise; and, whilst Vlysses slept, opened the bagg stuft with winde (which AEolus shut vp, and gaue to Vlysses) hoping it had been stoared with treasure. Lastly, a number of them drawen away with ambition and vayn-glorie, would haue yeelded to the deceiptfull sweetnes of the Syrenes, had not their Capten stopped their eares with waxe, as I sayd els-where, and caused himself to be bound to the mast of the ship: only Vlysses escaped, by heauenly help only, and liued with Circe familiarly. Horace,

> Rursus quid virtus, & quid sapientia possit,
> Vtile proposuit nobis exemplar Vlyssem,
> Qui domitor Troiæ, multorum prouidus vrbes,
> Et mores hominum inspexit, latumq; per æquor
> Dum sibi, dum socijs reditum parat, aspera multa
> Pertulit, aduersis rerum immersabilis vndis.
>
> Sirenum voces, & Circes pocula nosti,
> Quæ, si cum socijs stultus cupidusq; bibisset,
> Sub domina meretrice fuisset turpis & excors,
> Vixisset canis immundus, vel amica luto sus.
>
> Nos numerus sumus, & fruges consumere nati,
> Sponsi Penelopes, nebulones, Alcinoiq;
> In cute curanda plus æquo operata iuuentus,
> Cui pulchrum fuit in medios dormire dies, &
> Ad strepitum cytharæ cessatum ducere curam.

Atalantaes swiftnes is stayed, and her selfe out-run by golden apples: for, what cannot gold effect? She & Hippomenes are turnd to Lyons: lust is furius.

They being made Lyons, are afterwards tamed, bridled, and enforced to draw
Cybeles chariot: by olde age luſt and loue are calmed. Hyacinthus *his death*
teacheth vs not to toy; and Cypariſſus, *not to mourne too much for a thing of*
naught.
The Paſtors being now ouertaken by the Nymphs, began to beſtirre them-
ſelues: among others, Ergaſtus, *whoſe courſe was then come, ioyned* Hermaphroditus *to his mother* Venus, *much after this manner.*

L Ouing Lady *Venus,* bare *Mercury, Hermaphroditus,*
　Hermaphroditus, a youth ſo braue and like to the father,
Hermaphroditus, a boy ſo ſweete and like to the mother,
That, whoſoeuer knew *Hermes* and *Aphrodite,*
And lookt on braue youth, on ſweet boy *Hermaphroditus,*
Would ſay, Lady *Venus* bare *Mercury Hermaphroditus.*
　　Water-nymphs for a time brought vp this yonker in *Ida;*
But when ſixteen yeares were ſpent by the yonker in *Ida,*
Yonker could not abide, to abide any longer in *Ida.*
　　All his ioy was now his fortune for to be trying,
And forren countreyes with curius eye to be ſeeing,
And outlandiſh wells, and vnknowne ſprings to be knowing.
After much traueling, many ſtrange ſights, and many wonders;
At laſt, from *Lycian* borders his courſe he directed
Vnto the neighbor coaſts of *Caria:* where he ariued
Hard by a criſtall poole, poole criſtal-cleare to the bottome,
And ſo tranſparent, that a man might eaſily number
Euery ſmaleſt ſtone, from th'vtmoſt brim to the bottome.
There no barren recke, no pricking reede was abounding,
There no ſedge, no ruſh, no mooriſh weede had abiding:
But with fayre green turfe pooles brinck was chearfuly bordred,
Green turfe with freſh ſlowres & ſweet hearbs daintily painted.
There no boyes pluckt flowres their gay noſegaies to be making,
Nor no nymphs: but a nymph: one nymph, and only but one nymph,
One and only but one; but no ſuch one in a thouſand.
For, neither car'd ſhee ſarre-wounding bow to be bearing,
Nor with quick-ſent hounds by the green-hewd woods to be hunting,
Nor with water-nymphs by the ſmiling meades to be walking,
Nor to *Dianaes* court with tuckt-vp coate to be trudging.
　　Her ſeallow Fayries, ſtil prayd, and dayly deſired;
Salmacis, either take thee a darte, or a feathered arrow,
And intermingle theſe idle toyes, with a fruitfull
And commendable acte, and ſporte of mighty *Diana.*
Yet ſhe neither tooke her a darte, nor a feathered arrow,

Nor would intermingle her idle toyes, with a fruitful
And commendable act, and ſport of mighty *Diana:*
But contents her ſelf with dayly domeſtical Harbor:
Bathes her loued limmes, fit for ſo louly a water,
Sits on flowring banck, and combs her ſweetly beſeeming
Hayre, & lookes to the lake, and guides her combe by the water.
Now her fayreſt ſelf, with fineſt lawne ſhe adorneth,
And fayre ſelf, fine lawne on tender graſſe ſhe repoſeth:
Now fro the paunce to the roſe, fro the roſe to the lilly ſhe wandreth,
And herſelf with paunce, with roſe, with lilly ſhe paynteth.

 Whilſt ſhe bepaynts her ſelf with a paunce, with a roſe, with a lilly,
Hard by the pearl-bright brooke, ſhe beheld fayre *Hermaphroditus*,
Hermaphroditus a far; ſo like to a God, to a goddes;
That ſhee wiſht him a God, yet feard that he might be a Goddes.
But when man-like roabes declar'd that he was not a woman,
Salmacis all on fire his diuine beautie deſired,
Salmacis all on thornes, for ſo ſweete company longed,
Yet ſtayd, though on thornes, til her head, face, coate ſhe had ordred,
And made all things fine, and then to the boy ſhe repayred.

 O ſweete boy, whoſe more then mortall beauty deſerueth
For to be deemed a God, what God ſhal I call the my ſweete boy?
If that thou be a God, thou ſeemſt to be goodly *Cupido:*
If but a man, moſt happy the man, who might be thy father,
Happy the woman, whom thy ſweet ſelf mad'ſt to be mother,
Happy the Nymph, whom ſo braue brother cauſd to be ſiſter,
Happy the nurſe, whoſe milk did ſeede ſo chearful a ſuckling:
But much more bleſſed, but much more happy then all theſe,
Were that laſſe indeede, who might be thy wife, be thy bed-maker
If thou haue any wife, let mee be thy loue for a ſhort time,
If thou haue no wife, let mee be thy friend for a long time:
Whether a husband bound, or whether free as a batchler,
Giue me a lawfull ioy, or priuily doe me a pleaſure.

 Thus ſhe beſpake ſweete boy; but alas, ſweet boy was abaſhed,
Knew not what loue was, but bluſht, yet ſweetly he bluſhed,
And wel, too too wel that bluſhing beauty beſeemed.

 Salmacis askt but a kiſſe, when naught els might be procured,
And fayre Iuory neck with her Iuory handes ſhe beclaſped:

 Either let me alone, or I goe, ſaid *Hermaphroditus.*
Nay, ſweet friend, qd ſhee, ſtay here and play to thy pleaſure,
Stay and play by the poole, Ile goe: and ſo ſhe retireth,
And drawes back for a while, (yet looks back as ſhe retyreth)
Drawes back vnto a buſh; and there all cloſely ſhe lurketh,

N1

And through euery creeke, to the boy shee craftily peepeth.
Boy, vnspi'd, as he thought, as boys are wont, was a wandring
Here and there by the meade; and comes at last to the water;
Puts of his hose and shooes, and dips his feete to the anckles
In the bedabling waues, that seem'd his toes to be tickling.
By and by, draw'n on, by the coole and temperat humor
Of th'alluring lake, himselfe stark naked he stripped.

But when *Salmacis* once had seene fayre *Hermaphroditus*
Stript stark naked, alas her loue was turnd to a lusting,
Lust to a rage, and rage to a fire, and fire to a flaming.
Hardly she holdeth her hāds, she desires him now to be hādling,
And all impatient his snow-white skin to be tutching.

Stript boy leaps to the lake, lake serues as a veile to the stript boy,
Bright transparent veile, as a glasse to a rose, or a lillie.

Hid Nymph runs fro the bush, dispoyles her selfe in a moment,
Casteth away her Lawnes, and flings her selfe to the water,
Takes hold, embraces, clips, colls, clasps *Hermaphroditus*,
(Striuing and strugling and wrestling *Hermaphroditus*)
Feeles his naked lims, and sweete lipps all to be sucketh,
Sticks fast, spraules, and turnes, and windes him about, as an Yuie
Creepeth along on a tree, or a snake cleaues fast to an Egle,
Snake snatcht vp fro the ground, by the gryping clawes of an Egle.

Fond boy stil stil striues, and stil stil *Salmacis* vrgeth,
And bowes her whole-selfe, bends her whole-selfe to the fond boy,
Weighs him downe at last, and there lies all to be wrapped,
All intangled lies, all intermingled about him.

Peeuish boy, qd shee, now wrythe and wrest the a thousand
Wayes, no way shall serue, for thus wil I holde the for euer.
O, would God, would God, that I might so holde the for euer.

Her boone was graunted: they liu'd so ioyntly for euer;
They were one, not two: two coopled, yet not a coople,
Neither boy nor wench, but a wench-boy now, or a boy-wench,
Both, yet none of both; either, yet neither of either.

When poore youth perceau'd this transformation, and saw
Whereas he entred a man, that he turned back but a halfe-man:
Eyes, and heart, and hand, and voyce, (but now not a mans voyce)
Vp to the heau'ns did he lift, effeminat *Hermaphroditus*:
Father, Mother, graunt this fountayne so to be charmed,
That who goes in a man, may thence come foorth but a half-man.

Hermaphroditus chaunce, moude *Hermes* and *Aphrodite*:
And for a worthy reuenge, that well they speedily charmed,
That who goes in a man, comes alwayes foorth but a halfe-man.

ELpinus *was as briefe, as* Ergaſtus *had been tedious in his tale of his two wantons. If.*qd he, *at any mans birth, there be a coninnction of* Venus *and* Mercurie, *it maketh him neither man nor woman, both woman and man, given to inordinate and vnnaturall luſt,* noted by Salmacis. *For theſe two planets are ſo repugnant, that they can neuer be well conioyned; ſith* Venus *is all for the body, and* Mercury *onely for the minde.*

LA ſecreta intelligentia di queſta fauola, ſecondo alcuni, è, che nelle matrici delle donne ſono ſette le ſtanze che rioglieno il ſeme dell' huomo: tre dalla parte deſtra, che producono i maſchi, e tre dalla ſiniſtra, che producono le femine, & vna nel mezzo, laquale ricogliendo il ſeme, ha forza di produrre l'uno e l'altro ſeſſo inſieme. e per queſta cagione, vogliono dire, che Hermaphrodito naſceſſe di Mercurio, hauendo Venere raccolto il ſeme in quella ſtanza del mezzo: e pero ſono chiamati & ſono Hermaphroditi tutti quelli che ſono concetti nella medeſima ſtanza.

Meliboeus *now laſtly remayned of all the* Paſtors: *who thus ſent luſting* Bacchus *after wanton* Venus.

CAdmeian Semele was great with child by the thundrer,
Great with childe and quick. Whereat Saturnian Empres
Iuno, frets and fumes; and brawles and ſcoldes with her husband,
At laſt, what bootes it, qd ſhee, my winde to be waſting,
As though in fore-times *Ioue* gaue any eare to my ſcolding?
Nay nay, workes, not wordes muſt plague that drabbe, that adultres.
What? ſhall *Iuno* the Queene by a ſhameles queane be abuſed?
Iuno the Sou'raigne Queene? ſhal I raigne in skies with a golden
Mace and ſcepter in hand, and yet parte ſtakes with a ſtrumpet?
If that an outcome whore be my miſtres, why am I called
Ioues wife and ſiſter? Nay ſiſter alone: for I beare this
Name of a wife for a ſhew, *Ioues* ſecret ſcapes to be cou'ring.
Secret? nay ſhee vaunts, and takes a delight in her open
Shame; ſhee's bagd forſooth, and great with childe with a vengeance;
And lookes euery day and howre to be called a mother
Of ſome brat, by a God, by a greateſt God, by a thundring
Ioue; which ſcarce hath chaunc'te in ſo many yeares to a *Iuno.*
But let my miſtres no more take mee for a *Iuno,*
If that I make her not with her owne mouth aske for her owne death;
If that I make not *Ioue,* yea *Ioue* himſelfe, to be autor

Of

Of this death. This sayd, inclosde in a clowde, she remoued:
And to the huswifes house, in a ielous fury repayred.
Foltring toung, hoare hayre, suck eyes, legs lasily limping,
Face plowde with wrinckles, did make her like to the olde nurse,
Olde Beldam *Beroe, Semeles* nurse. And, of a purpose,
After long tatling, at length shee came to the name of
Iupiter, and then sight and sayd : Deare daughter, I pray God,
That this prooue to be *Ioue;* but I doubt : for, alas, many harlots
Vnder a fained name of Gods haue fouly deceaued
Good-naturd damsels, and them with follie defiled.
But suppose he be *Ioue* : yet that's not enough for a maydens
Minde, vnles that he shew himselfe to be truly the thundring
Ioue: for, a disguisde *Ioue* is no *Ioue :* aske him a token,
Aske him a signe thereof, deare childe : and surely, beleeue mee,
No signe's sufficient, vnles that he company with thee,
In that self-same sort as he doth with *Iuno* the Goddes,
In that Princelike guise, in that maiesticall order,
With Sou'raigne scepter, with fire and thunder about him.

Simple soule *Semele*, instructed thus by the Beldam,
Asked a boone of *Ioue*, as soone as he came to the entry,
But tolde not what boone: *Ioue* graunts, & sweares by the sacred
Horror of hellish *Stix*, that he would performe what he graūted.

Why then, qd *Semele*, let mee kisse *Ioue* as a thundring
And bright lightning *Ioue*, no lesse then *Iuno* the Goddes.
Ioue would fayne haue stopt her foolish mouth: but a fooles bolt
Was soone, too soone shot, which *Ioue* extreamly molested :
For, neither *Semele* could vnwish what she had once wisht,
Nor lamenting *Ioue* vnsweare that which he had once sworne.

Therefore sore displeased, he gets himselfe to *Olympus*,
And with a stearne countnance and grim look, heaps on a cluster
Thick clowds, blustring winds, black storms, fires fearfuly flashing,
And th'vndaunted dint of thunders mightily roaring :
And yet he makes himselfe as milde as he possibly may bee,
And allayes his Sou'raigne force, and leaues the deuouring
Fearful thunderbolt, that stroke downe griesly *Typhoeus*.
There is an other kinde of thunder: there is a lightning
Framed much more light, and of lesse might, by the *Cyclops*,
Cald the second scepter: this he takes, and comes to the chamber
Of longing *Semele:* who prowd and vayne as a woman,
With fond selfe conceit drew self-destruction onwards.
For, mortal *Semele* was quite consum'd in a moment
By th'immortal strength, and matchles might of a thundrer.

Yet,th'imperfect fruite fro the mothers wombe he remoued,
And (so ran the report) in his owne thigh strangely receau'd it,
Til by continuance of time it grew to a ripenes,
And the apoynted time by degrees was come to a fullnes.

Then by his aunt *Ino*,for a while was he charily fostred,
And soone after that,to the Nimphs of *Nysa*, deliu'red :
And good-natur'd Nymphs from *Iuno* warily kept him
In bowres and harbors,and gaue him milk for a season.

This same twice-borne babe at length was called *Iacchus*,
Sweete boy,pleasant impe,fayre lad,braue yonker *Iacchus*,
Neuer sad,free-tongd,free-hart,free-handed *Iacchus*,
And,when he wanteth his horns,as milde as a maiden,*Iacchus*,
But,when he hath on his horns,as fierce as a Tyger,*Iacchus*.

W*Hether* Melibœus *bee beholding to Bacchus, or Bacchus to* Melibœus,
I meane not to determine,said Elpinus : *but this I haue heard,that* Bacchus,*a mightie warriour ouercame* Lycurgus, Pentheus *, and diuers others,*
and subdued India,*riding thence in triumphant manner,on an Elephant. Yet*
his greatest fame was procured by his inuention of wine,which hath made him
painted and described accordingly, a yong mery youth,naked, crowned with an
yuy garland, hauing a branch of a vine in his hand, riding in a chariot drawne
by Tygers *and* Panthers : First, Bacchus *is mery,* Wine *moderately taken,*
maketh men ioyfull; he is also naked ; for, in vino veritas *: drunkards tell all,*
and sometimes more then all. Tygers *draw his chariot ; drunken men are fierce*
and outragious. Of Venus *and* Bacchus,Priapus *was borne : lust comes from*
wine and delicacie.

*

He is Semeles *sonne : that is,he is borne of the vine : for,* Semele *is so cal-*
led, ἀπὸ τῦ σείν τὰ μίλη, *of the shaking of boughes,her boughes being euer tossed*
and still wauering with the winde. Ioue *was his father ; for, wine hath a kinde*
of heate naturally incident vnto it : neither will vines growe in cold places. He
was sowed into Ioues *thigh,and so borne againe : for, wine is eftsoones pressed*
and troaden with feete. He is a companion of the Muses *: wine quickeneth the*
wit. Women be his priests : women are sooner ouercome with wine , then men.
He was, of the Ægyptians *called* Oliris *; and was torne in peeces by the* Titanes,*and seuered,and recouued,and had his seuered limmes laid together a-*
gaine : For, of euery twig or braunch or grift of the vinetree, cut off, and burie
ed in the earth,whole vinetrees spring forth againe. He hath sometimes hornes,
then is he intolerable,and fierce, like a Bull, being drunke immoderately. Sa-
tyres,and such wantons be his folowers ; and among the rest, Silenus *is his Tu-*
tor,a fat grosse stammering drunckard,balde,and flatnosde , with great eares,
short neck and swelling bely,riding on an asse,as not able, for swelling, to stand

on his feete; all effects of beastly carowsing. The water-nymphs tooke him
from the burnt ashes of his mother, and brought him vp: the vine-tree is
moyst of nature: or rather, the burning fire of Bacchus, must be quenched,
wine must be allaied. He is called Bacchus, ἀπὸ τὸ βαχεύειν, of raging. Bromi-
us, of βρεμειν, à fremendo, of roaring and hurlyburly. Lyæus, of λυειν, of freeing:
and thereof, liber in latine, for wine freeth men from care and thought. Iacchus ἀπὸ τὸς ἰαχῆς, of crying and showting.

> A strepitu Bromius, qd vociferetur, Iacchus,
> qd curis soluat corda, Lyæus erit.

Horace thus describeth his operation.

> Quid non ebrietas designat ? operta recludit,
> Spes iubet esse ratas, in prælia trudit inermem,
> Sollicitis animis onus eximit, addocet artes ;
> Fæcundi calices quem non fecère disertum?
> Contracta quem non in paupertate solutum?

Yuy is sacred vnto him : that being euer greene; and hee alwaies young
and fresh.

The Pastors hauing all made an end; Syluia, Dieromena, and Daphne,
had yet said nothing. Syluia therefore remembred Pomona : and Dieromena
in meane time, made herselfe ready for Rhamnusia: as for good old Daphne,
she was odd in number, and as odd in conceit, and therefore very like, either to
say nothing, or nothing like to that whish had been said before. Syluia spake, as
here ensueth.

IN King Procae's time, Pomona, the Lady of apples
Floorisht : faire Pomona, the brauest nimph of a thousand
Wood-nimphs: no wood-nimph was found so good for a garden,
None so circumspect, so cunning was, for an orchyarde.
No wells, no waters, no hills, no dales she frequented,
Fishing, and fouling, and hunting life she refused,
Fruite, and sruite-bearing branches Pomona desired,
Gardens were her ioy, and all her care was her orchyard.
Insteede of keene darts, shee arm's herself with a shredding
Hooke, and therewith cutts and pares the superfluus offsprings,
And ranck spreading boughes, which waste that naturall humor,
Which well sparde, makes stock to be strong, and fruit to be louely.
  Sometimes tender grifts from better tree she deriueth,
And to a baser stock commits them for to be noorisht.
Baser stock, full glad, so noble an impe to be fostring,
Giu's it sap for suck, and it most charily tendreth,
And from nipping frosts, with her owne barck dayly defendes it.

Sometimes

Sometimes crumpled ſtrings of thirſting roote ſhe bewatreth,
When raging dog-ſtar burnt fruite-yard all to be ſcorcheth ;
And this is all her ioy,and herein ſtil ſhe deliteth.
As for Lady *Venus*,no ſuch paſtime ſhe deſireth,
But walls her gardens,and orchyards warily wardeth,
And mens ſight ſhunneth, mens company dayly deteſteth,
Leaſt by the rurall folk,violence might chaunce to be offred
Vnto her owne ſweeteſelf,or force and ſpoyle to her orchyard.

What did not the Satyrs,that frisking luſty *Iuuentus*,
And *Pan* with pine-boughes on his horns,and fleſhly *Priapus*,
And old *Silenus*, well ſtuft with youthful *Iacchus*,
Old ſtaggring Toſpot *Silenus*, with many other
Rurall Gods,t'obtaine ſo ſweete and louely a goddes?
Yet more then the Satyrs,then *Pan*, then fleſhly *Priapus*,
Then th'old *Silenus* ; *Vertumnus* faithfuly ſeru'd her,
And more hartily lou'd,though nomore luckily lou'dher.

Howmany thouſand times did he turne himſelf to a reaper,
And in a reapers weedes,bare ſheaues of corne in a bundell,
And when he ſo was dreaſt,each man would deeme him a reaper?
Howmany thouſand times did he change himſelf to a mower,
And with long-toothd rake,with crookt ſithe went to the meddowe,
And when he thus made hay,each man tooke him for a mower?
How many times did he then transforme himſelf to a ploweman,
All in a leather pilch,with a goade in his hand,or a ploweſtaffe,
And ſo ſhapte,each man would ſweare that he were but a ploweman?
Yea how oft did he frame and ſhape himſelf as a gardner,
Preſt with a ſhredding hooke his vines and trees to be proyning,
And ſo dight,no-man did doubt,but he was but a gardner?
If that he met with a ſweard,or a ſouldiers coate,or a caſſock,
Caſſock,coate,and ſweard did make him march as a ſouldier.
And,when baits and hookes,and angling rods he receaued,
Fiſhers and anglers ſo well,ſo right he reſembled,
That both Nymph and fiſh might well therewith be deceaued.
So,and ſo did this *Vertumnus*,ſlippery turnecoate
Turne,and winde,transforme,and change himſelf to a thouſand
Shapes ; and all,to behold *Pomona* the Lady of apples.

At laſt,with gray heares his wrinckled browes he beſpreadeth,
Putts on a red thrumbd hat,with a ſtaffe goe's laſily hobling,
Like to an old Beldame : and thus ſhe begins to be tatling.

O braue ſweete apples,and ô moſt bewtiful orchyard,
O paradiſe-garden,fit for ſo louely a gardner:
And ſo giu's her a kiſſe ; (too wanton a kiſſe for a Beldame.)

O 2   *Than*

Then sits downe on a banck, and casteth her eyes to the garden
Stoarde with trees, and tree's with fruitefull burden abounding.

Ouer against this banck, where these two sate, was a goodly
Elme, that leant herselfe, as a louing prop to a vine-tree,
Vine-tree inclining, with clustred grapes, on her elme-tree.
See, said th'old Beldame, to the sweete fac'te Lady of apples,
See this loued sight, and marke there, how many thousand
Mutual imbracements, that vine-tree giu's to the elme-tree:
Vine giu's grace to the elme, and elme giu's strength to the vine-tree,
Either an others helpe, and either a ioy to an other.
But yet alas, if th'elme stoode single alone fro the vine-tree,
Or vine-tree be diuorct from her husbands company elmetree,
Elme shuld haue nothing, but fruiteles leaues for a burden,
Vine shuld lye on ground, which now mounts vp to the heauens.
Then let *Pomona* example take by the vine-tree,
Let *Pomona* loue, and ioyne herselfe to an elme-tree,
Ioyne herselfe to a mate, or shew herselfe to be willing
For to be ioynd to a mate. O how-many, how-many loues
Should shee haue, if shee once shewd herself to be louing?
Yea eu'n now (though now thou liue here sole in an orchyard,
Sole in an orchyard here, and all inclosd as an anckresse)
Sileni, Fauni, Siluani, all the delightfull
Crewe of rurall Gods, stil run to the Lady of apples.
But thou (if thou wilt haue this thy match to be well made)
Take heede, learne in time, and leand thine eare to a Beldame,
Who, as a woman, must of right, wish well to a woman,
And as an old woman, must needes know more then a damsell,
Disdaine these Demy-gods, that rome and range by the deserts,
Wood-gods, woodden gods, pide *Pan,* and filthy *Priapus,*
And take *Vertumnus* to thy mate, who, more then a thousand
Sileni, Fauni, Siluani, dayly desires thee:
And therefore (sith loue craues loue) more duly deseru's thee.
And take mee for a pledge: for, I know, that nobody better
Know's him then myself: his secreates all he reuealeth
Vnto me, and in mee his surest trust be reposeth.
And take this for a truth, *Vertumnus* goes not a gadding,
Is not an out-come guest, but dwells hereby as a neighbour.
Neither tak's he delite, his fancies dayly to alter,
Or seeke for new loues, or choyce once made to be changing:
Faithful *Vertumnus* loues with deuotion endles
First loue and last loue, *Pomona* the Lady of apples:
And can so conforme, and frame himself to be pleasing,

That.

That, what forme, or face, or shape Pomona desireth,
Into the same himself Vertumnus speedily changeth.
And, if like conceits are alwaies cause of a liking,
You two loue and like with like affection, one thing.
For, Pomona desires and loues faire plentiful orchyards,
And Vertumnus takes first fruites of plentiful orchyards.
And, though Vertumnus doe receaue these duetiful offrings,
And take in good part Pomonae's bewtiful apples,
Plummes, and grapes, and hearbs, and flowres: yet he chiefly desireth
Not those faire apples, but this faire Lady of apples,
Not Pomonae's goods, but sweete Pomona the goddes,
Not thine, but the alone. Therefore with mercy remember
Vertumnus torments, and thinke, that he mercy desireth
With my mouth: thinke, that with these mine eyes he afordeth
Teares: feare louely Venus, who wills each Nimph to be louely,
Feare Nemesis, that plagues such girles, as loue to be loueles.

Then she begins to recount many old wiues tales to the Lady,
How that Anaxarete, for scorning bewtiful Iphis,
Was transformd to a stone: with a thousand more: of a purpose
For to procure her loue: and bade her looke to the fatall
Fall of Anaxarete, and learne thereby to be louely;
So might budding fruite from nipping frosts be defended,
And halfe-ripe apples from blustring windes be protected.

But sith th'old trott's shifts, and tales were lightly regarded,
Turnecoate Vertumnus to a youth was speedily turned,
Braue youth, gallant youth, as bright and sheene, as Apollo
Seemes, when burning beames, which clouds had lately eclipsed,
Haue their streaming light, and blazing bewty recou'red.

Youthful Vertumnus to the chereful Lady aproached,
And now offred force: but no force needes to be offred:
Sweete face, and faire lookes, caus'd castles keyes to be yeelded.

VErtumnus, qd Elpinus, to end all in one word, noteth the diuers seasons of
the yeare: and is thus called of the Latine word, verto, which is, to turne,
and Annus, signifying the yeare, as if a man would say, vertannus, the turning
of the yeare. He is largely described and discoursed vpon by Propertius in the
second Elegie of his fourth booke. Vertumnus at last, by turning himselfe to a
youth, obteineth Pomona; that is, the spring comming on, the earth afordeth
varietie of fruites and flowres. The like is that mariage of Zephyrus and Flora, celebrated by Ouid in the fifth booke of his Fasti. Vertumnus transformde
to an old woman, goeth about to deceaue Pomona: it is good to abandon olde
bandes, which corrupt the mindes of tender girles.

The

The picture of Vertumnus.

Dicromena, *hearing* Syluia *make mention of* Iphis *and* Anaxarete, *tooke occafion offered: and,by difcouering her pride and plague,did thereby infinuate the reuenging might of the feuere Lady* Rhamnufia.

I Phis,a gentle youth (if a gentle minde be a gentry)
Poore,yet rich,but rich in pure affection only,
Loued a laffe of ftate,but alas vnluckily loued,
Loued a noble dame (if a noble birth be a noblefle)
Loued *Anaxarete*, whome pride ftil caufd to be loueles.

Oftentimes he retir'de ; yet loue ftil forced him onward,
Oft did he ftriue with loue,and yet loue ftil was a victor,
And a triumpher ftil. Then poore difconfolat *Iphis*
Yeelds perforce,and feekes his wounded foule to recomfort.
Sometimes vnto the nurfe his fecreate fmart he reuealeth,
And by the milk,by the pap,by the bleffed breaft,he befeecheth.
Sometimes vnto the friends of noble Dame he repaireth,
And their helping hand with ftreaming teares he defireth.
Sometimes wooing words in louing letter he writeth,
And ten thoufand times his lordlike Lady faluteth.
Sometimes greene garlands with deaw of teares he bemoyftneth,
And on pofts and gates,his garlands watery fixeth.
Sometimes tender fide on threfhold hard he repofeth,
And there,locks and barres with curfes vainly reuileth.
Scorneful *Anaxarete*,with a frowning face,with a hard hart,
Hart of flint,of fteele,contemns him dayly,for all this :
And to a difdaineful difgrace,to a furly behauiour,
Adds a reproachfull fpeech,and mocks him,leaft any fmalleft
Harts eafe,fmalleft hope might ftay contemptible *Iphis*.

Iphis,vnable now t'endure thefe plagues any longer,
Coms all impatient,and all inragd,to the damned
Dore of proud Miftres,there this laft paffion vttring.
Lady *Anaxarete*, ô now,fing, *io triumphe*.
Sing a triumphing fong : thou fhalt nomore be molefted
With vile woorme *Iphis*,poore pafthope,defperat *Iphis*.
Vaunt thy felf,and laugh,and let thy head be adorned
With frefh laurel leaues in ioyfull figne of a conqueft;
Iphis yeelds,yeelds breath,laft breath ; fing,*io triumphe*,
Feede that murdring fight with fight of murdered *Iphis*:
So fhal *Anaxarete*, eu'n in defpite of her hard hart,
Hardeft hart,confeffe,that I once yet wrought her a pleafure,
Blood-thirfting pleafure,when as *Iphis* murdered *Iphis*.

Yet let no man thinke, that I therefore leaue to be louing
Fayre-prow'd, louely-cruell, til I alſo leaue to be liuing.
With double darknes mine eyes ſhal at once be eclipſed,
Of ſuns burning beames and light vntimely bereaued,
And of *Anaxarete's* ſweete ſight vnkindly depriued.
Neither needes any man theſe tidings for to be telling;
Iphis wilbe the newes, and *Iphis* wil be the bringer
Of that ſelfſame newes : *Iphis* wil ſurely be preſent,
And in preſence dy: ſo *Iphis* ſhalbe reporter,
So this *Anaxarete* in like ſort ſhalbe beholder,
And feede murdring ſight with ſight of murdered *Iphis*.
Yet you gods (if mens affaires of gods be regarded,)
Vouchſafe forlorne wretch with ſome ſmalle grace to remember;
Let poore *Iphis* death, and cauſe of death be recorded:
And by how much now his liuing dayes be abridged,
Let, by ſomuch more his name and fame be prolonged.

  This ſaid, brawne-falln armes, and eyes all watred, he lifted
Vp to the poſts, which earſt with flowres he had often adorned,
And there faſtned a cord. Theſe, theſe be the crowns, be the garlands,
Theſe be the flowres, which yeeld ſuch pleaſant ſent to the ſcorneful
Lady *Anaxarete* : ſo thruſt in his head : yet he turned
Head, and face, and eyes, eu'n at laſt gaſpe, to the ſcorneful
Lady *Anaxarete* : and there hangd woefuly tottring,
With corde-ſtrangled throate; his ſprawling feete by the downefall
Knockt her dore by chaunce; knockt dore did yeeld a reſounding,
Yeelded a mourneful ſound, and made herſelf to be open,
Wide open, to behold ſo ſtrange and woeful an obiect.
Dead dore, ſenceles dore, ten thouſand times to be praiſed
More then *Anaxarete*, who by no paines of a louer,
By no intreating, by no perſwaſion, opn'ed
Thoſe dead eares, to receaue laſt words of deſperat *Iphis*,
Thoſe curſt eyes, to behold laſt teares of deſolat *Iphis*,
That prowd hart, to bewaile laſt fall of murdered *Iphis*.

  Dore once wide open, ſeruants ran forth with an outcry,
Ran, but ran too late; tooke vp diſfigured *Iphis*,
Cold *Iphis*, paleſact *Iphis*, nay, now not an *Iphis*,
And his poore mother with a ſight ſo deadly preſented,
Old mother, childles mother, nay, now not a mother.

  Woeful woman, alas, clipt, kiſt, embraced her *Iphis*,
Wept, cride out, hould, roard, performd al parts of a mother :
And to the graue at laſt with ſollemne funeral hornors,

Brought through th'open streetes her sons dead corps in a coffin.

Hard by the way, through which, this sad solemnity passed,
Lady *Anaxaretes* braue bowre stoode loftily mounted :
And, that dolefull sounde with mourning eccho redoobled
Came to her eares at last (for now at last, the reuenging
Goddes gan to requite) and forced her eyes to the windowe,
For to behold and see poore *Iphis* laid in a coffin :
Scarce she beheld and saw poore *Iphis* laid in a coffin,
But that sightles sight was starck and stiffe on a sudden,
And her purpled blood to a palenes speedily changed.
Back she remou's her seete, her seete will not be remoued,
Back she reflected her head, but her head would not be reflected ;
Feete and head stock fast : and that same merciles hardnes,
That same stone, which earst in her hard hart made his abiding,
Dwelled in euery ioynt, and each where tooke vp a lodging.

And least noble dames might deeme my tale, but a fable,
In towne of *Salamis*, where famous *Teucer* abided,
(Whence this scorneful dame her noble gentrie deriued)
Stony *Anaxarete*, for a lasting signe of a stony
Hart, stands fram'de of stone, in church of dame *Cytherea*.

Then let noble dames, let Ladies learne to be louely,
And make more account of a gentle minde, then a gentry.
Loue makes lowest high, and highest harts to be lowly,
And by these meanes makes both highe and lowe to bee louely.

THis reuenging goddes, qd Elpinus, was called Nemesis : she punished the insolencie of such, as in prosperitie bare themselues ouer arrogantly: especially those, who for their bewtie, were scornefull and disdainefull. She was also called Rhamnusia, of a place in Attica, where shee had a most sumptuous temple : and Adrastia, of one Adrastus, who was the first that euer did consecrate any temple vnto her. She was figured winged : for punishment commeth quickly. She stoode on a wheele, and sterne of a ship : for she rolleth and ruleth all vpside downe. She held a bridle, and a rule or measure : for, we must temper our tongs, and deale iustly, as the Greke Epigramme expoundeth it.

Ε' Νέμεσιν αγχλίγω τω πήχει, τώτι ερωτα,
μὴ δ μετριτη γρωσγ, μητ ἀχαλμα λεγων,

By Iphis wee may learne, not to looke too high : and by Anaxarete, wee are taught, not to disdaigne the lowly.
The picture of Nemesis.

DAphne seeing euery body silent; knew it was time for her to speake. Madame, qd she, I can neither sing nor say very well: but sith I must needes tell somwhat, it is good to begin betimes, that I may the sooner make an ende. The best is, I meane not to be so full of parables, as that *Elpinus* shall haue need to make any explication. I haue heard my mother many times in good sobrietie, make a long discourse of certayne schollers of *Cambridge*, who would needes finde out some way to mount vp to heauen, and vnderstand those mysteries which bee aboue the Moone. For this purpose they met together at Dawes crosse: where, after long debating of the matter, it was resolued by the full consent of the learned assembly, that they should seeke and search, passe and repasse, from East to Weast, some by lande, some by sea, till they had found the way to heauen. O, it was a sweete sight, to beholde so many sageheads and gentle spirites thus vnited and assembled together. All being ready, they all made haste: some embarqued themselues, some traueled by land: others stayed in villages adioyning, expecting some heauenly apparition or reuelation from aboue. They that were in the ship, began to consult of their attempt; when, loe, on the sodayn, (such grace the heauens afforde to them that be heauenly affected) there came a straunger, yet an *Academique*, vnto them: who perceauing that their resolution was, not to intermit their labour, till they had found the way how to goe to heauen aliue; toulde them, that peraduenture, himselfe could giue them best directions for that purpose: and that, if they would giue him the hearing, hee would discourse at large, both what himselfe was, and how diuers of his companions had attempted the like voyage, and what had befallen them in the same. They all thanked him, for his vnexpected courtesie; willed him to enter into the ship, and with this discourse helpe them to forget the daunger and yrksomenes of their trauel: which done, he thus began.

I was borne and bred fiue miles beyond S. *Michaels* mount, foure summers before the greene winter: *Saturne* was predominant at my natiuity: my father, a man of prouidence, perceauing my terrestriall disposition, would needes haue me admitted a scholler in the Vniuersitie, called the *Garden*, whereof we all were named Gardiners: Our Conuocation house was a Harbor sytuate directly vnder the Arctike pole, where, euery new Moone, my selfe and my fellow Gardiners assembled together, and sang such compositions as we had seuerally framed of the vertue of hearbs, the pleasaunt liquor of the vine, the sweetnes of fruits, the profite of husbandry, and dressing of Gardens and Orchyards: in such sort that our Vniuersity became famous, by reason of diuers learned monuments, daylie there deuised, and thence proceeding, to the publike profit of the common wealth, as, The vulgar Dioscorides, The Garden of Ladies, The moralization of the Georgikes, with many such wonderous workes. And as our selues

were

were delighted in dreſſing and keeping of Gardens; ſo did we chooſe vs
diſtinct names & additions of ſeueral hearbs accordingly: ſo that one was
called a Violet, an other a Thiſtle, this Lettuce, that Succorie; the reſt, either Borage, Hmlock, Paſnip, Cowſlip, Roſemary, or ſome like. But ſo it
fell out on a day, as we were thus buſied in our Harbour, we heard of a reporte ſcattered abroad, that a general deluge and inundation of waters
ſhould happen that yeare, as was foretolde by ſome idle Prognoſticators.
This ſtraunge newes troubled the whole countrey; and, among others, vs
poore Gardiners: who, hauing read this lewd Almanack, and conſidering
the floriſhing diſcourſes of theſe Aſtrologicall doctors (which threatned
the Vines, Gardens, and Orchyards, with blaſts, froſts, caterpillers, and a
thouſand ſuch phantaſtical dangers) layd our heads together, and dealt, as
I am about to tell you. Firſt we offered ſacrifice to *Bacchus* and *Priapus*,
and then concluded, to ſend ſome of our Vniuerſity as ambaſſadours to
heauen: who by this one iourney, might doe a double ſeruice: the one,
in ſeeing whether theſe tale-tell Aſtrologers had any ground for their
predictions; the other in obtaining grace & mercie of the Gods, by graun-
ting plenty & abundáce. Among others, *Succhory*, a pleaſant & mery có-
panion, had this conceipt in his head, to get vp to heauen. It were good, me
thinks, qd he, to finde out a great & mightie Egle, ſo ſtrong, that ſome two
of vs might mount on his back, & he beare vs vp to the skies: Mary, we had
need to look, that theſe 2 be not too heauy, or ouer-fat & corpulent, leſt the
Egle be ouercharged. Therefore the *Fennel*, and the *Violet*, in my fancy, be
the fitteſt for this purpoſe, as being deft and nimble fellowes, and as light
as may be. Nay, ſayd *Cowſlip*, there is no reaſon at all to vſe the help of an
Egle in this matter, becauſe you know that *Iupiter* himſelfe was once tranſ-
formed into an Egle, and caried vp to heauen an other kinde of burden, the
Fennell or *Violet*. Then out ſtept *Hemlock*, with his fryſe bonnet, and ſayd,
that he had found a better and more compendious way to heauen, then
that. It were not amiſſe, qd he, if we had a cart; becauſe the iourney is long:
and, the ambaſſadours may by this meanes trauel with greater eaſe and facilitie. Beſides this, they may therein conuey to *Olympus*, ſome of the beſt
fruites of our Gardens, to preſent the Gods withal when they come thither.
The graue aduice of this fore-caſting *Academike*, was generally wel liked
of: ſauing that they could not conceaue, who ſhould draw the Cart: and
therefore this inuention, the more pitie, came alſo to nothing. All the
Academike Gardiners deuiſed and muſed much, how it might be brought
to paſſe. Some remembring *Lucians* ſhip, thought it beſt to goe by water:
Others, rather by land, through ſome great forreſt, as *Dante* did: at laſt,
they all agreed, that the ſureſt way was, to make ladders of the poles
that bare vp their hoppes, and by the meanes thereof, to builde and
rayſe vp a towre that ſhould ouer-looke the whole worlde: and ſo might
they

they in short time pierce the clowdes: and by certaine engynes still draw
vp new stuffe to increase the height of their fortification, it occasion were.
The towre begun, and halfe ended (:or many hands make light worke)
wee made choyce of three, the most expert men in all our Vniuersitie;
in Astrologie, Mathematikes, and Philosophie; to weete, *Hemlocke*,
Pasnip, and the *Thistle*, to be ambassadors. These three gathered diuers
fruites, Raysons, and hearbs, to present the Lordes and Ladies of heauen
withall, and to request diuers boones in the behalfe of our Vniuersitie. So
we brought and accompanied them with great ioy, euen vnto the Ladders, & saw them mount vp chearefuly. *Hemlock* was one *Damœtas*, of the
Dearcles parck, *Fac-totū indeclinabile* to the Lady of the Lake. *Pasnip* was
a braue peece of a man, about soure and thirty yeares olde, fayre, streight,
and vpright, so nimble and light, that he might well haue walked on the
edge of a sworde, or poynt of a speare. The *Thistle* was more auncient,
as hauing passed full sortie yeares, and was wholly addicted to contemplation.

After much mounting, when the learned *Thistle* was almost at the first
heauen, he began to obserue and marke, whether *Strabo*, *Ptolomæus*, and
other measurers of the world, had made a good suruey thereof. He viewed
the toppe of the mount *Parnassus*, where *Lactantius* and *Plutarchus* apointed the limites of the deluge; and perceauing that from thence, it was a
thousand thousand myles vp to heauen, hee laughed at their sollie, and
made a mock of *Berosus*, who would needes finde out the centre of the
earth, by the Arke of *Noah*. Thus iesting at their ignorance, and hauing
his head full of Cosmographicall Proclamations, he began to discourse to
his companions, of the situation and distance of kingdomes, mountaines,
seas, riuers, & woods, of the eleuation of the Poles, the rising of the stars, &
the names of euery prouince, with their lawes, statutes, customes, and different kinds of discipline. He shewed new-found worlds, neuer known to
Africa, *Europe*, or *Asia*. He made *Aristotle* an asse, who neuer thought that
al the *Zone* vnder the *Zodiake* was habitable. With these & the like speculations and sweete sightes, they passed the time, and continued further on
their iourney. And further let them continue a while, sayd the ruler of the
company that came from Dawes crosse, in the mean time, whilst your Gardiners are mounting vp to heauen, let vs learne of you, what became of
the fearful prediction of those Astrological masters. Content, qd the straū-
ger, & thus it fell out. When these famous Astrologers with their nūbers,
poynts, measures, Astrolabes, signes, & instruments had concluded for certaine, that this inundation should ensue, which would ouerflow & drown
the whole world, so that not one person should escape aliue, publishing
this their conceit abroad, by printing of their Almanacks and Prognosti-

cations,

cations, shewing from day to day, in the houses of great men and palaces of princes, the signes, the eclipses of the moone, the coniunction of the planets, and other such fantasies, portending, as they sayd, this future inundation; they made euery man feare, and many run vp to hills, that, if they must needes dye, they might die last, and see others drownd before. Among the rest, the Prior of Saint *Bartholomews*, remoued from London to Harrow hill, and there bestowed an hundred markes, in fortifiyng and furnishing himselfe agaynst the flood. And now the time was at hand, when all should come to naught: When (I know not by what reuolution or influence) the ayre on the sodaine began to be black, clowds to lowre, and rayne to powre downe so fast, that euery man verily beleeued, the a-strologicall predictions would prooue true in the ende, sith they seemed so likely in the beginning. This made men, women, and children, tag and rag, to climbe vp to trees, to the tops of houses, castles, and steeples, to saue their liues. All the world being thus on an vprore, there came an odde Astronomer, peraduenture hauing lesse learning, but surely more wit then the others, who seeing, what a pitifull howling and lamentation was made on euery side, began with bitter words and vehemencie of speech to inueigh agaynst the former Astrologers, saying, they were seditious fel-lowes, worthy to be clapt by the heeles, and that all was starke false which they had put downe to the terror of the poore people, who of all other deaths were most vnwilling to be choakte with water. This new doctor was for his labour, accompted a foole of wise and foole: for, still as hee thus preached, it rayned still. At last, about two or three houres after, as God would, the ayre began to cleare vp, the rayne ceased, the storme was past, and all was well agayne. Then came foorth the amased people, from trees, rocks, and Castles, distracted betweene hope and feare, scarce resol-ued whether themselues were dead or aliue, as if they had come from the new-found worlde, or out of *Trophonius* den: and by degrees comming to their former sence and witte, made great feasts and bonfires, for ioy that they had escaped a daunger which neuer hangd ouer their heads. The Astronomer that gaue out this comfortable contradiction, seeing that all fell out according to his speech (although peraduenture himselfe thought as the rest did) bare himselfe loftily, was made a doctor, and dubbed a knight for learning, which was neuer in his head: and the rest were scorned for fooles, which had published the contrary Prognosticati-ons. Shortly after this, the first Astrologers, seeing themselues fouly ouer-seene, and that this other doctor, by some Seraphical instinct, had foretolde the trueth, came vnto him, reuereced him as a Demy-God, & desired him to imparte vnto them, the ground of this his knowledge, and conceipt: which done, they would acknowledge him for their onely master and

Capten

Capten in all their Aſtrological ſpeculations. What ground, qd he? Mary, the ſureſt ground, I aſſure you. For, are you ſuch ſottes, to imagin, that in this my prediction, I had regard to any aſtrological diuination, and not rather to a moſt ſure and vnfallible conſequence of reaſon, better then a thouſand obſeruations of ſignes and conſtellations? If this your vniuerſall deluge had happened, my grand maſters and doctors, who would then haue beene left aliue, to prooue me a lyer, all the world being drowned? If it happened not, (as in trueth it ſo falleth out) I was ſure of the generall applauſe of the people, for this my plauſible Prognoſtication. All the *Congregatio ſapientum* laughed hereat: And now, (qd the chiefe of their company) it is like that your fellow Gardners, are almoſt at heauen by this; therefore, continue your diſcourſe, as they, I hope, haue continued their iourney. With a good will, qd the ſtranger, and thus it came to paſſe. My fellowes at laſt came to a fayre and playne clowde, which tutched the very top of their tabernacle, thinking they had beene at their iourneies end, and that it had been an eaſie matter, to haue diſpatched the reſt on foote: but they miſſed their marke, and came ſhort of their account, which troubled them not a litle. And as they ſtoode thus conſulting with themſelues, how they might ſafely paſſe further, beholde, there came on a ſodayne, a man and a woman, riding on a litle clowde, as though it had beene a courſer: who ſaluted them courteouſly, and bade them welcome; demaunding what they ſought for, in ſo high a place, where it was very difficult to mount vp further, and more daungerous to goe downe agayne. We are *Academikes*, qd *Paſnip*, and being of late troubled and perplexed with the repugnant conceipts of Aſtrologers, and menaced and threatned with their vnhappy predictions, haue traueled hither of purpoſe to vnderſtand whether their diuinations be true or not: and if, as they ſay, the Gods haue determined to plague vs, and our gardens with ſterilitie and inundations, then haue we diuers petitions to be preferred to the immortal Gods, on the behalfe of our ſelues and our Orchyards: which being once peruſed, and accordingly conſidered by their diuine Maieſties, wee haue brought with vs ſuch ſimple fruites, as our poore abilitie could afforde, to preſent their cœleſtiall Deities withall. It is a ſtraunge thing, ſayd the man on the clowde, to ſee you here ſo high: but what contradiction finde you among your Aſtrologers? Me thinks you preſume very much, in daring to reprehend great clerkes, and mount vp to the skies, your ſelues being but Gardiners and ignorant men. Though we be Gardiners, qd the *Thiſtle*, yet let not that be preiudicial vnto vs: for my ſelfe am a doctor of Aſtrologie, & can yeeld you an accompt of the opinions of the *Chaldees, Ægyptians, Indians, Mores, Arabians, Iewes, Grecians, Romaynes,* modernes & ancients whatſoeuer: al whoſe conceipts I finde as variable as the moone, & themſelues altogether Lunatike. Before I make aunſwere hereunto, qd the man

that

that rode on the clowde, I will tell you my name: I am called *Intellectus*, vnderstanding, and this my sister is named *Fantasie*, or *Opinion*. Our duty and function is, to guide and conduct to heauen, all such persons as here ariue, but not as you haue aryued : though indeede, by reason of the small number of them that mount vp hither, we are not so pestred with busines, but that we haue leasure enough to conferre with you. Well then, my friends, you must know, that there be diuers wayes here, all which will bring you to one and the same ende. True it is, that there is one way, through which very few passe; because they see so many strange and most myraculous apparitions, that when they returne agayne to their companions below on the earth, they can meete with nothing there, to the which they may fully compare or resemble those heauenly myracles, when they seeke to make reporte thereof to their friends, or other company, desirous of their cœlestiall newes. And in trueth, for any one that commeth hither with a commendable desire, to reforme the disorders of mans life, there be fiue thousand, that ambitiously are driuen forward by a foolish curiositie.

When wee brought hither *Plato*, *Aristotle*, *Proclus*, *Auerrois*, and others that haue discoursed of the heauens, wee conducted them by such a way, that they saw but eight Sphæres: *Albertus magnus, Isake*, and many others were guided through an other passage, and found out nine Sphæres; and thus haue they euer from time to time, repugned their fellowes conceipts. Without doubt, qd *Hemlock*, I beleeue it is, as you say : for, so among vs below, if a man aske how many miles it is from *Tugford* to *Talley*; seauen sayth one, eight sayth another; nay, so many men, so many different numbers of miles : insomuch, that hee which would indeede know the trueth, had neede to bring a line with him, and measure the miles himselfe.

These aspiring wittes, quoth *Intellectus*, when they are thus eleuated, roame and wander about the incomprehensible quantity of the heauens, without my companie, and frame of their owne inuention, fiue hundred fooleries and monstrous imaginations in the heauens. Here they paynt a Bull, there a Dogge, here a Goate, there a Lyon, and such like, as beares, horses, and fishes : whereupon well might the Philosopher *Bion* reprehend their preposterus curiositie, who could not perceiue a fish swimming in a brook, before their eies, and yet would find out fishes aboue the cloudes : and *Thales* was as worthylie mocked by his mayde, for that, whilst he was tooting on the starres, he fell into a ditch, not knowing what was before his feete, yet inquisitiue in searching out the secrets of heauen without my assistance. Such phantastical and frantick fellowes, were for iust cause banished the court, by the good and learned *Alphonsus*, king of

Arragon

Arragon: for, it is truely fayd, that, The ſtarres rule fooles, and wiſe men rule the ſtarres. All theſe things, ſayd the *Thiſtle*, are to me very familiarly knowen, and I make no more accompt of theſe geſſing Aſtrologers, then of very Aſſes. Therefore, to let paſſe theſe Galaxiaes, Epicicles, Centres, Motions, Retrogradations, Acceſſes, Receſſes, and a thouſand ſuch trumperies; if it pleaſe you to directt vs in the playne way, we ſhall follow you as our guides, and honour you as our maſters. You ſeeme, qd *Fantaſie*, to be men of ingenuous and great conceipt, deſiring Honor, and aſpiring to high matters: come therefore, we will aforde you all the helpe we poſſibly may: mount on this cloude with vs, which ſhall protectt you from all anoyance of heate or colde. Incontinently, the clowde was eleuated vp to *Olympus:* and no ſooner had they ariued in heauen, but *Venus* and *Ganymedes* (as women and children vſe to doe) ran to them to ſee their flowers and fruites. *Paſnip* ſeeing *Venus* holde out her apron to receaue ſome of their prouiſion, gaue her leaue to take her choyce. Then came Lady *Luna*, who alſo tooke what ſhee would, and preſently departed, as being inioyned euery day twice, to cauſe a flowing and reflowing in the *Indian* and *Perſian* ſea: beſides a thouſand other matters, wherewith ſhe is euer occupied. *Ganymedes* was as buſie about *Hemlocke*, who there ſo liberally beſtowed the remnant of their fruites, that in the ende nothing remayned.

Iupiter ſeeing theſe ſtrangers aryued in heauen, in habite of ambaſſadors, bade them draw neare, himſelf then ſitting in counſayle. Where, the iolly proloquutor *Hemlock*, in the name of the reſt, began a braue oration: & when he came to the poynt to vſe theſe words: Loe here, the preſent which *Priapus*, the God of our earthly Gardẽs, hath ſent to your cœleſtial Maieſties: he foũd nothing at all left in his pannyers. *Iupiter* moued hereat, whould heare him no further; but catching him and *Paſnip* by the hayre of the head, threw them downe from heauen, to their Gardens on earth agayne: With this transformation, that they ſhould both thenceſoorth haue the forme and nature of that roote, and weede, whereof they bare the names. The *Thiſtle* being all this while in heauen, and perceauing how rygorouſly his fellowes were handled; ſcratched off all his tender haire from his head, for very griefe and anguiſh; ſo that it neuer after grew vp ſo firmly agayne, but that euery yeare once (for a memoriall of this admyrable accident) euerie little blaſt of winde blewe it all about the fieldes and Gardens.

Thus perplexed, hee intreates *Intellectus*, and humbly beſecheth him, that he would not forſake him in this extremitie. *Intellectus* pitying his wofull plight, excuſed him to the Gods, giuing them to vnderſtand, that hee had neither in worde nor deede offended their diuine Maieſtie.

Wherefore

Wherefore *Iupiter, Phœbus*, and *Mercurie* gaue him this prerogatiue and preheminence, that he might aſſigne new names to his nephews and ſucceeding poſteritie, as *Artichauks*, and ſuch like; which ſhould euer after be had in great eſtimation among other fruites of the Garden, and ſerued at mighty mens tables as a diſh of great dayntines and delicacie : and afterward gaue *Intellectus* leaue to leade him all about heauen ; and to peruſe his petitions, that his Patent might be ſealed accordingly. As the *Thiſtle* was about to view the heauens; Stay, qd *Intellectus*, thou muſt firſt obtayne the good will of *Time*; who muſt alſo haue a ſight of theſe thy demaundes : therefore reade them, and let me heare what they are.

The petition of the Gardiners.

INprimis, that Hemlock neuer grow in Gardens; but onely in ditches and ſuch like obſcure and vnpleaſant places, fitte for ſo vnſauorie and loathſome a weede.

Item, That none vnder the degree of an Eſquire, haue his bed ſtuft with the downe of a thiſtle.

Item, That whoſoeuer eateth buttered Paſnips without pepper, may dye without Auricular confeſſion.

Item, That no man, vnles he may diſpend foure nobles by the yeare in good free-holde, ſhall breake his faſt with an Artychauck pye.

Item, That none aboue the age of ſeuen yeares, if he nettle his hande, ſhall be ridde of his payne by rubbing the place with a Dock, and ſaying, In Docke, out Nettle.

Item, That if any maried man vſe any noſegay, wherein the flowers be odde in number, he may ſtand in daunger of *Acteons* penaltie.

Item, That whoſoeuer drinketh Claret wine without Borage, or Sack without a ſprig of Roſemary, may neuer be ridde of his Rheume by drinking Muſcadell before he goe to bed.

Item, That if a man be like to haue a Feuer quartane, for want of a figge, the maſter of the Garden, by the aduiſe of two Phiſitians, may giue him leaue to pluck and eate.

Item, That : Nay, qd *Intellectus*, no more Thats; for, this is too much already. Theſe fooleries muſt not be any part of thy petition : thou ſhalt onely demaund a good ſtomack and taſte, to the ende, that euery thing may be to thy good content and liking.

So they paſſed on, towards the auncient pallace of *Time. Time* was a great man out of all meaſure, ſhewing a kinde of maieſtie in his forehead. His face had three ſeuerall ſemblances : his browe and eyes reſembling middle age; his mouth and cheekes, youth : his beard, olde age. He had before him three great glaſſes, looking now in one, now in an other : and,
according

according to that which he saw in them,he framed his countenance: some-times ioyeus and mery,sometimes graue and moderate,sometimes sad and heauy.On his left side,was Weeping; on his right side,Laughing. His gar-ment was of such a color, as the *Thistle* could not possibly discerne it, al-though,as hee tolde mee, hee marked it seriously, neither knew hee how to tearme it.He sawe about him an infinite nüber of seruitors; the Day & the Night,with their daughter *Aurora,* betweene them,both, and Howres and Minutes their seruants:he sawe Peace,Warre,Plenty,Dearth, Life, Death, Riches,Pouertie,Loue,Hate, & other mighty potentates,euer looking on the face of *Tyme*, and conforming themselues to his countenance, were it mery,or sad. When he made any signe vnto them, they were all ready and prest to obey him ; and at his commaunde,wrought this or that impression in the earth. At the feete of *Tyme*,stoode *Desteny*,with a booke before her: which *Fortune* and *Chaunce* did tosse & turne incessantly, sometimes ouer-skipping fiue leaues,sometimes ten, sometimes an hundred, sometimes a thousand, as they thought good. *Tyme* caused *Desteny* to write and lay downe al his decrees; cõmaunding foure other personages to put the same in execution, toweet, Spring, Summer, Autumne, Winter: which foure, commaunde in like sorte,the Day and the Night: the Day and Night com-maunde the Howres; the Howres commaund the Minutes : the Minute bringeth this or that to passe in the world:and so doe they gouerne the hea-uens,the earth, and all. Oftentimes there come nessengers to the Day and Night,saying,such an one hath builded such a fortresse against the Maiestie and dominion of *Tyme:* another hath erected an image : a third hath com-posed a booke,all intending to be masters & triumphers ouer *Tyme. Tyme*, perceauing this,looketh in his glasses, held by *Verity*, and doth but smile at their attempts,willing *Desteny* to write his pleasure, and giuing authoritie vnto *Fortune. Fortune*,taking delite in such toyes for a time , committeth them afterwards to the power of fire or war , or else returneth them againe before the feete of *Tyme*,where,as soone as they are once set downe, they vanish away presently,and neuer apeare againe.

These last words were scarce vttered dy the stranger *Academike*,but so-dainely there arose an outragius tempest of snowe , hayle , raine , winde, thunder,and lightning all together : that, vnles by the good aduice of the fore-casting master,the double Canons, & al the great artillery of the ship, had beene presently discharged into the ayre, to counterbeate and dismay, the roaring and thundring cloudes; no doubt,the poore ship had been bea-ten to powder,and dasht to the bottome of the sea,with such like rage and violence,as if a man would breake with his fist, the shell of a nut, floating on the top of the water. The Lady Regent smiling, willed *Daphne*, to re-fer the pitifull description of so wofull a shipwrack , to some other time, when they might there meete againe, for the like celebration of *Amyntas* death. In meane time, for a conclusion of this dayes exercise (sith it , see-

med conuenient to end with him, with whome they began) *Amarillis* and
Cassinpaa sang these verses, which *Amyntas* liuing had made of the death of
Phillis: which ended, they all departed.

Amintas Phillidi consecrauit,
mortuæ moriturus.

Heu status instabilis, via deuia, κϊομοϲ ἄκιομοϲ,
Heu non parcentes parcæ, redit orbis in orbem,
Et resolutaruit perituri machina mundi.
   Omnia, quæ tellus, pontus, (t) æther habent,
   Nil, nisi perpetuus terror (t) error, habet;
   Una dies struxit, destruet vna dies.
Effugit vmbra leuis: quid non fugit, vt leuis vmbra?
Effluit vnda grauis: quid non fluit, vt grauis vnda?
Euolat hora breuis: quid non volat, vt breuis horá?
   Sic matura breui, sunt moritura breui:
   Sic velut vmbra fugit, sic velut vnda fluit,
   Plena labore dies, plena dolore dies.
Pallida mors æquo pulsat pede, magna, minora;
Pallida mors æquo pulsat pede? pulsat iniquo,
Semper inæquales quià sic pede proterit æquo.
   Proterit illustrem, magnanimumque ducem,
   Præterit exhaustum, decrepitumque senem,
   Proterit illa bonum, præterit illa malum.
Nullo delectu sæuit, discrimine nullo,
Sed pariter parui passim properamus & ampli,
Omnibus vna domus, læthi lex omnibus vna,
   Flos, fænum, sumus, somnus, & vmbra sumus;
   Quæ viguére, cadunt, quæ valuére, ruunt;
   Et redit in cineres, quod fuit ante cinis;

Qd si delectu,qd si discrimine sæuit,

Ipso delectu,dilectos sæuit in ipsos,

Alba ligustra cadunt,& deteriora supersunt.

   Si peragant plures pessima quæque dies,

   Si meliora ruant,alba ligustra cadant ;

   Delectus valeat,gratior error erat.

Delectus valeat ? fluitent mortalia casu?

Gratior error erat ? Quid dixi ? gratior error?

Ah valeat vox hæc ; hic ingratissimus error.

   Ille deus certa lege peregit opus,

   Perfectum certa lege mouetur opus,

   Et motum certa lege peribit opus.

Rector adest rebus,nec adest sine numine rector,

Numen inest summis,complectitur infima numen,

Numen inest medijs,penetratque per omnia numen.

   Et nihil est,casu quod perijsse putem ;

   Non est,cur casum rebus inesse putem ;

   Hoc est,cur casus nomen inane putem.

Crine quid est leuius ? nec abest sine numine crinis :

Passere quid leuius ? nec adest sine numine passer :

Vita quid grauius ? periet sine numine vita?

   Non est cur credam : numine vita venit :

   Non est cur credam : numine vita fugit :

   Numine natus homo,numine stratus homo.

Nascimur,& morimur,quia nascimur,vt moriamur :

Sed neque sorte sati,neque casu morte perempti :

Iupiter hoc iussit,mors tantùm iussa capessit.

   Iupiter hoc iussit,sunt rata iussa Iouis :

   Fatur,& est fatum: sufficit αὐτὸς ἐφα :

   Dixit,& edictum tempus in omne manet.

Ergò vale Phillis : longùm, formosa, valeto :
Digna Iouis solio, tauro Ioue digna, vel auro,
Digna minus misero, meliori digna marito.

   Tindaridis facies, Penelopæa fides,
Fædere iuncta mihi, funere iuncta Ioui,
Semper amans salue, semper amanda vale.

Errata.

Fol. 1. *b. for, in seueral harbor, read,* in a seueral harbor. Fol. 8. *b. for, the stoutest were tamed, Reade,* the stoutest are tamed. Fol. 11. *b. for, fore feare, reade,* for feare. Fol. 15. E 2. *a. for, sons beames, reade,* sons bright beames. Fol. 21. *b. for, sylogistical, reade,* syllogistical. Fol. 25. *b. faintly Ceres, reade* fainty Ceres. Fol. 26. *b. for, natrea deorum, reade,* natura deorum. 28. *a. for, sweare, reade,* sware. Pyriphlegeton, reade, Pyriphlegeton, 1. 2 *b. for, late, reade,* late. 1. 3 *a. for, γάνυμι, reade, γάνυμι.* 36 *a. last word, for, these, reade,* the. 37. *b last word, Iceu,* Ioue. 42. *a. first line, homed, reade,* horned. 43. *b. georgicwon, reade,* georgicwn. 44. *b. bare, reade,* beare. 51 *a. 4. lin. 3 ime, reade,* day. last line, swelling, reade, swilling. 54. *b. rolleth and ruleth, reade,* ruleth and rolleth.

THE
FOVNTAINE OF
ANCIENT FICTION.

Wherein is liuely depictured the Images and
Statues of the gods of the Ancients, with their
proper and perticular expositions.

Done out of Italian into English, by Richard Linche Gent.

Tempo è figliuola di verità.

LONDON,
Printed by Adam Islip.
1599.

To the right vertuous and well-dif-
poſed Gentleman, *M*. Peter Dauiſon *Eſquire*,
Richard Linche *wiſheth all affluence of worldly pro-*
ſperities, and the fruition of all celeſtiall graces hereafter.

Orſhipful Sir, the firſt thing that
I here wil requeſt at your hands,
ſhall be pardon, in preſenting
vnto your view a ſubiect ſo much
diſagreeing with your owne diſ-
poſition. The matter it ſelfe I graunt can chal-
lenge no ſuch graue Mecenas, being indeed
vvholly fabulous: but the willingneſſe of my
ſoule, to ſhew ſome ſigne of gratefulneſſe for
curteſies receiued, hath inforced me to aduenture ſo far vpon your acceptance, as to offer
this ſtrange-borne child of idleneſſe wholly vnto your fauourable patronage. And herein I imitate the faſhions and vſances of the ancient Perſians, vvho alwaies vvhen they ſaw
their king, vvould offer vp ſomething or other
that they had about them vnto him, as a token and teſtimonie of their loue, dutie, and
reuerence: and one day the king being abroad,

A iij   one

one of his ſubiects vpon the ſuddain met him, vvho hauing nothing in his hands to giue him, ran in all halt to the vvaters ſide, and brought him both his hands full of vvater, which the king graciouſly accepted, & gaue him thanks as for a greater preſent. This peece of work (Sir, may be compared to thoſe hands ful of water) being indeed of little vvorth and value, and alſo very haſtily performed, vvhich as it is, I offer in the fulneſſe of loue, and do deſire a fauorable cenſure for the ſame: for I knovv, that as a handfull of vvater is an vnmeet preſent for a king, ſo this matter ſo ſtuft and compacted of poeticall and vaine fiction, is not altogether beſeeming the countenance of ſo graue and ſo vvorthy a perſonage. But my error herein proceedeth vvholly of my vvillingnes to do ſomething that might merit your forepaſſed fauors, and to diſcouer a good meaning of gratefulnes, though the meanes it ſelfe perhaps proue not grateful vnto you. Howſoeuer it is, I conſecrate it vvholly vnto your ſelfe, and craue patience if any haſtbred imperfection therin offend your better iudgement. Thus recommending you vnto the ſafegard of the diuine Maieſty, I vviſh you all fortunes ſutable to your vertues.

Yours in all loiall fidelitie moſt aſſured.
Richard Linche.

To the Reader.

H E that beleeueth, that in his writings he pleaseth all mens humors, too much crediteth his owne opinion, and flattereth his owne iudgement : for men indeed that haue attained to the true maturitie of knowledge, & arts perfection, it is good to agree with, as for lame, and yet snarling censurers, it is matterlesse to satisfie : for so much as the prodigality of such their lauish opinions, hath his first conception of old father Ignorance, and is brought vp and educated by an infectious nurse, called Selfeglorie. This matter now handled, was vndertaken suddainly, and dispatched hastily, for which he craueth milder constructions, & in very deed had it not by an extraordinary accident happened into the hands of a stranger, it had not now (poore father forsaken child) endured the insupportable tyrantie of lawlesse censure. But when I found that it was so far gone, and as it were irreuocably escaped from out my hands, and euen ready to be thrust out naked & clothlesse into the world, I chose rather to father it, and re-entertaine such my wandring trauailler, and bestow some few lines in his behalfe vnto the reader, than that so bare a subiect should passe in his imperfections vnepistled, or not

befrien-

To the Reader.

befriended with the authors name in such his pri-
uatenesse and obscuritie. Such as it is therefore, either culpable in words too much affected, or in dis-
proportion being not methodically composed, or in
shallownesse in the not proper vnderstanding of the
first authors meaning, it must now passe, as for me
it is too late to recall it, and too needlesse to repent
it, for howsoeuer it is, it once neuer imagined to haue
been now subiect to the error-searching sight of a
generall eye, being only pend & translated for mine
owne exercises and priuate recreations. But herein I am something too tedious, for as it is an ab-
surd part in an architector to frame a long & vast
entry for a littl house and of small receit, so for me
to vse many words in this place, whose substance
(you will say) challengeth no worthines, they should
be friuolously bestowed, and time purpose-lesse entertained. For the indifferent Readers I cannot but
promise equal allowance: for any venom-lipt rough-
censuring Satires, I keepe sorrow for their wood-
borne inciuility and rustike imperfections, and do
arme my selfe with steele-mettald patience
to abide the shocke of their iniurious
toung-oppressions. And so
in hast I leaue you.

Rich. Linche.

The Images, Statues, and Pictures
of the gods of the auncients, vvith
their feuerall expofitions.

THere haue liued verie few people, or rather none at all, fince the
firft proportionlesse and indige-
fted heape of all things (whatfoeuer) was reduced by diuine prouidence into this admirable
forme: which haue not among
themfelues embraced a certaine and peculiar fort of
religious adoration. For the foule of man euen vpon
her firft entrance into this earth-framed and corrupted receptable of her celeftiall effence, doth feeme to
bring then with her a certaine kind of naturall religion, the diuinitie whereof procureth the difcrepance
betwixt men and beafts, which as they want the intellectuall fence and feeling of any fuch motion, do therfore neither worfhip or reuerence any deitie: Onely
man, whofe bodie is framed erect, with his eies ftill

looking

looking on that perspicuous and thought-amazing
composition of the heauens, is forcibly constrained
to beleeue, that there hath been some one of eternall
and infinit command, that hath had that vnspeakable
wisdome, and inexcogitable care, as first to compose,
then to gouerne and dispose this so rare and miracu-
lous wonderment : and him they entearme by the
name of G O D, as it were the giuer of al good things,
who by his infinitenesse is eternal, incomprehensible,
and inuisible . But such their beleefe extended not so
farre, nor was it so impressed in all mens hearts, as that
euery one therefore attained to this stainelesse and
truth-yeelding opinion. For at the first, the corruptible sottishnesse, and faith-wanting weaknesse of man
was such, as illustrating the heauens and their reuolutions, the earth and her encrease, the sea with her
strange courses, onely with the externall eies of their
faces, not admitting the same to anie contemplation,
or soule-obseruance, the vulgars, and such as blindfolded went groping vp and down in the dark for knowledge, were entangled in such an intricate garden and
Labyrinth of error, that they were firmely persuaded
that there was a god in this Statue, another in that
picture of earth, stone, and other mettals, and oftentimes in painted Images : from whence it proceeded,
that there were then in such friuolous and superstitious reuerence, so innumerable multitudes of gods
among the auncients. For not onely the seuerall humours of diuerse Nations, but euerie particular Cittie, caused their Image that they would worship, so to
be framed, according as they were then to craue and

request

request some especiall and extraordinarie boone of their wooden deities, or hauing alreadie obtained it, entended thereby to manifest their thankfgiuing and gratefulneffe. And being(as it we e) rockt asleep with the pleasing conceit of this their superstition, it grew so farre vpon them, that in the end they worshipped and deuoutly adored men like vnto themselues, such as were knowne to haue inuented and found out some speciall good and adiuvament for their easie and quiet liuing, or to haue(as it were) hewen out and forced from their deepe-searching capacities some strange and vncouth art, science, or profession. And to these men were erected and dedicated excellent grauen statues, in whose curious architecturie all those good things and deeds which they deuised or atcheeued here among men, were liuely and exactly set forth and interfected . And although this kind of Idolatrous veneration, firmly posseft the thoughts of men generally, yet vniuersally it extended not. For there then liued , who carried an irremoueable beleefe of the sacred deitie of one God onely, which was euer-during and inuisible , and therefore shaped not to themselues any further Image or representation (which who so feekes to entertaine, walketh in the erroneous paths of soule-endangering ignorance.) The Iewes(which among the ancients attained nigh-eft vnto the sure and infallible truth) worshipped one God onely , and him they adored not in counterfeit and stone-built Statues, difcerned onely with the eies of the body, but with the cleere-shining light of the mind, and were still rapt with premeditating and

contem-

contemplatiue thoughts of his ymeuſe and incom-
prehenſible diuinitie. And as *Cornelius Tacitus* affirmeth, they accounted them wicked and impious, who
of themſelues would make ſuch counterſhape or re-
preſentation of God, compoſing in it likeneſſe and
ſimilitude to the proportion of a humane and terrene
bodie: and therefore neither in their Citties, nor in
their Temples admitted they any ſuch vaine & ſenceleſſe adoration. *Lycurgus* (who in perfection and maturitie of true knowledge, did no way equalize the
Iewes) would not by any meanes that there ſhould be
contriued any frame or Idea of their gods, becauſe
(ſayth hee) they cannot bee likened neither to man or
anie other liuing creature, and being likewiſe inuiſi-
ble, who can depicture that which his eyes neuer
ſaw. *Lactantius* writeth, That the Ægiptians worſhipped with all deuotion the foure elements, and yet not
making any Image or picture of them. The Perſians,
the Scythians, and thoſe of Libia, neuer had Statues,
Altars, or Temples, but onely madetheir reſort in ſeuerall conuenticles to conſecrated woods & groues,
and to them onely they ſubmitted themſelues in reuerence, and powred out ther deuotion. And ſo likewiſe did thoſe of Maxilia in Gallia Narbonenſe, wor-
ſhipping in all humilitie certaine woods and groues,
which they purpoſely conſecrated for that intendement: and directed vp all their deuout praiers and
obteſtations to leaueleſſe trunkes and ſtocks of trees,
wherevpon *Lucan* writeth thus of them:

They worſhipt ſtockes, and armeleſſe trunckes of trees,
            Which

Cornelius Tacitus.

Licurgus.

Lactantius.

Which neither shape or due proportion haue,
And to these posts all reuerence they gaue.

Cornelius Tacitus (writing of Germany) sayth, That
the Germanes not onely denied all reuerence to any
pictures of their gods, but would not by any meanes
suffer any Temples to be built or dedicated vnto thē :
saying, that it was very incongruent and inconuenient to shut vp their deities within the wals of so small
a circuite, and that it was not a thing meet or agreeable for their infinite greatnesse to bee shaped out to
the small forme and proportion of a humane bodie.
As the Grecians did after that, and the Romanes, and
before them the Ægyptians, who all framed their
Images of their Gods to the due likenesse and proportion of a mans bodie. But yet they did not so farre
ouershoot themselues, as to thinke that their celestiall
gods had either heads, hands, or feet; but to shew (as
Varro sayth) That the soule of man, which is impriso- Varro.
ned here in the fleshly dungeon of the bodie, resem-
bles the diuine soules, which inhabite in the celestiall
dwellings of the heauens : and for that the mind or
soule cannot externally bee seene or proportioned,
they did prefigure it, and make it apparent by the
shape of a humane bodie. *Porphirius* sayth, as *Eusebius* Porphirius.
reporteth, That the Images of their gods were made
to the likenesse of men, because God (saith he) is a spirit and reason, whereof men, and no other creatures
doe participate. *Lactantius* giueth another reason of Lactantius.
these Statues, saying, that they were first made for the
conseruation of the remembrance of deceased kings

and

and gouernours, for the perpetuall eternisement of their famous and memorable atcheeuements: where-vpon *Eusebius* writing of the Ecclesiasticall historie, likewise writeth , That it was a generall custome among the Gentiles to honour the greatest personages, and men of best demerit , by representing their Ideas by Statues or Pictures, and so by that meanes keeping them as it were aliue by the memorious trophies of their neuer-dying worthinesse; wherby their succeeding posteritie might euidently perceiue what respectiue regard was had and cannonized of those who had in their life time adioined to their valerous approuements, ciuile and vertuous conuersation: you shall read in *Plinie*, that in Rhodes were found at one time more than three thousand Statues , and not many lesse in Athens, or in Delphos, and so also in manie other places of Greece. In which foolish superstition, Rome also (though not so lately) was vnto any of those nothing inferior, who had indeed gathered together so many pictures and supposed gods , that it was said, that in Rome there were another sort of people made of stone , for what pictures soeuer they could get, either of painters or ingrauers, they omitted no meanes to compasse , and with those would they beautifie their houses, not only in the Citie, but euen in their country or farme-houses : which indeed was iudged to bee too effeminat & soft for the strict and seuere life of the Romanes. *Lucullus* (as *Varro* writeth) had such delight in such Images, that almost euery day infinite numbers of people resorted to his farmes in the country to see his strange pictures and
curious

Eusebius.

Plinie.

Lucullus.

curious engraued Statues. And this note the ancients obferued, that thofe their Images were made with a deuife, as when they pleafed themfelues, they might take off their heads, and fet them vpon others. Wher-vpon *Suetonius* fpeaking of the glorious and infolent *Suetonius.* humor of *Caligula*, fayth, That he perceiuing himfelfe to haue furpaffed all other Princes and Gouernours his predeceffours in greatneffe and powerfull com-mand, began to footh himfelfe vp fo farre in that in-folencie and fuperarrogation, that hee commanded all thefe heads of their greateft Gods, which either for deuotion or rare workemanfhip, were moft ado-red, as that of Iupiter Olympius and others, fhould be taken away, and vpon them fhould bee placed the true portraiture of his owne, moft exquifitely hewed and engraued. And *Lambridius* likewife fayth, That *Lambridius* the Emperour *Commodus* tooke away the head from that famous and art-exceeding Image of *Nero*, which was fo cutioufly with fuch ingenious architecturie depictured, and vpon that likewife commanded his owne to be erected. Not long after this, the Statuaries of Princes were fo regarded & held in fuch reuerent embracements, as whatfoeuer (occafioned by what meanes you will) had fled to thefe priuelegious pla-ces, had ben freed from any purfuing danger whatfo-euer, and not to be inforced or brought away during his ftay in that fo regarded fanctuarie. Onely wee read of *Marcus Antonius* (who as *Suetonius* affirmeth) fly- *Suetonius.* ing to the Statue of *Iulius Cæfar*, for his better fafe-gard, was by *Auguftus* caufed violently to bee haled from thence, and afterwards ftopping his eares to all

praiers

praiers and entreaties, commanded him to bee slaine.
The Statues of Princes were oftentimes portraied
out naked, oftentimes also clothed, and most commonly gloriously depainted with gold : as wee read

Titus Li-
uius.

with *Titus Liuius*, who saith, That *Acylius Glabrio*
was the first in Italie that made any golden Statuarie,
and after that it was generally accustomed through

Alexander
Afrodiseus.

all the Country. *Alexander Afrodiseus* writeth, That in
those daies the Images of their gods, and of their
princes were made as it might seeme naked, & a greater honor therby was attributed vnto thē, as of those
whose clemencie and iustice lay open and manifest
vnto all men: signifying that Princes and Magistrates
ought to be naked as it were, and immaculate from
all corruptible vice, carrying in themselues a christalline and clear conscience, not cloked or couered with
any inward mischeef working or deceitful thoughts.
Vpon anie pompeous solemnitie of any exercises and
sports, not onely the Images of their gods were carried by seuerall turnes on mens shoulders, but also
the Statues of Emperours, valerous Captaines, and
farre famed commanders, were likewise presented on
those feastiuals. But *Alarius*, in that hee was ignoble

Salust.

by birth, and of meane discent (as *Salust* sayth) had not
then to carrie any picture of his owne, nor of his an-
cestors, but in steed of those, hee there manifested the
high and condigne rewards he had receiued for these
so honourable and renowned prises which hee won,
and triumphantly carried away in many gallant and
victorious expeditions. Assuredly, the Images and
Statuaries of the gods in those daies were almost

innu-

innumerable, and framed into fo many feueral and infinit fafhions, as to endeauour to fet them all downe,
were as difficult, as blindfolded to worke my felfe out
of fome intricate and ftrange-framed Labyrinth. Onely thofe whom approued and autentike Authors will
warrantife currant and paffible, we will now remember: and yet if all other Nations had obferued that
courfe which the Ægyptians vfed, happily we might
haue touched the moft part of them . For according
to the writings of *Plato* , in Ægypt were referued Plato.
among all their moft reuerend and facred reliques,
thofe engrauen or painted Images which were then
alreadie framed and left vnto them from their aunce-
ftors, neuer labouring or ftudying to inuent more, as
almoft all other Nations at that time bufied themfelues. In Greece for the moft part their gods were
fafhioned, according as the feuerall humour of the
people then affected, euery one enucleating thereby
their felfe-pleafing conceits, and inward delectations:
fo that becaufe the Lacedemonians were generally
martiall people, and verie oftentimes in wars imploy-
ments, their gods were alwaies depictured in côplete
armour. And the Phenicians (in that they were giuen to Marchandifes, and other worldlie gaine-pro-
curing trauels, accounting him onely bleft that poffeffed greateft treafure and abundance of wealth) caufed their gods to bee hewen out with a great fwolne
bag or purfe in each of their hands. And fo likewife in
diuerfe other difcrepant fafhions, were their Statues
in thofe ages framed, according as they then beleeued to be in them feuerall natures, powers, & effects :

C   by

by reafon whereof, (as *Eufebius* rehearfing the words
of *Porphirius* faith) The ancients to make the diuerfi-
tie of their gods appeare, depictured fome male, and
fome female, others virgines, and others married, and
fo accordingly habited them in their agreeable veft-
ments. The mettals and fubftance of which Statues,
Eufebius (taking it from *Porphirius*) thus fayth : That
God being abfolutely cleere, pure-fhining, and cor-
rufcant, whofe eies-dazelling luftre man cannot comprehend with terrene fence, they alwaies framed his
picture of the moft fine and precious tranfparent
chriftall, and of the moft pure and vnblemifhed marble that they could by any meanes and by all ftrict in-
ueftigation acquire and compaffe : fometimes alfo
they would frame his Statue of the moft glorious
gold, to fhew the eternall and diuine fire that burneth
continually where hee remaineth, and that his nature
is free from all corrupted ruftineffe of our humane
affections. Others that would haue his Statue of black
ftone, entend thereby to note his inuifibilitie. It is
written by *Plutarch* , That the making of thefe kind
of Statues, Images, and Pictures, hath been very ancient, but (fayth hee) the fathers in thofe daies, did make
them for the moft part of wood, becaufe it feemed to
them, that the hard and art-refifting mettall of ftone
was too ftubborn and harfh a ftuffe for them to make
their gods of, and that either gold or filuer were too
bafe, as being excrements of an vnfertile and fruit-
leffe foile, becaufe whereas the mines of thofe mettals are found, are fildome feene anie plant or root to
grow : and fuch ground as brought not forth flower,
hearbes,

Porphirius.

Porphirius.

Plutarch.

hearbes, and other fruits, they held as accurfed and vnfortunate. Thefe men indeed which liued in thofe daies, were not fo bewitched with the enchantments of the fweet-feeming, though foure-prouing delights of this world, nor regarded they the vfe of either filuer or gold in fuch ineftimable prife, but ftudied onely, and were laborious to fearch out fuch life-preferuing commodities, as they might thereby bee fed and nourifhed. *Plato* in like manner would haue fuch Statues altogether of wood, For (faith he) the earth being a place confecrated vnto the gods, there ought not to bee compofed thereof any Image or Picture, fo likewife neither of gold or filuer, for that among the poffeffours of thofe mettals, there is hatched and brought forth deteftable, eontentious, and malicious enuies. And *Lactantius* fayth, That fuch glorious and gold-emboffed Statues of their gods, did onelie fhew the auaricious minds of men, who vnder the fhadow of religion and deuotion, would bee continually poffeffed with infinit ftore of riches, both of gold and filuer, and other very precious ftones and iewels, whereof they made them fuch fumptuous Images, which indeed many of thē regarded & endeared, more for the ineftimable coft and charges beftowed vpon them, than for anie reuerence of thofe gods by which they were reprefented. But the opinion of *Plato*, as I haue faid, was to haue them altogether made of wood For Yron (fayth hee) and other fuch hard mettals are yfed and imployed in many fatall and horrible bloudie maffacres, and are the occafions of huge and infinite flaughters. *Tibullus* fpeaking of their domefti-

Plato.

Lactantius.

Tibullus.

C ij   call

call gods, whom they called Lares, thus fayth of them:
Maruell not you foolifh men to fee thefe our gods
made of ftockes of drie trees, for fuch (fayeth hee) in
the profperous daies of our contentfull fathers, when
religion, faith, and Iuftice were fincerely and louingly
embofom'd, were reuerenced with truer zeale of vnfained veneration, than are now adaies thefe gorgeous and gold-compofed Statues. It is written by *Pli-*
nie, That Images and Pictures be of great antiquitie
in Italie, yet they were not made of any other mettals
but wood: and fome few of ftone, fince Afia was vaf-
fallized and fubiugated to the Romanes. And for that
vnto all fuch Statues and Images of their gods, was
annexed and adioyned the picture of Eternitie, I
thinke it not amiffe in this place in fome fort to touch
it. Although *Boccace* writing of the Progenie of the
gods, fayth, That the auncients haue deriued it from
Demogorgon, as the principall and firft of them all, and
who inhabited in the middle center of the earth, en-
circled round about, & circumuefted with a dark and
obfufcate cloud, breathing from his mouth a certaine
liquid humiditie: but herein I will proceed no further, hauing no further warrant for fuch depicturance: onely I will now reuert my penne to the Statue of Eternitie, which what it is, the name doth
cleerely difcouer, containing in it felfe all worlds and
ages, and not limitted or meafured by any fpace of
time: And therefore *Trifmegiftus*, *Plato*, and the Py-
thagorickes, called Time the Image of Eternitie: in
that it is reuolued in it felfe, and admits no date.
Wherevpon for the more ample and copious manifefting

Plinie.

Boccace

Trifmegift.

festing thereof, we will heare the opinion of *Claudi-* Claudius.
us in his Stiliconyan comends, who there makes a description by a Serpent, that compasseth round with
her bodie the denne or caue wherin she lyeth, in such
sort, that making as it were a circle, she holdeth in her
mouth the end of her taile : by which is signified the
effect of time, which in it selfe alwaies goeth round :
which description is taken from the Ægyptians, who
before that the vse of letters and of writing was inuented, signified the circumference of a yeare by a Serpent, with her taile betweene her teeth : For that in
times there is the like coherence and depencie, for
the end of one yeare or time passed, is the beginning
of the other succeeding. And I remember the picture of Eternitie to be by some thus defigured : A woman clothed in rich robes downe to her feet, holding
in her right hand a round ball , and vpon her head is
instrophiated a thinne vaile, which spreads and casts
it selfe downe so farre, as both her shoulders are therewith wholly circumcinct and couered . The Image
weighed in the heedfull ballance of aduise , is not
much vnlike that reported by *Claudianus,* which wee
will endeauour (though not in his right colours) thus
to compose.

Downe in a vale (close hid from Phebus eie,
    Held in the arms of two heauen-threatning mountains,
From out whose bosome furiously their flie,
    With vnresisted force, two swift wing'd fountaines)
There dwels an aged Caue : that nere will die,
    Though death sits pictur'd in her horrid countenance,

The fountaine of ancient fiction.
She sends fourth Times, and cals them backe againe,
For Times and Ages aye with her remaine.

Vpon her lap a greene-scal'd Serpent lies,
  Whose hugenesse fils her wide rotunditye,
Darting forth fierie sparckles from her eyes,
  And what she finds, deuoures most hungrilie,
Her wrinckled taile fast twixt her teeth she ties,
  Euen which she seemes to gnaw most greedilie,
All in a circle thus she sits involved,
Whose firme tenacitie is ne're dissolved.

And at the gate of this so strange-fram'd denne,
  In Matrons habit, and in graue attire,
Stands gracious Nature noting with her pen,
  Whom she lets forth, and whom againe retire :
And round about the caue the soules of men
  Flie here, and there, as seeming to aspire,
And longing to recouer heauen ; but these
With Nature must remaine till death shall please :

In furthest nooke and corner of the cell,
  Sits an old man, whose colour'd hasre
Is far more white then any toung can tell,
  And whose cleere louely face exceeds all faire,
Writing downe lawes for those that here do dwell,
  That ignorance may neuer cause despaire,
And as he sits, each star he doth diuide,
And euery Plannet in his course doth guide.

Prescribing with immutable decree,

The fountaine of ancient fiction.

To euery one their courses as they lie,
By whom all liuing things (what ere they be)
That haue or life, or death, doo liue and die,
Then streight he turnes him round about to see
How Mars attends his course full busilie,
Who though through doubtfull paths he long doth stray,
Yet at the length all tends but to one way.

How Iupiter the worlds ne're-failing friend,
Directs his circuit through the azur'd skie,
How Luna at her brothers iournies end,
Rides in her purple coach most glorioustie,
How soure-fac'd Saturne his slow steps doth tend,
And how faire Venus through the aire doth flie,
And next to her succeeds heauens messenger,
Posting amaine as Phebus harbenger.

Who when (He) comes in his al-glorious shine,
Great Nature meets him in most reuerent wise,
To whom the aged man doth make a signe
In curtesie, as though he meant to rise,
When straight the gates of this same caue diuine,
Open themselues with wondrous subtleties,
Within whose adamantine cell is seene
What from beginning of the world hath been.

Here, euerie age of sundry mettall's framed,
Apactly seated in his due degree,
And of those mettals so they still are named,
Whether of wood, brasse, yron, or steele they be
Here shall you see, the siluer age so famed,

Staining

Staining the former in cleere puritie,
But when you see(that) of resplendent gold,
The other, but base mettals you will hold.

Boccace.   The description of this caue or denne (according to the opinion of *Boccace*) importeth thus much : That Eternitie hath an absolute and sole commaund ouer all times, and therefore she liues farre hence remoted in some vnknowne vale : where humane steps neuer approched, but is euen vnfound out of the celestiall inhabitants, that is, those happie soules which stand before the presence of the greatest, who onelie knoweth all things : shee sendeth forth times, and recals them backe againe, for that from her, all ages haue had their beginning, instantly possesse their being, and with her for euer shall continue : she sits incircled and inuolued in her selfe, as wee haue alreadie discouered in the former description by the forme of a Serpent, who continually with her taile in her mouth, turneth her selfe round with as great slownesse or leisure as is possible, shewing thereby that Time with a creeping and vnseene pace , steales by little and little cleane from vs. At the entrance of the caue (where Nature sits) the soules of men seeme to flutter and houer ouer her head : which importeth the infinite numbers of men that are euerie day created, bringing then with them their soules, and for that they appeare to flie directly ouer the bosome of Eternitie, it meaneth, that whosoeuer attaines vnto (that) excellencie of perfection, must first enter his aspiring steps by the means of Nature, and for that cause she is placed at the dore or portall.

portall. The aged man, which there fits deuiding and parting the ftarres, may be called God, not that hee is old, for time ouer him lofeth her vertue, and worketh no effect , who of himfelfe is perpetuall and euer-liuing: but that the auncients heretofore haue pleafed fo defigure him, and becaufe he effecteth all things by infinite wifdome, ruling and commanding all creatures whatfoeuer, by his vnfpeakeable power , they therefore attribute vnto him old age, wherein is commonly found more wifdome, grauitie, and experience than in youth. Thus farre *Boccace* reporteth, not touching any thing at all the explication of the ages and worlds, which followed in that his defcription, in that indeed they were not fo enigmaticall, but euery one might eafily admit the conceiuing knowledge of fo familiar intendements. Therefore now wee will proceed, beginning with the Image or Statue of Saturnus, according as it hath beene by the Auncients heretofore compofed.

Saturne.

SAturne being expulfed heauen by Iupiter (as hiftories record) and throwne downe from thence into this middle region: after many daies failing vpon the fea, at the length hee ariued in Italie, where hee liued manie yeares with Ianus, then king of that part of the Countrey where Rome afterwards was built: but poorely and meanely he liued , as indeed all the people in thofe times did, as hauing vnfound out the vfe of tilling and planting, whereby corne and other

fruits

fruits of the earth might suppeditate their wants of
necessarie food and victuall. The vse of which things
they now learned from Saturne, who painfully instructed them in the perfect knowledge of the nature of
each soile, and how, and by what industrious meanes
of art any ground (fruitlesse of it self by nature) might
become fertile and rich. This learned and powerfull
skill of Saturne, Ianus infinitely admired, insomuch,
as (manifesting his gratefulnesse, for so behoofefull
and commodious a good turne receaued) he commu-
nicated part of his kingdome for him to liue vpon :
affording him many other princely and respectiue re-
gards. And further commanded his people, that when
he died, they should with all reuerence honour him
as a god, a thing easily embraced by the ignorant Hea-
then in those daies, who in that they had receiued so
vnexpected a benefite from his meanes , willinglie
condiscended to ascribe and attribute vnto him all
godlike reuerence, and deuout adoration, as men indeed vnto whome the sole and eternall God had not
ministred the Key of vnderstanding, that their close-
shut hearts liuing in the darke caue of ignorance,
might therewith bee opened and vnlocked for the
admittance of the true acknowledgement of his sacred deitie: but they onely worshipped him for their
god, who by his humane knowledge had found out
some new means either for the earths better increase,
or other like profit that were most auaileable for their
labour-lesse and sluggish liuing. And therefore they
willingly adored Saturne as a mightie and puissant
god, dedicating vnto him manie sumptuous Statues
and

and temples. And him in his Statue they framed with
a hooke or fyth in his hand, demonftrating thereby
(as they meant it) the inuention of tilling of the
ground, becaufe with that the corne once recouering
his maturitie, is cut downe. Other writers there are,
that would haue him fignifie Tyme, as that with his
fythe he fhould meafure and proportionife the length
of Time, and therewith to decurtate and cut away all
things contained therein. Thofe alfo would haue him
to be in the fhape of a very aged man, as one who began from beginning of the world, holding in his
hand a child, which by peecemeales, hee feemes greedily to deuour, importing the reuenge hee tooke, being banifhed heauen by his owne children : thofe
which efcapt the furious gulfe of his maw, were onely foure, Iupiter, Iuno, Pluto, and Neptune, which intend the foure elements, Fire, Aire, earth, and Water,
which are not perifhable by the all-cutting fickle of
deuouring time. *Martianus Capella* depictures him,
holding in his right hand a Serpent, with the end of Martianus Capella.
her taile in her mouth, ftill turning round with a heauie and dead flow pace, and he hath his temples redemyted with a greene wreath, which feemeth ftill to
flourifh, his haire of his head, and his beard all milke
white, looking like one of many yeares, withering and
declining, and yet manifefting that it is in his power
to rebecome youthfull, frefh, and blooming. The
wreath on his head imports the beginning or fpring
of the yeare, his haire and beard the fnowie approch
of churlifh Winter, the flownefle of the ferpents paces the fluggifh reuolution of that planet, which as

it is of all the greateft, fo it asketh longeft time for his circular circumference, and in that from this plannet proceed dolorous and difmall effects, they fhape him to be old, louring, forrowing, hardfauonred and flug- gifh, his nature being cold, drie, and melancholie. The fame *Martianus* fayth, That the nuptials of Mercurie and Philologia, when fhe had fearched and perviewed each corner of the higher and lower heauens, fhee found Saturne fitting with great folitude in an ex- tream cold manfion all frozen & couered with yfe and fnow, wearing on his head a helmet, on which was liuely depictured three heads, the one of a Serpent, the other of a Lyon, and the third of a Boare: which three by many conftructions may fignifie the effect of Time, but in that it is by the Authors themfelues, but fleightly approued, we will wade no further in it. And yet *Macrobius* toucheth it very neerely, when hee de- fcribes him with a Lyons head, a Dogs head, and a Wolfes head: intending by the Lyons head the time prefent, which duly placed betweene that paft and that to come, preuaileth moft, and is of greateft force ; or difcouering thereby the ftormie troubles of mans life, by the rough, vnpleafing, and grim afpect of the Lyon: by that of the Dog, is meant the prefent time, who alwaies fawnes on vs, and by whofe alluring de- lights we are drawne vnto vaine and vnceitain hopes: The Wolues head fignifies the time paft, by his gree- die deuouring what ere he finds, leauing no memo- rie behind of what hee catcheth within his clawes: Aftarte the daughter of Celum, and wife and fifter of Saturne., made for her husband a princely helmet, which

Martianus

Macrobius.

which had foure eies, two before, and two behind, which continually shut themselues, & slept by turns, so that two alwaies were open, and vpon his shoul-ders were likewise made foure wings, two of them volant, and two couchant, which signified, that al-though he slept, he alwaies waked, and flying, conti-nued fixe and permanent; vnclouding hereby the na-ture of Time : these heads were cut out with exqui-site subtletie, and rare politure : *Eusebius* further saith, Eusebius.
That the same Astarte placed also vpon the head of Saturne two wings, demonstrating thereby by one of them the excellencie and perfection of the mind, and by the other he meant mans sence and vnderstan-ding. For say the Naturalists, the soule of man when she entreth into the humane bodie, bringeth with her from the spheare of Saturne the force of knowledge and discourse, so that the Platonickes vnderstand by Saturne, the mind, and the inward contemplation of things celestiall, and therefore called the time where-in hee liued the golden age, as a time, entertaining quiet, concord, and true content. And *Macrobius* Macrobius.
among the rest of his descriptions sayth, That his feet are tied together with the threds of woll, agree-ing thereby with the Prouerbe of the Latines, say-ing, That the gods doe not any thing in hast, nor make any forced speed to castigate the iniquities of men, but proceed with a slow and vnwilling progres-sion, as giuing them time and leisure of amendment. And thus concerning the Statues of Saturne.

Ianus.

IT lieth farre from my intendement in this treatife
to touch in any fort the life of the gods of the auncients , or to tell now how Ianus was one of the ri-
cheft kings of Italie, and how hee receiued Saturne
then an exile, and participated part of his kingdome
vnto him in lewe of thofe his knowledges difcouered:
for fo much as my purpofe onely extendeth to tell of
the Images and Statues which in thofe times of blindneffe and fuperftition were erected and confecrated
Macrobius. vnto their gods. According therefore to *Macrobius*,
Ianus was the firft that in all Italie caufed facred temples and fanctuaries of deuotion to bee built, ordai-
ning facrifices and fuch like rites of expiation to bee
vfed with all reuerence and zealous folemnization.By
reafon whereof hee himfelfe was afterwards among
thofe ignorant Plebeians, held and cannonized as a
god. And becaufe I fay that hee was the firft inuenter
and fetter vp of fuch facrifices, the auncients would
neuer offer vp any of their oblations vnto their gods,
vnleffe they had firft inuocated the helping affiftance
of Ianus. And this reafon alfo induced them the rather thereunto, for that hee was afterwards fuppofed
to be the god which continuallyfat at the dore or portall of heauen : fo that the petitions and praiers of
men below., could not paffe or afcend vnto the hearing of their gods, vnleffe he had firft granted and allowed fuch their acceffe and admittance. The gates
or dores of the heauēs are faid to be two, the one pla-
                                                    ced

ced at the Eaſt, the other at the Weſt; through the firſt the ſun entreth, when he commeth to illuminat with his brightneſſe the worlds obſcuritie; and through the other hee goeth out when hee deſcendeth to the Antipodes. Thoſe therefore that by the ſunne vnderſtand Ianus (as *Macrobius* and others) attribute vnto him the charge or keeping of thoſe gates, in that he is alwaies freely licenſed to enter in and go out through them at his pleaſure, and for this cauſe they ſhape him forth with two faces, for that the ſun alwaies looketh round about him, both before and behind in ech part and corner of the world: and in one of his hands they put a long rod or wand, and in the other a key; ſhewing by the one the rule and gouernement hee commandeth ouer all the world: and by the other hee openeth and vnlocketh it as it were from the cloſe priſon of vapourous cloudineſſe, when hee diſcouers the orientall reſplendencie of his radiance, and how he ſhutteth it vp againe when he leaueth it to the gloomy gouernment of the night. Neither is this to be vnderſtood by the day and the night only, but by all the yeare alſo, as wnen the ſun vnloſeth the ſpring from the ſtubborne embracements of the Winter, enamelling the pleaſant verdure of the earth with ſo many delicate and diuers-coloured flowers, where is found all choice of pleaſing pretineſſe in that gorgeous faire of bounteous Nature: which at his due time ended, the ſun locketh vp ſuch the ſumptuouſnes therof, ſuffering the earth to lie naked to the mercileſſe tiranny of yce and ſnow, whoſe all-periſhing coldneſſe benums her vſeleſſe and ſtiffe-

waxing

waxing ioints, which lately fo empreffe-like florifhed, and was fo glorioufly inuefted. The 2 faces of Ianus fignifie alfo Time, the one of thē being withered & hoary, intendeth the time paft, the other youthful & beardles, meaneth the times after cōming and fucceeding. *Plinie* writeth, That *Numa* king of the Romanes caufed the Statue of Ianus to be hewen out in fuch fort, that the fingers of his hands appeared to be three hundred threefcore and fiue, to demonftrate thereby that hee was God of the yeare, and had the fole rule and gouernement thereof. Wherevpon they called the firft moneth of the yeare Ianuarius, of Ianus, there then king. The Phenicians, as *Marcus Tullius* and *Macrobius* report, vnderftood by Ianus, the world: and therefore framed his Image in the forme of a ferpent, holding her taile in her mouth, continually turning round and circumfered: as that the world doth nourifh and feed it felfe, and the times thereof depending and cohering one of another. But returning to the two faces of Ianus, fome will haue fuch depicturance to fignifie the wifdome and graue intellect of prudent Princes, which befides that by their wife counfels they doe act things politikely and difcreetly, inftantly, and for the time prefent, carrie likewife in themfelues a fore-prouiding prefcience to preuent, and therby to remedie fucceeding mifcheefs and enfuing daungers: for that with the one face before, and the other behind, they continually behold and view round about them, recording things paft, and premeditating thofe likely to follow: the which things the ancients prefigure vnto vs by the Statue of
Ianus,

Plinie.

Marcus Tullius, and Macrobius.

intending (as *Plutarch* fayth) That Princes and Gouernors ought to bee the true patternes and mirrours
of gods among men. And as the Romanes worfhipped Anteuorta, and Poftuorta as companions and fellowes with their gods; the one pre-knowing what wil
come, the other remembring things paft, as that from
the diuine powers, nothing liue obfcured or vnreuealed : fo in the Image of Ianus, with two faces, is im-
ported the wifdome and knowledge of kings and rulers, which ought not to bee ignorant in any thing
whatfoeuer, which may tend to the quiet religious
and ciuile gouernement of their people and country.
There haue ben alfo who haue depictured Ianus with
foure faces, as there were Statues of the fame found in
diuerfe places of Tufcane : and vndoubtedly they manifefted thereby the foure feafons of the yeare, being
all of diuerfe natures and effects, but becaufe the defcription of the Spring, the Summer, Autumne, and
Winter are with euerie one very familiar, I will ceafe
to proceed therein, commemorating that onely of
Ouid, when he fpeaketh of the regall feat of Phœbus :

Before diuine Apolloes regall feat,
The beauteous fpring fits crown'd with curious flowers,
Next whom (with eares of corne about her head)
The fummer fits in her all-parching heat,
And Autumne (dy'de with iuice of grapes) downe poure
A world of new-made wine of pureft red,
Next whom (as placed all in due arow)
Sits grim-fac'd winter couerd all with fnow.

Thefe

These Stations are many times thus intellected: by the Spring is meant Venus : the Summer signifies Ceres: Autumne challengeth Bacchus: and for the Winter, wee oftentimes vnderstand Vulcan: & sometimes the winds with Eolus their commaunder : because from these proceed those tempestuous stormes, which are commonly predominant in that season. Vnder the feet of Ianus is oftentimes placed twelue altars, meaning thereby the moneths of the yeare, or signes of the Zodiake, which the sunne yearely in his expedition doth circulate. There was found in Rome a Statue dedicated vnto Ianus, which had as it might seeme, foure dores, and vnderneath foure columnes, which vnderpropped and supported the weightie heauinesse of the Image, in euery one of which columnes were set foure seuerall shels of fish, wherein were intersected the twelue months with greatest curiousnesse of art delimated and filed. And let this suffice for the Statues of Ianus, progressing to the Images and Pictures dedicated to the Sunne : for that he seemes to be the graund patrone of all Times, and that all things whatsoeuer haue their being and increase through his vertues and motions.

Apollo.

THe error that so possessed the vnsetled and wauering thoughts of the aunciencients, beleeuing that there were many and diuerse gods; proceeded from the opinion that they then carried of wise-appearing and learned-seeming men in those daies, who

who with their pleasing deliuerie of things, supposed
to bee reuealed vnto them, brought and seduced the
people into such a setled beleefe of those their absur-
dities, as long after it continued, ere they could free
their intangled conceits from such their bewitching
ensnarements : for they onely seeking from what originall cause the birth and encrease of things vpon the
earth might arise (wholly ignorant of the true con-
ceiuement thereof, as men guided only by others opinions, and common natures reasons, and therfore not
able to aduance their cogitations to the imbracement
of the true cause indeed, being the inuisible and euer-
liuing God) some of them iudged the elements to be
the cheefe and efficient workers of what the earth
yeelded forth and produced. Neither did all of them
attribute this vnto al the elements together, but some
only gaue the cause of such increase to the vertues of
the water, some to fire, some to the aire, and many also to the earth. Whervpon the Poets (as *Aristotle* saith) Aristotle.
being the first that chaunted forth the powers of such
their gods, induced the sillie and soon-perswaded people to thinke, that there were then in efficient power
many and diuers. By reason whereof, and vpon such
surmises, they called Neptune or Oceanus, the father
of the gods ; and the mother of them Vesta or Ops,
the wife of Saturne: whome likewise they entearmed,
La grand Madre, vnderstanding thereby the earth, in
that from her as from the originall proceed al increases whatsoeuer, and this was generally the opinion of
the Arcadians. *Thales Milesius* ascribed the cause of Thales Mi-
such generation of things vnto the vertues of the lesius.

water,

water, and so diuerse others were of diuerse and seuerall opinions: and in the end they brought the vulgars to beleeue likewise, that the Sunne, the Moone,
and the Starres, were the only causes of such encrease
on the earth : whereupon it issued, that they were afterwards regarded and worshipped as gods, hauing
Altars, Statues, and Temples consecrated vnto them.
And yet generally with the Assyrians this persuasion
preuailed not : For (say they) we may well erect Temples and Images to many other gods, but vnto those
whose true shapes wee may continually behold with
our eies, it shall bee very purposelesse : yet notwith-
Macrobius. standing (saith *Macrobius*) because some in those daies
affirme the sonne and Iupiter to be all one, in one part
of Assyria there was found a Statue made and erected
of the Sonne, all gloriously beautified and polished
with gold , in the forme of a young man without a
beard, who stretching out his armes, held in the right
hand a coachmans whip, and in the left a thunderbolt
with certaine eares of corne: shewing therby the powers, both of Sol and Iupiter. And because that of all
the celestiall bodies hee carrieth greatest force in the
creation of terrene things, the ancients through him
vnderstand many times many of their gods, as his vertues, natures, and effects are many. Whereupon it grew
that they framed him in so diuers and seuerall shapes.
But leauing such their opinions to themselues , wee
will now speake of him as he is Apollo, Sol, and Phebus, which three I doe make all one, him therefore the
auncients (as I haue already said) shaped with a very
youthfull countenance, beardlesse, and young-yeard.
Alciatus

Alciatus(speaking of that youthfulnesse which the ancients then framed and set downe in the shape of a
beauteous Nimph, with her apparell exquisitely well
wouen, excelling in curious worke of foliature, hauing her temples bound about , and instrophiated
with sweet-smelling garlands, resembling much the
goddesse Flora)depainteth there among such workes
of youthfulnesse the true forme of Apollo and Bacchus,as vnto which two it did onely belong to bee alwaies young :Whereof *Tibullus* likewise speaking,
among other his descriptions, thus sayth:

Bacchus alone, and Phebus aye are young,
Though both of them haue beards both white and long.

Where *Tibullus* depainteth Apollo with a beard,
though *Macrobius* and generally all others, set him
downe otherwise, as *Dionisius* the Tyrant of Syracusa
likewise approueth,when he (taking occasion to difcouer the sharpenesse of his conceited ieasts,) with
great furie pulled away the beard from the picture of
Esculapius,saying, That it was very inconuenient and
incongruent,that the father should be beardlesse, and
the sonne to haue one so wondrous huge and exceeding long:for that indeed it is read,that *Esculapius* was
the sonne of Apollo. Many that haue depictured the
shape of Apollo, make him holding in his hand a
Harpe with seuen strings , agreeing in number with
the planets of the heauens,which mouing with a due
destinction,yeeld forth a pleasing harmonie. *Macrobi-*
us sayth,That the sunne continually standeth amidst
the

the planets, commanding them to haften or enflacke
their reuolutions, in manner as in efficient vigor and
ftrength they receiue from him their vertues and o-
perations. And for this caufe likewife the auncients
called him the head or guide of the Mufes, which likewife were framed like vnto young virgines of beauteous and youthfull afpeet, habited as wandering and
filuane Nimphs, with diuerfe-fhaped inftruments in
their hands, melodioufly and with a foule-rauifhing
touch continually playing: and from thefe all the liberall fciences acknowledge their being, whereupon
they were entearmed the daughters of Iupiter and
Memoria, as inftantly becomming skilfull and perfeet
in what they vndertake to learne. They were impalled
with coronets, compofed of fundry-fhaped flowers
and leaues, to which were annexed beauteous garlands of palme : and oftentimes alfo they had their
temples curioufly adorned with feathers of diuerfe
and ftrange colours, by which is intended their victorious preuailement ouer the Piérides , contending
for the pleafantneffe of their voice to compare with
them in finging, which being afterwards foiled and
difgraced in fuch their fuper-arrogating challenges,
were for their fancineffe therein, metamorphifed into
tatling birds, which with vs wee call Pies, readie and
prompt to bring forth many familiar languages by
vfe and teaching . Some thinke alfo, that fuch their
coronets of flowers and palme, fignified the triumph
which they carried away from the Syrens, prefuming
likewife to compare with them for the cleereft and
moft delightfull voices. And in Rome of latter times

was

was feene a Statue dedicated vnto the Mufes, which on the head and calme of the picture had many and diukrs-fafhion'd feathers infixed ; and they were thought to bee thofe of the Syrens . The auncients when they intended to fet down how the liberall arts, and all other fciences, depended one vpon the other, and were as it were knit and coheared together, depictured the Mufes, holding one another by the hand, and heedfully dauncing (as it were in a round) lead and guided by Apollo: which meaneth that fuperiour light and vnderftanding, which illuminateth and enknowledgeth the intellectuall parts of men. The heauens (according to the opinion of the Platonickes) haue euery one their feuerall Mufe, called by them oftentimes Syrens, as moft harmonioufly and fweetly finging , alluded vnto the celeftiall orbes, which in number are likewife nine, and haue their motions according as they receiue their feuerall powers from the fon, which commandeth abfolutely both aboue him, here with vs, and in the lower center : by reafon whereof he is called *Dio del Cielo, della Terra, e dell'Inferno :* and the auncients attribute vnto him powerful commands ouer all the three. The Harpe which (as I haue faid before) he holdeth in his hand, denotateth the celeftiall and incomparable muficke of the heauenly orbes: his fhield or target by his fide, reprefents the circular compofition and rotunditie of our hemyfphere; for the ancients defigure him with a fhield on his arme, and fome alfo giue him a quiuer of arrowes on the other fide, which may fignifie, that as they once lofed from the bow, penetrate and enter

in

in with great force where they hit, so the forcible vertues of the Sunnes transparent raies, search out and
pierce through the smallest crase or voidance on the
earth. Others that say Apollo is called *Dio dell' Inferno*, and giue those arrowes so appropriated vnto him,
doe meane, that from the ouer-vehement ardour and
riscaldation of his beames, pestilences and infections
are engendred and nourished on the earth: but yet say
they, not so vniuersally dispersed, or vndoubtedly mortall, but with the moderate warmth and temperature
thereof, they are chased away, and healthie aires and
naturall increases spring vp and re-succeed. Among
other things appropriated vnto the Sun, the ancients
dedicated vnto him a Wolfe, and their reason was
this : That as the powerfull vertue of the Sunne sucketh vp and drieth the watrish exhalations of the
earth : so the voracious greedinesse of the Wolfe dis-
patcheth and consumeth that prey which in his famin
meeteth him by chance. Afterwards it grew that some
were of opinion, that the Sunne, the Moone, and the
Stars, fed themselues and were maintained and nourished with the moistures and humidities, ascending

Homer.

from the earth. And this *Homer* seemeth to affirme,
when he sayth, That Iupiter with other gods (meaning the Sun and certaine Starres) descended downe
to Oceanus to a banquet. It is reported, that the Wolf
is of so sharpe and cleere sight, that hee sees very perfectly in the thickest night, piercing through the va-
porous mistinesse of the same, as the Sunne vpon his
first apparence and second howers circuit, rarifies the
condensate aire, banishing the obfustate and conclu-
merated

merated cloudinesse thereof. In Delphos in the temple of Apollo, there was found the picture of a Wolf of stone and other hard mettals, exquisitely well cut out and hewen, and the liuely parts thereof were with such great cunning and curiousnesse of art intrauersed, as it possessed the beholders eies with an earnest and continuous admiration. And this picture there was held with such great veneration, for that *Latona* begot with child by Iupiter, and transformed afterwards to a Wolfe (as fearing to bee detected by Iuno) brought forth being so metamorphised, and in that strange shape, Apollo: or that as some others thinke, that picture was regarded there with such zealous observance, for that it was supposed to be a Wolf which discouered the sacriledge and robbing of certaine endeared reliques from that temple: howsoeuer, my opinion is, that the auncients vsed to appropriate the names of such beasts to their gods, as they perceiued to be in them any assimilitude or correspondencie of natures and effects. *Martianus* therefore sayth, That Martianus. vnto Apollo was consecrated the Crow, in token of his foretelling and propheticall diuination: and likewise the Swan, manifesting thereby by the contrarie colours of these two birds, that the perspicuous and corruscant tralucencie of the sun, maketh the aspect of the day in cleerenesse and brightnesse like to the feathers of the Swan, and after his departure from vs, absenting his irradiance from the worlds illustrement, he causeth the night to look of that pitchie and gloomie countenance, resembling in darkenesse and ietty hue those feathers of the Crow. *Pausanias* wri- Pausanias.

F teth,

teth, That in many places of Greece they reuerenced
with great deuotion a Cocke, as the bird of Apollo,
becaufe in his morning notes hee pre-warneth vs of
Homer. the appropinquation of the Suns returne. *Homer* maketh mention, That the Sparrow-hawke (as wee now
call them)was confecrated to Apollo,and hee calleth
hit his fwift-pofting meffenger.And in the fame place
hee writeth, That *Telemachus* returning home into
Ithaca, beheld a Sparrow-hawke in the aire eagerly
purfuing and chafing a Doue,which he tooke as a fpeciall diuination of fucceeding good hap,and that hee
fhould now free and emptie his houfe of thofe ouer-
earneft and importunate futers which daily remained
Eufebius. there for the loue of his mother. *Eufebius* reporteth,
That in Ægypt the Image of Sol was fo ftamed, that
it feemed to be fet in a fhip, carried vp, and fupported
by a Crocadile: meaning to fignifie by the fhip, that
quicke motion and liuely ftirring,which in each moi-
fture and humiditie worketh for the generation of
what it containeth:& by the Crocadile is vnderftood
that wholefome and fweet water from which the Sun
by vertue of his temperate raies exhaleth away all
corruptible and infecting humors. And further, touching the Sparrow-hawke this may bee fpoken: It is
Diodorus found written by *Diodorus Sycula*, entreating of thefe
Sycula. beafts and birds, which in the daies of the auncients
were worfhipped and regarded as gods,that in thofe
times a Sparrowhawke was feene in Thebes, a Cittie
of Ægypt, carrying in her mouth a booke written
with red letters, which fhee deliuered to the Priefts
and Churchmen there,containing in it in breefe,with
what

what zeale and vnfained veneration the gods ought
to be worfhipped and adored,and how neerely now it
concerned them to proceed with a heedfull and due
effectuating what was there propofed : Wherevpon
afterwards it grew,that their writers of facred and holy bookes did weare alwaies on their head a red cap,
with a wing of the fame bird infixed thereunto. The
auncients heretofore did not only vnfhadow the propertie of their gods, by beafts and liuing creatures,
but many times alfo by plants,flowers,& trees,which
they confecrated of purpofe,& dedicated vnto them:
wherevpon the lawrell or Bay was then appropriated
vnto Apollo, and therewith were made wreaths and
garlands, with which his temples were giit and redemyted in token (as fome think)of the ardent loue and
affection which he caried to Daphne the daughter of
Peneus,transformed into that tree by Neptune. The
Ægyptians,before the vfe of letters and writing was
found out,framed the fhape of the fun by compofing
a fcepter, in the vpper top whereof they infected an
eye, very curioufly and with great induftry of art engrauen : and they called it The eye of Iupiter, as that
he beheld and ouer-viewed the large fcope and compaffe of the world,ruling it with great wifedome and
due execution of rightfull iuftice, fo intended by the
fcepter,fignifying command and gouernement. The
Lacedemonians caufed the Statue of Apollo to bee
cut out with foure eares,and with as many hands, the
reafon that they fo fhaped him as many thinke , was
for that hee was feene to fight for them in that forme
and proportion:but others take it to difcouer & fhew

vnto vs the iudgement and prudencie of that god, as being flow to fpeake, and readie to heare, and thervp-on it grew as a Prouerbe among the Grecians, Heare him (fay they) that hath foure eares: meaning thereby the found knowledge and vnderftanding of him that heareth much and fpeaketh little. *Apuleius* affirming, That the funne with his deepe-fearching raies behol-deth any thing whatfoeuer, fayth, That in Theffalie were certaine witches, which when they had with their enchauntments and forcerifmes either bewit-ched any man, or theeuifhly ftolne any thing away, would prefently flie , and conuey themfelues into transfaced and vpreared caues, and many times into graues where dead carkaffes lay interred, feeking by fuch meanes to fhrowd themfelues from the view and fight of the fun, thinking it almoft impoffible to keep any thing hid from the farre-reaching and fin-difco-uering eie thereof. The Phenicians had the Statue of the fun framed of blacke ftone, large and fpacious at the bottome, but very fharpe and narrow at the top, the which *Herodotus* reporteth, they boafted to haue receiued from heauen, and they folemnely affirmed that to be the true Image or Idea of the fun, not made by any cunning of art, but fo defigured by the diuine powers. *Lactantius* fayth, That in Perfia the funne was the principall and cheefeft God they there adored, and him they worfhipped in a caue or denne, and his Statue was framed in this manner : Hee had the head of a Lyon, and was habited according to the Perfian cuftome, wearing on his head fuch tires & ornaments as the women of Perfia vfed to bee inuefted with, and

Apuleius.

Herodotus.

Lactantius.

he

he seemed to hold by main force, a white cow by the hornes. The head of the Lion meaneth, that the sun hath greater vertue and domination in that sign then in any other of all the Zodiake: or that he is of power and commaund among the planets so mightie as the Lyon is among beasts: the caue or den intendeth his eclipse: the cow may seeme to signifie the moone, for those reasons which hereafter in her description shall be discoue:ed. The sun seeming to inforce and constraine her, meaneth, that hee very oftentimes darkeneth her light, and cleane taketh away her brightnes, in that Nature (by her proposed lawes) commands her to obey and follow him. *Pausanias* writeth, That *Pausania.* in Patr:, a citie of Achaia, was found a Statue dedicated to Apollo, made of strange stones and other very hard mettals, and it seemed to haue the frame & proportion of an Oxe or Cow, which beasts as they said, were gratefull to Apollo: and *Homer* speaking how A- *Homer.* pollo was hired to keepe the heard of cattell for Laomedon, thus saith, when hee reported the speech of Neptune:

When first I laid the sure foundation
  Of those proud clouds-aspiring wals of Troy,
Nere to brought by force to ruination,
  Nor stooping her high lookes to dire annoy,
    Had she beleeu'd Cassandras diuination,
Thou Phebus, in thy shepheards weeds didst keepe
In pensiue solitude thy wandring sheepe.

Which shewes, that besides the many names

ascri-

aſcribed to Apollo, hee was likewiſe ſometimes called a ſheepeheard, from which it may be intended, that as from the temperat heat and vertue of the ſun al things here are nouriſhed and increaſed , ſo by the diligent care of the ſheepeheard, his flocke receiueth healthi-

Lucianus. neſſe, ſoundneſſe, and increaſe. *Lucianus* ſayth, That the Aſſyrians only defigured Apollo with a beard, re-prehending all others for ſhaping him otherwiſe, ſay-ing, that ſuch youthfulneſſe and greeneneſſe of years, diſcouered a certaine want and imperfection, which (ſay they) ought not to bee allowed in framing the Statues of their gods, and therefore they ſhaped him with a reaſonable long beard, as one attained to his true and perfect virility : and vpon his breaſt they pla-ced a ſhield, holding in his right hand a ſpeare, on the top whereof was ſet forth a figurelet of Victoria : in his left hand hee ſeemed to hold a very rare flower : downe from his ſhoulders depended a veſtement, wherein was curiouſly proportioned the head of Me-duſa, from which dangled and pointed downewards infinite ſwarmes of Snakes : on the one ſide of him were placed certaine Eagles volant : before his feet ſtood the liuely picture of a Nimph, which on either ſide of her likewiſe had two other Nimphs placed, whoſe bodies a Serpent with her flexible and often-turnings ſeemed to annodate and conioine. This cu-rious-compoſed Statue flowed with ſtrange varieties of eie-delighting and illuſtrious decoraments, that vndoubtedly the beholders eares asked as great ſatis-faction to vnderſtand the meaning, as their eyes cra-ued time to behold the matter. And for that *Macrobius*

ſets

·ſets it ſo forth, wee will heare what expoſitiue inter-
pretation he can deliuer it. His beard which from his
chin hangeth downe very long, ſharpening it ſelfe towards the end, reſembles (ſayth hee) the raies of the
ſun, which from the heauens reach downe vnto the
earth. The ſhield and ſpear intend the nature of Mars,
for that with ſome they are held to be all one. The figure of Victoria, ſheweth vs, that all things whatſoeuer, are ſubiect vnto the ſun, and haue their beginning
and being from the vertues thereof. The flower ſignifies the beauties and excellencies of thoſe things,
which the ſecret powers of the ſun with the life-giuing warmeneſſe of the ſame engendreth, nouriſheth
and maintaineth. The Nimph which ſtands before his
feet, repreſenteth the earth, the which the ſun from
aboue, comforteth with his moderat heat: The which
alſo the Aſſyrians themſelues did ſeeme to confirme
(as ſaith *Macrobius*) by the Image of their god, which
they called Adad, vnto whom they made ſubiect and
obedient the goddeſſe Adargate, and vnto theſe two
they beleeued all things to bee tied in ſubiection; and
by the one they vnderſtood the ſun, and by the other
the earth. The other two Nimphs which ſtand on
both ſides of him, ſignifie the mould or ſubſtance
whereof things are made, and Nature which ſhapes
them into proportion. The Serpent with her often
twining of her bodie, denotateth the many crooked
windings and turnings which the ſun with his raies
incircleth. The Eagles in that by nature they are ſwift
of wing, and couet alwaies to flie very high, are alluded vnto the wonderful velocitie, and exceeding alti-
tude

Macrobius.

tude of the fun: or as the Eagle commaundeth aboue
all other birds, fo the funne hath his abfolute dominion ouer the Planets. The habite which hee wore on
his fhoulders with the head of Medufa, fignifies Mi-
Porphirius. nerua, which is nothing elfe (as *Porphirius* fayth) but
that pure vertue of the fun, which cleareth and refi-
neth human intellect, and infufeth ingenious conceits
into the braines of men. The Ægyptians compofed
many Statues of the fun, and among the reft one was
in the fhape of a man, with the head of it(as it might
feeme) halfe fhauen, and the haire taken away, fo that
on the right fide only remained haires, which(accor-
Macrobius. ding to *Macrobius*)meaneth, that the fun is neuer abfent from Nature, but fhe continually feeleth the vertues and operations of his raies . And that that part
of the head that is fhauen, fignifies, that though the
fun for fome time detaine his glorious afpect from
the world, yet that he is to return and re-beautifie the
fame with as great brightneffe as at the firft, as thofe
haires fo fhauen wil againe fpring forth & re-increafe
to their true and full perfections. And in fome parts
of Ægypt they infixed on the Statue of the fun two
feathers, the one of them blacke and of a duskie hue,
the other bright and fhining: and the blacke they ter-
med *Penna infernale*, and the other *Penna celefte*, for
that the funne keepeth his abiding in the heauens all
thofe times when he paffeth through thofe fixe figns
of the Zodiake, whofe vertues make the ftation of the
parching fummer, being called *Segni fuperiori*, and
they report him to defcend down into the lower center of the earth(called Tartarius)when he beginneth

to

to take his circuit through the other sixe signes, entearmed *Segni inferiori*. And for that they placed those
feathers so vpon him, it signified (as *Macrobius* likewise
sayth) his swiftnesse and fast-flying circumference. It is
read, that in one part of Ægypt they vnderstood the
sun by the name of Serapides (which name likewise is
oftentimes taken for Iupiter) and him they shaped in
forme of a man, holding in his left hand a bushell, intending thereby that there ought to be a proportion
and due measure among men, obserued with an equal
and iust distribution of all things necessarie. And this
their god which they then tearmed Serapides, had a
Statue in the temple of Alexandria a cittie in Ægypt
dedicated vnto him, compacted almost of all sorts of
strangest and vnknowne mettals, and it was framed of
so exceeding huge and immeasurable extension, that
his armes (being stretched forth) reached to both sides
of the temple, at the one side of which was made with
subtle curiousnesse of art a windolet or smallest pro-
spectiue hole, into which the all-searching radiance
of the sun vpon his first apparance (hauing vnbolted
the purple-colour'd dores of the East) would penetrate and enter, glistering and shining with a maruellous reflection on the well-hewen and finely-polish'd
face of that Colosse, in such a sort, that the foolish and
faith-wanting vulgars in those times, credibly beleeued, that the sun came euery morning of dutie to sa-
lute Serapides, and to kisse his cheekes. This picture
was there adored with all reuerence and humble veneration, being made with such incredible art & work-
manship , that the stones and other hardest mettals

G   there-

thereof were so collaterally couched, and with such
priuie conclansture, as if they had ben waxe, or framed of other like flexible substance, being so exquisitely well disposed, and with such commodulat order
of discreet correspondencie. *Martianus Capella* spea-

Martianus Capella.

king of the marrying of Mercurie, sayth, That Mercurie and Vertue looking for Phebus for his aduise in
some matters, found him sitting gloriously in a regall
and tribunall seat, hauing before his feet foure vessels
of seuerall mettals, whose lids were closely shut and
couered, and these were made of diuers formes and
substances, the first was framed of the most hard and
durable yron, from which there seemed to euacuate
fresh-burning and liuely fires, and it was called, *Capo
di Vulcano* : The next was of cleerest and brightest siluer, filled with the puritie of well-tempred aire, and
this was called *Riso di Gioue* : the third was compacted
of solide and peizie lead, implete with raine, haile,
frost, and snow, called *Morte di Saturno* : the last
which stood neere to Phebus, was framed of the finest
and transparent glasse, containing in it the inuisible
seed which the vpper elements sprinckle on the earth,
and it had to name *Poppa ai Giunone*. Out of these vessels, sometimes from the one, and sometimes from the
other, would he call out such working vertues, as therby men here below receiued their health and life, or
their diseases and death: so that when hee intended to
send vnto the world a healthie temperature, and life-
preseruing aire, he would commixe some of that contained in the siluer vessell, with that inclosed in the
vessell of glasse : and when hee meant to plague the
world

world with peſtilences, infections, and mortalities, he
conioined the burning and ardorous flames of the y-
ron veſſell, with that inteined in the other of Lead.
Wherby it may directly appeare, that the diuerſities
and contrarious effects of Times, proceed from the
moderation of the ſuns forcible radiance, or from
the extremitie of his fierie riſcaldation: and that as
the one bringeth with it a generall healthineſſe and
encreaſe, purging the aire of groſſe and plagues-in-
gendring vapours, ſo the intemperature and ouer-
ſcorching furie of the ſame, poſſeſſing the earth with
a vniuerſall ariditie, poyſoneth the aire with infectious humors, and diſtilleth downe on the middle region all kinds of noiſome vnſoundneſſe and infirmities,
by whoſe ill-ſmelling odors and corruptions, the bodies of men and all other creatures, become lame, ſick,
putrified, and diſeaſefull. Among the auncients, Eſculapius (as is already ſaid) was held to be the ſonne of
Apollo, and hee was ſaid to bee the father of Higiea,
which interpreted, ſignifies ſoundneſſe of bodie, and
perfection of health. And *Pauſanias* taking it from the Pauſanias.
Phenicians, ſayth, That Eſculapius is nothing elſe
but the aire, which purged of ill humours by the ſun,
bringeth vigour and luſtineſſe to men on the earth:
whereupon alſo they called him many times god of
Phiſyke. But returning to the Images of Apollo, there
was found at Naples a Statue dedicated vnto him,
which (beſides many other curious ornaments and
beauties it was decked with) had depictured on one of
the ſhoulders with greateſt skill and diſquitition of
the inuenter, a liuely and excellent-proportioned

Doue:

Doue:and there stood before the Image a virgin, maruellously well cut forth , which seemed with wondrous earnestnesse to behold, and as it appeared to
reuerence the bird:which virgin among the ancients
was said to be Parthenope , who in her trauels from
Greece to Naples,was safely conducted by the good
guidance and leading of a Doue,perceiuing by many
manifest tokens comming from that bird, the good
successe and effect of that her iourny. *Martianus* (oftentimes busie in the descriptions of Phebus) thus
sets him forth: Vpon his head(sayth he) hee weares a
gorgeous and royall crowne,whereon were destinct-
ly disperpled, and apactly inchased many most precious, pricelesse, and corruscant gems, of such conspi-
cuous and bright-glittering lustre,as dazelled any humane eyes to gaze thereon: of which, three of them
beautified his all-glorious and far-shining forehead,
and these exceeded any of the rest in puritie of glister and daintinesse of colour; sixe other adorned his
temples,three on the one side,and three on the other,
with rare perspicuitie and incredible cleerenes,whose
vertues at certaine times of the year with diuers and
seuerall hues,compounding the pleasant and perfect
verdure of the spring with sundry-sorted colours of
straungest commixture, beautifies and depaints the
earth.The other three which were placed in the hin-
dermost part of the crowne, are of this nature, that
they are first engendred,and receiue their true and ful
perfection in the most cold snowie and yce-frozen
Winters: his tresses of haire which hang downe his
shoulders,looke like the most pure and refined gold,

his

his countenance feemeth at the firft view wholly fla-
migerous , and hee hath two wings infixed on his
heeles, befet with fparkling and ardent Carbuncles,
his vpper veftment is compacted of a wondrous thin
and fubtle fubftance, wouen & wrought in, as it might
feeme, with fineft purple and pureft gold . In his left
hand hee holdeth a bright fhield compofed of rich
ftones, and in his right hand a haftie and furious-fla-
ming firebrand : and thus farre among other his defcriptions, *Martianus* depictures him. *Eufebius* like- Eufebius.
wife writeth, That in Elefantinopolis, a city in Ægypt,
the Image of Apollo was framed to the due likeneffe
of a man throughout the bodie, faue onely that hee
had the head of a Ram with young and fmall hornes,
and his afpect was of a cerulean and blewifh-greene,
not vnlike that of the fea : which fignifies (as *Eufebius*
interprets it) that the Moone conioined with the fun
in the figne of Aries , becomes more moift and hu-
morous then at any other times, from whofe humiditie there fall on the earth watrifh mifts and thickned
vapours. But leauing thefe things to the Aftrologers,
I will impofe an end to the Statues of Apollo , concluding with that defcription of his and his fifters
birth, which *Claudianus* reporteth to bee fo curioufly
wrought in an vpper garment which belonged to
Proferpina. And although in the Italian it carrieth a
farre more pleafing grace than in the Englifh, yet
finding it there fet downe in verfe, I thought it not
irrequifite fo to difcouer it.

There might you fee with greateſt skill intexed;

T be

The fountaine of ancient fiction.

The portraiture of Phebus liuely drawne,
And his faire sisters shape thereto annexed,
   Whose beauteous parts seem'd shadowed o're with lawne:
And though with equall art both were explained,
   And workmans care gaue ech of them their due,
Yet to the view great difference remained
   In habit, shape, aspect, and in their hue:
For one of them must giue the day his light,
And th'other reigne commandresse of the night.

Both twins eu'n newly born th'are here set downe,
For so it pleasd the workman to deuise,
   And Thetis ready, when she sees them frowne,
With gently rocking them to still their cries:
There might you see the loue of their faire mother,
   Dandling the smiling babes within her armes,
Now kissith she the one, and now the other,
   With carefull studie to preuent their harmes,
And when she hath remou'd all troublous noice,
She charmes them fast asleepe with heauenly voice.

Thus was great Phebus in his tender yeares,
   Strengthlesse his vertues, and his lookes were mild,
Nor any fierie countenance appeares,
   More then is found in a quick-sprighted child.
Some blush-like tincture sometime dy'de his face,
   Much like a new-blowne red-leaud rose: his gesture
Such as beseemd one of so royall race:
   More pallid-hu'd and wan lookt his faire sister,
Whose pure-white yuorie forehead, there adornes
With wondrous grace, two new-sprung siluerie hornes.

                                And

And thus farre *Claudianus* touching the birth of
Sol and Phœbe. In this conclusion of the Statues and
and Images of Sol, may also be inserted a breefe touch
and description of Aurora, who although in the vpper region of the higher heauens, she goeth as it were
as herald and messenger of Phebus , discouering to
the world his gladsome comming and returne, yet I
thought it fittest in this treatise to postplace her, and
to speake of her after his mention, and succeeding
him: for so much indeed, as she is wholly engendred,
and receiueth her being frō the vertue of his beames,
and is no other but that rubicund & vermillion blush
in the skies, which the fierie ardencie of the suns first
apparence worketh in the orientall parts of the heauens, and from thence discending, beutifies with such
resplendant guilture the forehead of our hemysphere:
neither doe I find (although with the ancients she was
held and worshipped as a goddesse) that she hath anie
Statues, Images, or Altars dedicated vnto her. *Homer*   Homer.
describes her of the aspect of a young virgin, hauing
her haire disheueled, and hanging loose about her
shoulders, being of the colour of the purest gold, and
that shee sits in a glorious chaire , compacted also of
gold, with all the rest of her vestures of that colour,
hue, and glister. *Virgil* sayth, That vpon the instant   Virgil.
time of the sable-faced nights departure, shee commeth with one of her hands full of roses, gilliflowers,
and lillies, taken out of a little basket which shee carrieth in her other hand, and after that those twinkling
candles of the firmament are by her approch fled and
vanished, shee besprinkleth those flowers on the marble

ble pauement of the lower heauens , adorning the
same with a wondrous grace and vnspeakeable beautie. Others there are that describe her, holding in one
of her hands a flaming torch, and that shee is drawne
in a gorgeous and starre-bespotted chariot by winged
Pegasus, which fauour she obtained of Iupiter by many importunate requests, presently after the downefall of Belleseron: and thus farre touching the Statues
of Phebus, and descriptions of Aurora.

Diana.

FOr so much as among the auncients the Moone
was reuerenced and adored vnder diuers and seuerall names, so likewise did they then erect and dedicat
vnto her Statues, Altars, and Images of diuers and
seuerall formes, for that with some she was called Diana, with others Proserpina, with others Hecate, with
other some Lucina, and in Ægypt generally entearmed Isis. And according vnto such the proprietie of
her names they so ascribed vnto her, would they expresse her proportion of bodie, her habit, her natures,
vertues, and effects. And therefore according to the
Propertius. description of *Propertius*, shee was depictured in the
shape and due resemblance of a young and pleasant-
looking virgine of most amourous and beauteous aspect, hauing on either side of her forehead two small
glistering hornes, newly peeping forth: and that she
is most gloriously drawne through the aire in a pur-
ple-coloured coach by two furious and swift-paced
horses, the one being of a sad and darkish colour, the
other

other beautifull and white, which (according to *Boc-* Boccace.
cace) entendeth her powerfull operations, as well in
the day as in the night. *Festus Pompeius* writeth, That Festus
her charriot is drawne by a Mule, comparing her (be- Pompeius.
ing cold of nature) to the barrennesse and sterrillitie
of that beaft; and as her selfe giueth no light or splen-
dour of her selfe, but borroweth such her brightnesse
of her brother Phœbus , so the Mule neuer engendreth by any of her owne kind, but by asses, horses,
and other like beastes. There are also who depicture
the chariot of the Moone, drawne by two white bul-
lockes (as *Claudianus*) when he speaketh of that great
search and enquiry which Ceres made for the finding
out of her rauished daughter. It is read, that in many
places of Ægypt they reuerenced the Image of a bul-
locke with wonderfull zeale and veneration, which
they cut out and depainted of a sad colour , hauing
one of his flanckes bespotted with diuers white stars,
and on his head were placed two such sharpe hornes,
as the Moone seemeth to carrie in her cheefest waine,
and lights imperfection. And in those places they offered great Sactifices vnto her vpon the seuenth day
after any child was born and brought into the world,
as in token of their gratefulnesse and thanksgiuing
for the safe deliuerie of such new-borne infant : for
from the moisture and humiditie of the Moone (say
they) the woman receiueth speedier deliuerance, and
the child easier euacuation. And for these causes
would they oftentimes inuoke her gracious assistance,
entearming her the most mightie, mercifull, and most
sacred Lucina. *Marcus Tullius* writing against *Verres*, Marcus Tul.
H descri- lius.

describeth there a Statue or Picture of Diana, which he brought from out a temple in Cicilia, and he saith that it was of a wondrous heigth, and huge demension, hauing the whole bodie circumcinct with a thin vaile or couerture, the face of it of a most youthfull and virgineall aspect, holding in her right hand a liuely-burning torch, and in her left an yuorie bow, with a quiuer of siluer-headed arrows hanging at her back. The torch or firebrand (as *Pausanias* sayth) signifieth that brightnesse and day-resembling splendor, which she so graciously affordeth to the vncertaine steps of forren-nationed pilgrimes, and disconsolate trauellers: the sharpe-pointed arrowes meane those dolourous fits and passions that women feele at their childs deliuerance, which in this point is appropriated vnto her as she is Lucina. Among the Poets Diana is called the goddesse of hunting, and imperiall gouernesse of pleasant groues, shrub-bearing hils, and christal-faced fountaines: giuen vnto her as some hold, for that in the heauens she neuer keepeth any direct course, but wanders and stragles from that true and perfect circuit which the sunne alwaies obserueth, as likewise hunters in the chase and pursuit of their game leaue the most accustomed and trodden paths, posting through vncouth thickets and way-lesse passages: and they depicture her in the habit of a young nimph, with her bow ready bent in her hand, a quiuer of arrowes hanging at one side of her, and to the other is fast tied a most swiftfooted greyhound, with a coller about his necke set and inchased with many rich stones of infinite value, and after her follow a troope of siluan

virgines.

Pausanias.

The fountaine of ancient fiction.

virgines and light-paced huntreſſes , whoſe habites
and aſpects I remember to be by ſome thus deſcribed.

Early one morne old Tithons ſpouſe aroſe,
   And raiſd young Phebus from his quiet reſt,
Drawing the curtaines that did then diſcloſe
   Him faſt twixt Thetis armes whom he lou'd beſt.
He when he heard the ſummons of the day,
After ſome ſweet repaſt ſtreight ſtole away.

Scarce was he mounted on his glorious car,
   When thwart th'ambitious hils and lowly plaine,
Scouring a pace, you might perceiue a far
   A troupe of Amazons to poſt amaine,
But when they neerer came vnto your view,
You might diſcerne Diana and her crue.

A careleſſe crue of young-year'd Nimphs, deſpiſing
   The ioyous pleaſures and delights of loue,
Waſting their daies in rurall ſports deuiſing,
   Which know no other, nor will other proue.
Wing'd with deſire to ouertake the chace,
Away they fling with vnreſiſted pace.

Some haue their haire diſheuel'd hanging downe,
   Like to the ſuns ſmall ſtreames, or new gold wires,
Some on their heade doe weare a flowry crowne,
   Gracing the ſame with many curious tires,
But in their hot purſute they looſe ſuch graces,
Which makes more beautie beautifie their faces.

         H ij   Their

The fountaine of ancient fiction.

Their neckes, and purple-vained armes are bare,
　　And from their yuorie shoulders to the knee,
A silken vesture o're their skin they weare,
　　Through which a greedie eie would quickly see.
Close to their bodies is the same ingerted
With girdles jn the which are flowers inserted.

Ech in their hand a siluer bow doth hold,
　　With well-stor'd quiuers hanging at their backes,
Whose arrowes being spent, they may be bold
　　To borrow freely, so that none ere lackes:
They neuer need be niggards of their store,
For at their idle times they make them more.

Sometimes when hottest they pursue their chases,
　　You may perceiue how fast the sweat distilleth
In hasty-running streames adowne their faces,
　　Like seuen-fold Nilus when she prowaly swelleth:
For from the time that first Hyperion burneth,
They cease not till the widowed night returneth.

And in that swartish and estranged hue,
　　Causd by th'abundance of such blubbred heats,
They looke like youthfull men at the first view,
　　So are their beauties ouer-drownd with sweats.
Thus are those nimble skipping Nimphs displaid
That vse t'attend that Goddesse, Queene, and Maid.

　　And thus much touching the description of
those virgines, which are said to accompanie that
woods-delighting goddesse in her sports of hunting.

Pausa-

Pausanias writeth, That the bow in which *Diana* her *Pausanias.*
selfe vseth to shoot, is made of the saddest coloured
Ebonie, cleane contrarie to the opinion of *Ouid*, who *Ouid.*
directly describeth it to be of the purest gold: and hee
further writeth, that her chariot is drawne by two
white Hinds, (as *Claudianus* likewise affirmeth) when *Claudianus*
hee sayth:

Downe from the steepest clouds, o're-peering mountaines,
    Drawne in a chariot by two winged hinds,
Posts the commandresse of the groues and fountaines
    With greater speed than Eols angrie winds,
O're hils and valleyes, rocks, and roughest seas,
These golden-horned hinds goe where they please.

It is read likewise with *Pausanias*, that in Arcadia
was a Statue made of Diana, all couered ouer with
the skin of a Hind, and from her shoulders there hung
a quiuer of arrowes: in one hand shee held a burning
lampe, and the other shee leaned vpon the heads
of two gentle serpents, and before her feet there stood
a hound, cut out and proportioned with wondrous
great art and industrious labour of the workeman.
The auncients first began to consecrate Hinds vnto
Diana, since that time that shee sent such infectious
plagues among the Grecians, in token of her displeasure which shee conceiued against Agamemnon,
for killing a Hind. And afterwards also among the
Romanes they did commonly sacrifice a Hind vnto
her, adorning their holy sanctuaries and temples with
the hornes thereof. And hetherto for the description

H iij   of

of the Moone as she is Diana , who was oftentimes
also among the auncients called Triuia, and depictured with three heads, which indeed rather belongeth
vnto her as Hecate, and not as Diana. This Hecate the
auncients worshipped and adored, as she that had the
guard and keeping of all crosse waies, and such lanes
as in the end concurred and conioined themselues in
one, and for that cause they depictured her with three
heads, whereupon *Ouid* thus speaketh:

If in thy trauels thou doe misse thy way,
Doubtfull and wauering how to guide thy paces,
Enquire what Hecate to that will say,
Who for three seuerall waies hath seuerall faces,
Inuoke her aid, and she will guide thy feet,
Which alwaies after the true path shall keepe.

From whence likewise it proceeded, that *Virgil* oftentimes cals her Trigemina, Triuia, and Triforme.
And it is said, that Orpheus ascribed vnto her such faces, meaning to declare thereby the diuers and sundrie aspects which we oftentimes may discerne to be
in the Moone, and that her vertues and effects are powerfull and working, not onely in the heauens where
shee is called Luna, and on the earth where shee is
knowne by the name of Diana, but also extend down
euen to the bowels of Erebus, where shee is called
Hecate and Proserpina, where it is supposed shee remaineth during the time of her lights absence from
the worlds view and illustrement. And these things
Eusebius thus expoundeth: The Moone (saith hee) is
called

Eusebius.

called Hecate and Triforme by reafon of the many
fhapes and figures that appeare many times to bee in
her countenance, which proceedeth from the quantitie of the light which fhe receaueth from the beams
of Phœbus. The auncients appropriated the Lawrell
vnto her as due vnto her from her brother Apollo.
And thus much as fhee is Hecate. The Ægyptians (as
I haue alreadie faid) worfhipped the Moone vnder the
name of Ifis, and her they depiĉtured couered with a
blacke and fable vefture, in token that of her felfe fhee
giueth no light. And it is written by the Poets that
fhe was the daughter of the floud Inachus, and called
by the name of Io, and after that fhe loft her virginitie
to Iupiter, fhee trauelled into Ægypt, where among
them fhe was fo entearmed by the name of Ifis. And
they framed her Statue, holding in one hand a Cymball, and in the other an earthen veffell of water, wher-
vpon (as *Seruius* fayth) many fuppofed her to bee the Seruius.
Genius of Ægypt, in that through fuch her depiĉturance the nature of that country was opened and difcouered: vnderftanding by the Cymball which fhee
fo holdeth in one of her hands, that vncouth noife
and farre-heard murmure which Nilus roareth forth,
when with her tumbling and furious billowes fhee
ouer-wafheth the fpacious fields of Ægypt : and by
the other veffell of water, the many Riuers, Pooles,
and Lakes in which that Country excelleth. *Apuleius* Apuleius.
reporteth, that after his recouerie from his tranfmu-
tation into the forme of an affe, hee dreamed to haue
feene Ifis appeare one night before him in a vifion,
and hee there fo defcribes her, as it may bee eafily gathered:

thered that fhee was the very fame as I haue alreadie
fet downe Luna to be, and which the Ægyptians with
fo ftraunge and new-found ceremonies fo adored.
Martianus writeth, That Philologia entring into that
fpheare of the Moone, faw there many and diuers-fra-
med Cymbals, and likewife the torches of Ceres, the
bow of Diana, the Timbrell of Cibele, and a kind of
fhape alfo with three hornes, which I haue already
faid to bee in the Moone: all which things are appropriated and due vnto Luna. But returning to the defcription which *Apuleius* fo maketh of her in fuch his
vifion, he fayth, That fhee then feemed vnto him as it
were all wet and new come out of the fea, with her
haire hanging loofe about her fhoulders, and vpon
the crowne of her head was mounted a moft curious
and delicate chaplet, compofed of diuers fweet-fmel-
ling and fundry-forted flowers, in the midft of her fhining forehead appeared a certaine fquared and qua-
drangulate circle, glittering with wonderous luftre
and vnfpeakeable corrufcancie : on either fide of her
ftood certaine young whelpes of Serpents : her apar-
rell feemed to bee of diuerfe colours of a moft fubtle
and thin fubftance, fome part of it fhewing white, and
of an afhie hue, otherfome darkifh and fad, and in
fome other places of it, it appeared reddifh and high
coloured. And ouer this garment fhe wore one other
of all blacke, yet gliftering in that kind, and of a moft
perfe& iettifh hue, which was very thicke befpotted
and adulterated with true-fhapt ftarres of gold and
filuer, amidft the which was inferted a moft glorious
and bright-fhining Moone, formed out with inimitable

Martianus

Apuleius.

table art of the workeman, and round about the hem
or skirt of this vn-matchable vesture was interposed a
most curious and delicate border of verdent foliature,
intrauersed among the liuely depicturances of all
kinds and sorts of fruits. In her right hand shee held a
certaine instrument made like a Cymball, which of it
selfe would yeeld forth a most shrill and lowd report :
from her left arme hung downe a straunge-fashioned
vessell, compacted clean of gold, with the handle and
foot of it proportioned into the forme of a liuely serpent, which seemed mightily puft vp and swoln with
poyson : and before her feet there was placed a certaine ornament and skilfull deuise, made of the leaues
of palme. And thus farre *Apuleius* describes the apparance of Isis . The varietie of such her colours in
her apparrell, may be drawne into these naturall reasons : for that the Moone doth oftentimes turne her
selfe into diuerse aspects, which thereby denotate the
diuersities of the natures of seasons succeeding, as hir
rednes and high colour foretelleth the approch of furious and blustring winds, her dark and muddy-hued
looke the clustring together and conglomeration of
watrie clouds from which issueth ouer abundance of
raine and moisture , and her white and cleare aspect
pretokeneth calmes and serenitie of weather : her vpper garment being black, signifieth as I haue said, that
she hath no light of her selfe. Some thinke, that the
Cymball which *Apuleius* describes so to bee in one of
her hands, discouered those old vsances of the auncients, who in those times credibly supposed to haue infinitely pleased the Moone by making certain strange

I   musicall

muſicall noices which they cauſed by certaine inſtruments then in requeſt among them: others ſay,that it intended that pleaſant ſound which the Moone in her reuolution through the vpper heauens is heard to make,which is alſo the opiniõ of the Platonicks,who affirme, that the ſtirring of the celeſtiall orbes yeeldeth forth a moſt harmonious and delightfˑll muſick.

Herodotus. *Herodotus* ſayth , That in thoſe ſacrifices which the Ægyptians vſed ſo to offer vp to Iſis, the women accuſtomed to play on Cymbals,and the men on tabers, honouring ſuch their feaſtiuals with infinite ſorts of rites & ceremonies of ſolẽnization.The veſſell which hung downe from her left hand, ſignifies the liuely motion and ſtirring of the waters, cauſed by the operatiue humiditie of the Moone, wherevpon it is ſuppoſed,that according to her fulneſſe or decreaſing of her light, the ſea receaueth that prowd and loftie carriage of her billowes in her flowing, and that lowly and deiected demeanure in her ebbing : and for that the often changes and alterations of the Moone,may in ſome ſort touch the vnſtedfaſt and vncertaine remaine of all things in mans life, it is not amiſſe to re-

Ambroſius. member the ſayings of *Ambroſius*,who many times alludeth the goods, poſſeſſions, and pleaſures, which here men doe enioy to the inconſtant and mutable changes of the Moones aſpects, noting thereby,that there is nothing on the earth firme, permanent, or euer during,but that all the beauties and ornaments of the world are waſted and ſpoiled by the ſeuere tyrannie of all-deuouring time : wherupon(according to the opinion of manie) the Romanes afterwards

(ſuch

(fuch efpecially as were nobly defcended, and of auncient family) wore alwaies on the tops of their fhoes
certaine little Moons curioufly depainted, infomuch,
as that they being of mightie reuenues and of powerfull commands, might fo bee remembred and put in
mind of the cafualtie and doubtfull enioying of fuch
their world-bred felicities and terrene pleafures: and
that continually meditating on fuch the inftabillitie
of fortunes gifts and fauours, they fhould not grow
infolent, prowd, forgetfull of their being, or ouer-
highly thoughted. And thus much concerning the
Statues of Diana.

Iupiter.

THat euer-memorable and famoufed preuailement which Iupiter fo victorioufly carried ouer
his father Saturne, in expelling him from the
imperiall gouernement of the heauens, with manie
other valerous and haughtie performances by him
atchieued, purchafed and won vnto him fuch wondrous reputation and credite among the auntients,
that they not onely dignified him with all titles and
graces of warlike honour, but alfo deified him with
fuch reuerence and adoration, as they euer afterwards
held him as a moft mightie and powerfull God, exu-
perating any of the reft in the heigth of glorie, ftate,
and magnificence, and fo accordingly erected vnto
him moft fumptuous temples and coftly altars, repu-
ting him indeed to be the only and efpeciall god that
had the power and authoritie to befriend or profper

the eſtates of men here below, or to plague & ſcourge them with croſſes, miſeries, and mortalities, whereupon the Latines called him *Iupiter a iuuando*, for thoſe many benefits and good turnes wherewith hee poſſeſſed the people then liuing on the earth . The Platonickes vnderſtand by Iupiter the ſoule of the world, and that diuine ſpirit, through whoſe mightineſſe all things whatſoeuer firſt receiued their being, and ſtill ioiouſly increaſe and flouriſh in their inſtant continuance: and ſuch powerfull ſpirit and commander they

Orpheus. entearmed by the name of god. *Orpheus* (that farre famed Theologian among the Greekes) aſcribed thus much vnto Ioue, that he was the firſt before any thing in the world receiued forme, and ſhall continue the laſt after the conſumation and diſſolution therof, and that he ſitteth on the higheſt part of it , whoſe feet reach downe to the loweſt and baſeſt corner thereof, within whom is contained earth, water, aire, fire, day, and night: whoſe Image he thus ſetteth forth, his head (ſaythhee) with thoſe his golden-hued lockes; is the beauteous firmament gloriouſly adorned with ſuch infinite armies of tralucent ſtars, and from ech ſide of his temples peepe forth two yong golden hornes, ſignifying by the one the Eaſt, & by the other the Weſt, his eies are the Sunne and the Moone, his ſhoulders and breaſt the ſpacious compaſſe of the aire, and the wings thereon infixed, intend the furious ſwiftneſſe of the winds, his bellie downe to the knee, is the wide earth circūcinct with the waters of the ſea, & his feet diſcend down throgh the bowels of the lower center. This deſcription of Iupiter made by Orpheus, is not

much

much vnlike that of Pan, by whom the auncients alſo
ſignifie the vniuerſe, and tooke him and Iupiter to be
al one, as his Image or Statue in ſome ſort manifeſted,
which was erected (as *Iuſtine* writeth) in a temple in   Iuſtine.
Rome hard by the hill Palatine, which appeared to
the view almoſt all naked, ſaue that it was ſlightly en-
ſhadowed and couered with the skin of a goat . It is
read therfore that this Pan was reputed in thoſe daies
among the auncients to be one of thoſe gods that remained & kept his habitation among the hils, woods,
and groues, for that all of ſuch their gods as they then
ſo worſhipped, could not poſſibly haue roome and ſeuerall commands in the heauens, but that of neceſſi-
tie ſome muſt be enforced to deſcend downe and liue
below vpō the earth: among the which (as I haue ſaid)
was Pan , who was indeed moſt of any, adored and
worſhipped of the ſheepeheards, as hee that had the
peculiar care and gouernement of their flockes, and
of the encreaſes thereof, whoſe ſhape *Siluius Italicus*   Siluius Ita-
thus ſetteth forth :   licus.

Vpon the ſheepeheards cheefeſt feaſtiuall,
  When downe the floure-imbroder'd lawnes they trace,
Playing on Oten pipes moſt muſicall,
  To whoſe due ſteps they frame a true-kept pace,
In front of all the troope you there may ſee
Goat-eared Pan in this ſolemnitie.

From out his head two ſmall-tipt new-growne hornes
  Aduance themſelues, about whoſe ether ſide
A flourie garland twines, and there adornes.

I. iij   Hi

His curled temples with a wondrous pride,
His face is of a reddish blush and fierie,
From which doth hang a stiffe-rough beard and hairie.

And for his bodies vesture he doth weare
The finest skin of the most spotted Doe,
That euer any in those woods did beare,
Which from his shoulders loose hangs to his toe,
And when he walkes, he carrieth in his hand
A sheepeheards hooke made of a knotlesse wand.

After such his description hee progresseth further, and saith, That he is of that maruellous firme footing, that hee easily climeth vp , and ascendeth the most craggie and steepe mountaines that bee , and is of a most wonderfull speed and swiftnesse in his running, alluded therein to the nature of the world, which in his reuolution and circumference turneth aboutwith a suddaine and quicke dispatch of time. *Seruius* sayth, That the auncients so shaped Pan with hornes, as entending thereby the beames of the sunne , or those hornes of the Moone, which shee seemeth in her imperfection and lights decreasing to carrie . *Boccace* vnderstandeth by such his hornes , newly sprung forth and reuersed towards the heauens, the celestiall bodies which receaue knowledge and conceiuances by two manners ; the one by art, through which by Astrologicall skill and iudgement, the course and extrauancie of the starres is proportioned and knowne with their habitations, natures, and distances ; the other is that continuall proofe and efficient power
which

Seruius.

Boccace.

which is emploied here in things below: The rednesse
and high colour of his face, signifieth that pure and
liuely fire, which aboue the rest of the elements is adioined next to the heauenly spheres : his long beard
hanging downe ouer his breast, meaneth the two superior elements, Aire and Fire, which are of nature,
force, and operation, masculine, and they intuse their
workings and impressions in the two below , which
are feminine : The spotted vesture which hee weareth
ouer his shoulders, signifies the eight sphere, spotted
and bespangled with so many glistering stars, which
couer all things belonging vnto naturall encreases:
The Sheepeheards hooke which hee alwaies carrieth
in one of his hands, discouereth (according to *Boccace*) the rule and gouernment which Nature beareth
ouer all terrene things : And in that it is at one end
somewhat crooked and retorted, it vnshadoweth (as
Seruius sayth) the course of the yeare, which in it selfe | Seruius.
is circumfered and bended : And in the other hand
some place a whistle or pipe made of seuen reeds, demonstrating thereby the celestiall harmonie aboue,
which hath in it selfe seuen seuerall sounds, and seuen
differing voices, according to the reuolution & working of the seuen spheres, from which they receaue
such their musicall motion. And this *Macrobius* vn- | Macrobius.
derstandeth many times for Eccho, whom the auncients report to be most entirely beloued and endeared
of Pan, of whome (besides that which *Ouid* speaketh
of her in the transmutation of *Narcissus*) it is read,
that she was a goddesse, and the daughter of Speech,
and of the Aire, and therefore inuisible. Whereupon

Ausonius

Aufonius Gallus reporteth, That fhee hath oftentimes difluaded and reprehended him whofoeuer will vndertake to depicture her , and *Aufonius* repeats it there in an Epigram, whofe fence is thus reduced to a Sonnet.

Surceafe thou medling Artift thy endeuour,
  Who for thy skill haft reapt fuch long-liu'd fame,
Striue not to paint my bodies fhape, for neuer
  Did any humane eies behold the fame :
In concaue Cauernes of the earth I dwell,
  Daughter of th'aire, and of ech tatling voice,
In woods and hollow dales I build my cell,
  Ioying to re-report the leaft-heard noice,
To greefe-oppreft, and men difconfolate,
  That tell ech groue their foules vexation,
Their dying agonies I aggrauate
  By their plaints accents iteration,
And he that will defcribe my forme aright,
Muft fhape a formelefe found, or airie fpright.

But returning to Pan, I will proceed in his defcription, whofe lower parts of him are defigured, as it were ouergrowne with maruellous rough and ftubborne haire, with the feet of a Goat: fignifying hereby the nature of the earth , which in fome places is hard, craggie, bufhie, and vneuen, being befet with plants, trees, and briars, and in fome places champaine, in others full of deepe-difcented vallies , and other where very mountainous. Some alfo will haue Pans hornes fignifie the effigies and afpect of the
new-

new-changed Moone, his rubicund and fierie face the blushing countenance of the morning against the approch of Phebus, and likewise of the euening vpon his tramontana and discent to the antipodes, whose beames then seeming to reach downe vnto the earth, are vnderstood by his long and sharp-pointed beard. The spotted skin ouer his shoulders, explicates (as hath before been spoken of) the innumerable companies of starres which presently shew forth & aduance themselues vpon the sunnes departure towards the kingdome of Oceanus. The rod or sheepehooke in his hand, meaneth the rule and gouernement which he carrieth ouer all things. By the pipe of seuen reeds may be intended the musical melodie of the heauens, caused (as some hold) by the motion of the sunne. And so diuerse men varie and differ in their descriptions, similes, & applications. *Plato* vnderstandeth through Pan, Reason & Knowledge; and that it is of two sorts, the one of a man, the other of a beast : And for that (sayth hee) it is many times argued and reasoned both truly and falsely betweene two parties, hee entendeth by the vpper part of Pan the truth, accompanied with reason, which being of it selfe diuine, erecteth and lifteth vp it selfe alwaies towards the heauens; and that part below signifies the falsenesse of things, which being harsh, beastly and rude, liueth here in the world, and is onely delighted with the pleasures and foolish vanities thereof. But howsoeuer this description of Pan may be drawne into seuerall meanings, it pleased the auncients so to desigure him from the middle vpward (as I haue said) they framed him to the propor-

Plato.

K   tion

tion and fimilitude of a man, with his face ruddie and
fanguine, being very hairie, his fhoulders and breaft
couered with the skin of a fpotted Doe, Panther, or
Leopard. In the one hand he held a fheepehooke, and
in the other a whiftle , much vfed of fheepeheards,
when in their pleafant humors they carroll forth their
rurall notes of mirth and iouifance: from the middle
downewards hee carried the perfect fhape of a Goat,
both thighes, legs, and feet. After the fame forme and
portraiture alfo were the Faunes, Siluans, and Satyres
depictured and fet forth , hauing little fhort hornes
growing on their heads , with fmall eares, and fhort
tailes. And it is read that among fome people they are
held in very great regard and obferuance, and that
they are crowned by them with lillies, and other delicate flowers. They are of a moft wonderfull fpeed in
running, and inhabite among the fteepeft and high-
eft hils of India, (according to *Plinie*) being of that incredible footmanfhip, that they are neuer taken vnleffe by extremitie of old age, or other impedimen-
tall difeafe or fickeneffe. *Plutarch* writeth, That there
was one of thefe brought and prefented for a rare gift
vnto *Sylla*, returning from the warres againft *Mithri-
dates*. But regreffing to Pan, *Herodotus* writeth, That he
was one of thofe eight cheefe and principall gods
which were fo worfhipped and adored among the
Ægyptians, and among the Mendefians held in greateft regard and reputation. And vnto him there they
dedicated and confecrated the Pine, of whofe leaues
they compofed many curious garlands, and encom-
paffed his hornes therwith: the reafon hereof (as fome
fay)

Plinie.

Plutarch.

Herodotus.

say) was for the loue of a virgine called *Pitis* , afterwards metamorphised into that tree: as it is read also of Syrinx, turned into a reed, whereof Pan so frameth his pipes and rurall instruments. And now to the finishing of the Statues of Iupiter, beginning with that which is read with *Porphirius*, *Eusebius*, and *Suida*, who depicture the Image of Iupiter as it were sitting vpon a firme and irremouable seat; to signifie that that vertue which gouerneth and preserueth the world , is firme, permanent, and continuing: the vpper parts of the picture appeare naked and vnclothed, the lower parts couered and inuested: disshadowing therby, that the mercie and compassion of the diuine powers is alwaies manifest and apparent to those that are possessed with an vnderstanding spirit : the lower parts being clothed, meaneth, that all the while that wee are here in the world delighted, and as it were rockt asleepe with the illecebrous blandishments thereof, we cannot any way apprehend superior knowledges, but they are kept obscured, hid, and vnreuealed from vs. In his left hand he held a scepter, for that (say they) on that side of the bodie lieth the principall part of man, being the heart, from which are disperfed and sent out the vitall spirits and powers of the body: and as the king ruleth absolutely, and commandeth ouer his people at his pleasure, so the world, & al things cōtained therein, are tied in subiection and dutie vntō the will of the highest king . In his right hand they place a mightie Eagle, ioyned with the portraiture of Victoria, meaning thereby as by the other, that as the Eagle ouer all other birds whatsoeuer ruleth as cheef,

Porphirius.
Eusebius.
Suida.

so all the men in this world, and all other things inclosed within her spacious embracements, stand vassali-
zed and subiect to the all-commanding power of Iupiter. And this picture was erected in Piræus, a stately and magnifique gate of Athens. The Ægyptians
framed vnto themselues for the picture of Iupiter, a
peece of squared wood, wherein was proportioned
two round circles, as it were one ouer the other,
through which there seemed to creepe a Serpent, hauing the head of a Sparrowhawke. The circles intended the widenesse and rotunditie of the world : the
Serpent the great commander and conseruer of all
things therein ; for among the Ægyptians and Phenicians they held that Serpents were of a diuine and
supernaturall power, as hauing such speed and swiftnesse in their going, without the supportation of any
exterior lim, carried onely by an interior spirit and
liuelinesse, which makes them so often wrest & retort
their bodies with so many flexuous and winding turnings, and that they liue on the earth a wonderfull
long time, as disburdening themselues of their years,
by dispoiling and vncasing them of their vpper skins,
and so instantly againe rebecome youthfull and vigorous : the head of the Sparrowhawke signifieth nimblenesse, promptnesse, and agilitie. *Martianus* (when
hee writeth how Iupiter summoned all the gods to
the marriage of Mercurie and Philologia) depictures
him there impalled with a regall crowne, all adorned
with most precious and glittering stones, ouer his
shoulders he weares a thin vaile, wouen and made vp
by Pallas owne hands, which appeareth all white,

where-

Martianus.

wherein are inferted diuerfe fmall peeces of glaffe,
formed out into the due proportion of the moft refplendant ftarres: in his right hand hee holdeth two
round bals, the one wholly of gold, the other halfe
gold and halfe filuer: in the other hand an yuorie
Harpe with nine ftrings , his fhoes are made of the
greene Smarald, and he fitteth on a footcloth, wherein is wrought and intexed diuerfe ftraunge workes,
with the feathers of a Peacocke, and hard by his fide
lieth a tridentall gold-emboffed mafe. And fo farre
Martianus among manie other his defcriptions, fets
him forth. In many Countries the Statues and Images of Iupiter were fo depictured, as they thereby difcouered not only what hee was, and of what vertue,
power, and commaund , but gaue light as it were
and admonifhed Princes and Gouernours how to
proceed in the execution of their rule and authority,
as being on earth the viceroyes and vnder kings vnto
Iupiter, appointed and inftalled by him to fee iuftice
and equitie truly and effectually miniftred and performed. And *Plutarch* writeth, That in fome places of Plutarch.
Crete were Statues erected of Iupiter, which had all
the proportion and fhape of a humane bodie , faue
that they had no eares, fignifying thereby, that he that
commandeth in fuperiour authoritie aboue others,
ought not to be perfuaded or carried away by any priuate conference, or glofing infinuation, but muft
ftand vpright, firme, and ftedfaft, not leaning to one
fide more than to another, whereby he may be known
not to fauour or partialize. And contrarily, the Lacedemonians framed his picture with foure eares, as
K iij that

that Iupiter heareth and vnderstandeth all things, alluded also to the wisdome of Princes and Magistrats,
which ought to haue information of euery cause or
matter throughly before they deliuer out a definitiue
sentence or iudgement: and likewise that they receiue
and admit intelligences and notices how their lawes,
precepts, and edicts, are kept and obserued among
their subiects. *Pausanias* reporteth, That among the
Argiues there was erected in the temple of Minerua, the Statue of Iupiter made with three eies; two of
them seated in their right places, and the other in the
middle of his large forehead : vnderstanding thereby,
that he hath three kingdomes to gouerne and maine-
taine: the one the heauens, as that especially and in-
tirely commanded by him : the other Hell, which is,
there vnderstood by the earth, which compared with
the wondrous glorie and beauteous excellency of the
heaues, may in that respect worthily merit that name:
and the third kingdome is the sea , for so much as
Eschylus in manie places entitleth him with the name
of the lord and commander of the watrie gouernement and dominion. It is read also, that hard by the
pictures of Iupiter, was alwaies placed the Image of
Iustitia, as that kings and great potentates might not
commit anie thing wherin iustice and right were not
administred. And much to this purpose *Plutarch* writeth, That in Thebes were certaine Statues and Images of Iupiter made without hands, demonstrating
thereby the dutie of Iusticers, and authorised Officers,
for that indeed they ought to bee as it were without
hands ; that is, that they should not receaue any kind

of

Pausanias.

Eschylus.

Plutarch,

of bribe or reward, nor bee corrupted with the enticing proffers of bounteous gifts, whereby they might
become iniurious to the true deseruers of right and
equitie, and bee drawne to giue wrongfull iudgement
vpon the truth-inferring pledant. Some there are also
who haue defigured him without eyes, as by that
meanes Iusticers, and men authorised for deciding
lites and controuersies, might not see their deerest
friends in such times of pleading, and so not put in
mind either of friendship, kinred, or other occasion
to lead them to partialitie. And it is thought that this
Iupiter with the Romanes, was the same which they
then entearmed *Deus Fidius*, so reuerenced and adored among them, whose picture was alwaies kept
among their most sacred and regarded reliques, and
it was thus composed: There stood in the midst of a
Temple a great Colosse of marble, out of which was
framed and hewen with great curiositie of art, a win-
dow, in which were insculped three figures, whereof
one of them which stood and was placed on the right
hand, being in the forme of a well-yeard man, full of
modestie and grauitie, had these letters engrauen vpon it, *Honor*: The other on the left hand, formed into
the portraiture of a woman in Matrone-like habite,
carried these letters, *Veritas*. These two pictures seemed to hold one another hand in hand, before whom
there was placed the third figure, of the proportion
of a young man, of beauteous, yet sober aspect, on
whose head were infixed these words, *Deus Fidius*.
And thus much touching that note, taken from the
writings of *Pausanias*. There haue beene few Statues

compo-

compofed of Iupiter, to which hath not been annexed the fhape of an Eagle, which bird of all others the
Auncients haue moft often appropriated vnto him,
by which (as it is poëtifed) his glorious charriot is
fwiftly drawne and conueied through the airie paffa-
ges. Some hold, that Iupiter when hee warred & was
conuerfant here below in many fights & skirmifhes,
was by many fignes and tokens giuen by an Eagle, affured of profperous and fortunate fucceffe, which afterwards fell out true, he himfelfe victorioufly triumphing in thofe wars:Or that as he is feared and adored
among men, fo the Eagle carrieth a fuperioritie, and
raigneth as Empreffe-ouer all other birds. Among the
Eleans(a people in Greece) the Statue of Iupiter was
compacted of gold and yuorie , an d himfelfe fitting
vpon a regall and ftately feat, was impalled with a coronet,made with the leaues of an Oliue . In his right
hand hee held the Image of Victoria, crowned in the
fame manner: and in his left hand a fcepter,tempered
of diuerfe and fundrie mettals, on the top whereof
was mounted the true portraiture of an Eagle : his
fhoes were all of gold, whereon was fet forth and depainted the formes of diuerfe ftrange beafts and of rareft flowers. The feat it felfe was cleane gold,in which
was inchafed with moft excellent embellifhments
and curious politure,the liuely reprefentation of many vnknowne birds and fifhes . And this Statue was
vpheld and fupported by foure Images of Victoria,
hewen out and proportioned with inimitable skill of
the art Topiaria.And it is read,that in Caria(a region
in the leffer Afia) was erected a Statue of Iupiter,
holding

holding onely in one of his hands a Poleaxe, and *Plu-tarch* alledgeth this reason for it, saying, That *Hercules* after that hee had ouerthrowne and slaine *Hippolita,* Queene of the Amazones, tooke them from her and carried away among other her armes, this poleaxe, which afterwards he gaue to *Omphale* his wife, which by birth was of Lydia: and in this respect the kings of Lydia alwaies afterwards vsed to carrie with them in the warres such weapon, and held and regarded it as a thing sacred, and of a wondrous respect. This wea-pon through the succession of manie kings in the end came to *Candaules*, who not vouching to carrie it himselfe alwaies, gaue it in charge to one that accom-panied next vnto him, who afterwards with *Candaules* himselfe was slaine by *Giges*, then triumphant victor ouer those warres so vndertaken : who among other spoiles and reliques, carried and brought the same away into Caria, which first the Amazonian com-mandresse so lost to *Hercules*. And this was now infix-ed in the one hand of this Statue, which was dedica-ted vnto Iupiter. And thus much touching the Ima-ges, Statues, and Pictures consecrated vnto him.

Iuno.

THose that haue written, that the Auncients vn-der the names of diuerse gods haue worship-ped the foure elements, haue vnderstood by Iu-no the Aire, calling her the sister of Ioue, by whom is meant also that element of Fire. And as they then adored and worshipped him as supreame gouernour

of

of the heauens, so likewise they entearmed and entituled her the Queene and Ladie thereof, being both
indeed the superiour elements, which in themselues
haue greater strength, vertue, and operation in the
creation and encrease of things here below than the
other two: and oftentimes also they take Iuno for the
earth, and in that respect acknowledged as the wife of
Iupiter, in that (say they) there falleth from aboue a
certaine powerfull and engendring seed on the earth,
by whose strength and vertue it receiueth means and
abilitie to bring forth, maintaine, and nourish what
we see here produced. There are manie also who haue
worshipped and taken this goddesse the same as Luna, cognominating her by the name of Luna, as it
were signifying thereby, that she giueth light & guidance to the deliuerance of the new-borne infant:
From whence it grew, that the auncients parting(as
it were) and diuiding the parts of men seuerally and
asunder, giuing vnto euery god some one part, some
another, whereof they should take charge and care,
haue dedicated the eye-lids vnto Iuno, in that they
are placed and next adioined to our eies, by which we
receaue our light and steps direction, and that they
seeme to defend and protect the puritie of their vertues from any hurtfull and offensiue thing that might
otherwise fall downe, and get in vpon them. The
Statue of Iuno hath been framed by the auncients into the proportion of a woman of middle age, yet habited like a graue Matron, holding in the one had a siluer vessell, and in the other a sharpe-pointed speare:
and although it may seeme strange to place in the
hand

hand of Iuno this warlike weapon, shee being of her selfe naturally mild, peacefull, and gentle, yet the auncients haue so defigured her, in that she is many times also fierce, wrathfull, and furious, as shee shewed her selfe when shee conioined with the Grecians to ouerturne the prosperous estates of the Phrygians, aduenturing her selfe in person, accompanied with Minerua amidst the most perrillous and desperate skirmishes of those watres: as *Homer* among those his notes Homer. more copiously remembreth it, where also hee sayth, That her chariot (for in those times the greatest Captaines and especiall commaunders alwaies fought in chariots) glistered as it had been beset with purest carbuncles, the axletree was of solide gold, the wheeles of Ebonie, whose circulous plates with the nailes thereof were cleane siluer, the chaines whereunto the horses were tied, were gold, and the seat wherein she her selfe sat mounted, was of the most refined siluer, beautified, adorned, and bespotted round about with starres of gold. And although at all other times almost shee is depainted to bee drawne in her chariot by two gentle birds, yet at this approch shee is reported to bee carried by two furious horses. And *Virgil* Virgil. likewise describes her in such a chariot, when he saith that shee affected and fauoured Carthage very much, as to leaue there her chariot, horses, & furniture thereof. *Homer* by the many and sundry colours which appeare to bee depainted in that her chariot, vnderstandeth and meaneth the seuerall aspects of the aire. And Homer. *Boccace* taketh it otherwaies, saying, that she is so gloriously set forth and adorned with colours, to signifie Boccace.

L ij   that

that fhe is goddeſſe of riches, and ſuch her weapons
ſo belonging vnto her doe vnſhadow, that for riches,
wealth, honour, and aduancements, men vndertake
armes, and are conuerſant in the greateſt dangers of
the warres. And ſhee is alſo oftentimes pictured with
a ſcepter in her hand, to ſhew that ſhee hath the beſtowing of gouernments, authorities, & kingdomes:
as likewiſe ſhee promiſed Paris vpon ſuch his cenſure
of beautie betweene the three goddeſſes. Vnto her
alſo is dedicated among the auncients, the Peacocke,
as the bird cheefly appropriated vnto her, as that
men are ſo drawne and allured with the deſire of riches to the poſſeſſion and embracement thereof, as
the diuerſe-coloured feathers of this bird, enticeth
the beholders eyes more and more to view, & to gaſe

Boccace,

vpon them. And *Boccace* (ſpeaking of the progenie of
the gods) ſaith there, That men of mightie reuenues,
treaſures, and poſſeſſions, are alluded to this bird, as
that they are prowd, inſolent, deſirous to ouer-rule
all men, and well pleaſed to be ſoothed vp and flatte-
red in ſuch their thraſonicall humours and ouer-arro-
gant haughtineſſe, deſirous to be praiſed & extolled,
whether iuſtly or vndeſeruedly, it matters not : of
which ſort of people, as in thoſe times of *Boccace*, ſo I
doe not thinke alſo, but in theſe daies many of them
may be eaſily found out. Among the auncients it is
deliuered, that the meſſenger of Iuno is called Iris, by
which name alſo the Rainebow many times is vnderſtood, and that ſhee was the daughter of Thaumante,
which ſignifieth admiration, inſomuch as the ſtrange
varietie of the colours thereof, poſſeſſeth the beholders.

ders minds, with a continuing wonder and admiring
continuation . And shee is apparrelled in loose vestures for the more nimblenesse and dispatch of the
goddesses affaires and negotiations, who besides this
messenger had also fourteene other nimphs, continually awaiting vpon her, prest and readie to performe
all dutious seruices, and seruiceable duties : as *Virgil* Virgil.
affirmeth when he sayth, that shee promised vnto Eolus the fairest & most beautifull of all her handmaids,
if he would let loose his then imprisoned winds to the
dispersing and scattering of Æneas fleet, then bound
for the coasts of Italie. And these are said to bee the
causes of the changes and alterations of the aire, making it sometimes faire, sometimes tempestuous, rainie, and cloudie, and some other times sending down
haile, snow, thunder, and lightening. *Martianus* de- Martianus
painting Iuno sitting in a lower chaire vnder Iupiter,
thus describes her: She hath her head (sayth he) inuested and couered with a thinne white vaile, on the top
whereof is seated a stately coronet, inchased & adorned with many most precious and rare-found Iewels,
as the Heliotrope, the Smarald, Iacynth, and Scythis,
with manie other of more vnknowne vertues and
wonder-worthie operations : her inward vestures are
composed of some maruellous subtle substance, reflecting with a most starre-like glister, appearing as it
had beene made of glassie tinsell : ouer it depended a
mantle or vpper couerture of a sad & darkish colour,
yet yeelding forth (as it were) a secret-shining lustre
and beautie : her shoes were of a most obscure and
gloomie colour, as signifying the sable countenance

Hesiodus.

of the night, although *Hesiodus* and many others describe them to be of the purest gold. In her right shee holdeth a thunderbolt, and in the other a resounding and lowd-noiced Cymball, all which things cleerely explicate the natures of the aire, so as I need not now

Pausanias.

any further vnbodie the same. *Pausanias* writeth, That in a Temple in Corinth was a Statue erected vnto Iuno, made by *Polycletus*, of gold & yuorie, on the culme whereof was seated a glorious crowne, wherein were insculped and intrauersed the pictures of the graces. In the one hand it held a Pomegranate, and in the other a Scepter, on the top of which stood the portraiture of a Cuckow, for that it is storised that Iupiter when he was first enamoured of Iuno, transformed himselfe into that bird, and shee (then a yong virgin) desirous to take the bird, who glad of that oportunitie, was easily entrapped, and after that found meanes to satisfie his desired pleasure with her. Touching which tale *Pausanias* sayth, That although hee did not beleeue such things to be true, nor anie the like which are so written of the gods, yet (sayth hee) they are not altogether to bee reiected, in that there were no such things so reported, but were stuft and impleat with mysterie, and carried in themselues an inward meaning and secret vnderstanding, the which no doubt some haue by their writings exposed and vnshadowed, if by the tyrannie of fore-passed times, the memorious notes of such industrious fathers, were not blotted out and oblitterated: when in a certaine

Apuleius.

Comedie *Apuleius* bringeth in the iudgement of Paris vpon the hill Ida, hee setteth forth a young virgine

there

there of maiefticall afpect, encrowned with a princely Diademe, with a Scepter in her hand, and in her
company the two brothers Caftor and Pollux, which
on their heads wore ftately helmets , wherein were
depainted diuerfe fhining ftarres. And of thefe it is
read, that they were the fonnes of Iupiter, who were
fo louing one to the other in reciprocall affection and
kindneffe, that one died for the loue of the other, for
which they were afterwards by Iupiter feated in the
heauens, where they are knowne now by the name of
Gemini . The one of thefe was famoufed for wreft-
ling and other fleightfull excercifes of recreation, the
other excelled in horfemanfhip and good riding:and
both of them manie times are depictured and fet
forth, riding on two white horfes, as (it is read) they
were fo feene fighting hard by the riuer Sagra, in a
certaine battell there. *Eleanus* reporteth them to bee E'eanu∾
verie ftrong-bodied, of great ftature and manly countenance, yet both of them beardleffe and young, and
one fo like the other, as is poffible to fuppofe thé:they
were futed with warlike accouftrements, with fwords
by their fides, and fpeares in their hands, and on their
helmets were depainted in ftead of ftarres certaine
ftreaming flames, for that it is written, that the Argo-
nauts being once in great mifery on the fea, tired with
the long continuance of a forcible and all wracking
tempeft , and expecting euery minute to deliuer vp
their bodies to the churlifh embracement of the angrie billow, vpon the praiers of Orpheus there were
then feene in the element on the heads of Caftor and
Pollux, two moft bright and fierie-ftreaming ftarres,
                                                    which

which suddaine wonder the afflicted and waue-tossed sea men tooke as an assured token of insuing safetie, as it afterwards fell out. Whereupon it came to passe, that alwaies afterwards that starre was inuocated and called vpon by distressed Mariners, as *Seneca* and *Pliny* likewise report, That the appearance of that star foretelleth serenitie of weather, and peaceable calmes. And because this star is seated in the aire, and so Iuno her selfe many times taken for the aire, it pleased *Apuleius* (as I haue alreadie written) as he tooke it by tradition from the auncients to accompany this goddesse with those two brothers Castor and Pollux. It is found with *Pausanias*, that in a certaine place of Beotia there was a temple dedicated vnto Iuno, in the which was erected her Statue, of a wondrous heigth and extension, and it had to name as the Italian giueth it *Giunone spesa*. The reason of such name may be this: Iuno on a certaine time vpon some occasions displeased and discontented with Iupiter, in a great choller and furious rage departed from him and went away euen to the furthest parts of Eubea, he willing to pacifie and calme such the conceaued anger of his wife, asked aduise of *Citheron* then lord of that Countrey, how she might be won, called home, and reclaimed: hee presently aduised him, that hee forthwith should cause to bee built an Image or picture of the wood of an Oke, in the due likenesse and proportion of a yong virgine, and couering it ouer with some nuptiall vestments, should procure the same cunningly to be caried along with him to the place where marriages were then vsed to bee solemnised, that by such meanes it might

Seneca.
Plinie.

Pausanias.

might bee blased abroad how a new marriage was intended, and the old spouse for euer reiected and forsaken. Iupiter liking of this new-deuised plot, instantly proceeded to the execution thereof. And in the end when all matters were readie, and hee himselfe going with this picture in great solemnitie to the accustomed place of marriages, Iuno vnderstanding thereof, suddenly approched, and fearing indeed to bee now cast off for euer, in great anger and iealousie violently tore away the garments of the supposed bride, and finding it to bee a counterfeit Image, and a deuise made onely to reduce her to her old husband, conuerted such her displeasure into new liking & fancie, and at this conceited ieast infinitely reioiced. Afterwards among the auncients, this day was (in remembrance of the reuniting of Iupiter and Iuno) held and obserued in great solemnization. This fable *Eusebius* reporteth to bee by *Plutarch* thus vnclouded : The discord (sayth hee) which so arose betweene Iupiter & Iuno, **Plutarch.** is nothing else but the distemperature and strugling contention of the elements, from whence issueth the destruction, death, and ouerthrow of all things whatsoeuer; as by their quietnesse, concordance, & agreement, they are produced and conserued: if therefore Iuno (which is as much as a watrish, moist, and windie nature) in such their striuing and disagreements ouermaister and subiect Iupiter , there ensue most wonderfull flouds, and rainie wetnesse on the earth, as once happened in the Countrey of Beotia, being all ouercouered and drowned with the superabundance of such flouds and waters , till by the reuniting and

knit-

knitting together of the old kindneſſe betweene Iupiter and his ſpouſe, the waters decreaſed, ſhruncke
away, and diſſipated themſelues into ſeuerall armes of
the ſea, which indeed fell out euen vpon that verie inſtant when Iuno pluckt away thoſe cloths, ſo inueſted
vpon the Image, and diſcouered the ſubſtance and bodie of an Oke: of which tree alſo it is written, that it
was the firſt of all others that ſprouted forth of the
earth after the departure of the vniuerſall deluge and
inundation ofthe whole world, and which (as *Heſiodus*
ſayth) then brought vnto mankind manifold and ſun-
drie profites and conueniences, as that by the fruits
thereof, men in thoſe daies liued and receaued nutri-
ment, and by the wood of it built and compoſed their
manſions houſes and temples. The aunciemts heretofore haue conſecrated vnto Iuno the Lillie , and
thereof haue framed for her diuerſe wreaths and garlands, and they called it the Roſe of Iuno, becauſe being beſprinckled with her milke, they turned & were
preſently made white, being before of a ruddie and
ſanguine colour, & it is thus fabulized: Iupiter (knowing of the old hatred, and ſpightfull malice which
his wife alwaies carried towards *Hercules*) one day (as
ſhe lay aſleepe) ſo deuiſed and brought to paſſe, as hee
conueyed *Hercules* with great ſecrecie to the paps of
Iuno, that thereby he might ſucke and draw from her
ſome of her milke, whoſe vertues ſhould diſanull and
fruſtrate her old conceaued ſpight, and change the
ſame into a new-made loue and kindneſſe. But *Hercules* ſucking ouergreedily, and belike pulling too hard
vpon her paps, Iuno ſodainly awaked, and perceiuing
him

him so vnexpectedly there, whom from her soule she so much hated, distractedly as it were started frō him, and by that meanes of violence her milke spurting forth, and making through the element a certaine white list and streake, called by the Astrologers *Via lactea* discended downe on the earth, and fell vpon those Lillies, then growing sanguine and reddish, which afterwards grew discoloured, pale, and milkie white. *Tertullian* writeth, That in Argos a Cittie of ^{Tertullian.} Greece, was erected a Statue vnto Iuno, all couered ouer, and behung with the bowes of a Vine, and vnderneath the feet of it lay the skin of a Lyon, which discouered thereby the hatred and disdaine she caried towards *Bacchus* and *Hercules*, both which were highly seated in her greatest disfauour; much like the kindnesse vsed of such in these our daies, for it is poetised indeed, that shee was Stepmother vnto them both ; Some haue depictured the Statue of Iuno in Matrones habite, holding in one hand the head of the flower Poppie, and at her feet lying a yoke as it were, or a paire of fetters: by these was meant the marriage knot and linke which coupleth the man and wife together; and by the Poppie the innumerable issue of childrē, which in the world are conceaued & brought forth, alluded to the numberlesse plentie of seed contained in the head of that flower. And this was so appropriated vnto her, for that with many she is supposed and held to be the goddesse of Mariage. And thus farre concerning the Images and Pictures dedicated vnto her.

M ij

Terra.

Terra, o la gran Madre.

THe earth among the Auncients was taken and held to bee the first, and of greatest antiquitie of all other their gods, and in that respect they tearmed her to be the mother of them all. And as they perceiued in her sundrie natures, and diuers properties, so they ascribed vnto her diuers and seuerall names, and erected Statues and Altars vnto her , according to those names, vnder which they then so worshipped and adored her, who (as I haue alreadie written) was with many taken and vnderstood for Iuno: and those statues and images which were dedicated vnto her, were made also many times of many other goddesses: whose properties signified them to bee in nature the same as the earth, as first *La gran Madre, la Madre de i dei, Ope, Rhea, Cibele, Vesta, Cerere, Proserpina,* anb manie others which of their places and habitations where they then remained, had their names accordingly, all signifying one & the same thing, being as I haue said, the Earth, frõ the which indeed, & from whose fruits, all things here in the world seeme to receaue their life and being, and are nourished & conserued by the fertilenesse thereof , and in this respect shee was called the mother of the gods , insomuch, as all those gods of the Auncients, which were so supersticiously adored and held in that respectiue regardance, liued here once on the earth, and were fed and maintained by the increases, fruits, & suppeditaments thereof. But to returne to speake of those her seuerall names , first shee was called Ope, (who also was

the

the wife of Saturne)for that it fignifies affiftance, aid, and adiuuament, in that there is nothing fo commodious, helping, or auaileable to the preferuation of human life, as the earth with her encreafes: wherevp on *Homer* cals her the giuer of life , becaufe by her Homer. meanes all liuing things doe breath and enioy vitalitie. And *Martianus* defcribing her fayth, That fhee is Martianus. enaged, and of many yeares, and growne vp to a great bignelle and corpulencie, and faith, that notwithftanding that fhe is old, fhe continually bringeth forth iffue from her wombe , being as it were encompafled and fet round about with her fonnes and daughters: fhe goeth for the moft part in greene veftures, with her vpper vaile ouer her bodie, befpotted with diuers and fundrie colours, wherein is wrought & fet forth infinite curious knots , among which are inferted all thofe things which with mortall men are moft efteemed, as precious jems, ftones, pearles, and other moft rare mettals of vnknowne, and therefore vnfpeakeable values. *Varro*(as S. *Auguftine* reporteth in his booke Varro. calle *de Ciuitate dei*)fayth, that the earth is called Ops, becaufe by mans helpe, induftrie, and labour, it becommeth more rich, fertile, and increafefull, and that the oftener it is wrought vpon, tilled, and manured, it reacheth ftill to more plentie, perfection, and fecunditie. Shee is called Proferpina (according to the opinion of many) in that the blades and ftalkes of corne fpring forth and grow with fuch ftealing and vnfeene progreflion and fafhion of encreafe, as the Serpent in her fliding paces fmoothly creepeth , and fnekingly conueyeth her felfe away . Shee is entearmed Vefta,

M iij becaufe

becaufe fhe fitteth alwaies clothed and inuefted. And
Varro. *Varro* defcribeth the picture of Ops,(as it is taken out
of *Boccace*)to be thus, and he thus expoundeth it: On
her head(fayth he)fhe weareth a ftately crowne, made
in the forme of many towers and caftles , in that the
circuit and compaffe of the earth is round, like the
fhape of a crowne, and is replenifhed and filled with
Citties, Caftles, and Villages : her apparrell is wouen
and compofed of greene hearbes, all ouerfhadowed
with frondiferous boughes, difcouering thereby the
infinite numbers of trees, plants, and flowers, growing on the earth. In one of her hands fhee holdeth a
Scepter, which fignifies, that in the world are manie
riches,kingdomes,and gouernements,as alfo the powerfull commands and mightineffe of terrene Lords
and Potentates.By the ball which fhee holdeth in her
other hand, is meant the roundneffe of the earth,diui-
ded into two fpheres:and hard by her is placed a chariot with foure wheeles, which difcouereth, that although fhe hir felfe remaineth for euer firme and irremoueable , yet the workes and negotiations of the
world are continually altering, changing, and vnfta-
ble,according to the natures and powers of the foure
ftations of the yeare. This chariot is drawne by foure
Lyons, which enucleateth either the fubtiltie which
husbandmen vfe ouer their ground, to couer & hide
the feed fo foone as it is fowne,from the greedineffe
and narrow fearch of the birds : as Lyons(according
Solinus. as *Solynus* reporteth) are accuftomed, when they are
chafed and hunted by woodmen to fweepe & difperfe
the duft with their tailes,that fo the print and impreff-
fion

sion of their footing, might not detect their course of
escape, or else to shew, that there is no ground so barren, stubborne, and fruitlesse, but may in time by often
cultiuation, & industrious manuring, be made a plen-
teous & fertile soile , as the Lyons themselues in the
end become gentle, tame, and tractable. The emptie
and void seats which are placed round about the picture, doe import, that there is no countrey so popu-
lous and abounding in people, but are by pestilences,
infections, dissentions, and warres, wasted, spoiled,
and depopulated ; or to shew that in many places of
the earth are diuerse countries vnpeopled and deso-
late. And thus farre *Varro* in his description of Ops.
It is read with *Isiodorus* , that the Image of this god- Isiodorus.
desse, called *La gran Madre*, is framed holding in one
of her hands a key, signifying thereby, that the earth
in the time of Winter and cold season , is locked vp
(as it were) and incloseth within it the seed which is
dispersed and throwne downe into it, which at the approch of the Spring and Summer doth peepe forth,
and shew it selfe againe, at which time it is said, that
the earth is again vnlocked, and openeth her bosome.
Cornelius Tacitus reporteth, That certaine people of Cornelius
Germanie worshipped and adored this goddesse, as Tacitus.
she that of all other was the most friendly & helping
to mankind , supplying their wants and necessities
with her manifold fruits and encreases. And in that
they erected not vnto her (as I haue in some places alreadie written) any Statues, Images, or Pictures, they
performed such their adoration in cosecrated groues,
wherein they placed a chariot or coach, couered all

ouer

ouer with sacred vestures, vnto which no man might
be suffered to approch and touch, but only a certaine
Priest appointed to speake to her, as hee onely that
knew the goddesse to be there, & was further acquainted with all her vnreuealed matters of secrecie, and in
this respect they all gaue him preheminence, place,
and dignitie. And this chariot was drawne very so-
lemnely (and with all obseruancie of reuerence done
vnto it by the people) by two white Cowes. It is to
be pre-intended, that the world in those daies was not
afflicted with warres, stratagemes, contentions, intestine broiles, and fatall massacres, neither knew it the
vse of yron or steele, the daies and yeeres were then
circumfered in ioy, tranquilitie, and hearts content,
all places were free, peacefull, secure, and quiet, & vnto this sight and solemnitie the people came flocking
in, with great humility deuoting vnto her their poore
seruices, with many gifts, presents, and oblation. And
after that this goddesse afterward intended to end
such her progresse, and to abide no longer below in
the world, the chariot with the cloths thereof, was
suddainely by some sleightfull art throwne violently
into a Lake or Riuer, with the picture of the goddesse
in it, and the seruants so appointed for this deuise, all
ouerwhelmed and drowned in the water. And it is
thought, that this fond ceremonie encreased mightily their opinion and beleefe of such their religion,
and caused that she was alwaies among them adored
and worshipped as a mightie goddesse. And this goddesse was also called (as I haue alreadie written) Cibele, which name (according to the opinions of
many)

manie)came of a certaine mount so entearmed. But *Festus Pompeius* giues her the same nature and ver-tues, and the same Statues, Images, and Pictures as she hath being Ops,with her chariot likewise drawne by two furious Lyons: which *Aristotle* likewise affir-meth, when writing of many wonders and miracu-lous things in the world, he remembreth in such his description a certaine stone which groweth on the hill Sipilus in Phrygia, the which who so had found and caried away any part of it into the Temple of Ci-belè,he should become instantly most dutifull obedi-dient and regardant vnto his parents,although he had before infinitely hated, despised, and by violent and impious hands beaten them: and vnder her picture there in that temple,were placed with great curiosity of art, two stately and maiestical Lyons. But *Diodorus* and manie others are of opinion, that the Lyons so dedicated vnto her, signified, that she was once fed and nourished by them on that Mountaine Sipilus, as it is read also of many others that haue beene kept aliue and preserued by Wolues, Harts, Beares, and Serpents. The Naturalists, and such as haue laboured for the vertue and nature of things produced,say that the elements admit in themselues such a coherence, communencie,and coniunction,that the one is easily changed into the nature of another, according as the aire becommeth indensate and grosse,or pure and ra-rified.And in that regard there ought to follow lesse admiration among vs of such intricate names,effects and properties of the gods of the auncients , as the one sometimes vnderstood for one thing, and some-times

times for another, and yet all signifying vnder seuerall names and titles one and the same thing: as Iupiter oftentimes is taken for the element of Fire, sometimes for the aire, and so likewise the Sunne and the Moone in many places taken for the same, and yet exposed vnder diuerse names. The waters also had diuerse gods, shewing forth their sundry qualities and effects in the same manner, as the earth, from whose bosome ascend vp mistie and vapourous exhalations , and are setled and remaine in the lower part of the aire, composing there thicke and conglomerated clouds, from whose moistnesse afterward issue downe on the earth great vents and abundance of raine. And for this cause (according to *Fornutus*) the earth is called Rhea, as it were guiltie, and being the cause and occasion of such showers and rainie moistures. And the Image of this goddesse was set forth with many Cymbals and vessels of water, as also torches, lampes, and firebrands, meaning thereby the many lightenings and suddain flashes which immediately precede the approches of violent and tempestuous showers. The Statue of the earth (as she is Vesta) is proportioned in the shape of a young virgine, with her apparrell beautified and bedecked with many curious ornaments, and attires of sundrie and diuerse colours, as wee see the earth vpon the comming of the Summer to bee so gloriously bespotted with seuerall-sorted flowers. But it is to bee obserued, that among the auncients was also another Vesta, which as the first (as I haue said) signified the earth, this intended the fire, that is, that liuely & nourishing heat, from which (being dispersed into the

bowels

Fornutus.

bowels of the earth) euerie thing therein contained,
receiueth his being and encrease, and of this the auncients shaped not any Image or Statue, in that it could
not be discerned by any outward eies, but with diuine
and contemplatiue thoughts, being of it selfe wholly
celestiall. And besides these names of the earth, it was
called also, when of it selfe it proued not fertile, but
industriously manured by the labours of man, by the
name of Ceres, and her Statue was framed to the assimilitude of an aged Matron, hauing her head circumcinct and redemyted with eares of corne, holding in
her hand the stalke of a Poppie, in that this flower signifieth fertilitie and great encrease . And *Orpheus* Orpheus!
writeth, That her charriot is drawne by two furious
Dragons of most fierce and indomitable nature. And
the reason of it as *Hesiodus* reporteth is, in that in the Hesiodus
Island Salamina, seated by the Euboicke sea, there liued a most powerfull, angrie, and deuouring Serpent,
of a most admirable, strange, and vncouth hugenesse,
by which indeed all that Countrey became wasted,
spoiled, and depopulated, vntill afterwards by the valerous prowesse of *Euricolus* it was ouermatched, chased, and expelled the Countrey, which vpon that fled
into the next Prouince called Eleusis, where at that
time Ceres remained, as hoping by her to bee protected and safe guarded. And from that time it long after continued there in the temple of Ceres, as her at-
tendant seruant and minister. Many also haue depictured Ceres with many torches, lights, & firebrands
in her hands, as in the same manner in a temple seated vpon a promontarie of Attica was a Statue so depainted

painted by *Praxitiles*. The reason was, as some hold,
in that she had been so seene raging vp and downe in
the search and enquirie of her daughter Proserpina,
rauished and stolne away by Pluto . And hetherto
concerning such Statues , Altars, and Depicturances.

Neptune.

A Mong the auncients Neptune was held and supposed to bee him of the three brothers to whose
share the kingdome of the waters fell and was allotted, and therefore and in that respect they entearmed
him god of the sea, depainting him with diuerse and
seuerall countenances , setting him forth sometimes
with mild and pleasant lookes, at other times louring
and sad, and at other times with a mad, furious, and
ang ie aspect:which is giuen him (according to *Virgil* & *Homer*) in that the sea it selfe at sundrie times,
so sheweth her selfe. And they describe him manie
times to bee naked , holding in his hand a siluer
Trident, or forked Mace , and standing vpright,
as carried in the concauitie of a huge marine shell,
which in steed of a Charriot , is forciblie drawne
by two monstrous horses , which from the middle
downeward haue the due proportion and shape of
Fishes, as *Statius* at large describeth them . Sometimes they depaint him with a thinne vaile hanging
ouer one of his shoulders of a cerulean or blewish
colour. *Lucianus* (speaking of certain sacrifices offred
by certaine people of Greece vnto Neptune) setteth
him

Lucianus.

him downe there with maruellous long hair, hanging down ouer his shoulders, being of a very sad & darkish colour. And yet *Seruius* and many other writers doe ~Seruius~ affirme, that among the auncients all their gods of the sea were for the most part depainted in shape of old men with white and hoarie haires, as that their heads were so died with the froth and spume of the sea. Whereupon *Philostratus* (describing *Glaucus* being ~Philostra-~ a god also of the sea) sayth, That he had a long white ~tus.~ beard which was very supple, gentle, and soft, & that the haire of his head was also very white, and hung downe wet & dropping about his shoulders, his eyes to be greene, and maruellously glistering, being hollow, and set farre into his head, his brow full of furrowes, wrinckles, and greene spots, his breast all ouergrowne also with a greenish coloured sea weed or mosse, something like that which hangs to the bottomes of ships after long voyages, his bellie, and from thence downeward both thighes, legs, & feet, became fish-like full of fynnes and scalie, and that hee had a wonderfull long taile, all glistering with scales, which he alwaies lifted vp and aduanced aboue the waters. The three-forked Trident so giuen to Neptune, signifieth the three gulfes of the Mediteranean sea, which from the head thereof mainely tumbleth downe into the Ocean. Others allude it to the three seuerall natures of the waters, as that those of Riuers and Fountaines are in the tast sweet and pleasant, those of the sea saltish, sharpe, and hard, and those of lakes, pooles, and standing meres are neither bitter nor salt, nor yet pleasing, sweet, or gratefull to the tast. Vnto Neptune

N. iij   also

also the auncients gaue the Trumpet or horne, as belonging vnto him, which they deuised in respect of that shrill and loud-noised shell which the Tritons vsed alway to carrie & sound before him : which Tritons were supposed also to be gods of the sea (according as *Solinus* deliuereth) but most writers entearme them the sea-trumpeters, or els the Heralds of the great Emperor Neptune. *Higinus* writeth, That when the Giants warred and contended with the gods of the heauens, Iupiter in great earnestnesse sent downe vnto Neptune for some of those his Tritons, which being come, made forthwith such a horrible & fearefull noise with such their crooked and retorted shels, as the Gyants neuer before hearing any such like noise, all astonied and amased, not being able to endure the terrible and affrighting sound thereof, instantly retraited, fled away, & departed. *Solinus* reporteth, That on the top of a certaine Temple dedicated vnto Saturne, the people of Lydia erected and placed one of these Tritons, sounding forth with with his Trumpet: vnshadowing thereby (as *Macrobius* expounds it) that from the times of Saturne, hystorie and letters began first to speake(as it were)sound forth and to be heard, which vntill those daies slept dumbe vnreuealed, mute, and speechlesse. These Tritons as some affirme, were not altogether fained and deuised by Poets, for that(as it is credibly written)there now remaine in the sea, fishes which haue the due proportion and shape of men from the middle vpwards. *Plynie* writeth, That in the time of *Tiberius* the Emperor,

there

Marginal notes:
Solinus.
Macrobius.
Plinie.

there arriued at Rome certaine Embaſſadours , ſent from the Cittie of Lisbona in Portugall,concerning ſome priuate negotiations of their eſtate, who there credibly reported , that they themſelues had heard ſuch Tritons ſo to ſound their crooked ſhels, hard by the ſhoare where they dwelt. *Alexander Neapolitanus* Alexander reporteth, That a certaine Gentleman a neere neigh- Neapolita- bour of his,and a man of worth and credite,conſtant- nus. ly affirmed, that hee had ſeene a ſeaman taken by cer- taine fiſhers, which at that time being dead, was all couered ouer and ſeaſoned with honny, to the end it might laſt,and continue ſweet:and that he ſaw it then in Spaine , being ſent thither from the furthermoſt parts of Affrica,as a preſent of great wonder and ad- miration, and much after this manner hee deſcribeth it:It had the face of an aged man (ſayth hee) with the haire of his beard and head wondrous rough , ſtub- borne, and long, of a cerulean or azure colour, his ſtature exceeded the proportion of a man, vpon his ſhoulders grew two wings, ſuch as vpon many other fiſhes are now commonly knowne,&his skin,though wonderous rough,and of great thickneſſe,yet ſhined and gliſtered very brightly. The ſame Authour adioy- neth,That *Theodorus Gaza* likewiſe affirmed, that hee had ſeene a ſea-nimph or water-maid (one of thoſe which we call Nereides)by great fortune caſt a ſhore on the coaſt where hee inhabited,which ſayth he,had the true aſpect & countenance of a woman of a moſt pleaſing & beauteous face, but from her necke to her thighes ſhee was couered all ouer with ſcales, and ſo downeward became wholly like a fiſh: wherevpon it
grew,

grew, that the Poets fained fuch Nereides to be moſt beautifull and gracious Nimphs, attending the gods and goddeſſes of the ſea, as Oceanus, Nereus, Neptune, Thetis, Dorida, Galatea, and others, which Galatea as *Heſiodus* writeth, is ſo entearmed by reaſon of the whiteneſſe of her ſkinne, who alſo deſcribes her haire to be milke white. *Ouid* ſayth, That *Poliſemus* being bewitched with her incomparable beautie, deſcribeth her to bee more cleere and faire than the pureſt Lillie. *Philoſtratus* in a certaine tablet which hee maketh of the Cyclops, depictureth Galatea drawne in a ſtraunge-framed chariot by two mightie Dolphins, on a quiet and gentle ſea, which Dolphins were guided by two ſiluer raines, held in the hands of old Tritons daughters, ouer her head was carried a Canope made of Purple ſilke, and Siluer, to enſhadow her delicious face from the beautie-ſcorching furie of the ſunnes irradiance: her haire hung diſperſed ouer her ſhoulders, which with the reflection of Phœbus beames ſeemed like ſmall wires of gold, with the fauourable and gentle breath of Zephirus diſſipated and ſpread abroad. The preſcribed *Alexander Neapolitanus*, credibly deliuereth, that one of thoſe Tritons which before we ſpake of (or as wee may tearm them) marigenous men, hauing by chance from a little caue or hollowneſſe of a rocke where he lay, eſpied a yong woman fetching water from a fountaine there hard by, vpon a ſodaine leapt out of his watry denne, ſet vpon her, and forced her violently with him into the ſea, notwithſtanding her vehement ſhrikes, and all-endeuoured reſiſtance: which being by ſome of the inhabitants

Philoſtratus.

habitants thereabouts perceaued, though a farre off, they laid plots, & consulted among themselues, how they might again entice him to the land by any means whatsoeuer: which afterwards they accomplished by sending another maid to that fountaine, & spreading that place all ouer with subtle nets, in the end they ensnared him therein, and so brought him aliue into the Towne; which within three daies, not being able so long to endure the land died. Not altogether vnlike to these Tritons (in respect of human shape) but more neerely indeed resembling those Nereides, are those which wee entearme by the names of Syrens, in that (as it is poëtised) they haue also the face and countenance of a woman, & so the rest of their bodies aboue vnto the middle, from which downward they become fishes. And it is written with some, that these haue wings, and that their feet are like those of a Cocke. *Seruius* describeth that lower part of them to bee in the shape of a bird: as *Ouid* also remembreth, when he   Ouid. sayth, That those were the companions of Proserpina, which after that she was rauished by Pluto, were metamorphised into such formes, being halfe women, & halfe birds. But howsoeuer the Poets varie in their opinions, they generally vnderstand by those Syrens the delicate purenesse of beautie, wantonnesse, pleasure, & enticing allurements to the daliancie of amorous embracements. And it is read, that they sing so melodiously, and with such a sence-besotting sweetnesse, that the suspectlesly inchaunted sea-trauellers are infinitely beguiled and lulled asleepe with the harmony and pleasing blandishment thereof, and by

O   that

that meanes are murthered and deuoured by them, as indeed it often times befalleth vnto those miserable and vnfortunate men, who bewitched with the ille-cebrous and honny-dewed tongues of harlots, suffer themselues to be(as it were)cast into a sleep, shutting the eyes of vnderstanding and reason , and by that meanes are made a prey to those deuouring & gree-die vulturs, & in the end vtterly eaten vp, wasted, and consumed. Whereupon *Boccace* reporteth, That the Auncients heretofore depictured the Syrens daun-cing and sporting in a greene meade , which was all ouer spread and strewed with bones and carkasses of dead men: vnclouding thereby the assurednesse of ruine, decay, and perishment to those that so voluptu-ously addict themselues to the vnbridled affection of such lasciuious and soule-hazarding concupiscence. As there are many most ouglie monsters and strange-formed creatures in the sea (thought indeed to bee much more then on the land) so *Homer* also maketh especiall mention of one, which hee calleth by the name of Scilla, which (sayth hee)liueth in a fearefull darke and secret cauerne hid in the sea, in the nature of some huge rocke, and who with her vncouth and lowd barking and howling, make the waters therea-bout mightily resound with an incredible report and eccho of such her strange vlulations. And this mon-ster sayth he, hath twelue feet, six neckes, & six heads, and in euery mouth are placed threeranckes of most wonderfull huge teeth, from whence continually issu-eth and gusheth forth a most deadly venomousfome: her heads are alwaies peeping forth with greedie vigilancie

Boccace,

Homer.

gilancie to see if any ship doe passe by that way, that thereby shee might make a prey of the poore, miserable, and distrust-lesse passengers, as once happened to the most afflicted and hard-fortuned companions of Vlisses.

Of the before-mentioned Nereides, *Plato* writeth, that there are supposed to bee a hundred, maiestically riding on Dolphins, and alwaies attending on Neptune, which number of them hee also remembreth, when he describeth that stately & magnifique temple which the Atlantickes dedicated vnto Neptune, where hee himselfe was depictured, seated in a sumptuous chariot, holding the raines of the bridle in one hand, and a whip in the other, and his sea-horses galloping with incredible swiftnesse & celeritie of pace: and this Statue was made with such immeasurable extensure and height, being also adorned with many pillars round about, that it seemed a most wonder-worthie & huge piramides, the top whereof reached vp euen to the vppermost roofe of the temple.

Martianus (when hee speaketh of the concouation of the gods to the marriage of Philologia) describeth Neptune of a greenish complexion, wearing on his head a white crowne: signifying thereby, the spumie froth of the sea, being troubled and boisterously tossed with the ouer-furious blasts of Boreas. Among the Auncients also the picture and portraiture of Neptune was shaped out, not much vnlike that of Oceanus, whome they called and held as the father of the watrie gods, and vnderstanding by him all the whole powers, natures, and effects of the sea.

Plato

O ij

Thales

Thales Milesius iudged to bee the first and cheefe pro-
ducer of all things whatsoeuer, and which opinion
the Poets afterward embracing, supposed Oceanus as
I haue alreadie said, to bee the father of all such their
gods: whom they depaint riding on the sea, drawne in
a glorious Car, accompanied & attended vpon with
a mightie troope of Nimphs, and those before-speci-
fied Tritons, ioyfully sounding forth their shrill-voi-
ced Trumpets: after these doe follow a wonderfull
heard of marine beasts, commanded & kept together
by Proteus; for it is read, that in the Carpathian sea
are found great numbers of beasts, which for the most
part haue the vpper part of them like calues, and the
rest like fishes, which with vs are called sea-calues. Of
these and many other such semi-fishes, the Poets ascribe the charge and gouernement to Proteus. The
chariot in which Oceanus is so decribed to ride, signifieth the compasse which the sea maketh about the
bodie of the earth, the rotunditie of which, is represented by the wheeles of that chariot. By these nimphs
is meant the propertie and nature of the waters, and
the diuers and seueral operations and effects thereof,
the which by the Auncients were vnderstood, not
onely vnder the name of Oceanus, Neptunus, Thetis,
Dorida, and Amphitrio, but also many times vnder
the title and name of Achelous, Alpheus, and diuers
others: for by the first is intended onely the nature of
the salt waters, & by these, that of Fountains, Springs,
and Riuers, which likewise by the Auncients in those
daies were formed and depictured in humane shapes.
But before I proceed any further concerning the waters

ters, I will here somewhat touch the description of the winds, because hauing spoken of the sea, I thinke it not here incongruent to insert them, for that vpon the waters they commonly shew forth their force and power more than on the land. And although I might haue before among the treatises of Iuno conuenient-ly remembred them, in that (according to the opinion of the Naturalists) the aire it selfe being moued and troubled, is the very wind, and that Iuno is oftentimes also taken for the Aire, yet it shall not bee ouer-much digression in this place to capitulate some opi-nions, as they are deliuered vnto vs by the writings of others.

The winds therefore among the Auncients, were held and worshipped as gods, and Sacrifices and ob-lations offered vnto them accordingly, with great zeale, and many rites and ceremonious obseruances, for so much as they reputed & iudged all prosperous and successefull voyages of nauigation to proceed by the fauourable quietnesse and gentle disposition of the winds, which they depictured with two small wings infixed on their shoulders, and with a fierie and high-coloured countenance, with their cheekes puft vp and swolne like one that with maine force striueth to send forth some forcible blast, their natures and qualities are discrepant, in that some ingender and thicken clouds, some againe with their breath expell and chase them away, othersome occasion the fall and sprouting forth of great abundance of raine, and others againe drie vp the aire, making it thin, subtle, and cleere. And as in diuers manners they shew forth

O iij   their

their properties, natures and powers, so are they of
the Poets diuersly described and set downe, of whom
it is written, that foure onely are the cheefe and principall which blowe from the foure quarters of the
world, euery one seuerally from his owne seat & quarter, as they are touched by *Ouid* in his diuision and
partition of the vniuersall frame of the world. And

Strabo.

yet (according as *Strabo* reporteth) with many there
are acknowledged onely two : the one called Aquilo
or Boreas, being the wind that blowes frō the Septen-
trionall, which also (as *Pausanias* writeth) had a most
stately and excellent Statue curiously cut out and engrauen in the Temple of Iuno in Greece, frequented
by the Eleans : and the other is called Auster or No-
tus, predominating the Southerne region of the aire,
and because commonly proceed from his blasts darke
showers and stormy tempests, he is thus, or to the like
effect described :

All gloomie-faced, lookes the Stormie South,
   Whose euer-weeping eye, drop showers of raine,
Who with his strong-breath'd all ore-turning mouth,
   Kings stone-built temples tumbles downe amaine,
Whose furious blasts the waue-tost seaman feeleth,
   When vp aloft his ship is hoisd to heauen,
Whose storme-cras'd sides ech churlish waue so reeleth,
   That her right course she neuer keepeth euen.
He neuer lookes with any cleere aspect,
   His temples are adorn'd with clouds, his seat
Of terrifying thunderbolts compact,
   Which when he sends, he denotates huge heat.

He

He neuer breaths or sighs with any paine,
But from the same doe issue showers of raine.

Of these winds, the third is called Eurus, whose
blasts proceed frō the Orientall parts. And the fourth,
whose mild and gentle breath procures so temperate
and pleasing aire, is called Zephirus, who (for that his
warme calmenesse and moderate blowing, is the cause
of the flowers and hearbes better increases) is supposed by the Aunciēts to bee the husband of Flora, the
goddesse and ladie of all sweet-smelling flowers. And
this shall be sufficient for the winds in this place, returning now to the finishing of those descriptions of
the flouds and riuers, which according to the Auncients, were framed in the shape of a man, wearing
long haire, and with a long milke white beard, and
leaning vpon one arme, (as *Philostratus* remembreth)
when he sayth, that riuers are neuer streight, or runne
out right: and as *Statius* likewise depictureth the floud **Statius.**
Inachus , which passeth through the continent of
Greece, saying thus:

Amidst a fertile flowre-adorned Dale,
  Wal'd round about with banckes of sedge and willow,
Lies horned Inachus, dreirie and pale,
  Leaning his head and arme (as on a pillow)
Vpon a vessell full of water filled,
Which thorow fertile Grecia is distilled.

The Riuers (according to *Seruius*) are framed with
hornes, either because the murmure and noise of the
                                                    waters,

waters, fomthing refemble the foft bellowing of buls, or elfe becaufe wee alwaies fee, the bankes and fides of riuers to be retorted(as it were) winding and croo-ked like hornes: whereupon *Virgil*, where hee calleth Tiber the king of all the flouds and riuers of Italie, calleth him there cornuted(as it were)hauing horns. And with fome alfo the riuer Po is fafhioned into the fhape of a bull, for thofe reafons belike before fpoken of and mentioned. And hitherto in this treatife it fhal be fufficient to haue proceeded.

Virgil. *(margin note)*

Pluto.

THe ancients heretofore allotted vnto euery feue-ral place a perticular king, gouernor, or cõman-der, who of that place fo committed vnto him, fhould take vpon him an efpeciall care and charge, who there commanded and ruled as an abfolute lord, as it is poetifed of the kingdomes of the heauens, the waters, and the earth: in the partition of which, it fell out, that the gouernement of the lower center which is vnder vs, happened and was allotted vnto Pluto, which alfo with vs is called Erebus. He therefore was amongft them then accounted the king and lord of the dead, and that hee according to the lawes of Iu-ftice gaue them their punifhments & tormentsaccor-ding as they had deferued, when they liued vpon the earth. Yet many writers doe affirme, that vnto that of-fice were appointed, and did belong the three iuft iud-ges, Eacus, Rhadamantus, and Minos, of which three, fome little here in this place fhall be commemorated.

Plato

Plato therefore fayth, that in the times of Saturne thofe lawes and orders were in practife and exercifed which alfo in the firft daies of Pluto were held & obferued,and his words are thefe : There was a law(faith he)in thofe times, that thofe men which in their life time had liued well, and according to the rules of vertue and her commandements, fhould after they were dead bee fent and tranfported vnto the Ifland of the fortunate: and that thofe which had liued vicioufly and lewdly, fhould bee conueyed to the place of horror,there to receaue condigne punifhments, according to their merits and qualities of offences.And in thofe times (fayth hee)when alfo Iupiter began to raigne with vfurped authoritie, all men wee adiudged to punifhments,pains,or elfe to happie pleafures, euen the very day before the parties died. By meanes whereof many were wrongfully condemned,& fome alfo fent to the bleffed Ifland, that had deferued intollerable paines and tortures. The which thing Iupiter vnderftanding by the information of *Plato*,who complained of that abufe, thus anfwered.Well(fayth hee) I wil find out a remedie for this inconuenience prefently,and therewith feemed to be wondrous angry. This proceeds(fayth he)in that men are adiudged,being then liuing,and who knowes not that this man, or that man hath friends and great alliances,who wil not fticke to bribe and corrupt the Iudge for fauour and partialitie, and that this other man hath deadlie enemies and ill-wifhers, who continually are aggrauating the offence,and prouoke by vnlawfull meanes fome wrongfull fentence to bee denounced. As for

P　　　　　　　　great

great mens faults, they are couered and hid with glorious abillements, with wealth, authoritie, noble discent, gentrie, and parentage, And then the Iudges themselues being earthly, (and therefore imperfect) must needes giue wrongfull iudgement and verdict. We must therefore take some such order, that in these cases mortals must not bee pre-acquainted with the times when they must die, as now they doe, and thereupon commaunded *Prometheus* to performe it accordingly: for after that (sayth hee) they shall be thus despoiled of their earthly robes, riches, and power, and being dead and naked, shall appeare before Iudges likewise dead and naked, (which then shall bee void of friendship, partialitie, or fauour) it shall be an easie matter in this case to giue true and rightfull iudgement, according to the qualitie and height of their offences. For the confirmation of which my purpose and intended decree (which I haue now resoluedly concluded within my selfe) my pleasure is, that my three sonnes, two of them borne in Asia, being Minos and Rhadamantus, and another in Europe, which is Eacus, standing in a certaine greene meade, out of which doe part and are diuided two seuerall waies, the one into Hell, and the other into Elisium (for so we may now call them) shall bee appointed there as Iudges of the soules of mortals, Rhadamante iudging those of Asia, and Eacus those of Europe. And that, if it fortune that any doubt or vndecided scruple, shall arise betweene them, that then the same bee referred presently vnto Minos, that thereby hee may giue his censure and opinion of it: for so much as wee intend to deale and proceed vprightly in thefe cafes, & that there be not admitted therein any fauour, coufenage, or deceit. This (fayth *Plato*) was the order and decree of Iupiter, which afterward was prefently effected & put in execution. Firft vpon the examination of their fins, Rhadamantus and Eacus fate together in two yron chaires, holding in either of their handes a white rod. And Minos (diuided from them both) was feated all alone, holding in his hand a golden fcepter, who feemed to meditate and ponder with a mufing & fad countenance vpon the punifhments, torments, or pleafures, to be denounced & due to the offenders. As *Vliffes* (according as *Homer* reporteth) gaue out that at his being in that infernall kingdome, hee there faw the three Iudges in fuch manner fo to doome the foules of men: and thus farre are the words of *Plato.* *Martianus* writeth, (where he fpeaketh of the lower Martianus, region) that *Pluto* himfelfe fitteth moft maieftically in a mightie ebon chaire, holding in one of his hands a blacke imperiall fcepter, and on his head feated a ftate-ly and fumptuous crowne. At his left hand fitteth his Ladie Proferpina, attended with many furies and vg-ly fpirits, at whofe feet lieth chained the dog Cerbe-rus. And further the fame Authour proceedeth not. Vnto *Pluto* alfo the Auncients haue giuen a trium-phant chariot, drawne with foure furious blacke hor-fes, from out whofe fierie nofthrils proceedeth won-drous thicke and ill-fauoured fmoakes: which is alfo the opinion of *Claudianus.* Although *Boccace* fpeaketh Boccace, only of three horfes, and that his charriot hath but three wheeles. Some write alfo, that *Pluto* hath his

head

head redemited and compassed about with a garland
or wreath made of the leaues of Cipres trees, which
signifie sadnesse and horror, and which are vsed in burials, massacres, & about dead carkasses. Others affirm,
that the same garland is made of the Narcissus leaues,
for those also are held gratefull, and are employed
about dead bodies, in memorie of the vntimely death
of that youth, afterwards transformed into that flower. And the like garlands also did those furies weare
which were attending on Pluto, and which were appointed by him to afflict the soules of men with such
measure of torments and paines, as their vicious and
leaud life had merited and worthily deserued, their
names were Alecto, Tisiphone, and Megæra: who in
stead of haire to adorne their heads, had venomous
Snakes and Adders encompassing the same, whose
winding and crooked tailes hang downe dissipated
and disparckled all about their shoulders, faces, and
breasts. Some writers doe alledge a fourth furie, adioined to these three, which they entearme by the
name of Lissa, which is as much to say as madnesse, &
therefore they hold, that from her proceed all luna-
cies, distractnesse of sence, & forgetfulnesse of vnder-
Euripides. standing and reason. Wherupon *Euripides* reporteth,
that Iris (commanded by Iuno) brought this furie to
her sonne in law Hercules, because shee intended to
bewitch him with a braine distempering passion of
madnesse, furie, and rage. And this Lissa is alwaies depictured with an yron stringed whip in her hand. Poets also haue in some sort annexed vnto these furies,
as partaking something of their natures, those monsters.

sters which are called Harpiæ, for that the Ancients
beleeued, that these also were employed by the gods
in punishing the sinnes of mortall men, who are said
also to remaine & inhabite in the infernall kingdome:
although *Virgil* reporteth, that they dwel in the Islads *Virgil.*
called Strophades, enuironned with the Ionian sea, &
are described to haue the face and countenance of
beauteous and faire women, yet leane and something
meagre , the rest of their bodies framed in the due
proportion and shape of birds, with mightie broad
wings, and crooked and sharpe talents, for so *Virgil*
describeth them, which afterwards was most excellently imitated by Ariosto. Of these Harpiæ are engendred those birds which are called Striges, which
alwaies flie in the night, and (as it is written) in the
dead of silence get into mens houses where young
children are, and priuily sucke their bloud, whereby
oftentimes by losse of too much bloud, they miserably pine away and perish. *Statius* sayth, That these
haue also the face of women, and do remaine & breed
in the infernal region. Some also haue writ, that those
spirits which are called Lamiæ, with the Grecians are
held to be the verie same as the other, which they called by the names of inchantresses or deuillish old women alwaies practising mischeefe, hurt, and villanie.
Philostratus sayth, That they are ill spirits, or wicked
diuels, cruell, bloudie, and luxurious without measure, and most hungrie and greedie after human flesh.
Suida and *Fauorinus* report of one Lamia, who was a Suida and:
most louely and beauteous woman, on whom Iupiter Fauorinus.
became exceedingly enamoured , who had also one
goodly

goodly and faire child, at whose delicate feature and
well-shaped lineaments, Iuno exceedingly repined,
and in the end by her infinit spight and iealousie, caused it to be by such night spirits most cruelly murthered: vpon which vnexpected and vnluckie accident,
the woe-afflicted mother became almost frantike and
distracted of her wits, who since in that miserable passion of phrensie vseth to wander vp and downe, working and contriuing all the mischeese, hurt, and de-
spight to all other young children whatsoeuer. Others
write, that these Lamiæ had the faces of women, and
the feet of horses. But *Dyon* the historian describeth
them in another sort, which also with many is held to
be the most probable.

Dyon.

It is read therefore with him, that in certain desarts
& vnhabited places of Lybia, are certaine most fierce
rauening, and most furious beasts, which (sayth hee)
haue the face, necke, & breast of a woman of the most
loue-alluring faire and delicate hue, that any art of
man for a most perfect colour can any way inuent,
who in their countenance and eyes doe retaine so
pleasing a grace, and such attractiue and enticing
smiles, that they doe enwrap & ouercome (as it were)
the beholders sences euen with an entranced wonderment, and amased admiration. The rest of their bodie
is all couered ouer with most hard glistering & bright
scales, whose forme downeward is of the shape of a
most vglie serpent, fearefull and terrible. They haue
not any wings, nor haue they any voice, onely like
snakes they doe hisse, and make some soft noice with
their lips: they are so infinite swift and nimble in running,

ning, that no other beaſt is thought able to ouertake
them, they make their prey of wild men, by laying
open, and diſcouering their delicious ſnow-white
breaſts, which who ſo ſeeth, becommeth inſtantly ſo
beſotted with the beautie thereof, that hee preſently
deſireth the taſt of thoſe pleaſures which are promiſed by ſo faire outward ſhewes , and in comming to
embrace them, they themſelues altar not in any point
their countenance, vnleſſe by ſeeming to bee baſhful,
modeſt, and ſhameſaſt, they fixe their eies downward
on the earth , alwaies keeping hid and ſecret their
ſharpe talents and ſerpent-ſhaped tailes, vntill by ſuch
their inueagling and deceitfull demeanures, they fully are poſſeſſed of the prey betweene their embracements, which preſently they impoyſen to death with
the venome of their ſting, and afterward doe eat and
deuour them moſt greedily, whoſe mans fleſh-coue-
ting maw is neuer filled or ſatisfied. *Homer* ſpeaketh of **Homer.**
a certaine beaſt which was called Chimæra, which
was deſcribed to haue the head of a Lyon, the bellie
or middle part of a Goat, and the taile and feet of a
Dragon , and from whoſe mouth iſſued forth fierie
ſparckles , which alſo *Virgil* affirmeth in more large
allowance. The neerer coniectures are, that this Chimæra was not a beaſt, but a certaine high mountaine
in Licia, from whoſe top ſeemed to aſcend & mount
flames of liuely fire (not vnlike the nature and qualitie of thoſe of the hill Mongibell) in the vpper parts
of this mountaine, in cerraine hollow caues & dens
liued many Lyons of an extraordinarie, furious, and
cruell kind: towards the bottome of it, which was in-

compaſſed

paſſed about with many high trees, buſhes, and thickets, were found infinite numbers of Snakes, Serpents,
and Dragons, in that abundance, as the Country therabouts was altogether vnfrequented and diſinhabi-
ted of any human dwellers. For which inconuenience
(proceeding from the number of thoſe rauenous
beaſts)it is written, that *Belleferon* found out a remedie, and endeuoured ſo far, as he draue all thoſe beaſts
cleane out of that country: for which cauſe(it ſhould
ſeeme) the Poets afterwards ſuppoſed, that the beaſt
Chimæra was ſlaine by *Belleferon*.

Concerning the ſiſters, which wee call Parcæ, and
which are ſaid to attend on Pluto, there are alſo three,
whoſe names are Clotho, Lacheſis, and Atropos,
whereof the firſt(according to the opinion of the ancients)taketh charge of the birth & natiuities of mortall men : the ſecond, of all the reſt of their life : and
the laſt, of their inſtant deaths, and departure out of
this world: all which three are depictured ſitting on a
row, buſily employed in their ſeuerall offices, the yon-
geſt ſiſter drawing out of a diſtaffe a reaſonable big
thred, the ſecond winding it about a wheele, and turning the ſame till it became little and ſlender, and the
eldeſt; which ſeemed decrepit and far in yeares, ſtood
readie with her knife, (when it ſhould bee ſpun)to cut
it off:and they are deſcribed to be inueſted with white
vailes, and with little coronets on their heads, wreathed about with garlands, compoſed of the flowers of
Narciſſus. And now to conclude with theſe deſcriptions of the Inferi, wee will end with that of Charon,
ſuppoſed to be the ferry man of Acheron , with the
expli-

explication thereof, as both *Boccace* and *Seruius* haue deliuered, as also *Virgil* and *Homer*, and diuers others affirming the same.

By Charon therefore is vnderstood Time, which *Boccace.* Time(according to some opinions) is the son of Erebus,(which is taken for the diuine and celestiall counsell, held priuately before the world began) and from which, since, all things haue been produced: and as the Ancients(as I haue said) supposed it to bee the father of Time, so likewise they held the Night to be the mother thereof, insomuch, as before time there was neuer any matter whatsoeuer, nor any light or apparance of day could bee discerned, and therefore this Erebus by the Auncients is placed now in darknesse, which is the infernall region. And whereas Charon is supposed to haue the transportation and passing ouer of the soules of mortall men from the one side of the riuer Acheron, or(as some call it) Stix vnto the other, it is enucleated(as it were)& vnclouded thereby, that Time so soone as wee are borne and brought forth into the world, doth carrie vs along by little and little vnto our deaths, and setteth vs ouer the riuer of Acheron, which word interpreted, signifieth sorrowfulnes, for that indeed we passe this life with miseries, aduersities, and laments. He is described old, and yet exceeding strong, for that Time neuer looseth his strength or vertue by the ouer-ruuning of yeares, and hee is apparrelled with a blacke and most noisome stinking mantle, which hangeth loosely ouer his shoulders, whose smel nothing is almost able to endure, al which signifieth, that while men are here in this world sub-

Q   iect

iect to time, we neuer respect the glorie of the celestiall habitations, only deuoting our selues to the riches,
wealth, and pleasures of this world, which indeed are
most vile, filthie, and stincking, compared to those ioi-
ous and happie blessings of heauen, whereunto wee
should wholly addict our selues, and direct our studies, endeuouring by all endeuours to acquire & pur-
chase the same vnto vs: but wee are so couered ouer &
inuested with this cloake and vaile of mortalitie and
mundane affections, that wee are carried away blindfolded into a thousand miserable and disordinate desires. For the canckred rust of effeminate desires hath
so deepely eaten into this our yron age, as notwithstanding the infinite labourious endeauours of many
artificiall workemen, haue most largely extended, yet
est tali rubigine tincta vt oleŭ & opera perdiderunt, Who
euer assaied the varnishing thereof. For such an irra-
dicable habite hath it attained vnto, that as the pestiferous shirt, wherein the treble-nighted brood was
enwrapped, effused a venomous contagion, which
did incorporate it selfe into the flesh, fretted the sin-
newes, and festered into the marrow, so this en-eating
yron mole, wherewith the insensate of-pring of this
time is attainted, admitteth a remedilesse infection,
that staineth the christalline puritie of our minds, &
dooth eneruate the contexed ground of our sences:
onely wee herein differ from him, that the poyson
wherewith hee was infected, wrought in him such
torment, as hee instantly sought a remedie: but perceauing it so deepely rooted, that otherwise he could
not bee thereof dispatched, hee sacrificed himselfe

in

in a fire, whose ascending flames mounted him vp to
the heauens: whereas contrariwise wee (as entoxicat
with Circæan drugs, and lulled asleepe by the villai-
nous deceits of the sweet-seeming delights wherwith
wee are besotted)seeke by all meanes possible to pam-
per and feed vp our humourous conceits, and loath
death, for nothing so much as wee thereby are depriued and dispossessed of our pleasures,which wee willingly would neuer forsake, from whence while wee
draw backeward, with all our forces still clinging to
our foule desires, wee are by the weight of wicked-
nesse throwne downe headlong, and precipitated
into hell . And thus much shall suffice for the descriptions and expositions necessarie in this Treatise.

Mercurie.

IT hath beene alreadie largely declared, that among
the Ancients manie, yea infinite numbers of gods
were held and worshipped in most strange and supersticious adoration, of which, as many of them had
many places and charges to take care of,protect, and
gouerne, so likewise they were to vndertake many fun-
ctions, offices, and duties. By reason whereof,it proceeded, that also they had so many names, titles, and
degrees appropriated vnto them, which is the cause,
that the Ancients oftentimes shape forth & engraue
the effigies and forme of one god in diuerse and seuerall fashions, according as they were at that time to
shew forth the qualitie,nature, and condition of such

Q ij   their

their then presented deitie and working vertue . By
meanes whereof,becaufe vnto Mercurie (of whome
we now entreat)they attributed thefe natures, as that
hee fometimes was taken to be the god and patron of
gaine and profit,fometime of eloquence, and fome-
time alfo of theft,fubtiltie, and deceit, they haue depainted him now in this fhape and now in that forme,
and alwaies diuerfly : but the trueft draught and fimilitude of his portraiture is, wherein hee is depictured
and fet forth as the meffenger of the gods : of which
office alfo there were two forts held. and obferued
among the gods, the one was executed by Mercurie,
and the other by Iris, betweene both which, all the
embaffages and errants difpatched wherefoeuer, were
done and performed: onely this diffe:ence there was,
that Iris more particularly attended vpon Iuno, and.
was for the moft part commanded by her onely, vnleffe when the gods among themfelues had intended.
to afflict mortals with peftilences,wars,or fome other
all ruinating mifcheefes,then was Iris commonly imployed in thefe fatall meffages . And about other
matters of fports, meetings, marriages, or pleafant
affaires , Mercurie was folelie vfed and commaun-
   The Auncients therefore depictured his forme in
the likeneffe & fhape of a yong man without a beard,
with two fmall wings infixed on the tops of his eares,
his bodie almoft all naked, faue that from his fhoul-
pers depended a thinne vaile, which winded & compaffed about all his bodie : in his right hand hee held
a golden purfe, and in his left his Caducæus or Snakie ftaffe: behind him was depictured a liuely Cocke,

and

and with wings alfo on his heeles: with the Ægyptians his ftaffe was thus defcribed, Hee hath (fay they) in one of his hands a flender white wand, about the which two ferpents doe annodate and entwine themfelues, whofe heads doe meet together euen iuft at the top thereof, as their tailes alfo doe meet at the lower end, and the one of them is a male, & the other female. And this depiĉturance with them was called *Concordia*, or *Signum pacis*. VVhereupon afterwards it grew, that Embaffadours and great parfonages (employed in matters of ftate) carried alwaies in their hands fuch like ftaffe, and were alfo called Caduceators. Many who would haue depiĉtured the portraiture of Peace, haue taken and fet downe this for the verie fame, adioining vnto it fome certaine branches of the Oliue tree. VVherevpon it is written by *Virgil*, Virgil. that *Æneas* fending certain Embaffadours to the king of the Latines, caufed them all to bee crowned with greene Oliue branches. *Statius* alfo fayth, That when Statius. *Tideus* went to demand of *Etheocles* the kingdome of Thebes in the name of *Polinices*, hee held in his hand an Oliue branch, as a token of a peaceful Embaffador. And that (when he could not obtaine his requeft and demand) he violently threw it frõ him on the ground, and in a furious manner ftampt vpon it with his feet, as the figne of a moft fatall and bloudie warre, which afterward was profecuted accordingly. But now, hauing taken this occafion to fpeak of the Oliue branch, it fhall not be much digreffion fomwhat to touch the Statues of *Concordia* or Peace, who (according as *Ariftofanes* deliuereth) was framed in the fhape of a Ariftofanes.

Q iij yong

young woman, holding betweene her armes the infant Pluto, taken fometimes for the god of Riches, in that by Peace they are acquired and confenued, and by warres wafted and confumed. And this Peace was by the Ancients held to be a very fpeciall and louing friend to the goddeffe Ceres , from which two procced the encreafes of fruits and corne,& all other nutriments whatfoeuer. And *Tibullus* thus fpeaking of her fayth :

Tibullus.

All-plenteous,faire,and well-difpofed Peace,
  In whom all learning finds eternall fpring,
Through whom Bellonaes ftratagems doe ceafe,
  Thou waft the firft of all that ere did bring
The ftiffeneckt bull vnto the crooked yoke,
  Making the fields yeeld plenty euery where,
Who with thy gentle mildly-gouern'd ftroke
  Exempteth all the world from further feare.
By thee, all profpers well conferu'd, and cherifht,
By furious war, all's loft, confum'd, and perifht.

Wherevpon *Claudianus* reporteth, that Ceres by no entreaties would marrie her daughter either to Mars or Phœbus, being importunately fued vnto by both of them: in that fhee held Mars as her profeffed and open enemie, and excepted alfo againft Phœbus, for that with his ouer-ardent and fierie beames, her encreafes were parched, burned, and confumed. But returning to our firft intended treatife, it hath ben already fpoken, that Mercurie was depictured & drawn forth with two wings on the top of his eares, and alfo

(as

(as some hold) two lesser infixed on his heeles, & with his white rod or wand in his hand, as *Homer* alledgeth when hee sayth:that Iupiter sent him to Calipso to releafe Vlisses and others of his companie from these mischeeuous and diuelish enchauntments, and when he was sent also at another time to conduct Priamus through the Grecian campe to demand the body of his slaine sonne Hector. And at another time when he was dispatched to Æneas, then remaining and soiourning with Dido the Carthaginean Queene. And indeed generally of all writers hee was described in that forme: vnto those feathers or wings so placed vpon Mercurie (who as I haue said, is oftentimes taken for learning and eloquence) is compared and alluded the nature of speech, discourse, and words ; in that they are no sooner pronounced and deliuered from the prison-like mansion of the mouth, but they doe as it were flie away, and are so sudainely vanished and departed, as if they had wings (as a man may say) to carrie them away both out of sight and hearing. And in that regard *Homer* oftentimes calleth them winged or feathered words. Almost all writers agree, that Mercurie was depictured with very long hair on his head, and that it hung downe about his shoulders : wherevnto also some hold, that his wings were fastened, yet *Apuleius* describes it otherwise, (when hee writeth of the Comedie of the goddesses, striuing for the golden ball) where hee sayth, that Mercurie was sent vnto them by Iupiter, and that he appeared there like a verie youth, hardly attained to full virillitie, and that hee had very short haire on his head, which looked

like

Homer.

Apuleius

like the colour of amber, and was curled, and that for his vestures he had only a subtle & thinne vaile, composed of purple silke . *Martianus Capella* describes

Martianus Capella.

him to bee young also, but of a maruellous strong & actiue constitution, and of a well-disposed bodie, of well-knit artures, ioints, and sinewes, and on his chin sayth hee, begin to sprout forth and shew themselues, certaine young haires of a yellowish colour. According to his opinion is *Statius*. But *Lucianus* describeth

Lucianus.

him without either his Caduceas, or any such wings so infixed vpon him, or that hee had any such yellow haire, but sayth, that hee lookt like a lustie yong man, powerfull and vigorous, and that hee was very skilfull and well exercised in running, wrastling, and actiuitie

Philostratus.

Wherof likewise *Philostratus* speaketh when he sayth, that Palestra was the daughter of Mercurie (which since wee haue entearmed by the name of wrastling) and that shee was so indifferently formed, that it was very hard to iudge her either for a man or woman: for sayth hee, her countenance seemed both youthfull & maidenly, her haire not altogether so long as a womans, nor so short as a mans, her breasts were delicate and white, and yet small and slender, her generall proportion euery way pleasing, and yet nothing effeminate, and hee describes her there, sitting in a greene meade, holding betweene her naked breasts an Oliue branch, gratefull and acceptable vnto her, in that the wrastlers (called also Palestrians, which did customably vse those kind of exercises) vsed to annoint their bodies before they attempted their sports, with the oyle of Oliues. And thus *Philostratus* depainteth her,

saying

saying, that fhe was the daughter of Mercury, becaufe
it is read indeed, that he was the firft inuenter & fetter vp of thofe exercifes of wraftling, leaping, & other
actiue & agile performances. And for this and other
caufes the Ancients worfhipped and adored as a god,
Mercurie, vnto whom alfo, they attribute the firft de-
uifing and finding out of Letters, Muficke, and Geo-
metrie. Hee was taken alfo for the god of Trafficke &
Marchandifes, as that vnto thofe kind of profeffours
it is fit and neceffarie to haue eloquence, knowledge,
and fubtiletie of wit for the better managing & handling their deceitfull affaires, wherevpon *Fulgentius* Fulgentius.
fayth, That the wings fo depictured on the heeles of
Mercurie, fignifie the courfe of thofe that do traffick,
which (fayth hee) is alwaies vncertaine and full of
doubt, now profperous, and anone vnfortunate, and
that they themfelues are carried vp and lifted vp (as it
were) with the wings of hope, and affurance of good
fucceffe, and many times alfo defpairing, & that they
are continually vexed with vn-affured thoughts, and
difquieting vigilancie; the which thing the Cock, placed behind this god, doth fignifie & difclofe, although
with fome it is held, that this Cocke rather meaneth
the watchfulneffe and waking ftudies of learned men,
for fo much as for thofe kind of men that profeffed
letters, it was held an odious thing in thofe daies to
fpend the whole night in fleepe and drowfie cogitations. And therefore Mercurie was often taken for that
light of knowledge, & fpirit of vnderftanding, which
guides men to the true conceauement of darke and
enigmaticall fentences . And yet notwithftanding,

R naturall

naturall and seasonable rest and repose was altogether also in those times allowed as the refresher of
mens wits. *Pausanias* writeth (speaking of the Countrie of Corinth) that with the Trezemyans there was erected an altar, on which were performed & offered certaine Sacrifices and oblations to the Muses, and vnto Sleep, as ioining them both together, & accounting Sleepe to bee a greater friend, and more agreeable to the Muses than vnto any other god or goddesse whatsoeuer, vnto which Sleepe also they erected Statues, Images, and Pictures, adoring him with great zeale, reuerence, and veneration, as supposing him to be a great god, and the giuer of ease and quiet, & the mittigater and allaier of great and heauie labors. According to *Homer* & *Hesiodus*, Sleepe was accounted the brother of death, the which thing also the Images insculped in the curiously-engraued chest of Cipselus, liuely explained, wherein was inchased and set forth the true resemblance and portraiture of a woman, of a most soure, louring, & sad aspect, something growne in yeares and elderly, who in her left hand held a young child, of a reasonable & ordinarie beautie, and in her right arm another child of a most swartish, blacke, and dull complexion, hauing his legs and armes growing maruellous crooked; both these children were cut out and fashioned with their eies shut, the first was Sleepe, and the other Death, being both brothers and twinnes : the woman that held them so in her armes, was Night, and mother vnto them both. This Night also hath been desigured by the Ancients in forme of an old woman, hauing two great wings
growing

growing on her shoulders, all coleblacke and spread
abroad, as if they seemed to offer a flight, and that she
is drawne also in a charriot, whose foure wheeles are
made of Ebonie. *Boccace* sayth, That the wheeles therof signifie the foure parts of the night so diuided and
distinguished by Marriners, as also of souldiors vpon
their guards. And hee there also affirmeth, that shee
looketh with a very heauie and sad countenance, but
her vpper garment or vaile being of a black substance
is notwithstanding depainted and adulterated with
sundrie spots of siluer, made to the true assimilitude
and shape of starres, which (sayth hee) is alluded to
the beauteous ornament of the heauens . *Tibullus*
sayth, That the Night like a graue Matron is alwayes
attended & waited vpon with all her children, which
are said to be, Death, Sleepe, the Starres, Melancholie,
and many others. *Philostratus* in a Tablet (which hee   Philoſtra-
made for *Amphiarus*) depainteth there the portrai-   tus.
ture of Sleepe in the shape of an aged woman, all la-
zie, slouthfull, and sluggish, and that shee was habited
with two seuerall vestments ; that aboue was white,
and the other vnder that, all blacke, by the one is vnderstood the day, and the other the night : & she held
in one of her hands a horne, from which shee seemed
to poure forth vpon mortall men the seed of rest, ease,
and quiet. *Ouid* describing her place of her habitati-   Ouid.
on, sayth, That she dwelleth with the Cimerians (people which by reason of the absence of the sunnes illu-
mination) haue continuall darkenesse. *Homer* setteth   Homer.
downe her dwelling place to bee in Lemnos, an Island
embrac'd by the Egean sea . *Statius* sayth, That shee   Statius.

abideth with the people of Ethiopia . And *Ariosto* writeth of her abode to bee in the furthermost nooke or corner of Arabia. But *Ouid* (as I haue said) speaking of her habitation to bee with the Cimerians, sayth also, That the bed shee resteth vpon, is made of the hardest and blackest Ebonie, couered all ouer with blacke vestures or attillatures, & that on the top of the bedstead are framed forth in most excellent and curious manner, an infinite multitude of dreames, of diuerse and seuerall natures figured out and exposed. But of this it shall be sufficient to haue said thus much, reuerting my pen to the perfecting of our former matter of Mercurie.

It is read therefore, that vnto the Statues and Images dedicated vnto Mercurie (those especially which were erected in publike streets and high waies) it was the vse and custome for euery passenger that passed by, to throw stones, stickes, or other such like, according as vpon the first veiw, or by chance they happened vpon them, by reason whereof, about those Statues in very short time, were raised very great hils only of stones: by which is either signified, that the gods (so adored in those daies) were to bee reuerenced and worshipped with all those things , which at the first sight presented themselues, thereby offering them vp (as it were) as an oblation vnto them ; or else it did meane, that Learning, Discourse, and Knowledge, is compacted and made of little parcels and peeces of phrases, figures, and sentences, as that hill was grown to mightinesse & huge proportion, by heaping and entermingling of those little stones so particularlie

gathe-

gathered together, and accumulated by the paſſengers.

The Auncients alſo haue aſcribed vnto Mercurie the charge, care, & protection of ſheepheards, which *Homer* likewiſe ſeemeth to confirme, when hee ſayth, that Phorbus was the richeſt in cattell and heards of beaſts of all the Troians whatſoeuer, whome Mercurie (ſayth hee) fauouring and affecting, had raiſed and aduaunced to that wealth and happineſſe. *Pauſanias* writeth, That in a certaine Prouince of Corinth in a high way, was erected an Image or Statue of Mercurie, wholly compoſed of braſſe, at whoſe right ſide was depictured forth a Lambe, lying on the ground. The ſame Author alſo ſayth, That there was another of the like held in great reuerence among the Tanagreans, people of Beotia, on the ſhoulders of which picture was drawne forth, ſitting, the portraiture of a Ram with golden hornes, and the reaſon of it was, in that (as they held) Mercurie was ſeene to go in ſuch ſort with a Ram on his ſhoulders, round about the wals of a Cittie in Beotia, when hee cauſed a moſt greeuous and infectious peſtilence to ceaſe, which had almoſt periſhed and conſumed all the inhabitants of that citty. Wherevpon it was alwaies afterward obſerued, that vpon the celebration and ſolemnizing of the feaſt of Mercurie, there was appointed a beautifull young man, who ſhould that day three times go round about the wals of the cittie, with a Ram on his ſhoulders. *Pauſanias* ſpeaketh alſo of another kind of Statue, which was brought from Arcadia vnto Rome, and there erected in the temple of Iupiter Olympicus,

Pauſanias.

Pauſanias.

R iij

cus, which on his head had a helmet of engrauen Steele, and ouer his shoulders was cast a Souldiours coat, who held also vnder his arme the shape of a Ram.

Macrobius. *Macrobius*, who is of opinion, That by all the gods of the Auncients were vnderstood the seuerall vertues of the Sunne, sayth, that the wings so giuen to Mercurie(as is before touched) doe signifie the swiftnesse, and velocitie of the Sunnes expedition in the Zodiake. And that whereas it is written, that hee slue Argos the guardian and keeper of the daughter of Inachus, transformed afterward into a Cow, he sayth, that that Argos supposed to haue so many eies, is nothing else but the heauens; beautified with so many starres, which beholdeth and gouerneth the earth: which earth also the Ægyptians in their sacred letters framed in the likenesse of a Cowe, so that Mercurie (who is also oftentimes taken for the sunne): thus killing Argus, is only the banishing, vanquishing, or putting to flight of the stars in the firmament, which (as it were) hide themselues vpon the first appropinquation of the suns all glorious resplendencie. *Marti-* **Martianus** *anus* sayth, That Philologia entering into the second heauens, saw there comming towards her a Virgine, holding in one of her hands a certaine tablet, wherein were intersected many descriptions, properties, conditions, and figures of Mercurie. In the midst of which was liuely proportioned a certaine Birde of Ægypt like vnto a Storke, which with them was called Ibis, and also the head of a young man with long yellow haire, & round about it seemed to twine two

young

young Serpents. Vnder that was drawn a white wand
all gilded at the top, in the midſt of it of a greeniſh
colour, and towards the end coale blacke. On the right
hand of it was depictured a great ſhel of ſome ſtrange
fiſh, and alſo a Scorpion: and on the left ſide was depainted a Goat, & a little bird, much like vnto a Sparrow-hawke all which depicturances containe within
themſelues the myſteries and darke meanings of the
Ægyptians, with whom Mercurie was worſhipped &
adored vnder the name of that god, which with them
was called Anubis, and was depictured alſo with his
Caduceus, as *Apuleius* likewiſe (where hee writeth of   Apuleius.
certaine tales of thoſe people which trauelled with
Iſis) depainteth him. And ſayth, that Anubis (which
the Ægyptians called Mercurie) was ſet forth & depictured ſometimes of a blacke and ſwartiſh complexion, ſometimes alſo very beautifull, and of a faire aſpect. And among ſome of them alſo they framed his
Image, as hauing the head of a Dog, in his right hand
holding a Snakie wand, and with his left ſhaking a
greene bough of Palme. By the head of the Dog was
vnderſtood the ſubtiletie & craftineſſe which proceeded from Mercurie, for ſo much as there is thought
no beaſt to be ſo wiſe, capable, and wilie as the Dog :
Or elſe they ſo ſhaped him with the head of a Dog,
for that (as it is written by *Diodorus Siculus*) this Anu-   Diodorus
bis was the ſonne of Oſiris, who long before that fol-   Siculus.
lowing his father in the warres, ſhewed himſelfe ſo
valerous and approued hardie, as that indeed after he
was dead, hee was worſhipped & honoured as a god.
And for that in his life time, hee alwaies carried de-

painted

painted in his fhield the portraiture of a Dog, defi-
guring the fame alfo vpon all his other armes , his
Image or Statue was afterward in that manner drawn
and fet forth with a Dogs head , demonftrating alfo
thereby, that hee was louing, faithfull, and obedient
to his father, defending him alwaies from all dangers,
abufes, and perrillous accidents, which alfo is commonlie feene in that beaft towards his maifter or
keeper.

There be fome haue written, that Mercurie was taken & held for the very fame as *Hercules*, or not much
different frō him, as his Image or Picture held among
the French men manifefted, which people likewife a-
dored him as the god of Wifdome & Eloquence, and
his Statue was thus compofed:

There was hewen, and cut out with moft exquifite
skill and care of the workmen, an excelently well proportioned Image, in the fimilitude and fhape of a very
aged man, euen decrepit as it fhould feeme, and in the
extremitie of yeares, his head almoft bald, fauing that
on the fides remained fome few haires, fhort, and curled, his countenance feuere, grim, and foure, his complexion of a tawnie and time-worne hue, his vpper
vefture was the skin of a Lyon, and in his right hand
he held an vnweldy and huge poleaxe, in his left hand
an yron bow, and at his backe hung a quiuer of fteele-
headed arrowes, to the end of his tongue were faftened and annexed many fmall chaines & linkes of gold,
with which hee feemed to pull and draw vnto him infinite multitudes of men of fundry Nations , which
were alfo tied and faftened to thofe chaines, and yet

of

of themfelues feemed voluntarily to follow him, the picture looking alwaies backeward to behold fuch innumerable troopes flocking towards him. And this peece of worke was framed with inexplicable & rare perfection of knowledge, beautified & adorned with delicate politure and true couching and conclaufture of thofe hard and almoft impenetrable ftones. By the defcription and fetting forth of which, is difcouered and vnript(as it were)the all-drawing force, and attractiue power of eloquence, fo attributed & afcribed by thefe people vnto *Hercules*. In framing him old and in yeeres, is vnderftood, that in men of experience and long ftudies, eloquence is of more vertue and power, as attained vnto naturitie of perfection, being indeed raw(and therefore not well digefted)in yonger yeeres which of neceffitie muft want iudgement and a fetled experience to adioine vnto it , by which it is made more forcible, preuailing, and gracious, as *Homer* at large & copioufly fpeaketh thereof in his commends and praifes of Neftor. From whofe mouth(fayth hee) moft fluently rufhed forth ftreames of dulcet honny, and whofe penne diftilled fugred drops of delicious fweetneffe, and whofe workes and fruits fo compleat & adorned with golden fentences, affuageth the malice of time, and mittigateth and allaieth her fpight of forgetfulneffe, whofe perpetuitie is engrauen in the braffe-leaued bookes of neuer-dying memorie. And thus much concerning the Statues, Images, Pictures, and Defcriptions made of Mercurie, held among the Ancients to be the god of craft and eloquence.

S   Minerua.

Minerua.

IT is manifeſt, that the knowledge of neuer ſo many things without either a grace, or a certaine kind of pleaſing deliuerie of the ſame, is not abſolutely exquiſite in praiſe; yet merritting due commends, though not in the excellencie or height thereof : ſo likewiſe to ſpeake much, and to enter into the handling or diſcourſe of many matters for one that knoweth little, & is but ſleightly trauelled in the truly-conceaued paths of literature, not only diſcouers an ineducated rudeneſſe, and lame ignorance of letters, but oftentimes induceth vnto himſelfe danger, and may offend very highly, as *Marcus Tullius* at large and learnedly hath written. As therefore among the Ancients Mercurie was taken and held (in reſpect of his melliſluous and honny-dewed tongue of deliuerie) for the god of eloquence : ſo likewiſe was Minerua reuerenced and adored amongſt them, for the Queen and Goddeſſe of Wiſedome, Learning, and Knowledge. And to let vs vnderſtand, that it is requiſite (as before is ſomething touched) to know very well what we vndertake to ſpeake and diſcourſe of; and to apprehend a right conceauement what wee ſuppoſe wee know indeed, to argue with ſhort and pithie diſputes, thereby to pull on attention, and auoid the miſerie of being thought to be tedious; to contend mildly, and laſtly, to write methodically, and with a good grace, (being indeed a ſpeciall introducement of a reading ſpirit) the Ancients haue thought fit to conioine the

Sta-

Statues of this god & goddeſſe together, as betweene whom reſted a kind of Sympathie and concordance of diſpoſitions, and they called it by a Greeke name, *Hermathena*, for that the Grecians entearmed Mercurie Hermes, and Minerua they called Athena. And they vſed to erect this Picture or Image, alwaies in ſchooles, intending thereby to put ſchollers in mind, that they ought to embrace knowledge with eloquence, making thereof a compoſed medling and entermixing , as that by the one, the other receaued farre greater vertue, grace, and perfection by the combination of both their powers together.

And it was held among the Auncients, that Wiſdome and Knowledge was not only neceſſarie, and to be acquired ſolely in Citties, and in priuate & domeſticall gouernements, but alſo to be entertained & imbraced abroad in the warres, among Generals, Captaines, and all ſorts of commanders: therefore they attribute vnto Minerua the care & charge of the wars, and depicture her in her Statue all armed like a valiant commandreſſe, as it is recorded that ſhee ſhewed her ſelfe very gallant, valerous, and forward in the warres, held betweene the gods & the Gyants, wherin (as it is written with ſome) ſhee hand to hand ſlew Pallantes the moſt fierce, terrible, and mightieſt of them all. Whereupon ſhee afterwards got the name of Pallas, and was ſo entearmed. But other writers affirme, that ſhee was called Pallas, for ſome other reaſons, whereof it ſhall bee now needleſſe to ſpeake, only it is ſufficient, that they all agree, that Minerua and Pallas were all one and the ſame.

Many

Many haue written also, that Bellona was goddeſſe
of the warres, and the ſame as Minerua, but by their
Statues and Images dedicated vnto them, theſe diffe-
rences doe appeare: By Minerua was vnderſtood and
intended the wiſe councels and aduiſed prudencie of
Captaines and Officers, in managing their militarie
affaires: and by Bellona were meant all bloudie ſtrata-
gems, maſſacres, ſurpriſes, executions, and fatall meetings of the enemie whatſoeuer, and therfore ſhe was
depiĉtured to hold in one of her hands a whip of red-
hot yron ſtrings, and in her other hand a great earthen
baſen, filled vp with conicaled bloud, ſhee was held
alſo to be the goddeſſe of wrath, furie, and anger, and
many times depainted with a trumpet at her mouth,
as ſhee that gaue the ſigne of battell, and of generall
encounters. But moſt writers doe agree, that ſhee was
moſt commonly depiĉtured with a flaming firebrand
in her hand, for that the Auncients (as it is read with
Licoſrones.) before the vſe of the Trumpets was found
out, when they intended to giue a ſignall or token of
battell, accuſtomed to ſend a ſlaue before the campe
of the enemie with a flaming torch or firebrand in his
hand, the which after that hee had ſhaken three times
in his hand, would throw it downe towards the face
of the enemie, and preſently after begun their battell
& furious encounters on both ſides. *Claudianus* & *Sta-*
tius doe report, that this Bellona was the firſt that was
ſeene to carrie in her hands this fierie token of fight.
And thus much ſhall ſuffice for her deſcription as ſhe
is taken for Bellona.

Minerua by moſt writers was depiĉtured in the
ſhape

shape of a young woman, of a liuely and freſh countenance, yet ſomething threatening and angrie in hir
lookes, her eyes were very fixe, aſſured, and ſtedfaſt,
and much like the colour of a blewiſh greene, or that
of a troubled ſea, and ſhee was armed complete at all
peeces, with a long ſpeare in one hand, & on hir other
arme a ſhield or target, made of the pureſt Chriſtall,
on the top of her helmet was placed a garland, made
of Oliue branches, and hard by her ſide were drawne
forth, and portraied two young children with naked
kniues in their hands, ſeeming (as it might appeare by
their lookes) to menace one another, the one was called Feare, the other Horror, as that thoſe two alwaies
waited, and were conuerſant in warres and bloudie
controuerſies. Wherevpon *Statius* (writing that Mars Statius.
commanded by Iupiter to ſet warres and quarrels betweene the Argiues and Thebans) ſayth there, that
Mars ſent before him thoſe two, Feare, and Horror.
Pauſanias writeth, that the picture of Feare was ſha- Pauſanias.
ped forth in ſeuerall formes by the Auncients, as that
ſometimes it was made with the head of a Lyon, terrible and furious; which manner was vſed much by the
Grecians , and which forme was engrauen on the
ſhield of Agamemnon : with ſome other it was framed with the face and bodie of a woman, but of ſo vgly and deformed countenance as is poſſible to imagin.
The Corinthians dedicated this picture ſo maʼe, vnto
the ſonnes of Medea, ſlaine and murthered for bringing ſuch fatall gifts to the daughter of old Creon,
whereby ſhe and all that regall familie periſhed, and
were for euer extinct.

The

The Oliue tree was confecrated to Minerua, for that (as *Virgil* fayth) the Athenians vfed to crown the heads of Conquerors and triumphant commanders, with garlands thereof. Many writers doe difagree in the defcription of Minerua, and efpecially thofe of Greece. Touching the birth of her, it is written, that fhe was borne without a mother, and that fhee iffued and came forth into the world out of the head of Iupiter (according to the opinion of all fantafticke Poets.) By which is meant & vnderftood, that all human knowledge and vnderftanding proceedeth from the fuperior and diuine guidance aboue, whereby thefe intellectuall parts become celeftiall, and defpifers of terrene delights. But *Martianus* interpretes it to the difgrace of women, (being indeed a great and fore, enemie vnto all that fexe) but (his expofition being too feuere and rigorous in that behalfe) it fhall not be pertinent further to declare it. Whofe opinion alfo *Ariftotle* himfelfe fomething embraced, affirming (being too much opinionated therein) that as Minerua was borne without a mother, fo all women generally are of themfelues without wit, knowledge, fecrecie, or affured conftancie : but fuch inuention proceedes onely of malice, and fome other feed of rancour, which was indeed irradicated in his breaft againft that praife-worthie fexe. Wherin I dare in fome fort contradict *Ariftotle*, in that (it is apparent) that there are in the world women of as great fpirit, wit, capacitie, and fetled refolutions as moft men are, and are as eloquent in deliuery of their thoughts, & as fcholler-like in chufing fit and fignificant words, in compofing &

annexing

Virgil.

Ariftotle.

annexing their pithie, fententious, and well-placed
phrafes, as moft men are whatfoeuer (exempting fome
famous profeffed Doctors, and daily Students.) But
returning to Minerua, the Auncients (as I haue faid)
framed her Statue to be all armed throughout, in the
fafhion of a moft valerous and hardie warrior : & fhe
wore on her head a wonderfull rich helmet, all made
and hammered of maffie gold, which with the beauty
thereof fhined moft glorioufly, fending forth a moft
excellent luftre, and delicate tranfparencie . *Homer* Homer.
fayth, That by this helmet fo infixed on her head, is
fignified, that the wit and policie of man (which alwaies refteth in the braine of the head) is (as a man
may fay)fo armed, and at all times prouided & readie,
that it defendeth the bodie from all eminent dangers,
mifcheefes, and inconueniences, & that it doth fhine,
& is made beautifull with vertuous & worthie works,
ftudies of contemplation, and diuine meditations.
The fame *Homer* fayth, That the excellent wit of man Homer.
doth neuer difcouer all that it knowes, nor yet leaueth
all that it difcourfeth of, eafily to be vnderftood & conceiued: wherein fuch words are compared to the doubtfull anfweres of an Oracle, or the darke and intricate
fpeeches of Sphinx: whereby belike it came, that in a
certaine part of Ægypt, they placed in the temple of
Minerua, the Statue and portraiture of this Sphinx,
which the people there reuerenced & adored, beleeuing it to be the goddeffe Ifis.

Paufaniæ (fpeaking of the Athenians)fayth, That Paufanias.
there was in that countrie a very ftately, and curioufly
built Image of Minerua, which had engrauen on the
top

top of the helmet the shape & forme of Sphinx, and
on both sides of it were cut out & carued the portraitures of two Griffins, which are held indeed to be neither beasts nor birds, but doe equally partake of both
kinds, for they haue the vpper part (as the head, necke
and wings) of an Eagle, and the rest of their bodies
shaped to the true similitude of Lyons. These strange
formed beasts are found to remaine (though *Pliny* sets
them downe as fabulous) in the furthermost parts of
Scythia, where (as it is written) are certaine mines of
gold and siluer, which these Griffins doe continually
guard and keepe, so that the people of that Country,
being called Arimaspes (which as many writers affirm
haue but one eye in their forehead) cannot without
great danger and hazard of their liues dig or seach for
any of that gold.

On the top also of that helmet so made for Minerua, someimes they placed the forme of a Cocke, as in
one part of Greece (inhabited by the Eleans) there
was such a Statue erected & made by Phidias, which
was wholly framed of gold and yuorie, which was so
consecrated and dedicated vnto Minerua, because
that bird of all others is most fierce, bold, and hardie
in his fight, as likewise in Captaines and men of war,
is requisite and required: or els it did demonstrat therby the vigilancie and wakefull cogitations of great
commanders and wise Gouernors, in whom is required great foresight, watchfulnesse, & care. And herein I must somewhat digresse from this treatise of Minerua, to obserue my Authour, who in this place hath
inserted some few capitulations of other abstracts, the
first

firſt beginning with the deſcriptions of *Veritas*, or Truth, with the explications thereof.

It is written with many Authors, & eſpecially with *Hippocrates*, that the effigies and portraiture of Truth was framed in the due ſimilitude & likeneſſe of a beauteous young woman, attired with very graue & modeſt abillements, and yet for that kind of elderly habite, very rich and coſtly. And the ſame Authour alſo depainteth there the ſhape of Opinion, likewiſe reſembling a young woman, not altogether ſo faire & louely, and yet not deformed or ill proportioned: who (ſaith he) ſeemed rather impudent than modeſtly bold, in all her demeanures, with her hands reaching forth to take and receaue whatſoeuer is offered and preſented.

Philoſtratus (ſpeaking of Truth) ſayth, that ſhee remaineth in the caue of Amphiarus, clothed all in white garments, gliſtering, and of a beautifull hue, where alſo ſhe was taken and ſuppoſed to bee the mother of Vertue, which Vertue, the Auncients reuerenced and worſhipped as a ſacred Goddeſſe, & conſecrated many Temples, Statues, and Altars vnto her, whoſe Image they erected directly before the Temple which was dedicated vnto Honor, meaning thereby, that none could enter or haue acceſſe thereunto, but by meanes of the other, and that there was no way or meanes to get true honour, but by the way & line of vertue, as that honour, dignitie, and aduancement were the rewards and recompences of vertuous and well-gouerned actions: and this picture of Honor alſo (as diuers write) was oftentimes ſet forth with

T two

Hipocrates.

two wings on the shoulders thereof, intending & vn-shadowing thereby, that honour and glorie doe as it were lend wings vnto men of vertue and merit, to lift vp and aduance themselues aboue the ordinarie pitch and seat of vulgar and desertlesse people, euen to the wonder and admiration of all men.

Lucianus   *Lucianus* speaking of a certaine Temple dedicated vnto Truth, sayth, that in the midst thereof was ere-cted her Image or Statue in the forme of a young wo-man, all sorrowfull, sad, and discontent, habited in vn-seemely rags and base attire, and (as it should seeme by certaine superscriptions ouer the head) shee com-plained, that she was ill-intreated, abused, & wronged by Fortune.

In many places (especially in Greece) Vertue hath been shaped forth in forme of a Pilgrime or trauel-ler, in that she findeth no resting place, secure abode, or certaine habitation, being sometimes vexed & op-prest by the gouernement of Tyrants, sometimes of Vsurers, and auaricious commanders, sometimes by luxurious Rulers, & sometimes also by the furie and chances of warres, intestine seditions, & ciuil broiles. Sometimes she is desigured forth like a graue and au-stere Matrone, sitting vpon a foure-squared stone, all solitarie, pensiue, and melancholie, and leaning her head vpon her knees, as though shee seemed wearie of her life, being so full of crosses, miseries, and per-turbations.

Zenophon   It is written with *Zenophon* and *Marcus Tullius*, that Hercules when he was in his adolescencie, and prime of his blooming daies, wandering by chaunce

in

in a defart and vnfrequented wood, came where two feuerall waies diuided themfelues in two contrarie courfes, the one leading directly into the wood, and the other enclining on the one fide thereof: Hercules as vncertain which of thefe two he fhould take, ftood pondering and confidering of the choice, hee had not long ftood thus reuoluing within himfelfe, but there appeared before him (all on the fudaine) two women, the one of which was called Pleafure, who indeed was wondrous beautifull to the eye, and of a louely afpect, wanton in her demeanure, and exceeding pleafing in all her geftures, and fhee was apparrelled with verie glorious and gorgeous abillements, whofe eye-dazeling brightneffe amafed Hercules with huge admiration thereof, fhe was fo adorned and decked with refplendant iewels, and gliftering ftones, & this woman feemed to perfuade him to take the way of fenfualitie & delights, which at the firft entrance appeared vnto him very large, faire, and eafie, befet with very pleafant and greene hearbes, and diuers-coloured flowers, but towards the end it grew very ftreit, ftony, rough, and full of fharpe-pricking thornes: the other woman (fomewhat more graue & fetled in her countenance) was called Vertue, who was clothed with verie fimple and meane garments, and fhee with her finger pointed vnto that way which fhee would wifh Hercules to take, which indeed at the beginning fhewed it felfe very narrow, full of rockes, and fteepe-afcending banckes, verie crooked, and almoft in-acceffable; but after towards the midft it fhewed very plefant, and at the very end of it was a moft delicat green

mead,

mead, all befet and enwalled with trees of the rareft and daintieft fruits that could bee wifhed for, the vale it felfe all befpangled (as it were) with field-flowers of fundry forts and colours, entermixed with the odoriferous rofe, gillowflower, marigold, & pinke: through the midft of this greene plot, glided and ftole along a foft-murmuring chriftall fpring, through the puritie of whofe cleereneffe (by meanes of the reflection of the funnes beames) an infinite number of golden hewed peble ftones, daunced as it were, & leaped on the fands, as moued and ftirred with the fwift-paced current of that faire-running water: and vnto this path Hercules betooke himfelfe, labouring & ftriuing very eagerlie to paffe in at the firft entrance, which at the length, with continuing and laborious endeauours, he recouered, & fo attained to that delicious & beautifull medow, which his choice fo elected, afterwards purchafed vnto him euer-liuing fame and glory, regiftered by time in the braffe-leaued booke of endleffe perpetuitie.

The Auncients alfo made and dedicated Images and Statues for the adoration and worfhip of Honor, **Alciatus.** which (as *Alciatus* giueth vs to vnderftand) they framed in the fhape of a little child, clothed and apparelled with a purple garment, hauing a garland of Lawrell, wreathed about his head: with whome was depainted to hold hand in hand the god Cupid, who feemed to lead and guide the child vnto the goddeffe Vertue, which was depictured right ouer againft it, hewen forth and engraued with exquifite and rare intaliature.

Among

The fountaine of ancient fiction.

Among the Auncients likewise was reuerenced and adored as a great goddesse , the Ladie *Volupia*, which they held to bee the goddesse of pleasures and delights: and her Statue was depainted, as hauing a pallid and leane countenance, yet sitting in a pontificall and maiestike chaire, all embrodered and embossed with starres of refined gold . And vnder her feet was drawne out the picture of Vertue , looking as though she had ben deiected, troden downe, and despised by her.

It is written with *Plinie* (as also *Solinus* and *Macro-* *bius* affirme the same) that in a certaine temple dedicated vnto this goddesse *Volupia* , was cut out with egregious skill of the workeman (as sitting vpon an Altar)the goddesse Angerona, looking with a heauie and sad countenance, which also was framed with her lips tied together, and fast conioined, to shew vs therby, that in all pleasures or other mattets whatsoeuer, it behoueth vs to hold our peace, & to keepe silence. *Macrobius* expounds it thus, that whosoeuer knoweth how to vse secrecie , silence, and to dissemble his greefes, and discontents, shall in the end ouercome them, and shall lead a most pleasant, easefull, and quiet life.

The Ægyptians did much reuerence and worship their god of Silence , which with them was called Harpocrates, and according to the Greekes, Sigaleon: whose Statue and Image (as *Martianus* and *Apuleius* record) was made in the likenesse of a young child, who close to his lips held one of his fingers, as a signe of secrecie . Whereupon it comes, that the same

T iij   fashion

fashion is now also obserued when men would signifie by signs, that a thing should not be vnreuealed or spoken of . Sometimes the portraiture of this God is drawne without any face at all, all couered ouer with the skin of a Wolfe, on which were depainted as many eyes and eares as could bee inserted thereon: signifying thereby, that it was needfull to see and heare much, and to speak little, in that he that speaketh not, offendeth not. By the Wolues skin is vnderstood the propertie of that beast, who when it hath stolne anie prey, presently conueyeth himselfe away, and runneth with such heed, feare, and quietnesse, that hee dares not in all that time so much as drawe his breath, or pant, with such slie secrecie doth he escape and steale away.

But now it is time to returne to our first intreatie of Minerua, whom (as I haue alreadie said) the Auncients all armed, with a Speare or Dart in one hand, and a Christall shield in the other. By the shield (in that Minerua is taken for Wisdome and Knowledge) is vnderstood the roundnesse aud compasse of the world, gouerned with wise decrees, politike lawes, & discreet commandements. By the Dart or Speare, is vnshadowed the force, vertue, and power of wisdome, & that the words and speeches of a learned man do preuaile, and are effectual throughout the whole world: or that the sharpenesse and vigour of an excellent wit, & all-apprehending capacitie, is able to penetrate & make entrance into the hardest and obscurest enigma whatsoeuer; as the Dart being furiously deliuered from the hands of a powerfull bodie, pierceth very deepe into

any

any hard ground or other mettall of good proofe or refiſtance.

Pauſanias writeth, that in a certain place of Greece was erected a moſt huge and great Coloſſus, out of which was cut forth and carued the picture of Minerua, ſitting as it were on a little ſtoole, & drawing forth ſmall threds from a diſtaffe: for that the Ancients ſuppoſed her to bee the firſt inuentreſſe and deuiſer of ſpinning, as alſo of weauing in ſilke, and other like inuentions.

They attribute alſo vnto her the firſt finding out of almoſt all kind of Arts and Sciences : vnderſtanding thereby, that the wit and inuention of man (for which Minerua, as I haue ſaid, is taken) is the beginner and diſcouerer of all ſorts of trades, faſhions, ſciences, or profeſſions whatſoeuer : touching which the Poets do faine, that Prometheus with the helpe of Minerua went vp to the higher heauens , and ſtealing away ſome part of the fierie chariot of the Sunne, gaue and beſtowed it on men below, whereby afterwards they contriued new arts, and mechanicall trickes of cunning and skill, euery one after his owne maner, deuiſe, & humor: in working of which arts (as *Pliny* writeth) is requ'red two things, the firſt is Wit, and Conceit, and the other, Heed, Care, and true effecting of what is propoſed : the firſt is meant by Minerua, the laſt by Vulcan (which is as much to ſay as fire) for vnder the name of Vulcan, wee oftentimes read the nature of fire to bee vnderſtood , being the inſtrument and meanes to forme and faſhion almoſt all things whatſoeuer.

Many

Many writers haue deſcribed the portraitures of Vulcan and Minerua both in one Statue and Image, as *Plato* in one place ſayth, That theſe two were equallie ſuppoſed to bee the gods and protectors of Athens, for ſo much indeed as in thoſe times the ſtudie and practiſe of Sciences, was no leſſe vſed and followed than the profeſſion and inward exerciſes of letters and learning.

Plato,

Others write, that Neptune and Minerua were the ioint-protecters of Athens, ſo appointed by the order and decree of Iupiter, wherevpon the Athenians ſtamped and imprinted vpon their coine the picture of Neptunes Trident, and on the other ſide the portraiture of Minerua.

But (as I ſaid before) Vulcan was many times vnderſtood for fire, or at the leaſt for the force, propertie, and nature thereof, as *Euſebius* in many places alloweth . *Alexander Neapolitanus* reporteth, that in one place of Ægypt was erected the Statue of Vulcan, which held in one of his hands the true and liuely proportion of a certaine beaſt, which we call a Mole, and in his other hand a thunderbolt: and the Ægyptians ſo placed a Mole in his hand, for that they ſuppoſed that Vulcan had ſent into one part of Ægypt infinite and vnſpeakeable numbers of Moles of purpoſe to eat, gnaw, and deſtroy the ſadles, bridles, targets, and ſuch like furniture made of Leather, belonging to the Arabians their enemies, who then were entred into their Countrie with huge armies of ſouldiours, to ouerrun and depopulate the Country, which notwithſtanding afterwards by the innumerable ſwarmes

Alexander Neapolitanus.

as

as it were of these Moles, (so noisome and offensiue vnto them)were constrained to retire,leaue, & abandon the countrey: which thing is not altogether vnlikely, for so much as many autentike and approoued Authours haue verified the like.

Elianus reporteth, that the rootes of trees and hearbes in certaine parts of Italie,were eaten and destroyed in such sort with multitudes of Rats, that the inhabitants in the end(although they daily endeuoured tokill them) were notwithstanding for penurie, faine to leaue and forsake their Countrey. *Marcus Varro* writeth, That there was a Towne in Spain scituated on a sandie ground,which was so vndermined by Connies,that in short time it sunke, and was vtterly decaied.Neither haue these chances happened only in wild Countries and many continents,but in places also enuironned with the sea, as that it is written,that one of the Isles Cyclades, called Giare, was by the ouer-abundance and multitudes of Rats and Mice, left void and destitute of inhabitants, being so tormented and annoied with them, that very necessitie caused them to forgoe their Countrie.It is also reported, that in Fraunce a very famous towne was by the said vermine(so abounding therein)left void & vnfrequented of any Inhabitants. The like chance also(as it is written) happened in a certaine country of Affrica by the swarmes of Locusts and Grashoppers.*Plinie* reporteth, That in a certaine Prouince adioining to the confines of Æthiopia, Ants,and other small vermine, exiled thence all the inhabitants thereabout. The people of Megaris in Greece, were constrained

Elianus.

Marcus Varro.

Plinie

V by

by bees to leaue and forsake the countrey. Theophra-stus speaketh of another Countrey, which was de-stroyed by Palmers, which are little wormes, long and rough, hauing many legs, and in Latine may be called *Bruchi*, *Campe*, or *Multipede*. *Antenor* writing also of the Isle of Crete, sayth, That a certaine multi-tude of Bees, chased out of a great Cittie all the inhabitants thereof, vsing their houses in the stead of hiues.

But returning to our former matter, which was, that the people of Ægypt verily beleeued, that those Moles were sent by Vulcan into their Countrey to destroy and driue away their enemies the Arabians, then entred into the land : It is crediblie written by *Plutarch* and others, that the people of Arabia do at this time infinitely abhor & hate those kind of beasts, and doe lay all plots and deuises to kill & destroy them wheresoeuer they heare them to remaine, which kind of vermine also the Ethiopians, & especially the con-iurers of Persia hold an opinion to be very odious & displeasing to their gods. But it is not written, that the Ægyptians beleeued that Vulcan should send them those Moles, nor what reason moued them vnto that conceit in the embracing of such opinion : but it is so recited as is before spoken of by that Author *Alex-ander Neapolitanus*, without any further explication of it. Although with some writers it is thus expoun-ded : By Vulcan (say they) is meant the drinesse and extreame heat of that season, which was summer : or else indeed the naturall drinesse and warmth of that Countrey of Æthiopia. And *Plinie* writing of those

vermine

Plutarch.

vermine fayth, they doe encreafe and multiply in moft aboundant manner, alwaies coueting thofe places, which by the ardent furie of the funnes vertue, become drie, fandie, and crafed, as likewife moft of the countrey of Æthiopia is, and further expofitions are not found to bee deliuered by anie Writers, touching that opinion and conceit of the Ægyptians.

The opinions and writings which the Ancients haue made of Vulcan, remaine diuerfe & many, and in that refpect hee is fhaped forth fometimes in this forme, and fometimes in another: with fome hee is depictured, ftanding, working, and hammering in a Smiths forge on the hill Etna in Sicilia, framing thunderbolts for Iupiter, and fafhioning arrowes for the god of loue, and was taken to bee the rareft workman that euer liued, vnto whome when the gods had anie occafion to vfe fuch maner of weapons, they prefently repaired: as Thetis went vnto him to defire him to forge an armor for her fonne Achilles, and Venus for her fonne Æneas.

Some depicture him lame of one leg, and of a very blacke and fwart complexion, as one all fmokie, & of a general ill-fhaped proportion of all his lineaments. It is not read, that vnto Vulcan were appropriated any beafts, plants, or trees, as vnto all other of their gods, onely *Elianus* writeth, that the Egyptians confecrated Elianus. vnto him the Lyons, in that thofe beaftes of all other are moft hot, drie, & fierie by nature, by which abundance of heat within their bodies, it comes to paffe, that they doe fo exceedingly feare and are aftonied at the fight of fire, which they can by no meanes indure,

but

but run from it with great affrightment. It is read also, that on the hill Mongibell in Sicillia there are certain great dogs, which do there guard and keepe the Temple of Vulcan, which is seated hard by a woods side, adioyning to that Mountaine, and the people thereabouts doe worship and adore Vulcan in that Temple, and in those consecrated woods and bushes.

It is written by the Poets, that Vulcan was the husband of Venus, as lawfully married vnto her, and that they are alwaies depictured together, as accompanying one the other. By which is vnderstood, that the generation and birth of creatures (meant by Venus) cannot bee effectuall without a moderate heat & warmenesse (which is also vnderstood by Vulcan.) Some also doe adioine Mars as the companion to Venus, meaning by him the heat of the Sunne, whereupon the Alcitans (people inhabiting the furthermost parts of Spaine, as *Macrobius* reporteth) made the Statue and Image of Mars, so adorned and beautified with the beames of the sunne, in as liuely manner as could bee deuised; which picture was there reuerenced with wondrous zeale and adoration. *Macrobius* also sayth, That the gods (being the substance of the celestiall fire) were onely different in name, and not otherwise: and that Mars was generally taken for that heat and warmenesse which proceeded from the vertue of the Sun. By reason whereof, the liuely heat and bloud which is within vs, is easily set on fire & enflamed with anger, furie, and desire of warre: of which things Mars also is held and supposed to bee the god. And after that fashion the Auncients worshipped &

adored

adored him, dedicating vnto him many sumptuous
Statues, Images, and Pictures, and they shaped him
of aspect, most fierce, terrible, and wrathfull, with hollow red eyes, very speedie and quicke in their reuolutions, his face all hairie, with long curled lockes on
his head, depending euen to his shoulders, of a coale-
blacke colour, he stood all armed throughout, with a
speare in one hand, and in the other a whip, and sometimes they depicture him riding on a horse, sometimes
drawne in a chariot, whose horses were called Feare
and Horror: And some other say, that his chariot was
drawne with two men, which alwaies accompanied
him wheresoeuer he went, and they were called Furie
& Violence. The which thing *Statius* imitateth when Statius.
he sayth, That Iupiter sent for Mars, and commanded
him to raise and stirre vp bloudie warres and quarrels
between the Argiues and Thebans. And in this place
Statius describeth the armes of this god to bee these :
He wore (sayth hee) on his head a helmet most bright
and shining, and of so fierie a hue and glister, as it seemed there issued out of it great flashes of lightning,
his breastplate was of solid gold , reflecting with a
most glorious and eye-delighting lustre , and there
was insculpt thereon many figures and shapes of most
fierce and vgly monsters, his shield was depainted all
ouer with a red or bloudie colour, inchased also with
most strange-shaped and deformed beastes, cut out
and engrauen with rare-inuention, & puritie of work-
manship , excelling in the topiarie art . And thus
hee rode with a speare and scourge in either of his
hands, in a most costly and gold-embossed Charriot,

whofe horfes(called Furie and Violence) were guided
by the two churlifh coachmen, Wrath and Deftru-
ction : directly before this chariot was depainted the
portraiture of Fame, ftretching abroad her wings,
& feeming to proffer a flight, which at the firft view,
feemed to mount, and afterward to roue abroad, and
fearch into all corners of the earth , and this picture
appeared(a little off from it)to be very fmal, but comming neere vnto it, it was of a great bigneffe, which
workemanfhip was performed with great cunning
and precife curioufneffe of art . The Auncients alfo
pictured this Fame in the forme of a woman, apparelled with a thin and fleightly-wouen mantle of purple
filke, which was clofe girted about her bodie, that fhe
might with more fwiftneffe runne and fcour through
the Countries of the world, in both her hands fhee
feemed to hold a crooked fhell, long and hollow like
to an inftrument, which wee call a Cornet, which fhe
held to her mouth. With fome fhe is depainted with
two wings on her fhoulders, and her face befet full of
eyes, and ouer all her bodie were infinite numbers of
eares, and tongues liuely fet forth and depictured, as
Virgil moft excellently hath deliuered, who alfo fayth,
that fhee flieth alwaies in the night without taking
fleepe or repofe at any time, and that fhee commonly
feateth her felfe on the top of a high turret, where fhe
vttereth and babbleth foorth all that either her eyes
haue feene, or her eares haue heard, being indeed fo
many, that nothing can efcape them, whereby fhee
was entearmed the tatling Ladie, & miftreffe of news.
But touching the former defcriptions of Mars : It is
written

Virgil.

written with some, that such his glorious and sumptuous chariot whereon hee vsed to ride in the warres,
was commonly drawne with foure mightie strong
horses, which were so furious, hot, and prowd, that
euen very fierie sparkles seemed to issue forth frō their
nosthrils. *Isiodorus* sayth, That the picture of Mars was   Isiodorus.
oftentimes set forth and depainted, with the breast of
it all naked and vnclothed, to vnshadow thereby, that
in the warres and chaunces of danger, men ought not
to be timorous, but should expose themselues to all
hazardous and vncertaine aduentures whatsoeuer.
Herodotus writeth, that the people of Scithia hung vp   Herodotus.
a sword in the middle of a temple, and worshipped it
as the Image of Mars, as people ignorant, how to represent the god of warre otherwise. *Statius* describing   Statius.
the house of Mars sayth, That it is built in an obscure
corner of Thracia, where the people wholly giue and
addict themselues to warres and stratagemicall policies, and that it was wholly made and composed of
yron, all rustic, blacke, and foule, and that the porters
there which kept the gates, were called Horror and
Madnesse, within the house inhabited Furie, Wrath,
Impietie, Feare, Treason, and Violence, of all which,
the gouernesse and commandresse was Discord, who
there was seated in a regall and princely throne, holding in one of her hands a bright shining sword, and
in her other a great yron basen full of humane bloud.
Of this Discord it is written, that shee was the ouerthrow and ruine of that famous towne of Phrygia in
Asia Minor, called Troy, & the reason (as some write)
was, in that shee was not inuited to a certaine great
feast.

feaſt made on the Mountain Pelion by Iupiter for the
ſolemnizing and celebrating of the nuptials between
Peleus and Thetis, where almoſt all gods and goddeſſes whatſoeuer, were conuented; and where alſo ſhee
appeared, but notwithſtanding was commaunded by
Iupiter to depart from that marriage, and not allowed to bee at the ſolemnization thereof: and this great
meeting was not ten daies before the contention betweene the three goddeſſes for the golden ball, ended
and decided by Paris, which proued the deſtruction
of all the houſe of Priamus, and ſlaughter of the Troians; for of this marriage was begotten that euer-fa-
med knight Achilles: but as I told you, becauſe Diſcord could not be admitted to this feaſt, prepared only for merrie, pleaſant, and for familiar agreements,
ſhe afterward raiſed ſuch miſcheeuous occaſion, and
ſo laboured day and night in her diuelliſh plots, that
by her meanes grew that long-continuing warre and
enmitie betweene the Phrygians and Pelaſgians, pro-
ſecuted, maintained, and ended, by the proweſſe of
this new-borne child Achilles. *Virgil* ſayth, That this
Diſcord was by many writers framed and ſet forth in
the likeneſſe of one of the furies of hell: as likewiſe
Petronius. *Petronius* and *Ariſtides* affirme, ſaying, That ſhee hath
the aſpect and looke of an infernall hag, with hollow
and bleared eyes, far ſunke into her head, from which
euermore diſtilled downe many watrie drops, her
lips are pale and drie, her teeth all furd with lothſome
corruption, her breath all-infected, ill-ſauoured, and
thicke, her cheekes diſcoloured, wan, and thin, & that
ſhee ſtretched forth her long & leane hands, as readie

to

to catch and take hold of any occasion profered, in her breast she carried a naked knife with a sharp point, her legs were wondrous crooked, and little, as scarce able to support the burthen of her withered bodie, for her garment she wore a mantle made of black rug, and thus *Petronius* describes her leaning vpon a staffe. *Pausanias* writeth, that in a lid of a chest giuen to Cipselus, was engraued & carued the combat of Aiax and Hector, performed in the presence of Discord, which (sayth hee) was an old and hard-fauoured woman.

Ariosto vpon some occasion speaking of Mars (from Ariosto, whom now we haue a little wandred, describeth there his pallace or court where hee vsed to abide, saying, that through euery part and corner of the same, were heard straunge ecchoes, resounding most perfectly, which of themselues without anie former speech, would yeeld forth voices most plainely and distinctly, which commonly were fearefull shrikes, threatnings, and dismall cries: in the midst of this pallace was erected the Image of Vertue, whose lookes seemed to bee sad and pensiue, and her soule all sorrow-beaten, discontented, and melancholie, and shee stood leaning her head on her arme in most distressefull maner: hard by her was seated in a chaire the picture of Furie, triumphing in ioy, pleasure, and delight, and seeming prowd with good fortunes, and happie successes. Not farre from her sat Death, with a bloudie and stearne countenance, whose face was ouerwasht with bloud, and hackt with many and cruell slashes, where vpon a stately altar, he was offering sacrifices in goblets made

with

with the skuls of men, and filled vp euen to the brim
with humane bloud; wḷich oblation was confecrated
to god Mars, with coales of fire (which set on flame
the facrifice)fetcht from many Citties, Townes, and
Holds,burnt and ruinated by tyrannie of the Warres:
round about the Court were hanged vp (as pictures
to beautifie the fame)many famous fpoiles and glorious enfigns of victorie,brought from all the parts &
corne of the world : In his bed chamber were depainted forth with wondrous curious workmanfhip,
fatall maffacres, burning of townes, difmall flaughters of men, caftles won by treafon,murther,and villanie,with many fuch like all in row conioined and fet
together.

Vnto Mars was confecrated by the Auncients, as
gratefull vnto him, a Cocke, either to fhew thereby
the vigilancie and carefull watch which fhould bee in
fouldiours,or elfe (as *Lucianus* writeth)becaufe that
Alectrio(a fouldiour entirely beloued and endeared
of Mars) was by the gods transformed and chaunged
into this bird. Some alfo haue appropriated vnto him
the wolfe, being a moft rauenous & deuouring beaft,
and therefore attributed vnto him; in that all fouldiers
and men of warre, vpon their firft furie and heate are
giuen much to fpoiling and confuming of goods, ruinating and ouerthrowing all things whatfoeuer,that
happen vnto them in the pride of their choler, & firft
inflamation of their bloud : or elfe becaufe this beaft
(as I haue in other places remembred)feeth moft perfectly in the darkeft night, as wife and prouident captaines and commaunders ought to doe, that is, that
they

they with an all-foreseeing aduisednesse and circum-
spection, preuent and frustrate the secret, darke, and
hidden plots, and close-contriued stratagemes of the
enemie whatsoeuer, for by the sharpe-sighted eyes of
this beast is vnderstood the farre-reaching capacitie
and wittie braine of a politicke commaunder, in discouering and seeing through the secret and concealed intendemennts of his aduersarie. And thus much
shall suffice for the natures and properties of Mars,
imposing also an end to the Statues, Images, and Pictures dedicated, erected, and consecrated to him, as
also to Minerua, so taken by the Auncients to bee
the goddesse of Wisedome, Learning, and of Wars.

Bacchus.

HIstories doe deliuer vnto vs, that this Bacchus
(of whome wee now entreat) was held among
the Auncients in great repute and esteeme for
a most valerous, hardie, and well-approued Captaine,
performing in those his times many worthie, haughtie, and gallant seruices, which gained vnto him the
report and title of a victorious and all-conquering
commander: as *Diodorus Siculus*, and many other autentike Authours haue written. But in the end, whether in regard of such his valiancie, or other perticular propertie and knowledge, he was amongst others
of their supersticious errors, cannonized & worshipped as a god, dedicating temples, and erecting Altars
and Statues vnto him: among whome also hee was
knowne and called by diuerse and seuerall names, as

some-

sometimes Bacchus, sometimes Dionisius, & at other
times *Liber pater*, & many other, and by reason thereof was sometimes depictured in this form, and sometimes in that shape, according to the seuerall opinion
of the people with whome hee was so worshipped.
Philostratus sayth, That his Statue was framed in the
likenesse of a young man without a beard, of a corpulent & grosse bodie, his face of a high colour, and
very big, and about his head was wreathed a garland
of yuie leaues, from his temples seemed to peepe
forth two small hornes, and close by his side lay a certaine beast, called a Panther. The which description
made by *Philostratus*, is in some sort drawne from the
nature and qualitie of Wine, of which indeed, the
Poets faine that Bacchus is the god, for so much as he
(as it is written) was the first that euer found out the
commoditie thereof, and discouered vnto men, (then
abiding in ignorance thereof) the manner of gathering grapes from the vinetree, and to presse and bruse
them together, of whose iuice and licour afterwards
Wine was made. But some affirme, that Icarus the father of Erigonus, first inuented the making of Wine,
and that it was first of all drunke in Athens, where he
himselfe being drunke with the force thereof, was miserably slaine by the people. And it is also written that
in Italy Saturne was the first that euer instructed them
in the true vse of the grape, which hee before had practised and learned in Crete. *Plutarch* sayth, That in
France one Arras, an Etruscian was the first that caused it to bee vsed. But concerning the truth of the first
inuention thereof, it is infallibly certaine, that it was
found

Philostra-
tus.

found out by *Noe*, which *Lactantius* and *Iosephus* affirme, befides, that place alfo in the nineteenth of Genefis approoues it, which is fufficient watrant againft all allegations whatfoeuer. *Iaques de Bergamus* in his second booke of the Chronicles of the world, fayth, That *Noe* by this meanes found out the nature of the grape: *Noe* (fayth hee) on a certaine day viewing and marking the feeding of beafts on a mountaine of Armenia called Coricus, among the reft efpied a young bull brouſing on the berries of a wild vine, of which he had not long fed, but that hee became exceeding wild, furious, and mad. *Noe* wondring at the force and effect of thofe berries, planted them afterwards on better grafts, and fo had the experiment and triall of the vertue and propertie of them, of which prefently after hee cauſed Wine to be made, and for that cauſe, was among the Scyth ans called Ianus, which fignifieth in that language, the giuer of Wine.

Iaques de Bergamus.

But proceeding with the depicturanees of Bacchus, *Claudianus* fayth, that his Image or Statue is made and fet forth (as it were) all naked and without clothes, meaning thereby, that the furie and working power of wine ouer-abundantly taken, cauſeth a man to difcouer, lay open, and (as it were) make naked, anie feceret or concealed thing whatfoeuer, which before that time with neuer fo much labour, induftrie, and care, was kept priuate, cloſe, and vnreuealed : with fome Bacchus is depictured in the fimilitude of a very aged man, anatomifing and vnſhadowing thereby, that the exceffe taking of wine, haftneth on, and is the cauſe of the fudaine and vntimely approch of old

X iij

age,

age , as debillitating and eneruating the contexed
ground of our fences and finnewes, with the fucking
vp and drying of the humiditie and naturall moisture
of youth-maintaining humours : for fo much as it is
manifeft, that the vnexpected failing, and weakeneffe
of our fences, (by that meanes admitting a more feeble eftate of our bodies) being old age, is nothing elfe
but the abfence and vtter decay of a naturall moiftnes
within vs, and a generall ficcitude throughout the
whole compofition of our bodies; which wee feeking
to recouer and re-poffeffe , accept no meanes fo fit,
nor thinke any prefcription fo auaileable , as the vfu-
all drinking of wine, wherein indeed men are infinitely deceaued, and inuelloped (as it were) with clouds
and mifts of blindneffe, and of error : for fo much as
though wine bee in the firft taft and receit thereof into our bodies, fomething moift and engendring rume
and raw humours , yet it is in the operatiue vertue
and power fo maruellous hot and fierie, that it drieth
vp, and concocteth all the noiftneffe and humiditie
whatfoeuer, before ingendered and bred : for *Galen*
(that euer-famous Doctor) fayth, That the greateft
drinkers of Wine, the more they drink, the more drie
and thirftie doe they find themfelues, & by how much
the more they thinke and doe beleeue to quench and
allay their thirft by drinking more Wine , fo much
doe they encreafe and augment their drineffe and defire thereof.

 Not much vnlike that former defcription of Bacchus, was that depicturance which wee read to bee
made of one Comus , held and reputed among the
           Aunci-

Galen.

Auncients to bee the god of Feasts, Banquets, and mirth, ministring conuenticles: whose Statue or Image was likewise drawne forth and framed in the resemblance and likenesse of a very young man, whose face seemed to thrust out a few small haires; his countenance pleasant, gracious, and smiling, and his complexion rubicund and high coloured. And *Philostratus* describes him standing at the dore of a great chamber full of guests, inuited to a most sumptuous banquet, wherein was much drinking and feasting, with great excesse, and too much superfluitie, as solemnising and celebrating the espousals of a new-married virgine: and sayth, that hee stood there leaning on a staffe, with his eies halfe shut, and halfe open, so that by little and little his head declined towards his bosome, and his bosome towards his arme, then resting on the staffe, which was indeed verie vncertainly placed: and thus betweene falling, and a weake supporting of himselfe, hee reelingly wauered and mooued to and fro: about his head (sayth hee) was wreathed a garland of smeet-smelling flowers, and also ouer most part of his bodie, at the one side of him was placed a great goblet of wine, and hard by that a musicall instrument like to a Cymball: the flowers so redeniting his temples, signifie ioy, mirth, and pleasance, and the instrument the lightnesse of heart, and contempt of sadnesse and melancholike cogitations: his pleasant, fresh, and liuely countenance shewes, that by the operation and stirring vertue of wine, mens spirits are awaked and made ioifull, as without doubt a moderat and temperate receit thereof, quickeneth & reuiueth

drousie

drousie and drooping sences, infusing into their spirits a more loftie and aspiring thought. *Plinie* writeth, that discreet taking of wine, encreaseth & contexeth a mans forces and sinewes, purifies the bloud from conicaled corruption, sharpens the sight, comforteth the stomach, procureth appetite, prouoketh vrine, nourisheth sleepe, forceth vomites, purgeth melancholie, expelleth sorrowfulnesse of heart, and to conclude, exceedingly reioiceth and dooth letificate the spirits of men. *Plato* sayth, That as raine temperately affoorded, nutrifieth and giueth encrease to all kind of herbage whatsoeuer, and that ouer-much abundance thereof, and extraordinarie inundations, destroyeth, drowneth, and spoileth them : euen so wine taken with moderation, and discreetly, comforteth the heart and spirits, whereas ouermuch vsed, it scorcheth, inflameth, and consumeth it : *Apuleius Paniasis* (that writ of the diuers operations of meats) sayth, That one cup of wine a man may drinke after meales with health, and the preseruatiue meanes thereof, but the second quickeneth and prouoketh venerous lusts, and the third bringeth shame, dishonour, & infamie. The Grecians neuer put any water into wine, but caused a little wine to bee medled with a great quantitie of water. *Hesiodus* commandeth, that one cup of wine bee intermingled with three of water. The auncient Romanes absolutely forbad the vse of Wine to anie women or children, as *Valerius* reporteth.

Plinie writeth, That wine was so highly forbidden in Rome, and with such seuere penalties imposed on the breakers of such law, that on a time a certaine maid

Plinie.

Plato.

Apuleius
Paniasis.

Plinie.

maid hauing ftolne the keyes of her maifters wine-
feller, priuily to haue drunke and tafted thereof, (or
perhaps a defire onely to infringe the commaunde-
ment, according to the humours of many of that fex)
was for the fame (without anie further intent therein
meant by her) adiudged by famine to loofe her life,
and that alfo not without the confent and well-liking
of many of her friends, kinsfolkes, and parents.

It is written of Romulus, that when hee had made
any great feaft or banquet, and inuited many guefts
therevnto, would haue great plentie of wine at the table, but would neuer himfelfe fo much as taft thereof,
faying, that to morrow he was to determine of weightie affaires.

It is read, that Iulius Cæfar neuer drunke wine: and
yet that famous Alexander, that true fubiect of wars-
hyftorians, almoft neuer abftained it, but in the end
it ouerthrew him, and depriued him of further vfe
thereof.

Anachrafes fayth, That Wine prefenteth vnto Anachrafes.
vs three grapes, the firft of pleafure, the fecond of
drunkenneffe, and the laft of teares, forrow, and
difgrace.

Diodorus Siculus fayth, That Bacchus was depictured among the Grecians in two feuerall formes,
the one of a verie aged man with a very long beard,
growing ftiffe and thicke, the other of youthful years,
of a pleafant and amorous afpect: by the firft is vnfol-
ded the nature of wine, being immeafureable taken,
which maketh men looke furious, wild, and of a fterne
countenance, and by the fecond (as when wine is mo-
Y derately

derately and temperately taken)is meant, that it maketh men pleasant, discoursiue, and full of merry pa-

Macrobius. stimes. *Macrobius*,who(as I haue alreadie many times
remembred)alwaies vnderstood by the nature of such
their gods,the seuerall properties and vertues of the
Sunne,sayth, That Bacchus was framed sometimes in
the likenesse of a young child,sometimes of a youth,
sometimes at the full age and growth of a man, and
sometimes in the forme of one very aged and decrepit, with a long white beard, to signifie that all these
seuerall ages and encreases are seene to bee in the sun,
for in the time of the winter Solstitium,whē the daies
doe then newly begin to lengthen and grow longer,
it may bee said,that hee is then a young child, dailie
encreasing and growing.And that at the Equinoctiall
of the Spring hee hath attained to the yeares of adolescencie,and may bee called a young man. Then afterwards at the Solstitium of the Summer, when daies
are fully at the longest,and can lengthen no more,hee
is said to be at the estate of entire virilitie and manlie
growth,and hath then a full beard,without further in-
creasing or growing. But because after that time the
daies begin againe to shorten,by reason of the sunnes
withdrawing himselfe from our horison, and obscu-
ring his bright irradiance and glorie from the world,
he may be called an old man, as shortening and lesse-
ning his daies declining and drawing to an absolute
obscuritie and departure from this life, and thus *Macrobius* hath expounded his application.

Diodorus. 　*Diodorus Siculus* describeth Bacchus with two
Siculus. homes on his head,which(sayth *Macrobius*) signifie
the

the raies and beames of the fun, but *Diodorus* fayth,
That by them rather is vnfhadowed and intended,
that Bacchus was the firft that inftructed and taught
men how to till their grounds , by fubiugating and
coupling their Oxen for the performance thereof.
Some writers vnderftand by thofe hornes fo infixed
on Bacchus, audacitie, impudencie, boldneffe, and
fierceneffe , approoued by the ouermuch taking of
wine, which makes men hardie and aduenturous, as
alfo impudent and fhameleffe,as is generally affirmed
by *Philoftratus, Feftus Pompeius, Porphirio, Perfius*, and
others that haue writ thereof. *Mufonius* a Greeke wri- Mufonius.
ter fayth, That vnto Bacchus were not onely hornes
giuen, but that hee was of many Poets defcribed and
defigured in the fhape and likeneffe of a bull, the reafon was, for that(as Poets deliuer) Ioue (transformed
into a ferpent) lay carnally with his owne daughter
Proferpina, the which by him being great , brought
forth Bacchus in the forme of a young bull, wherevpon with the Cizenians (people inhabiting the further parts of Perfia) his Image and Picture was framed to the true fimilitude and likeneffe of a bull. But
Theopompus and other writers fay , that they gaue Theopom-
thofe hornes fo vnto Bacchus, in that in Epirus and pus.
many places thereabouts, were buls of that hugenes
and mightie bodies,that with their hornes (being an-
fwerable alfo in bigneffe)the people there made them
their great veffels to drinke in, which there was a generall cup or veffell throughout all thofe Countries
thereabouts,and which fafhion alfo fpread it felfe afterwards into many other Countries round about
them,

them, among which they alwaies vſed and accuſtomed to drinke out of hornes. The Athenians afterward taking hold of that cuſtome and manner, framed their ſiluer veſſels and bowles wherein they vſed to drinke, in the faſhion and proportion of crooked and retorted hornes.

But it is vnderſtood with ſome, that ſuch hornes on Bacchus, ſignified certaine few haires, which from either ſide of the head were left growing in thoſe daies, which likewiſe now at this time the Prieſts and holy men of Armenia (and in many places of India) doe vſe to weare, and obſerue, which doe ſhaue all the vpper part and top of their heads, and alſo behind in their neckes, (reſeruing onely two mightie long lockes, growing on either ſide before, towards their temples) which they vſed to bind with a fillet or lace very hard, and ſo made them to ſtand of themſelues erect and out right. For which cauſe and faſhion alſo *Moſes* was ſaid among the Hebrewes to haue had hornes, and ſo was King *Liſimachus* with the Perſians.

Philoſtratus writeth, That Bacchus was oftentimes depictured and drawne forth in his Statues and Images, clothed with womens garments, and in effeminate habite, when hee reporteth, that hee went in ſuch manner apparrelled, with a long purple robe, beautifully ſet forth and adorned with tires of ſilke, vnto his loue Ariadne, and that then he wore on his head a cotonet of roſes, curiouſly compoſed & made, his companions and followers alſo were all in like wanton and looſe abillements, faſhioning themſelues

some

some like rurall Nimphs, as the Driades, Oriades, and such like; some like the sea Nimphs, as the Nereides, Syrens, and others; and some also in the shape of Satires, Faunes, and Siluans, and all these attended him, going to his amorous delights, and sports with Ariadne. The clothes and garments of women, so said to bee on Bacchus, signifie, that the inordinate taking of wine weakeneth and debillitateth the naturall forces and powers of a man, making him feeble, vnconstant, and strengthlesse, like a woman: or that (as some hold) he was so depictured, because on certaine daies of the yeare hee accustomed so to habite himselfe, when those great feasts, which were called Bacchanalia, were solemnised and kept, at which almost all the women thereabout would meet, drinking and carousing in that abundance and immoderate excesse, as they would become with the force thereof euen furiously mad, brainesicke, and wild, with dauncing and leaping, singing loud canticles, beating one another, running among the woods, vallies, and mountaines, and vsing all strange and rude gestures, and behauiours, worse than people extreamely mad and lunatike. And in this manner almost all the hither part of Thessalie for the space of tenne daies vsed to banquet and riot, delighting in their barbarous custommes, and vnciuile obseruances.

Pausanias writeth, that among the Eleans the picture of Bacchus was there cut out, as hauing a long beard, with a garment or gowne couering all his bodie euen to the feet, and that hee held in one hand a hooke or sharpe sythe, and in the other a goblet or

Pausanias.

bowle

bowle of wine, and round about him were depainted
forth many vinetrees, and other fruitfull and commodious plants. And with some hee was called Bacchus
Baſſareus, by reaſon of that long garment which vſu-
ally hee wore, and which was called Baſſara, ſo named
of a certain place in Lidia, where thoſe kind of cloths
were made, or els it was ſo called of the skinnes of
wolues, which thoſe women in their Bacchinall feaſts
vſed to weare about their ſhoulders, for that in the
Thracian language a wolſe is called Baſſara. Neither
did thoſe women vſe onely the skins of VVolues, but
of Panthers and Tygres alſo, which they careleſly
wold hang about their ſhoulders in their fits of drun-
kenneſſe and furie, tearing vp the graſſe and hearbes
with their nailes as they went along, their haire hanging ouer their faces, which they ſet forth with diuerſe and ſundrie-coloured flowers; ouer one of their
armes they wore a garland made of yuie leaues, or the
white Poppie, for that this Poppie was ſuppoſed to be
an infernall flower, and growing on the banckes of
Acheron, and therefore the Ancients appropriated it
vnto the companions and followers of Bacchus, for
that among ſome he was held alſo and taken to be the
god of the infernall region, whereupon (as I haue already very lately deliuered) the Poets doe affirme that
hee was borne of Proſerpina, which was Queene of
the lower kingdome, wife to Pluto, and daughter to
Iupiter and Ceres.

Diodorus
Siculus.
It is written with *Diodorus Siculus*, that Bacchus
was not alwaies conuerſant and merrie in drinking
and in feaſts, but ſayth, that hee ſhewed himſelfe in
many

many feruices a very valerous & couragious captaine, and followed the warres with great fortunes manie yeares together, in which time, he would commonlie weare for his vpper garment the skinnes of Panthers, and such like beasts. He victoriously ouercame in battell (sayth *Diodorus*) many kings and great commanders, as *Licurgus Pentheus*, and others, and also subiugated and reduced vnto his commaund all the hether India, returning from thence with mightie triumph and victorie, carried on the backe of a huge Elephant, with all his whole armie celebrating and extolling the praises and worthy exploits of their lord & commander. Neither is it read, that before his time there was euer any king or Prefect that euer triumphed in the warres, or was led home with such ceremonious signes and testimonies of victorious preuailement ouer his enemies. And therefore vnto Bacchus, as vnto the first triumpher, was confecrated the bird Pica, being a bird full of prattle, and apt to speake any familiar language, for that in those triumphs it was lawfull for any one to reprooue anothers vices with any dispightfull tearmes, or disgrace whatsoeuer, euerie one crying out, and obiecting what might bee said to the defence or deniall thereof.

The Auncients also haue attributed vnto this god the first innention and making of garlands, who also was the first that did weare any, and for himselfe hee made them of yuie leaues, which afterwards was confecrated also vnto him : whereupon *Alexander* the great minding to imitate him therein, caused all his armie in his returne from the conquest of India , to
make.

make them garlands and wreaths thereof. This plant
or tree was for diuerfe reafons attributed vnto Bacchus. *Plutarch* fayth, That it hath in it felfe fuch a hidden and fecret power and vertue, that being applied
in a certaine fafhion, obferued by the Phyficians, it
caufeth men without either beere or wine to bee exceeding drunke and giddie in the braines. *Euftathius*
writeth, That yuie according to the Greeke word
thereof, which is *Liſſo*, fignifieth luft, or defire of carnall voluptuoufneffe, and in that refpect was giuen
vnto Bacchus, for that men being drunke and ouercome with the braine-diftempering furie thereof, are
fooner drawne and enclined to thofe defires, than at
other times.

Plutarch. (margin note)
Euftathius. (margin note)

The Statues of Bacchus alfo was fometimes (as
fome writers report) fet forth and adorned with coronets made of the leaues of a Fig tree, in memorie (as
fome hold) of a Nimph which was called *Syca*, which
word with the Greekes fignifieth as much as *Fico* in
Italian : which Nimph was entirely beloued of Bacchus, and metamorphifed by the gods into that plant.
As it is read alfo of *Staphilis*, a Nimph on whome
Bacchus was likewife exceedingly enamoured, and
who afterwards was transformed into a vine tree : fo
that it fhould feeme from thence it comes, that thefe
plants are fo pleafing & grateful vnto Bacchus. With
fome alfo hee is crowned with the leaues of the flower Narciffus, and many other fragrant and fweet-
fmelling flowers. Wherevpon *Statius* fayth, That his
Chariot wherein hee was vfed to bee drawne, was all
adorned and beautified with flowers, hearbes, and
young

young plants. *Boccace*(by the Charriot which is fo giuen vnto him)expoundeth,that bythe extream taking
of Wine,mens heads,and alfo their bodies goe tumbling and reeling vp and downe like the wheeles of a
charriot: which fayth hee,)being drawne with Panthers and Tygres,fignifieth, that the working power
of Wine maketh men feeme furious, cruell, and terrible in their lookes, and wild behauiours,according
to the qualities of thofe beafts fo appropriated vnto
him. *Philoftratus* fayth, That thofe Panthers are fo gi- Philoftra-
uen vnto Bacchus, for that they are of a moft hot and tus.
drie conftitution, (as commonly the drinkers of wine
are) and that they are light and fpeedie either in leaping or running,as men likewife find them more nimble and light when they are drunke and haue fomewhat ouergone themfelues in too much wine , than
they doe at any other time . The fame Authour alfo
fayth (in a certaine place where hee depainteth the
fhip of Bacchus)that the prow or forepart therof was
framed in the likeneffe and proportion of a Panther,
round abound which were Cymbals and Shalmes depainted,and plaied vpon by many young men : in the
midft of the fhip was placed a long and ftreight tree,
on the top of which were hung purple garments,wo-
uen with pure gold of Triolus,which the frantike women in the Bacchinall feafts vfed to weare,which alfo
were depictured there with rare perfection of true
cunning and workemanfhip : on both fides of the
fhip were fet forth with great life many yuie trees full
of berries,as alfo many vines,whofe verie braunches
with plentie of fruit, feemed to crafe and breake off

Z   from

from the ftocke, whofe greene leaues and new ripened
grapes were depainted forth with vnfpeakeable curioufneffe and labour. Towards the bottome of the fhip
was hewen and cut out a moft liuely and perfect fountaine, flowing and ftreaming with pure Wine, whofe
fweetneffe certaine men (moft exactly drawne forth
vnderneath it) feemed to taft, and eagerly receaue,
wherein was difcouered by admirable skill of the
workeman, a moft liuely reprefentation of an exceeding thirft and defire of drinke : and thus *Philoftratus*
defcribeth the fhip of Bacchus, whofe verie like by all
defcriptions and particular refemblances, was long
time kept and preferued in Rome, in the temple there
called *La chiefa di Santa Agnefe*, and afterward called
the temple of Bacchus.

It is written of Bacchus by ancient Authours, that
when hee was a young child, the three fatall fifters
compaffed him about as he lay in his cradle, and caft
ouer his face two moft venomous and vgly ferpents,
which as hiftories mention, neuer offended him : from
whence it afterwards grew, that the Bacchinall women, in celebrating their rites and ceremonies, vfed
to eat and deuour young Snakes. And *Catullus* fayth, Catullus.
that thofe frantike women in performing and executing the ceremonious obferuances of their feaft, vfed
to carrie in one of their hands fome member & part
of a young heyfar, all mingled and cut in peeces: and
the reafon was for that (as it is read) *Pantheus* king of
Thebes (being a great enemie to all thofe cuftomes
and fafhions) defpifed and fet at nought all fuch honours fo dedicated vnto Bacchus, neither would hee
admit

admit by any meanes any fuch ceremonie to bee performed within his rule and gouernement, who to de-
rogate the more from Bacchus, and difgrace his obferuances, one day as they were bufily employed in
great reuerence and zeale amidft their cheefeft oblations, caufed a mad heyfar (or as *Ouid* repo eth, a wild
Beare) to bee driuen in amongft the thickeft troope
of them, fo to difturbe and affright them in their cere-
moni us intendements, who at the firft being fomewhat fuddainely furprifed, fat aftonied, but remembring themfelues, and being alfo halfe drunke, they
furioufly fet vpon the beaft, and with fhort bils and
kniues, and other fuch like weapons as they had, hewed and cut it into a thoufand little peeces, and euery
one ioying and reioicing in their victorie & triumph,
fell prefently again to drinking, of which being ouercome and fubdued, in great furie they ranne vp and
down, carrying in their hands fome peece or other of
the flaughtered beaft, with making ftraunge fhrikes,
fhouts, and vncouth noife for the victorie therof, and
thus through the woods, bufhes, hils, or vallies would
they in an extreame furie, and forgetfulneffe of fence,
confufedly and out of order run galloping together.
And euer afterward to eternife this their preuailemēt
ouer that beaft, would they in their bacchinall feaftes
and drinking, carrie in one of their hands fome ioint
or other of a new kild heyfar. And thus much fhall
fuffice for the Statues, Pictures, and Defcriptions that
ancient writers haue made and deliuered of Bacchus.

Fortune.

L Actantius writeth, that this Fortune is nothing els but a vaine, idle, and fenceleſſe name, which ſheweth foorth the ſhallowneſſe and weakeneſſe of mans wiſedome, in attributing the ſucceſſe or euent of any thing whatſoeuer, to her vertue, power, or pleaſure. Which opinion alſo *Marcus Tullius* confirmeth, ſaying, that this name of Fortune was firſt brought in and vſed to couer and ſhadow the ignorance of man, who (ſayth hee) giueth the ſucceſſe of all haps and accidents vnto her, of which hee himſelfe by naturall iudgement can ſhew no reaſon: which onely proceedeth from the barrenneſſe and dulneſſe of wits and capacities, for ſo much as thoſe things and euents, whereof hee could giue any likely reaſon or coniecture of probabilitie for the effect thereof, hee neuer aſcribed vnto this goddeſſe Fortune. But the Auncients were no more deceaued in this, than in other the gods and goddeſſes, and therefore conſecrated and dedicated vnto her many Statues, Altars, Temples, and Pictures, adoring her as the abſolute diſpoſer and diſpenſatrix of mundane affaires and buſineſſes. And they ſuppoſed, that as well all euill, and bad miſcheefes and inconueniences, as good and happy proſperities proceeded from her. By reaſon whereof, there was held to be two Fortunes, the one good, the other bad, and from the one came riches, happineſſe, quiet, content, and pleaſures: from the other all miſery, war, affliction, croſſes, and diſaſter calamities whatſoeuer.

Where-

Wherevpon fhe was depictured with fome, as hauing two faces, the one white and well-fauoured, the other blacke and difproportioned . *Alexander Neapolitanus* reporteth, That at Preneftes was a temple dedicated vnto Fortune, wherein was drawne out & portrayed a Picture or Image in the fhape and forme of two Siſters, both conioined together in the fame Statue, and that it was there held and worfhipped in high reuerence and adoration : And it was taken for the reprefentation of Fortune . But yet amongſt moſt people, and according to moſt writers, there is acknowledged but one Fortune. *Paufanias* fayth (writing of the monuments of antiquitie) that the moſt auncient Statue and Image of Fortune was that which *Bupalus* (that farre-famed Architector & Ingrauer) compofed and made in Greece, which picture afterwards the Smyrneans (people alfo of that Countrey) bought with a great fumme of money . And the fame was cut out and proportioned in the fhape and likeneſſe of a woman, on whofe head was infixed a round and circular ball, and in one of her hands fhe held the horne of plentie and abundance, called Cornucopia: by which depicturance is plainely vnderſtood the office & propertie of that goddeſſe, which is to haue the beſtowing and giuing of great riches, wealth, and treafures, the which notwithſtanding fhee beſtoweth on men with fuch vncertainety, that they neuer remaine long with them, but are vnfetled, vnfure, and quickely rowled from them againe, as the heauens are toſſed and circumfered by the two poles, refembled thereunto by the ball fo placed vpon her head. *Lactantius* fayth,

Alexander Neapolitanus.

Paufanias.

Lactantius.

Z iij   that

that vnto Fortune was giuen the sterne or rudder of a ship, to signifie, that shee doth rule, commaund, and gouerne all humane things whatsoeuer, as the ship is gouerned by the rudder: and sayth, that shee is vnconstant in all her gifts, mutable, and neuer assured, fauoring and affecting for the most part wicked and irreligious persons, and aduancing men of meane worth, vertue, and learning, deiecting and oppressing the true children, and rightly begotten of the muses, and those in whom perfection of merit abideth. And shee is oftentimes also called the blind goddesse, and the vncertaine and partiall Ladie, and that she is humourous, and must be pleased by submission and acknowledgement of her power and superioritie, as certaine verses much to the same effect, doe demonstrate and testifie, which englished are these, or much agreeing with the true meaning of the Authour:

Imperious ruler of the worlds desseignes,
Ladie of sollace, pleasure, and of paines,
Who in thy well-pleasd humours, kings erecteth,
And when thou list, them down againe deiecteth:
Powerfull in all, in few things constant, alluring
Base men to greatnesse, though nothing assuring:
Those which true vertue truly doe embrace,
Not subiect to the smiles of beauties face,
Nor seating vaine-built hopes on glassie frame,
Of big-swolne titles of thy glorious name,
Thou doest seuerely scourge with vniust rigour,
Shewing in their afflicts thy powerfull vigour.
Like tennis-bals thou beat'st vs to and fro,

The fountaine of ancient fiction.

From fauours to difgrace, from ioy to woe,
From wars to peace, from rule to be commanded,
Till at the length cleane out of fight w' are banded:
When ftreight frefh bals (cald Fauorits) come in place,
Which (being new) looke with a fmooth-white face,
And for a while are pleafing and well-liking,
And gently toft with mild and eafie ftriking,
Till in fome humor (wearied with that play)
Some ftiffer racket bandies them away,
    O Fortune, that thy facred deitie,
    Should fo confift in fuch varietie.

And in another place a difcontented perfon railing
againft her crueltie, thus fayth :

How long fhall thefe my foule-bred forrowes laft
    Which hoarely thus increafe and multiplie ?
Tell me (prowd Fortune) fhall they neuer waft ?
    Is there no date of this my miferie ?
Wilt thou needs fhew enfample of thy pride
    On my o're-burdened wo-poffeffed heart,
Which thoufand times far better might abide
    Deaths all-concluding momentanie dart.
But yet if in the end thou fhew me grace
    (As thou delight'ft in inftabillitie)
And looke on my deuoires with fmiling face,
    Changing thefe greefes to ioies tranquillitie,
O then how gladly would I thefe endure,
If of thy fauour I might fo be fure.

Forc'd by vile Fortune, I feeke out new waies,

                                                    And

The fountaine of ancient fiction.

And range in vncouth corners of ech wood,
Where darkeneſſe, and ſad ſilence ſpend their daies,
And melancholy liues in angrie mood,
There ſit I penning Satyres gainſt theſe times,
Railing gainſt Fortunes malice in my wrongs,
Compoſing Odes, and rage-expreſſing rimes,
Sad madrigals, and heart-vnburdening ſongs:
There as a man all dead with diſcontent,
I feed on ſighs, and drinke mine owne ſalt teares,
When ſenceleſſe trees ſhed ſap, and doe relent,
And floures do hang their heads, as though th'had eares
To heare my plaints, and all doe ſeeme to ſay,
We waile thy hap thou Image of decay.

The chriſtalline and ſiluer-faced Brookes
Their ſoft-toucht muſicke to the dancing ſtones
Doe ceaſe, they wonder ſo at my ſad lookes,
Ech ſauage Beaſt doth bellow forth my mones,
The vales-delighting Nimphs, and hill-borne Faunes
That wonted were to leape and lead the hay,
Croſſing the flourie verdure of the Lawnes
To hearken to my mones would reſt that day,
The ſhrill-voic'd Birds ſing forth a dolefull ditty,
And warble out ſome dreirie note of mourning
To ſhew how much my greefes they all did pitty,
As one in fires of woes for euer burning,
The woods grow wearie of my wretchedneſſe,
Nimphs, Brookes, Beaſts, Birds, admire my heauineſſe.

By all which wee may euidently perceiue what
ſway and power ouer humane affaires, is aſcribed
vnto

vnto Fortune . And in another place a certaine *inamoretto* paſſion-rent (as a man may ſay)and full of melancholie, partly complaining of his miſtreſſe, but eſpecially inueighing againſt the fooliſh partialitie of Fortune, in aduauncing the deſertleſſe and illiterates, leauing and forſaking the vertuous and learned to miſeries,and all-deſpiſed pouerties,(as alſo accuſing the world and the children therof with two much forgetfulneſſe of themſelues, in regarding ſo decrely the fruition of many riches and pleaſures, wholly neglecting,or rather ſcorning the embracement of vertue, letters,or knowledge) thus ſayth . But firſt the Poet ſetteth downe the place where this diſcontented louer vnbowelled (as it were) and anatomiſed his hearts oppreſſions.

Downe by that prowd ambicious Riuers ſide,
On whoſe enameld bankes were wont to lie
The weeping ſiſters of that daring guide,
That needs would rule the chariot of the skie.
Vnder the ſhade of a frondiferous beech,
Sits greeſefull Dolio breathing out this ſpeech:

The daughters of Clymene,and ſiſters of Phaeton.

Sleepe Phebus,ſleepe,reſt in thy watrie bed,
Looke on vs this blacke and diſmall day,
Wherat he pauſd,and hanging downe his head,
Greeſe ſtopt the paſſage of his ſpeeches way :
All ſorrow-wounded thus,he lookt like one,
Whom heau'ns had metamorphiz'd to a ſtone.

Such ſtone,within whoſe concaue boſome dwels,

A a   Some

The fountaine of ancient fiction.

Some thin-cheekt Fountaine, leane and hollow-eyed,
From out whose loines spring forth a thousand wels,
Which closely sneke away for being spide,
So stealingly there creepes downe Dolios face
Two small deuided streames with silent pace.

At last, when inward greefes had almost slaine him,
 (For vn-reuealed woes soone kill the heart)
Viewing the blushing East, he thus gan plaine him,
 O thus he waild, as though his life should part:
Sleepe Phebus, sleepe, rest in thy watrie bed,
O rest in Thetis lap thy drowsie head.

And thus he often woo'd, and stil entreated
 The sun to hide the glorie of his face,
Which words he iterated and repeated,
 To shew the blacke disasters of his case,
Sad night (he knew) best fitted his dull spright,
The wo-tormented soule doth hate the light.

O cruell Fortuue, stepdame to my ioies,
 That dishinherits them from sweet content,
Plunging their hopes in seas of dire annoies,
 Depriuing them of gifts which Nature lent,
When will thy prowd insulting humor cease,
That freed frrom cares, my soule may liue in peace.

But why doe I entreat thy ruthlesse heart,
 That knowes thy greatest pleasure, thy delights,
Consists in aggrauating my soules smart,
 Poyson'd with woe by venome of thy spight?

The fountaine of ancient fiction.
No, let me rather curse thy bloudie mind,
Which executes the wrath of one so blind.

So blind as will aduance ech low-bred groome,
    To haughtie titles of a glorious place,
Lifting him vp from nothing, to the roome
    Where those of honours, and of vertues race
Should seated bee, and not th'illiterate :
Learning, not place, doth men nobillitate.

But what thou wilt, must stand, the rest must fall,
    All human kings pay tribute to thy might,
And this must rise, when pleaseth thee to call,
    This other perrish in a wofull plight :
Thy courses are irregular, thy kindnesse
Misplac'd, thy will lawlesse, all is blindnesse.

Thou filst the world with hell-bred villanies,
    Dis arming vertue of all true defence,
Leauing her naked midst her enemies,
    That are both void of learning, wit, and sence :
Only this sence they haue, for e're to hold
Their high-pil'd heapes of all-preuailing gold.

And that is it that chokes true vertues breath,
    Making it die, though she immortall be,
Fruitlesse it makes it, subiect vnto Death,
    That's want : or else it liues eternally,
But men doe count of vertue as a dreame,
Only they studie on some golden theame.

                    A a ij   Neuer

The fountaine of ancient fiction.

Neuer was any thing so pricelesse deemed,
   So louingly embosom'd in mans thought,
No not religious rites are so esteemed
   As gold, for which both earth and hell are sought,
All paines are ease, so wee may it obtaine,
All ease is paine, when wee should vertue gaine.

Where haue you seene one of the Muses traine,
   Whose mind is impleat with vertues seed,
Scorning this worldly soule polluting gaine,
   But that he liues in euerlasting need,
And yet not basely, though in meane estate,
For vertue scornes base meanes with deadly hate.

But there's no thought of vertue, no regard,
   Whereas this guilded idoll beares the sway,
Men of desart from fauours are debard,
   And churlishly thrust from preferments way,
When some base Gnatoes sleepe in Fortunes lap,
Whose wealth, not wit, procures such fooles such hap.

Then come you wounded soules, conioine with me,
   In some obumbrate thicket let vs dwell,
Some place which heau'ns faire eie did neuer see,
   There let vs build some sorrow framed cell,
Where weele cast our sighs and sum our cares,
Penning them sadly downe with sea-salt teares.

Eccho.   Wearying the lowd-toungd daughter of the aire,
   Infusing trembling horrors in ech beast
With suddein-broken accents of dispaire,

                                      With

The fountaine of ancient fiction.

With deepe-fetcht grones, as signes of our vnrest:
And if the Satyres aske why we complaine,
Fortune commands, and vertue now is slaine.

Thus in these raging fits of true-felt passion,
  This melancholike louer vsd to crie,
Railing gainst Loue and Fortune in such fashion,
  As if twixt both there were one simpathie
Of natures and of humours all one kind,
Both being false, mutable, and both blind.

And in this inuectiue and selfe-afflicting vaine, the
same Louer in another place further complaineth of
the ouermuch rigour of his Ladie, preseruing and
continuing in hate and scorne of his loue: which
words reduced to a Sonnet, are these, or to the like
effect.

Hard is his hap who neuer finds content,
  But still must dwell with heauy-thoughted sadnesse,
Harder that heart that neuer will relent,
  That may, and will not turne these woes to gladnesse,
Then ioies adue, comfort and mirth, farewell,
  For I must now exile me from all pleasure,
Seeking some vncouth caue where I may dwell,
  Pensiue and solitarie without measure,
There to bewaile my such vntimely fortune,
  That in my Aprill daies I thus should perish,
And there that steele-hard heart still still t'importune,
  That it at last my bleeding soule would cherish,
If not, with greedie longing to attend,

And thus farre haue I continued the exclamations
of an vnhappy louer, who in the same place also writ
many other inuectiues againg Fortune and Loue, ioining them both together, which I will here preter-
mit , hauing already too much digressed from our
cheefe intendement: reuerting therfore from whence
we left you, it is written, that the Thebans in a certain
statue which they dedicated vnto Fortune(being also
in the shape & similitude of a woman) placing in one
of her hands a yong child, which they tearmed by the
name of Pluto, which with many is taken to bee the
god of riches : so that it discouered, by representing
Pluto in the forme of a child, that in the hands of Fortune was the bestowing and disposing of wealth, riches, possessions, and aduancements, commanding the
and hauing that absolute authority & rule ouer them,
Martianus. as mothers gouerne and rule their children. *Martianus*
thus describes her to appeare at the mariage of Philologia. There was(saith he)among the rest a young and
beautifull woman, more talking and more abounding
in idle discourse and words then any of the rest, who
seemed to be full of gestures and of fantastike carriage
of her bodie, and alwaies mouing and stirring vp and
downe, her vpper garment was of the thinnest silke,
whose lightnesse the least breath of wind would puffe
vp, her steps and paces as shee went, were very vncertaine, & she neuer would abide long in one place, or
in one companie, and hee sayth, that her name was
Chaunce, which also is the same in sence as Fortune,
and

and which likewife with fome is called Nemefis: fhee carried in her lap (which was very fpacious & wide) almoft all the fund ie kinds and forts of all the beauties, ornaments, riches, and graces of the world, of which, fome fhee feemed to offer with her hand to fome that ftood by, but in fo haftie manner, and fo fuddenly as was poffible, as that if they did not inftantly take hold and accept of her curtefie, all what was offered was loft, to fome fhe feemed very familiar & kind, dallying with them and playing with their locks, and vfing many other fuch wanton and alluring behauiours: but to fome others againe fhe would feeme maruellous angry and difpleafed, ftriking them ouer the faces and heads with a white wand, which fhe held in her hand, and with fuch figne and token of reuenge, as if fhe had ben highly prouoked and incenfed, and would affuredly acquite her felfe on the offenders whofoeuer.

In a temple in Greece was erected a Statue of Fortune, which was made in the forme and fimilitude of a graue Matrone, habited and clothed in garments futable to the defires and fafhions of elder yeeres, and in her countenance fhe feemed very fad and penfiue: a little before her was placed the Image and portraiture of a young virgine, amourous in afpect and pleafant, which feemed to giue & offer her hand to the picture of the other: behind thefe (euen hard at their heeles) was engrauen forth another Image in the likeneffe of a yong child, which with one of her armes feemed to leane on the picture of the fad Matrone, which looking fo dolefull and heauie, fignifies her felfe to bee

that

that Fortune which is alreadie paſt and ſlipt by , and therefore ſhe ſits lamenting and bewailing the departure thereof. The other which ſeemed ſo pleaſant and offered her hand, is the preſent Fortune, and the yong infant behind them both, is that which is to come and ſucceedeth.

A mong the Ancients and among the old writers, Fortuna and Nemeſis were oftentimes taken to bee all one , yet at other times they made this difference and ſeuerall natures to appeare for Nemeſis : as *Amianus Marcellinus* ſayth) was held and taken to bee the goddeſſe, to whom only it belonged to puniſh and caſtigate the offences of the wicked and malefactors, afflicting them with paines and torments, according to the qualitie of their ſins; and alſo rewarded the vertuous and well-liuers with aduancements, honour, and titles of place and dignitie: and that ſhe did know and ſee all things euen into the darkeſt and moſt priuate corner of the world, & therevpon was by the Auncients ſuppoſed to be the daughter of Iuſtitia, who (ſay they) dwelt & inhabited in a very ſecret corner, within the houſe of Eternitie, where ſhe noted downe in her books of memorie, the offences and wicked deeds of the euill. *Macrobius* ſayth, this Nemeſis was adored and worſhipped among the Ægyptians, as the reuenger and cheefe enemie of pride, inſolencie, & haughtineſſe, and that ſhe was alſo with many called Rhamnuſia, ſo tearmed of a certain place among the Athenians; where alſo was erected and dedicated vnto hir a moſt ſtately and magnifique Statue of marble, and that ſhee was alſo ſometimes knowne by the name of

Amianus Marcellinus

Macrobius.

of Adraſtia, of king Adraſtus, for that he was the firſt
that euer cauſed her to be held in that worſhip and reuerenced regard, and that euer conſecrated any altars
or temples vnto her.

The ſame Author alſo deſcribeth her, ſaying, that
her picture was depainted and ſet forth with wings
on her ſhoulders, to ſignifie, that ſhe was alwaies readie and at hand amongſt men : hard by her ſide was
placed the rudder of a ſhip, & ſhe her ſelfe ſtood vpon a round wheele, holding in hir right hand a golden
ball, and in the other a whip, manifeſting thereby, that
where ſhe fauoured or diſliked, either aduancements,
wealth and honour, or miſeries, croſſes, and afflictions
followed and enſued.

She is oftentimes alſo depainted, as holding the
bridle of a horſe in one of her hands, and in the other
a ſmall and long peece of wood of a certain meaſure,
which we call an ell or a yard: vnſhadowing thereby,
that men ought to rule & reſtrain their tongues from
euill and corrupting ſpeeches , and that they ſhould
adminiſter iuſtice and true meaſures with whom they
deale or doe conuerſe.

It is written with Pauſanias, that Nemeſis was the Pauſanias.
moſt ſeuere and cruell puniſher of arrogancie & vain-
glory of all others, & ſaith, that ſhe abaſed & brought
downe the inſolencie and ouer-weening boldneſſe of
the northerne barbarous people, who with an aſſured
conqueſt and victorie (as they thought) entered into
the countries of the Athenians, and there (ſcorning
as it ſhould ſeeme) their ſmall forces and reſiſtances,
fell to ſpoile and rifeling , and preſently ſet vp and

erected

erected their huge Coloſſus, or piller of marble,
which they of purpoſe brought with them to ingraue
and ſet forth their victories, trophies, and ſpoiles that
they ſhould make of their enemies : but being afterward ouercome themſelues, & beaten back into their
countries, the ſame ſtone the Athenians cauſed to be
conſecrated vnto Nemeſis, whoſe picture and coun-
terfet by the incomparable skill of Phidias, was moſt
curiouſly and exactly ingrauen thereon, to ſhew therby, that ſhee only was the cauſe of the cleane ſubuer-
ting and expelling their fatall enemies out of their
Countrey, and that ſhee therein extended her power
and office to the reuenging and aboliſhing the ouer-
haughtie attempts of pride, & foole-hardie preſump-
tion. And in that ſhe was thus held to be puniſher of
vaine humors, and prowd demeanures of mortals, the
Ancients alſo held and ſuppoſed her to bee the verie
ſame in nature and propertie as the goddeſſe Iuſtitia,
whoſe deſcription (as *Aulus Gellius* affirmeth) was by
Chriſippus thus ſet forth and compoſed.

Aulus Gel-
lius.

Her Statue (ſayth hee) was framed out in the due
proportion and ſimilitude of a beauteous young virgine, who was not of any prowd, loftie, or diſdaineful
countenance, nor baſe or deiected in her looke or ca-
riage, but carrying ſo ſetled and modeſt demeanures,
as ſeemed worthy of all reuerence, loue, and due commendation, her eyes ſeemed moſt quicke in their circumference, cleere and liuely, which ſhe often turned
this way, and that way, looking and prying into euery
place round about her, and for that cauſe the Auncients entearmed her the all-diſcerning Ladie. *Apuleius*

oftentimes

oftentimes vfed to fweare & take his oath by the light
of Phœbus, and eye of *Iuſtitia*, adioining them both
together in equalitie of cleereneſſe. By which may be
vnderſtood, that there ought to be in Iudges and ad-
miniſters of iuſtice, a ſharpe & cleere eye to find out
and inueſtigat the truth, & as it were to ſee into (with
the ſight of capacitie) any offēce or crime perpetrated
whatſoeuer: whoſe cleereneſſe and far-piercing manner of examination, diſcouers and laies open what
before hath ben long kept hid, & in darke and obſcure
couertures. And in framing her like a virgine, is alſo
meant, that ſuch officers, and men authoriſed for execution of iuſtice, ought to reſemble a virgines chaſti-
tie, by not ſuffering themſelues to be tempted and ſo
led away by corruption of bribes, by partialitie, flatte-
rie, or inſinuation, but to remaine vnmoued, conſtant,
and ſtedfaſt in ſinceritie of conſcience, proceeding in
their profeſſion according to right, equitie, & reaſon.
Pauſanias writeth, that in a certaine place in Ægypt **Pauſanias**
was portraied forth the Image of *Iuſtitia*, in reſemblance alſo of a faire young virgin, which ſeemed to
draw after her with her left hand, another blacke and
hard-fauoured woman, which ſhe haled and puld forward, euen by maine force, & ſtriking her many times
ouer the face and head in moſt deſpightfull & ſeuere
manner, ſeeming therein (as it were) to reuenge ſome
wrong or iniurie offered vnto her. The young virgin
was *Iuſtitia*, and the other *Iniuria* : which intellecteth
vs thereby, that Iudges and ſuch like officers for ciuile
& domeſtike gouernments, ought continually ſtriue
by all endeuours to ſuppreſſe wrongs, iniuries, and

miſ-

The fountaine of ancient fiction.

misdemeanures , and that no man receiue molesta-
tions, violence, ot hard vsages of the stronger partie.
And that they also carie an equall hand ouer all matters and complaints exposed vnto them, and not to
giue forth and denounce sentence, till both sides may
bee produced to plead for themselues, alledging lawfull reasons for their innocencie, and purgation of
those crimes obiected against them: vnlesse they will
reseble that Iudge which Apelles drew forth in a certaine peece of worke of his, which (according to *Luci-*
anus) is thus described, with the occasion and reason
of the depainting and setting out thereof:

Lucianus.

After that Ptolomie king of Ægypt had deliuered
Apelles out of prison, and restored him to libertie,
when indeed he had once thought to haue punished
him with seuere tortures of death. (hauing ouerlight-
ly beleeued the vniust information of Antiphilus,
who meerely of malice had accused him of a certaine
rebellion and insurrection in that Countrey) & after
that in lieu of such his wrong of opprobrie and false
imprisonment, he had giuen him a hundred talents, as
part of amends for such his trouble, & had commanded that Antiphilus should alwaies afterwards be his
slaue and bondman: for requitall of such his iniurious
practises, and slandering his integritie of life, hee in a
fantasticall humor, betooke himselfe to his art, intending by some curious deuise thereof to shew forth the
depicturance of the danger & perill of his life, which
at the time of such his accusation hee then stood in,
which was in this manner with incomparable knowledge of skil performed, being called *Calunia di Apelle*:

There

There was placed in a iudiciall and high feat, made (as it were) for the determining & deciding of ciuile caufes and affaires, the Statue of a man, with maruellous long ears, fuch as Midas is reported to haue had, who there reprefented the prefence of a graue & reuerend Iudge. Vnto this Iudge two women (one of the one fide, and the other on the other fide) feemed to whifper fome matter or other in his eares, the one of them was called Ignorance, the other Sufpition, and hee held forth his hand towards another woman, called Calumnia, being of the fhape of a beautifull, rich, and young woman, then comming & approching towards him, fhee was maruellous gorgeous in her habit, and of a paffing faire afpect, fauing that at that inftant fhe feemed fomewhat angrie, difdainefull, & difcontented, infomuch, as her eies looked very red and fierie: In her left hand fhe held a flaming torch, & with her right fhee feemed forcibly to draw & plucke after her a young man by the haires of his head in moft tyrannicall fort, who miferablie and dolefully with both his hands erected toward the heauens, bemoned & lamented his woe-afflicted condition and ftate : a little before her approched Enuie, which was in the forme of a wondrous leane old man, with pallid & meagre face, on whofe withered cheeks it fhould feeme Time with the all-cutting plow-fhare of his remorfe-leffe crueltie had wrought deepe furrowes, & inuolued wrinkles. And immediately after her (Enuie vfhering them all) came two young women more, which feemed to flatter and glofe with her with perfuafiue and infinuating phrafes, extolling her beautie, and (as it were, forcing her to assume a strong opinion of her owne incomparable fairenesse,& seemed also to adore and decke her abillements and cloths with many conceited and curious toies of fantasie and delight:& the one was called Deceit,and the other Trecherie,both sisters,and of one humor.After all these followed also another woman(whose name was Penitence)habited with vild ragged and base attirements,who infinitely deploring her beeing,seemed to crucifie her self with strange impassionated fits beyond all measure, who looking backe, and seeing another poore woman making haft to ouertake her(called Truth)euen for verie sorrow shame & greefe,fell into diuers sounds,& was readie to die and depart from the world.And thus *Lucianus* describes that picture,which was called *Calumnia di Apelle*. By which this little may bee obserued, that the meaning of it is nothing else but a false & malicious accusation, entertained and supported by the Iudge of one, that is not there himselfe in presence to purge and cleare himselfe of that which is obiected against him,whose accuser is oftentimes Enuy: seconded and coadiuted by Deceit and Trecherie: the cause of the Iudges rash sentence, is Ignorance, together with Suspition,and the imbracing of calumniation or slander of the innocent:the bewailing & teares of Penitence at the discouerie of Truth, shews the greefe and shame that the guiltlesse and true persons receiue by bringing their reputation in question of villanie and dishonesty.And this shall suffice for the description of this Picture of Apelles, with the explication thereof,returning to the finishing and concluding of

the

the Statues and Images dedicated vnto Fortune.

Quintus Curtius fayth, That Fortune was depictured among the people of Scythia, in the forme of a
woman without feet, & that there was placed round
about at her right hand a number of little wings, firſt
to ſignifie,that ſhee cannot ſtand faſt or firme,& that
her gifts and fauors are no ſooner giuen, but are preſently loſt,& doe (as it were) ſudainely flie from a man
before theybe fully intertained or poſſeſſed. *Alexander*
Neapolitanus writeth, That with certaine people of
Greece her Picture or Statue was wholly framed and
compacted of glaſſe, as ſhewing thereby, that vpon
euery ſmal occaſion,riches, and happineſſe are decaied,conſumed,and periſhed. And yet all the Ancients
for the moſt part ſo abſolutely relied & confided vpon
her power and vertue, that they referred and attributed all luckie ſucceſſes of battels &other pleaſures alſo vnto her fauor,kindnes, and good liking. In Rome
(as *Liuie* reports) was erected a very ſumptuous temple by Camillus,which he dedicated vnto Fortune after the victorious ouerthrow hee gaue vnto the He-
truſcians.

Plutarch alſo ſpeaketh of another Temple which
was dedicated vnto Fortune , which was built two
miles out of Rome in that very place, where Coriola-
nus,approching like a gallant captain inarms(though
then againſt his country) met with his owne mother,
and others of his kinred,at whoſe vrgent intreaties &
praiers,hee ſurceaſed to proceed in his (till then) im-
placable furie and wrath, and ſo that glorious Metro-
politane of the world , was no doubt preſerued
from

from ſaccage and ruine at that time, for that before he had reſolutely vowed to burne & conſume it to aſhes. And in this place(as I haue ſaid) was erected a temple vnto Fortune, where ſhe was portraied forth in braſſe to the reſemblance and true proportion of a woman, which afterwards(ſome Deuill hanting the ſame) was taken and held by thoſe faith-wanting Idolaters in great reuerence & adoration, as a moſt infallible and true Oracle.

It is written of Galba, that whē he had taken away a certaine chaine or bracelet of gold from this Image of Fortune (which was then hung about her necke)& had placed it on the Statue of Venus, that ſhee (that ſame very night following) appeared vnto him in his ſleepe with threatening meanes & words of reuenge, which ſo appalled & confounded his ſences, that not many daies after in a great affrightment and terror, he departed from this life ſpeechleſſe and dumbe many houres before he died.

With many Authors it is written, that in a certain country of Ægypt Fortune is depictured, as turning round a great wheele made of glaſſe, on the top wher-of are ſet forth the pictures of many men playing ioi-fully, and in the pride of mirth and iolitie ſome others alſo climing & endeuouring to aſcend to the top ther-of, and others hauing newly attained it, precipitating and tumbling downe backe againe.

Spartianus writeth, that almoſt all the Romane Em-perours were ſo addicted to an opinion, which they embraced of the powerfull mightineſſe of this For-tune, that they kept euermore her picture or Image

in

Spartianus.

in their bed-chambers, and other priuat places of re-
trait, & that when any of them died, the same Image
was presently caried into the lodging of the knowne
successor.

The first (as *Liuie* affirmeth) that caused in Rome   Liuie.
any temples to be erected vnto Fortune, was *Seruius*
Tullius, the sixt king of the Romanes. And yet *Plu-* Plutarch.
tarch saith in his bookes intituled (The fortune of the
Romanes) that *Marcius*, which was the fourth king
(after their computation) was the first that dedicated
or built any Statues or temples vnto this goddesse ; &
that as this Empire attained higher and higher vnto
her puissance and glorie, so the superstitious deuotion of these people, increased for the reuerencing and
worshipping of Fortune, which afterwards spread it
selfe throughout all Italie, though it continued no
long time.

The Philosopher *Cebes* resembled Fortune very fitly Cebes.
vnto a Comedie , in which many actors appeare, oftentimes in likenesse and similitude of kings & great
monarchs, and presently after performe the part of
some rogue or villan,& are become poore fishermen,
slaues, and bondmen,and such like. *Socrates* compared Socrates.
her also vnto a common place of meeting, conuenti-
cle,or theatre,where without all order or obseruation
as they come,men are placed and haue their seats;no-
thing respecting the worthinesse or dignity of any
among them whatsoeuer,all being intermingled, and
confusedly thronged together: shewing thereby, that
Fortune without either respect of gentrie,worthines,
or merit,but all vnaduisedly, & without order or reason bestoweth her fauors, riches,and felicities.

The fountaine of ancient fiction.

It is read, that *Vnpal* was the first that in all Greece caused any Statues, altars, or temples to be consecrated vnto this goddesse Fortune, and that in the towne of Smyrna he erected one most stately temple, in the midst whereof, the portraiture of Fortune was placed; which picture was cut out & carued with incredible curiousnesse of the workeman, and beautified & graced with diuers delicat embellishments, and almost art-exceeding politures.

In Egira a city of Achaia, the Image of Fortune was drawn forth in the shape of a maruellous fair woman, who held in one of her hands the horn of abundance, called Cornucopia, and in the other the boy Cupid : all which (as *Pansanias* interpretes it) signifieth, that it little auaileth any woman to bee of a beautifull, amorous, & well-composed feature, if fortune in that bodie be wanting and absent: meaning that beauty without riches or honor, loseth partly her value & esteem among men, which riches are intended by that Cornucopia, signifying abundance of wealth, and enioying of much treasure. And indeed he is very fortunate & happy, that in his loue shall find beauty to be counterpoisd with riches, and that the fruition of that shal be accompanied with the graces of Venus, and those all-ouercomming accomplements.

Giraldus.

Giraldus (writing of the gods of the ancients) saith, that with some Fortune is depictured riding on a horse, who with his wonderfull and strange swiftnes of gallop, caries her away almost inuisible : and after her posteth Destiny, with great furie and exceeding celerity, holding in her hand an yron bow ready bent, and aiming to strike Fortune euen at the very heart.

This

This breefe depicturance may vnfold vnto vs the vn-
ftaied and changing mutabilitie of Fortune, and her
fudain & moft fwift departure from thofe whom euen
now fhe fauoured & highly aduanced: or that it fignifies, that fhe is alwaies flying from deftiny, feeking all
means to auoid her cōpany, for that indeed thefe two
can neuer accord or agree together; for fo much as
where Deftiny fets hir foot, Fortune is there as it were
inchanted & coniured, as hauing no power, efficacie,
or vertue. And thus much fhal fuffice for the depicturances & defcriptions, with the feuerall explications
adioined, which are read in autenticke writers to bee
made and deuifed by the Auncients of this their goddeffe Fortune.

Venus.

BEfore it bee difcended to the defcriptions of the
images & ftatues dedicated vnto this goddes Venus, it fhall not be impertinent fomwhat to touch the
feueral natures & conditions vnderftood & fignified
by her, as being a furtherance & light to conceiue the
reafons why fo many diuers ftatues & pictures were
fo diuerfly fafhioned & compofed of her. According
therfore to the opinion of the Poets, Venus was taken
to be the goddeffe of wantonnes & amorous delights,
as that fhe infpired into the minds of men, libidinous
defires, and luftfull appetites, & with whofe power &
affiftance they attained the effect of their lofe concu-
pifcence: whervpō alfo they entermed her the mother
of loue, becaufe that without a certaine loue & fimpa-
thie of affections, thofe defires are fildome accomplifhed. And vnto hir they afcribe the care and charge of

matria-

marriages and holie wedlockes, of which likewise it is
written, that Himeneus & Iuno are the protectors &
rulers. But according to the works of nature, which
vnder this name, are indeed diuersly vnderstood, Venus doth signifie that secret & hiddē vertue by which
all creatures whatsoeuer are drawne with association,
effectuating thereby the art of generation: wherevpon
Macrobius. *Macrobius* saith, that from Venus is brought the desire
and humor of carnall lusts and voluptuousnes, which
afterward taking root more deeply, conduceth vnto a
true accomplishment therof. Some that haue written
of these naturall causes, haue affirmed, that Venus, Iuno, Luna, & Proserpina haue ben al one, retaining only different names and titles, in that many effects and
issues proceeding from them, haue ben diuers and seuerall. But leauing these opinions, let vs now enter into the Images & Pictures made and composed of her.

It is written with *Philo* (an Hebrew author of great
antiquitie) that this Venus was born and ingendred of
the froth of the sea, taking force and vertue of the pri-
uities of Celum, which his son Saturn cut off & threw
down therin: and her statue is framed in the shape of a
most beautiful and amorous yong woman, which seemed also to stand vpright in the midst of a huge shell
of a fish, which was drawn by two other most vgly &
Ouid. strāge fishes, (as *Ouid* at large noteth it) who also saith,
that vnto her was consecrated the Iland of Ciprus, &
especially in it the city of Paphos, standing by the sea
side, for that she was seen and discouered vpon hir first
apparance out of the sea, to go on land on that part of
the country: by reason wherof, the people therabouts
adore and worship hir with great zeale & veneration,

and

and erected and dedicated vnto her a most rich and stately temple very gorgeous and costly.

Pausinias saith, that Venus is drawne in a coach through the airie passages, with two white Doues (as *Apuleius* also affirmeth) being birds of all others most agreeable and pleasing vnto her, & are called the birds of Venus : for it is written indeed, that they are most abundantly inclined to procreation, & that almost at all times of the year, they ingender, increase, and bring forth their young, of whome it is obserued, that vpon their first assocation and coupling together, they do kisse one another, and as it were embrace, and friendly intertain their acquaintance and friendship; alluded to the fashions and customes of amorous louers, in their first salutes, and times of daliance. *Eleanus* writeth, that these birds are so cōsecrated vnto Venus, for that (saith he) it is read, that on a certain mountain of Sicilia, called Erice, were kept and obserued certain daies as holy daies and times of pastime and disport, the which the Sicilians tearmes The daies of passage ; insomuch (as the Indians report) that Venus passed and took hir iorney in those daies from thence into Libia, at which time not one doue was seene to remain behind in the country, as attending & accompanying the goddesse in hir voiage, which being performed and ended, they al returned and came back again vnto their old haunts and accustomed places as before: whervpon after that, certain solemnities and rites were on that mountaine kept and celebrated.

Horace and *Virgil* affirme, that the chariot of Venus is drawn by two white Swans, wherof *Statius* also maketh mention, saying, that those kind of birds are most

mild,

Eleanus.

mild, innocent, and harmelesse and therfore giuen vnto Venus: or that their harmonious & pleasant notes, which they sing a litle before the approch of death, are compared to the amorous & delightful discourses and conferences of louers , which commonly afterward proue & turn into sorrow, misery, or death. VVith the Grecians the image & picture of this goddesse was set forth naked & without cloths, as Praxitiles also an excellent ingrauer in the Island of Guidos composed it: meaning therby, that al venerous & licentious people are by such their inordinat lust, like beasts, depriued of sence, & left as it were naked and despoiled of reason and the cloths & garments of vnderstanding; & oftentimes also stripped and wasted of their pristine & former riches, and goods. And this picture there framed in that Isle of Guidos, was wrought and cut out by the same Praxitiles with such exquisit art & deepe-knowledged skil, that the desire of the veiw and sight therof drew and allured many passengers and voiagers by sea to saile to Ciprus to satisfie their eies of what their eares so highly had heard commended.

The ancients vsed to dedicat vnto this goddesse many plants & flowers, among the which, specially were the roses, whose fragrant and sweet odor is resembled vnto the pleasing delights & outward faire shews and colours of loue, & in that they are of that blushing and rubicund colour, and that they can hardly bee pluckt without their pricks, and molesting mens fingers: they are likened vnto luxurious people, & such as giue theselues ouer to the vnbridled affections of carnality, for that such vnlawful & foule desires are sildome effectuated without shame & blushing, & that there accompanieth

panieth and conioineth with them, dolors, afflictions,
paines, greefes, horrors, and a polluted confcience, or
els they are fo compared, for that the color & delicat
hue of thefe rofes is foon faded, perifhed, & decaied, as
the beuties of women, as alfo the delights & pleafures
therof fudainly fall away and are confumed. But concerning thefe rofes, the Poets do inuēt, that at the firſt
they were of a milkewhite colour, & grew verie pale
and difcoloured: vntil Venus on a certain time hauing
intelligence that Mars (for fome iealoufie conceaued)
had complotted & determined a deuife to haue murdered her fweethart Adonis, and fhe in great haft and
rage running to preuent & difanull the intended mif-
cheef, greeuoufly prickt hir foot on the ftalks of thefe
flowers, of which wound (fending forth abundance of
bloud) they were prefently turned into that frefh colour which now at this time they do retaine.

It is read with *Paufanias*, that Marcellus erected and Paufanias.
dedicated a moft fumptuous temple vnto this goddes
Venus: which he caufed to be built two miles off from
Rome, that thofe kind of humors & wanton pleafures
ought to bee remoted a farre off from the minds and
thoughts of all chaft virgines of Rome.

Lactantius writeth, that the Lacedemonians framed Lactantius.
& compofed the Image of Venus all armed like a warrior, holding in one hand a fpeare, and in the other a
fhield or target, which depicturance they deuifed in
regard of a certain ouerthrow which the women of
that coūtry gaue vnto their enemy the people of Mef-
fenia, and with fucceffe they fuppofed to haue proceeded from the power and affiftance of Venus, as infpi-
ring into thofe womans hearts manly courages, ftout-
nefse,

The fountaine of ancient fiction.

nesse, and resolutions. In memory whereof, they alwaies afterward reputed Venus to be of most forcible power and mightinesse in arms, and after that beleefe reuerenced, adored, and worshipped hir. Concerning which depicturance and setting forth of the statue of Venus, *Ausonius* in a certain Epigram made by him to that purpose, saith, that Pallas was most wonderfully incenst, and mightily stomacked such description set out in that maner, and that she presently fel into great contention and quarrell with Venus, for allowing it so to be done, that she of her selfany way should seem therby to take vpon her any martiall performances or exploits, derogating and detracting from her honor, dignity, and worthinesse. In which Epigram also *Ausonius* declareth how prowdly and gallantly Venus answered her thereunto: as that she wondered and stood amased how Pallas durst now be so rash, bold & ouerhardie, as to accuse or braue her therein, considering that she stood then all armed, and had much more aduantage against her, than she had vpon the mountain Ida, wherein likewise by the verdict of Paris, she vtterly then confounded and ouerthrew her mightinesse, and made hir depart away ashamed, angry and discontented. All which argumentation & striuing controuersies, the same authour most exquisitely there hath set down and depainted. And thus far only in this treatise shal be progressed, as not aduenturing to displease the modest in capitulating such ouer-wanton and too lascious expositions and meanings which the Auncients made and vnderstood of the natures, qualities, properties, and conditions, of this their goddesse Venus.

Ausonius.

FINIS.